AF443074

# Advanced Randomized Neural Networks for Pattern Analysis

# ADVANCES IN PATTERN ANALYSIS AND INTELLIGENT SENSING

Series Editors:  David Zhang
*(The Chinese University of Hong Kong, Shenzhen, China)*
Baoyuan Wu
*(The Chinese University of Hong Kong, Shenzhen, China)*
Bob Zhang
*(University of Macau China)*

*Published*

Advances in Pattern Analysis and Intelligent Sensing – Volume 1

# Advanced Randomized Neural Networks for Pattern Analysis

**Chenglong Zhang**
The Chinese University of Hong Kong, Shenzhen, China
University of Science and Technology of China, China

**Shifei Ding**
China University of Mining and Technology, China

**Yang Wang**
Guizhou University, China

**David Zhang**
The Chinese University of Hong Kong, Shenzhen, China

## World Scientific

NEW JERSEY · LONDON · SINGAPORE · BEIJING · SHANGHAI · TAIPEI · CHENNAI

*Published by*

World Scientific Publishing Co. Pte. Ltd.

5 Toh Tuck Link, Singapore 596224

*USA office:* 27 Warren Street, Suite 401-402, Hackensack, NJ 07601

*UK office:* 57 Shelton Street, Covent Garden, London WC2H 9HE

**Library of Congress Cataloging-in-Publication Data**

Names: Zhang, Chenglong (Data scientist) author | Ding, Shifei author |
Zhang, David, 1949- author | Wang, Yang (Data and computer scientist) author
Title: Advanced randomized neural networks for pattern analysis /
Chenglong Zhang, Shifei Ding, Yang Wang, David Zhang.
Description: Singapore ; Hackensack, NJ : World Scientific Publishing Co, [2026] |
Series: Advances in pattern analysis and intelligent sensing ; vol. 1 |
Includes bibliographical references and index.
Identifiers: LCCN 2025015467 | ISBN 9789819814688 hardcover |
ISBN 9789819814695 ebook for institutions | ISBN 9789819814701 ebook for individuals
Subjects: LCSH: Neural networks (Computer science) | Machine learning | Artificial intelligence
Classification: LCC QA76.87 .Z4345 2026
LC record available at https://lccn.loc.gov/2025015467

**British Library Cataloguing-in-Publication Data**
A catalogue record for this book is available from the British Library.



For any available supplementary material, please visit
https://www.worldscientific.com/worldscibooks/10.1142/14354#t=suppl

Desk Editors: Soundararajan Raghuraman/Veronica Lee

Typeset by Stallion Press
Email: enquiries@stallionpress.com

# Preface

With the rise of large language models (LLMs), deep neural networks (DNNs) have achieved unprecedented success in feature representation, image classification and pattern recognition. However, DNNs rely on gradient descent to optimize neuron weights, involving complex architectures and numerous parameters. In recent times, using random learning theory to design DNNs with random weights has shown benefits like fewer parameters and faster modeling.

What are advanced randomized neural networks, and why do we need them? This book addresses these questions comprehensively. Randomized neural networks can be classified into data-dependent and data-independent categories based on their parameter learning mechanisms. Advanced randomized neural networks (ARNNs) utilize data-dependent stochastic configuration algorithms to assign random parameters and incrementally construct network structures, thereby maintaining the universal approximation property (UAP) of randomized neural networks. To further enhance the performance of ARNNs in various pattern analysis tasks, our research presents systematic solutions for neural network optimization, robust data analysis, and deep fusion learning of ARNNs.

This book is rooted in our research, offering a comprehensive introduction to the three dimensions of ARNNs. We then delve into our recent advancements in neural network optimization, robust data analysis, and deep fusion learning of ARNNs. Experimental results across various pattern analysis tasks have demonstrated the superiority of these advanced models. This book is invaluable for researchers, professionals, and graduate students in pattern analysis, medical diagnosis, and computer vision, and will also benefit those engaged in interdisciplinary research.

Our team has been working on advanced randomized neural networks for pattern analysis more than a few years. We appreciate the related grant support from the China Postdoctoral Science Foundation (2025M772940); National Natural Science Foundation of China (NSFC) (No. 62276265, No. 62172347); the Science and Technology Development Fund, Macao SAR (No. FDCT0028/2023/RIA1); the Guangdong Basic and Applied Basic Research Foundation (No. 2024A1515011539); the Guizhou Provincial Science and Technology Project (No. ZK[2024]-035); the Shenzhen Science and Technology Innovation Program (No. ZDSYS20211021111415025); and the Foundation of State Key Laboratory of Public Big Data (No. PBD2023-34 and No. PBD2023-35).

We would like to extend our sincere appreciations to the following collaborative professors and students for their invaluable contributions and unwavering support throughout the development of this book (in alphabetic order): Dawei Cheng, Shicheng Dai, Yuan Gao, Chaoxun Guo, Lili Guo, Jie Hu, Shaobo Li, Zihao Liao, Bingbing Tang, Guanci Yang, Jian Zhang, Zi Zhang, Zichen Zhang, Peng Zhou, and Jianglan Zhu.

Chenglong Zhang
*The Chinese University of Hong Kong, Shenzhen*
*University of Science and Technology of China*

Shifei Ding
*China University of Mining and Technology*

Yang Wang
*Guizhou University*

David Zhang
*The Chinese University of Hong Kong, Shenzhen*

# About the Authors

**Chenglong Zhang** (Member, IEEE) received his B.Sc. degree from the Qufu Normal University, Rizhao, China, in 2014, his M.Sc. degree from the Guizhou University, Guiyang, China, in 2017, and his Ph.D. degree from the School of Computer Science and Technology, China University of Mining and Technology, Xuzhou, China, in 2023. He is currently a Postdoctoral Fellow with the Chinese University of Hong Kong, Shenzhen, and University of Science and Technology of China. His main research interests include randomized neural networks, deep stochastic configuration networks, multi-modal data fusion, and medical biometrics. He serves as a Young Editorial Board Member of the *Journal of Artificial Intelligence & Control Systems* (JAICS) and the *Journal of Shandong University of Science and Technology* (Natural Science). He has published more than 30 papers in international conferences and journals.

**Shifei Ding** (Fellow, CAAI; Senior Member, IEEE) received his Ph.D. degree from Shandong University of Science and Technology, Taian, China, in 2004. He received Postdoctoral Fellow from the Key Laboratory of Intelligent Information Processing (IIP), Institute of Computing Technology (ICT), and the Chinese Academy of Sciences (CAS). He is a professor and Ph.D. supervisor at the China University of Mining and Technology. His research interests include intelligent information processing, pattern recognition, machine learning, data mining, and granular computing. He has published 6 books and more than around 200 papers in international conferences and journals. Prof. Ding has been selected as a Fellow of the Chinese Association for Artificial Intelligence (CAAI) in 2024.

**Yang Wang** received his B.Sc. degree from the Xuchang University, Xuchang, China, in 2011, his M.Sc. degree from the Guizhou University, Guiyang, China, in 2014, and his Ph.D. degree from the Chinese Academy of Sciences, Chengdu, China, in 2018. He is currently a Lecturer at the State Key Laboratory of Public Big Data, Guizhou University. His main research interests include stochastic configuration networks, industrial artificial intelligence, and deep learning.

**David Zhang (Corresponding Author)** (Life Fellow, IEEE) graduated from Peking University, Beijing, China, in 1974, and received his MS and first Ph.D. degrees in computer science from the Harbin Institute of Technology, Harbin, China, in 1982 and 1985, respectively. He also got his second Ph.D. degree in electrical and computer engineering from the University of Waterloo, ON, Canada, in 1994. From 1986 to 1988, he was a Postdoctoral Fellow at Tsinghua University, Beijing, and then an Associate Professor at the Institute of Automation, Chinese Academy of Sciences, Beijing. He has been a Chair Professor at the Hong Kong Polytechnic University, Hong Kong, where he is the Founding Director of the Biometrics Research Centre (UGC/CRC) supported by the Hong Kong SAR Government since 1998. He is currently a Distinguished Presidential Chair Professor at the Chinese University of Hong Kong, Shenzhen, China. Over the past 40 years, he has been working on pattern recognition, image processing, and biometrics, where many research results have been awarded and some created directions, including medical biometrics and computerized TCM, all of which are famous in the world. He has published 20+ monographs, 500+ international journal papers, and 50+ patents from the USA, Japan, and China. For eight years, he has been continuously listed as a Global Highly Cited Researcher in Engineering by Clarivate Analytics. He is also ranked 73rd with H-Index 130 in the Top 1,000 Scientists for International Computer Science in 2024. Prof. Zhang has been selected as a Fellow of both the Royal Society of Canada (RSC) and the Canadian Academy of Engineering (CAE). He is also a Croucher Senior Research Fellow, a Distinguished Speaker of the IEEE Computer Society, and an IAPR and AAIA Fellow.

# Contents

## Part 3  Deep Fusion Learning       209

## 10.  Deep Stochastic Configuration Networks Ensemble via Hyper-Parameter Optimization      211



## 11.  Deep Stochastic Configuration Networks Ensemble via Boosting Negative Correlation Learning      229

# List of Figures

# List of Tables

# Chapter 1

# Introduction

In the era of large language models (LLMs), deep learning has achieved unprecedented success. However, most deep learning models use gradient descent to update model parameters iteratively, resulting in more complex network structures, slower training speeds, and a larger number of network parameters. Using random learning theory to train deep learning models demonstrates the advantages of fewer network parameters and faster modeling efficiency. In this chapter, we first elucidate why advanced randomized neural networks? and review the theories of traditional randomized neural networks and advanced randomized neural networks with stochastic configuration algorithms. Additionally, we analyze the current state of advanced randomized neural networks for neural network optimization, robust data analysis, and deep fusion learning.

## 1.1  Why Advanced Randomized Neural Networks?

In recent years, the development of information technologies such as the internet, internet of things (IoT), cloud computing, 5G, and artificial intelligence (AI) has led to an exponential increase in data volume, ushering in the era of big data (Marx, 2013; McAfee *et al.*, 2012; Sagiroglu and Sinanc, 2013). AI has rapidly advanced in fields such as intelligent manufacturing, biological computing, and object detection. A critical challenge now facing AI development is how to quickly and effectively analyze and process large-scale, complex data across various industries (Liang *et al.*, 2022; Mao *et al.*, 2019; Schadt *et al.*, 2010).

Neural networks have experienced significant growth due to their strong feature learning capabilities and nonlinear approximation characteristics (Abdi *et al.*, 1999; Chen and Chen, 1995; Cybenko, 1989; Hornik *et al.*, 1989; Park and Sandberg, 1991). Deep learning (DL) models can extract multi-level abstract features from high-dimensional, large-scale data by constructing multi-layer network structures, achieving groundbreaking success in feature representation, image classification, and pattern recognition (LeCun *et al.*, 2015). However, deep models such as deep belief networks (DBNs)(Hinton *et al.*, 2006), deep Boltzmann machines (DBMs)(Hinton and Salakhutdinov, 2012), and convolutional neural networks (CNNs) typically require the back-propagation (BP) algorithm to iteratively solve gradients and update weights layer by layer (Krizhevsky *et al.*, 2012). These models have complex network structures, slow training speeds, and a large number of network parameters.

Randomized learning methods have shown great potential for rapid and efficient modeling in machine learning (Lukoševičius and Jaeger, 2009; Mahoney *et al.*, 2011; Scardapane and Wang, 2017). Using randomized learning techniques to training neural networks originated in the late 1980s and were further developed in the early 1990s (Lowe and Broomhead, 1988). For instance, Pao *et al.* (1994); Pao and Takefuji (1992) proposed a random vector functional link neural network (RVFLN), and Schmidt *et al.* (1992) introduced a feedforward neural network with random weights (FNNRW). The training process of randomized neural networks (RNNs) usually consists of 2 parts: (1) randomly assign input weights and biases to hidden layer nodes; (2) use the least squares method or its regularization method to calculate the output weights of hidden layer nodes, thereby simplifying the training process and improving learning efficiency. Subsequently, Igelnik and Pao (1995) proved the universal approximation property (UAP) of RVFLN for continuous functions under the condition that the input weights and biases of the hidden layer nodes satisfy the uniform distribution. RNNs have great development potential because of its random parameter allocation method and efficient learning method, especially for high real-time data pattern analysis scenarios.

However, recent studies have shown that the UAP of RNNs depends on the number of hidden layer nodes and the range of input weights and baises. If set improperly, the model cannot approximate the target function with high probability (Husmeier, 1999; Li and Wang, 2017; Tyukin and Prokhorov, 2009). To ensure the UAP of RNNs and maintain their generalization performance, Wang and Li (2017b) proposed stochastic configuration networks (SCNs) in 2017, which employ data-dependent supervisory mechanism to assign input parameters and incrementally generate network architecture, ensuring the UAP of the learning model and improving its learning accuracy and efficiency with less human intervention.

Subsequently, SCNs have gradually attracted the research interest of a large number of scholars both domestically and internationally and have been rapidly promoted and developed, showing significant advantages in computational efficiency and accuracy in areas such as hardware implementation (Gao *et al.*, 2020a; Li and Wang, 2024b; Pan *et al.*, 2020), computer vision (Alsahanova *et al.*, 2025; Li and Wang, 2024a, 2019), medical data analysis (Li *et al.*, 2024b; Zhu *et al.*, 2024), system modeling and prediction (Dang and Wang, 2025; Deng *et al.*, 2024a; Li *et al.*, 2023b, 2025; Wang and Dang, 2024a; Zhao *et al.*, 2023). However, the generalization and robustness of SCNs still need improvement for complex and diverse pattern analysis scenarios, especially in terms of neural network optimization, robust data analysis, and deep fusion learning. Therefore, designing data-dependent stochastic configuration based advanced randomized neural networks for pattern analysis will help promote the development and application of randomized neural network fields. This will contribute to the further promotion of supervised mechanism-based randomized neural networks and intelligent information processing. The difference between advanced randomized neural networks and traditional randomized neural networks is illustrated as Fig. 1.1.

## 1.2 Traditional Randomized Neural Networks

Random vector functional link neural network (RVFLN), proposed by Pao and Takefuji in 1992 (Pao *et al.*, 1994; Pao and Takefuji, 1992), which is a classical randomized neural network model. The architecture of random vector functional link neural network, as

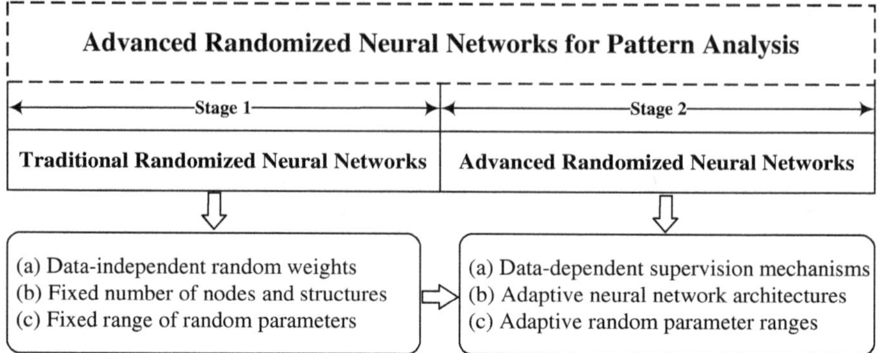

Fig. 1.1.   The difference between advanced randomized neural networks and traditional randomized neural networks.

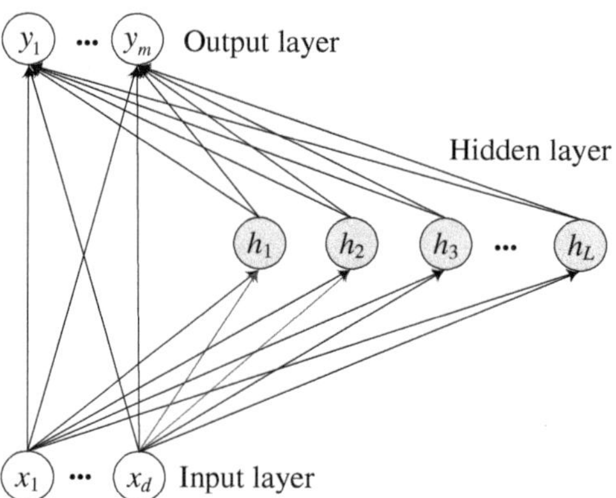


Fig. 1.2.   The architecture of random vector functional link neural network.

shown in Fig. 1.2, consists of two parts: linear mapping and non-linear mapping. The nonlinear mapping occurs between the input layer and the hidden layer, ensuring the model's nonlinear fitting ability; the linear mapping occurs between the input layer and the output layer, which helps reduce the risk of model over-fitting.

Given training data $\{X, Y\}$, in which $X = \{x_1, x_2, \ldots, x_N\}$, $x_i = [x_{i,1}, x_{i,2}, \ldots, x_{i,d}] \in \mathbb{R}^d$, $d$ represents the feature dimension; $Y = \{y_1, y_2, \ldots, y_N\}$, $y_i = [y_{i,1}, y_{i,2}, \ldots, y_{i,m}] \in \mathbb{R}^m$, $m$ denotes the label dimension; $i = 1, 2, \ldots, N$, $N$ indicates the number of samples.

Assume the number of hidden layer nodes in RVFLN is $L$, the input weights $W$ and biases $B$ of the hidden layer nodes can be randomly assigned according to Eqs. (1.1) and (1.2), respectively:

$$W = 2 \times rand(d, L) - 1. \tag{1.1}$$

$$B = 2 \times rand(1, L) - 1. \tag{1.2}$$

The output matrix $H$ of the hidden layer can be calculated by using Eqs. (1.3) and (1.4):

$$H = [X, H_L] = \begin{bmatrix} x_{11} & x_{1d} & \phi_1(x_1) & \cdots & \phi_L(x_1) \\ \vdots & \vdots & \vdots & \ddots & \vdots \\ x_{N1} & x_{Nd} & \phi_1(x_N) & \cdots & \phi_L(x_N) \end{bmatrix}, \tag{1.3}$$

$$H_L = \phi(XW + B), \tag{1.4}$$

where $H_L$ is the output of the hidden layer nodes, which can be calculated by Eq. (1.4); $\phi(\cdot)$ represents the activation function.

Finally, the output weights of the model can be calculated using the objective function in Eq. (1.5):

$$\beta = \arg\min_{\beta} \|H\beta - Y\|^2 = H^\dagger Y, \tag{1.5}$$

where $H^\dagger$ represents the Moore–Penrose inverse of $H$.

To reduce the risk of over-fitting, $L_2$ regularization term (Saunders *et al.*, 1998) is introduced into the objective function of Eq. (1.5), Eq. (1.6) can be revised as follows:

$$\beta = \arg\min_{\beta} \|H\beta - Y\|^2 + C\|\beta\|^2. \tag{1.6}$$

Taking the partial derivative of Eq. (1.6) with respect to $\beta$ and setting it to 0 as Eq. (1.7), we can obtain the output weights of Eq. (1.8):

$$\frac{\partial J}{\partial \beta} = 2H^T H\beta - 2H^T Y + 2C\beta = 0, \tag{1.7}$$

$$\beta = \begin{cases} \left(H^T H + CI\right)^{-1} H^T Y, N \geq L + d \\ H^T \left(HH^T + CI\right)^{-1} Y, N < L + d \end{cases}, \tag{1.8}$$

where $C$ represents the $L_2$ regularization parameter.

Therefore, the output $f$ of RVFLN model can be calculated by Eq. (1.9) as follows:

$$f = H\beta. \tag{1.9}$$

Igelnik and Pao (1995) employed the Monte Carlo method with the limit-integral representation of the target function to theoretically prove the universal approximation property of RVFLN as Theorem 1.1.

**Theorem 1.1.** Igelnik and Pao (1995) *For any compact set $D \subseteq \mathbb{R}^d$, and define $f \in C(D)$ as the set of all continuous functions over $D$. Suppose the activation function $g$ satisfies $\int_{\mathbb{R}} |g(t)|^2 dt < \infty$ or $\int_{\mathbb{R}} |g'(t)|^2 dt < \infty$. If $W$ and $B$ are randomly distributed over $\chi$ and follow a certain distribution, there exists a sufficiently large number of nodes $L$ and corresponding network output weight matrices $\beta_1, \beta_2, \ldots, \beta_L$, as well as a probability space $\chi$, such that $f_i = \sum_{j=1}^{L} g_j \beta_j$ approximates $f$ to any desired degree of accuracy with probability one.*

*This result can be expressed as Eq. (1.10):*

$$\lim_{L \to \infty} E \left( \int_D |f(x) - f_i(x)|^2 dx \right) = 0, \qquad (1.10)$$

*where $E$ represents the expectation operator over the probability space.*

Subsequently, Husmeier (1999) explored the universal approximation property of RVFLN with random parameters based on symmetric interval distribution. The results indicates that this property only holds for target functions that satisfy the Lipschitz condition. Furthermore, empirical evidence shows that most practical modeling scenarios fulfill the Lipschitz condition. Therefore, the theoretical results of Theorem 1.1 hold significant theoretical importance for the construction of randomized neural networks.

## 1.3  Advanced Stochastic Configuration Networks

### 1.3.1  *Stochastic Configuration Algorithms*

For randomized neural networks, when the number of hidden layer nodes is small, the accuracy performance of neural networks cannot be guaranteed. Conversely, a large number of hidden layer nodes can easily lead to over-fitting, thus reducing the model's generalization performance. To address this issue, constructive neural network schemes have gradually attracted the attention of researchers.

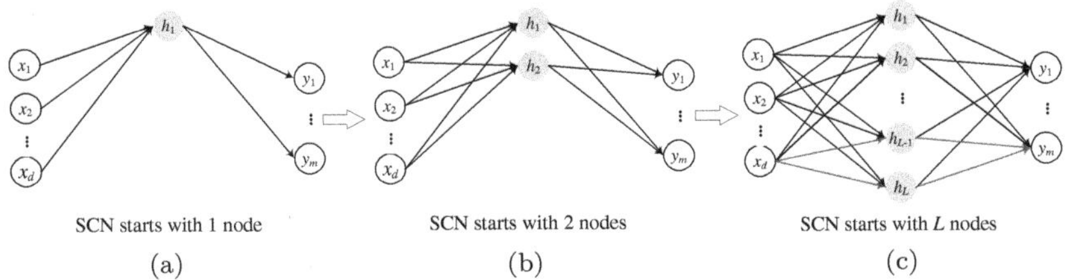



**Fig. 1.3.** The architecture constructive process of SCNs.

These schemes start with a smaller network size and progressively generate hidden layer nodes and calculate their output weights until an acceptable error range is achieved (Barron, 1993; Kwok and Yeung, 1997). Recent years, to address the above questions, Wang and Li (2017b) proposed stochastic configuration networks (SCNs), which use data-dependent supervision mechanism to configure neuron parameters and construct network architecture incrementally. The architecture constructive process of SCNs can be illustrated in Fig. 1.3.

In brief, the incremental constructive process of SCNs can be demonstrated as follows (Wang and Li, 2017b):

For the objective function $f = [f_1, f_2, \ldots, f_m] : \mathbb{R}^d \to \mathbb{R}^m$, suppose that we have established is a learning model with $L-1$ hidden layer nodes, i.e. $f_{L-1}(x) = \sum_{j=1}^{L-1} g_j(xw_j + b_j)\beta_j$, where $f_0 = 0$, $L = 1, 2, \ldots, L_{\max}$, $\beta_j = [\beta_{j,1}, \beta_{j,2}, \ldots, \beta_{j,m}]$. We define the current network residual as $e_{L-1} = f - f_{L-1} = [e_{L-1,1}, e_{L-1,2}, \ldots, e_{L-1,m}]$, which is far from an acceptable level of accuracy. The SCN framework can successfully provide a fast solution to incrementally add node $L$, resulting in $f_L = f_{L-1} + g_L\beta_L$ until the residual $e_L = f - f_L$ falls within the expected error range.

To determine the output weights, Wang and Li (2017b) presented three implementation modes of SCNs based on different stochastic configuration (SC) algorithms. SC-I maintains the output weights of previous nodes unchanged and only calculates the output weights for newly configured nodes. SC-II solves the output weights of some nodes by calculating local least squares according to the set shift window. SC-III calculates the output weights of all nodes by solving global least squares (Wang and Li, 2017b).

**Theorem 1.2 Wang and Li (2017b).** *Suppose $\Gamma = \{g_1, g_2, g_3, \ldots\}$ represents a set of real-valued functions, span($\Gamma$) denotes a function* *space spanned* $\Gamma$. *Assume that span($\Gamma$) is dense in the $L_2$ space and $\forall g \in \Gamma, 0 < \|g\| \le b_g, b_g \in \mathbb{R}^+$. Given $r \in (0,1)$, and a non-negative real number sequence $\{\mu_L\}$ with $\mu_L \le 1 - r$ and $\lim_{L\to\infty} \mu_L = 0$. For $L = 1, 2, 3, \ldots$, define:*

$$\delta_L = \sum_{h=1}^{m} \delta_{L,q}, \delta_{L,q} = (1 - r - \mu_L) \|e_{L-1,q}\|^2. \tag{1.11}$$

*If the random basis function $g_L$ satisfies the following inequality constraints as Eq. (1.12), the output weights of node $L$ can be determined by Eq. (1.13).*

$$\langle e_{L-1,q}, g_L \rangle^2 \ge b_g^2 \delta_{L,q}, \quad q = 1, 2, \ldots, m. \tag{1.12}$$

$$\beta_{L,q} = \frac{\langle e_{L-1,q}, g_L \rangle}{\|g_L\|^2}, \quad q = 1, 2, \ldots, m. \tag{1.13}$$

*Thus, we have $\lim_{L\to\infty} \|f - f_L\| = 0$.*

Theorem 1.2 (Wang and Li, 2017b) provides a new construction scheme for randomized neural networks.The weights $w_L$ and biases $b_L$ of node $L$ are randomly assigned based on data dependence supervised mechanism of Eq. (1.13). However, the output weights $\beta_L$ is analytically evaluated by $\beta_{L,q} = \langle e_{L-1,q}, g_L \rangle / \|g_L\|^2$. This determination scheme may result in a very slow convergence rate for the constructive process. Thus, to address this, Theorem 1.3 (Wang and Li, 2017b) provides a result on the universal approximation property if the least squares method is applied to update the output weights in the proceeding manner.

**Theorem 1.3 Wang and Li (2017b).** *Suppose $\Gamma = \{g_1, g_2, g_3, \ldots\}$ represents a set of real-valued functions, span($\Gamma$) denotes a function space spanned $\Gamma$. Assume that span($\Gamma$) is dense in the $L_2$ space and $\forall g \in \Gamma, 0 < \|g\| \le b_g, b_g \in \mathbb{R}^+$. Given $r \in (0,1)$, and a non-negative real number sequence $\{\mu_L\}$ with $\mu_L \le 1 - r$ and $\lim_{L\to\infty} \mu_L = 0$. For $L = 1, 2, 3, \ldots$, define:*

$$\delta_L = \sum_{q=1}^{m} \delta_{L,q}, \delta_{L,q} = (1 - r - \mu_L) \|e_{L-1,q}\|^2. \tag{1.14}$$

*If the random basis function $g_L$ is generated to satisfy the following inequality constraints as Eq. (1.15):*

$$\langle e_{L-1,q}, g_L \rangle^2 \geq b_g^2 \delta_{L,q}, \quad q = 1, 2 \ldots, m. \tag{1.15}$$

*While the output weights are calculated by Eq. (1.16):*

$$[\beta_1, \beta_2, \ldots, \beta_L]^T = \arg\min_{\beta} \left\| f - \sum_{j=1}^{L} g_j \beta_j \right\|^2. \tag{1.16}$$

*Then, we have $\lim_{L\to\infty} \|f - f_L\| = 0$.*

In Theorem 1.3, (Wang and Li, 2017b), the evaluation of output weights $\beta_1, \beta_2, \ldots, \beta_L$ is straightforward with the use of Moore–Penrose generalized inverse. However, when the data scale is large, this calculation method has large computational complexity. To improve the efficiency of large-scale data modeling, the concept of moving window is used in the global least squares method in Theorem 1.4 (Wang and Li, 2017b). When the number of hidden layer nodes exceeds the set window size, only part of the output weights are optimized, which is of great significance for large-scale data processing.

**Theorem 1.4.** *Suppose $\Gamma = \{g_1, g_2, g_3, \ldots\}$ represents a set of real-valued functions, $\text{span}(\Gamma)$ denotes a function space spanned $\Gamma$. Assume that $\text{span}(\Gamma)$ is dense in the $L_2$ space and $\forall g \in \Gamma, 0 < \|g\| \leq b_g, b_g \in \mathbb{R}^+$. Given $r \in (0,1)$, and a non-negative real number sequence $\{\mu_L\}$ with $\mu_L \leq 1 - r$ and $\lim_{L\to\infty} \mu_L = 0$. For $L = 1, 2, 3, \ldots$, define:*

$$\delta_L = \sum_{q=1}^{m} \delta_{L,q}, \delta_{L,q} = (1 - r - \mu_L) \|e_{L-1,q}\|^2. \tag{1.17}$$

*If the random basis function $g_L$ is generated to satisfy the following inequality constraints as Eq. (1.18):*

$$\langle e_{L-1,q}, g_L \rangle^2 \geq b_g^2 \delta_{L,q}, \quad q = 1, 2 \ldots, m. \tag{1.18}$$

*When the number of hidden layer node $L \leq K$, the output weights can be calculated by Eq. (1.19):*

$$[\beta_1, \beta_2, \ldots, \beta_L]^T = \arg\min_{\beta} \left\| f - \sum_{j=1}^{L} g_j \beta_j \right\|^2. \tag{1.19}$$

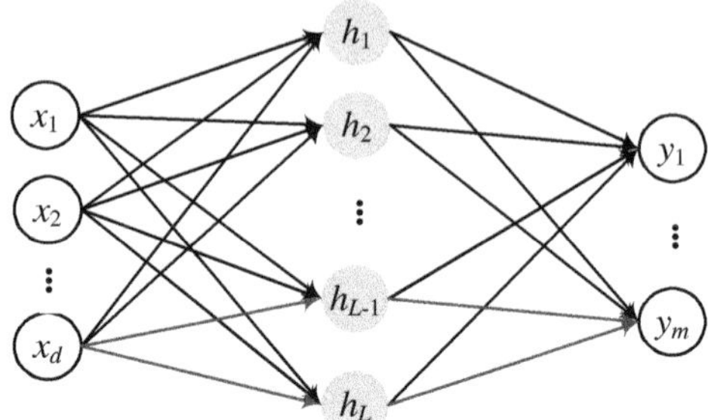

**Fig. 1.4.** The architecture of stochastic configuration networks.

*Otherwise, when the number of hidden layer node $L > K$, $\beta_1, \beta_2, \ldots, \beta_{L-K}$ will be selectively calculated unchanged and update $\beta_{L-K+1}, \beta_{L-K+2}, \ldots, \beta_L$ according to Eq. (1.20):*

$$[\beta_{L-K+1}, \beta_{L-K+2}, \ldots, \beta_L]^T$$

$$= \arg\min_{\beta} \left\| f - \sum_{j=1}^{L-K} g_j \beta_j - \sum_{j-L-K+1}^{L} g_j \beta_j \right\|^2. \tag{1.20}$$

*Then, we have $\lim_{L \to \infty} \| f - f_L \| = 0$.*

### 1.3.2 *Stochastic Configuration Networks*

In this section, we give the description of stochastic configuration networks (SCNs), i.e., SCN I–III in detail, which are associated with Theorems 1.2, 1.3, and 1.4, respectively. In general, the architecture of stochastic configuration networks, as shown in Fig. 1.4, the main components of our proposed SCN I–III can be summarized as follows (Wang and Li, 2017b).

**(1) Configuration of hidden parameters:** randomly assigning the input weights and biases to meet the constraints, then generating a new hidden node and adding it to the current learner model.

**(2) Evaluation of output weights:** constructively or selectively determining the output weights of the current learner model.

Given the training data $\{X, Y\}$, where $X = \{x_1, x_2, \ldots, x_N\}$, $X_i = [x_{i,1}, x_{i,2}, \ldots, x_{i,d}] \in \mathbb{R}^d$, $d$ represents the number of feature dimensions; $Y = \{y_1, y_2, \ldots, y_N\}$, $y_i = [y_{i,1}, y_{i,2}, \ldots, y_{i,m}] \in \mathbb{R}^m$,

$m$ indicates the number of label dimensions; $i = 1, 2, \ldots, N$, and $N$ expresses the number of samples.

Assuming that $L - 1$ hidden layer nodes of SCNs have been generated, the current outputs can be calculated by Eq. (1.21):

$$f_{L-1}(X) = \sum_{j=1}^{L-1} g_j \left(X w_j + b_j\right) \beta_j, \quad (L = 1, 2, \ldots, f_0 = 0), \quad (1.21)$$

where $\beta_j$ represents the output weights of node $j$ in the hidden layer; $g_j(\cdot)$ is the activation function; $w_j$ and $b_j$ denote the input weights and biases of the $j$th node of the hidden layer, respectively.

The current network residual can be defined as shown in Eq. (1.22):

$$e_{L-1}(X) = f - f_{L-1}(X)$$
$$= [e_{L-1,1}(X), e_{L-1,2}(X), \ldots, e_{L-1,m}(X)] \in \mathscr{R}^{N \times m}. \quad (1.22)$$

If the $\|e_{L-1}\|^2$ does not reach the preset error $\varepsilon$ or the maximum number of nodes $L_{\max}$, the node $L$ will be added incrementally, we first generate $T_{\max}$ candidate input weights $w_L$ and biases $b_j$ of node $L$ randomly as Eqs. (1.23) and (1.24):

$$w_L = \lambda \times (2 \times \mathrm{rand}(d, T_{\max}) - 1), \quad (1.23)$$

$$b_L = \lambda \times (2 \times \mathrm{rand}(1, T_{\max}) - 1), \quad (1.24)$$

where $\lambda$ is the scale scope of candidate parameters, which can be determined by supervision mechanism adaptively.

According to Theorem 1.2, the output weights of $\beta_{L,q}$ becomes as Eq. (1.25):

$$\beta_{L,q} = \frac{\left(e_{L-1,q}(X)^T \cdot h_L(X)\right)^2}{h_L(X)^T \cdot h_L(X)}, \quad q = 1, 2, \ldots, m, \quad (1.25)$$

where $h_L = h_L(X) = [g_L(x_1 w_L + b_L), \ldots, g_L(x_N w_L + b_L)]^T$, the current output of hidden layer can be expressed as $H_L = [h_1, h_2, \ldots, h_L]$.

For the sake of brevity, we introduce a set of variables $\xi_{L,q}$, $q = 1, 2, \ldots, m$ as Eq. (1.26), the candidate parameter that satisfies the maximum value is taken $\xi_L = \sum_{q=1}^{m} \xi_{L,q}$ as the $L$th node parameter.

$$\xi_{L,q} = \frac{\left(e_{L-1,q}(X)^T \cdot h_L(X)\right)^2}{h_L(X)^T \cdot h_L(X)} - (1 - r - \mu_L) e_{L-1,q}(X)^T \cdot e_{L-1,q}(X),$$
$$(1.26)$$

where $\lambda$ denotes the parameter scale of the weights and biases; $r \in (0,1)$; $\{\mu_L\}$ represents the sequence of non-negative real numbers, where $\mu_L \leq 1 - r$, $\lim_{L \to +\infty} \mu_L = 0$.

SCN - I employs Eq. (1.25) to determine output weights of each nodes, keep the previous output weights of nodes unchanged, only calculate the output weights of the new node will be added.

SCN - II employs Eqs. (1.27) and (1.28) to calculate the output weights of nodes, as $L \leq K$, $[\beta_1, \beta_2, \ldots, \beta_L]^T$ can be determined as Eq. (1.27), while as $L > K$, $\beta_{L-K+1}, \beta_{L-K+2}, \ldots, \beta_L$ can be determined as Eq. (1.28).

$$\beta = \arg \min_{\beta} \|H_L \beta - T\|^2 = H_L^{\dagger} T, \tag{1.27}$$

$$\beta^{\text{window}} = \arg \min_{\beta} \|H_K \beta - T\|^2 = H_K^{\dagger} T, \tag{1.28}$$

where $H_K$ is composed of the last $K$ columns of $H$, i.e., $H_K = [h_{L-K+1}, h_{L-K+2}, \ldots, h_L]$, and the left (previous) $\beta_1, \beta_2, \ldots, \beta_{L-K}$ remain unchanged.

It is easy to see that SCN-II and SCN-III become consistent once $K \geq L_{\max}$ as Eq. (1.27).

## 1.4 Advanced Deep Stochastic Configuration Networks

### 1.4.1 *Deep Stochastic Configuration Algorithms*

As deep models can extract more efficient representation information through multi-level feature learning, to smartly choose the architecture of the DNNs, improve the learning speed and reduce the computational burden (Alvarez and Salzmann, 2016; Wang and Li, 2018) utilized stochastic configuration theory to construct deep version of SCNs (DSCNs).Different from other deep neural networks, DSCNs can be constructed incrementally starting from a small architecture (one hidden layer with one node), where the input parameters of the nodes can be calculated by data-dependent supervision mechanism. Subsequently, additional nodes and layers are gradually added to construct a deep model. As illustrated in Fig. 1.5, (DSCN with two hidden layers), all nodes are fully connected to the outputs and the output weights are determined by least square approach to maintain generalization performance of DSCNs (Wang and Li, 2018).

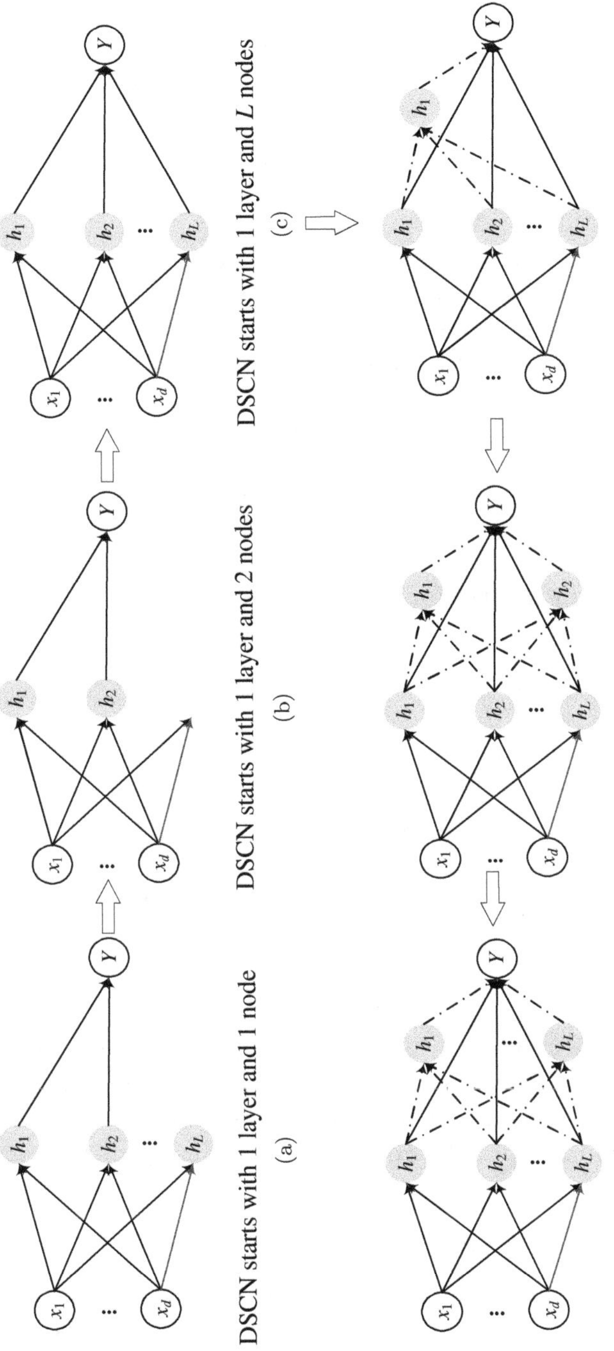



**Fig. 1.5.** The architecture constructive process of DSCNs.

Given a target function $\mathscr{F} : \mathbb{R}^d \to \mathbb{R}^m$, suppose that a DSCN model has $n$ hidden layers and the number of nodes in each layer is $L_k$, where $k = 1, 2, \ldots, n$.

$$\mathscr{F} = \sum_{k=1}^{n} \sum_{j=1}^{L_k} \phi_{k,j}\left(x^{k-1}; w_j^{k-1}, b_j^{k-1}\right) \beta_j^k, \tag{1.29}$$

where $\beta_j^k$ represents the output weight of node $j$ in the hidden layer $k$; $\phi_{k,j}(\cdot)$ is the activation function of node $j$ in the hidden layer $k$, where different layers can employ different activation functions; $w_j^{k-1}$ and $b_j^{k-1}$ denote the input weight and bias of node $j$ in layer $k$, respectively.

The inputs of each hidden layer can be illustrated as Eq. (1.30):

$$x^0 = x, x^k = \Phi\left(x^{k-1}; W^{k-1}, B^{k-1}\right) = \left[\phi_{k,1}, \phi_{k,2}, \ldots, \phi_{k,L_k}\right],$$

$$\tag{1.30}$$

The input weight matrix for all nodes of the hidden layer $k$ is as Eq. (1.31):

$$W^{k-1} = \left[W_1^{k-1}, W_2^{k-1}, \ldots, W_{L_k}^{k-1}\right], \tag{1.31}$$

The input bias matrix for all nodes of the hidden layer $k$ is as Eq. (1.32):

$$B^{k-1} = \left[b_1^{k-1}, b_2^{k-1}, \ldots, b_{L_k}^{k-1}\right], \tag{1.32}$$

Therefore, the current residual of DSCN can be expressed as Eq. (1.33):

$$\mathscr{E}^n = \mathscr{F} - \mathscr{F}_{S_n}^n = \left[\mathscr{E}_1^n, \mathscr{E}_2^n, \ldots, \mathscr{E}_m^n\right]. \tag{1.33}$$

**Theorem 1.5** Wang and Li (2018). *Assume that span$(\Gamma)$ is dense in the $L_2$ space and $\forall \phi \in \Gamma, 0 < \|\phi\| \leq c, c \in \mathbb{R}^+$. Given $r \in (0, 1)$, let $\{\mu_l\}$ denote a sequence of non-negative real numbers such that $\mu_l \leq 1 - r$ and $\lim_{l \to \infty} \mu_l = 0$. For $n = 1, 2, \ldots$ and $j = 1, 2, \ldots, L_n$, define:*

$$\delta_{j,q}^{(n)} = (1 - r - \mu_j) \left\|\mathscr{E}_{j-1,q}^{(n)}\right\|^2, \quad q = 1, 2, \ldots, m. \tag{1.34}$$

*Stochastically configuring the $j$th hidden node $\phi_{n,j}$ within the $n$th hidden layer $(j = 1, 2, \ldots, L_n)$ to satisfy the following inequalities as*

*Eq.* (1.35):

$$\left\langle \mathscr{E}_{j,q}^{(n)}, \phi_{n,j} \right\rangle^2 \geq c^2 \delta_{j,q}^{(n)}, \quad q = 1, 2, \ldots, m. \tag{1.35}$$

*Fix the random basis functions* $\phi_{n,1}, \phi_{n,2}, \ldots, \phi_{n,L_n}$ *and start to add the first hidden node* $\phi_{n+1,1}$ *in the* $(n+1)$-*th hidden layer according to the following inequalities as Eq.* (1.36):

$$\left\langle \mathscr{E}_{L_n,q}^{(n)}, \phi_{n+1,1} \right\rangle^2 \geq c^2 \delta_{L_n,q}^{(n)}, \quad q = 1, 2, \ldots, m. \tag{1.36}$$

*Keep adding new hidden nodes within the* $(n+1)th$ *hidden layer based on Eq.* (1.36), *followed by generating the first hidden node in a new hidden layer via Eq.* (1.37). *After adding one hidden node (either in the present hidden layer or starting a new hidden layer), the read-out weights are evaluated by the least squares method, that is,*

$$\beta^* = \arg\min_{\beta} \left\| \mathscr{F} - \sum_{k=1}^{n} \sum_{j=1}^{L_k} \phi_{k,j} \beta_j^{(k)} \right\|^2. \tag{1.37}$$

*Then, we have* $\lim_{n \to +\infty} \| \mathscr{F} - \mathscr{F}_{S_n}^{(n)} \| = 0$, *where* $\mathscr{F}_{S_n}^{(n)}$ *is defined by Eq.* (1.29).

### 1.4.2 *Deep Stochastic Configuration Networks*

In 2017, Wang *et al.* proposed a novel data-dependent stochastic configuration theory for training random neural networks (Wang and Li, 2017b). In 2018, to enhance the feature learning representation capability of SCNs, Wang et al. designed DSCNs with multi-layer structure (Wang and Li, 2018). Different from other deep neural networks, DSCNs can be constructed incrementally starting from a small architecture (one hidden layer with one node), where the input parameters of the nodes can be calculated by data-dependent supervision mechanism. Subsequently, additional nodes and layers are gradually added to construct a deep model. As illustrated in Fig. 1.6, (DSCN with two hidden layers), all nodes are fully connected to the outputs and the output weights are determined by least square approach to maintain generalization performance of DSCNs (Wang and Li, 2018).

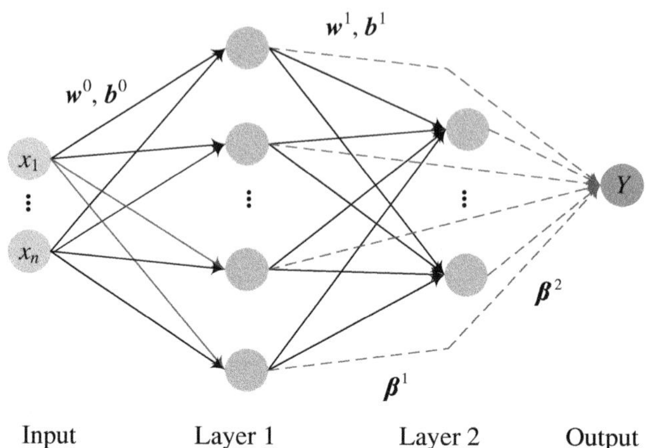



**Fig. 1.6.** The feedforward framework of DSCN with two hidden layers. Among them, the input parameters of nodes are generated by data-dependent supervision mechanism, and all the nodes are fully connected to the outputs (Wang and Li, 2018).

In brief, the algorithm description of a classical DSCN model can be summarized as follows, furthermore, the specific theories and the proof of universal approximation capability are elaborated in Wang and Li (2018):

The input feature with $d$ dimensions is denoted as $X = \{x_1, x_2, \ldots, x_N\}$ for a given training set $\{X, Y\}$, while the corresponding label with $m$ dimensions is represented by $Y = \{y_1, y_2, \ldots, y_N\}$. Here, $N$ represents the number of training points.

Assume that $L_n - 1$ nodes have been generated in hidden layer $n$ of DSCN, the current outputs can be defined as $f^n_{L_n - 1}$. Consequently, the residual error vector $e^n_{L_n - 1}$ can be calculated using Eq. (1.38):

$$e^n_{L_n-1} = Y - f^n_{L_n-1} = [e^n_{L_n-1,1}(X), e^n_{L_n-1,2}(X), \ldots, e^n_{L_n-1,m}(X)], \tag{1.38}$$

where $X$ is the input feature of training data when $n = 1$, while if $n \geq 2$, $X = H^{n-1}$; $H^{n-1}$ represents the outputs of hidden layer $n-1$.

Initialize the candidate weights and biases from a uniform distribution over $[-\lambda, \lambda]^d$ and $[-\lambda, \lambda]$ respectively, we choose the input weight $w^{n-1}_{L_n}$ and bias $b^{n-1}_{L_n}$, which satisfies the condition of $\xi^n_{L_n,j} \geq 0$ and maximizes the value of objective function $\xi^n_{L_n} = \sum_{j=1}^{m} \xi^n_{L_n,j}$, as the parameters of node $L_n$.

$$\xi_{L_n,j}^n = \frac{\langle e_{L_n-1,j}^n, h_{L_n}^n \rangle^2}{\langle h_{L_n}^n, h_{L_n}^n \rangle} - (1-r)\langle e_{L_n-1,j}^n, e_{L_n-1,j}^n \rangle, \tag{1.39}$$

$$h_{L_n}^n = \phi[X(w_{L_n}^n) + b_{L_n}^n](X = X, n = 1; X = H^{n-1}, n \geq 2), \tag{1.40}$$

where $h_{L_n}^n$ represents the outputs of node $L_n$; $j = 1, 2, \ldots, m$; $r \in (0,1)$.

The output weights vector $\beta$ can be calculated based on least square method as Eq. (1.41):

$$\beta = \arg\min_{\beta} \|Y - H\beta\|^2 = H^\dagger Y, \tag{1.41}$$

where $H = [H^1, H^2, \ldots, H^n]$; $H^n = [h_1^n, h_2^n, \ldots, h_{L_n}^n]$; $H^\dagger$ expresses the Moore–Penrose inverse of $H$.

## 1.5 Outline of This Book

In this book, we present a comprehensive summary of our work on advanced randomized neural networks (ARNNs). The book is structured into three main parts, each focusing on a distinct area of research progress in ARNNs. Excluding Chapter 1 (Introduction) and Chapter 15 (Book Review and Future Work), the remaining thirteen chapters are organized as follows:

**Part 1: Neural Networks Optimization:** This part explores neural networks optimization techniques for ARNNs across four chapters:

- **Chapter 2:** Introduces an adaptive decay regularized stochastic configuration network with multi-level signal processing for predicting battery remaining useful life.
- **Chapter 3:** Proposes a novel regularized stochastic configuration network combining ridge methods with residual error feedback.
- **Chapter 4:** Presents an efficient block-incremental stochastic configuration network with group lasso regularization.
- **Chapter 5:** Demonstrates greedy stochastic configuration networks for addressing ill-posed problems.

**Part 2: Robust Data Analysis:** Focused on robust data analysis in ARNNs, this part comprises four chapters:

- **Chapter 6:** Introduces intuitionistic fuzzy stochastic configuration networks for binary classification problems.
- **Chapter 7:** Develops weighted deep stochastic configuration networks based on M-Estimator functions for regression problems with outliers.
- **Chapter 8:** Proposes noise-robust regularized deep stochastic configuration networks with $L_1$ norm loss.
- **Chapter 9:** Demonstrates robust semi-supervised stochastic configuration networks for semi-supervised regression problems with noise.

**Part 3: Deep Fusion Learning:** This part delves into deep fusion learning techniques for ARNNs, spanning five chapters:

- **Chapter 10:** Introduces deep stochastic configuration networks ensemble via hyper-parameter optimization.
- **Chapter 11:** Demonstrates deep stochastic configuration networks ensemble via boosting negative correlation learning.
- **Chapter 12:** Proposes an explicit ensemble model of intuitionistic fuzzy deep stochastic configuration networks.
- **Chapter 13:** Illustrates stacked deep stochastic configuration networks with multi-level feature fusion.
- **Chapter 14:** Presents stochastic configuration networks with long short-term memory feature embedding.

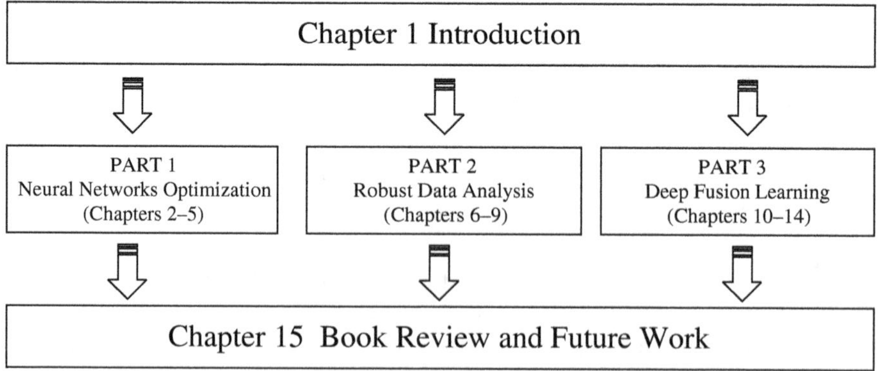


**Fig. 1.7.** The main structure arrangement in this book.

The structure of the book is visually summarized in Fig. 1.7, highlighting the connections between its different parts. Chapter 1 provides an overview of the book, followed by the three parallel parts (1, 2, and 3) that present the latest research on neural network optimization, robust data analysis, and deep fusion learning in ARNNs, respectively. The book concludes with Chapter 15, which offers a review of the content and outlines future research directions.

# Part 1
# Neural Networks Optimization

# Chapter 2

# Decay Regularized Stochastic Configuration Network with Multi-Level Signal Processing

A robust and effective health management strategy for battery power systems is crucial to ensure the reliable operation of unmanned aerial vehicles (UAVs). This chapter introduces an adaptive decay regularized stochastic configuration network (DRSCN) integrated with multi-level signal processing for predicting the remaining useful life (RUL) of UAV batteries. We first propose a multi-level signal enhancement framework (MLSEF) designed to efficiently extract critical battery health indicators from complex signals. A key innovation lies in the enhancement of the SCN model's output layer through decay regularization, which sparsifies the weights and significantly mitigates the risk of over-fitting in later prediction stages. To further optimize DRSCN, we employ the convex lens and dual-mechanism enhanced sand cat swarm optimization algorithm (CLDM-SCSO) for precise hyper-parameter tuning, thereby enhancing prediction accuracy. Extensive experiments conducted using the NASA HIRF battery dataset demonstrate the framework's superior accuracy and reliability compared to existing methods, providing an efficient and dependable solution for UAV battery health monitoring.

## 2.1   Introduction

With the widespread adoption of unmanned aerial vehicles (UAVs) in sectors such as military, logistics, surveillance, and entertainment, there is a growing emphasis not only on enhancing battery performance and reliability but also on aligning with the principles of the green economy. As the energy core of UAV operations, accurately assessing the battery's remaining useful life (RUL) and health status is paramount. The transition towards green energy solutions further underscores the need for batteries that are efficient, reliable, sustainable, and recyclable, reflecting a commitment to minimizing the environmental impact of UAV technologies (Saha *et al.*, 2011).

Recent research has increasingly focused on identifying and predicting key indicators of battery performance degradation (Li *et al.*, 2024a). Analyses of UAV battery signals reveal significant nonlinear and non-stationary characteristics, with flight operations and environmental factors introducing additional complexity and randomness (Lipu *et al.*, 2020). Addressing these challenges requires advanced signal processing techniques (Lipu *et al.*, 2020; Wang *et al.*, 2020a), which are particularly effective in analyzing nonlinear and non-stationary time series. These techniques significantly enhance signal processing outcomes, improving the accuracy and robustness of prediction models (Luo *et al.*, 2024). For instance, Zhang *et al.* (2023) developed a dual-layer decomposition mechanism based on the Pearson correlation coefficient (PCC), utilizing complete ensemble empirical mode decomposition with adaptive noise (CEEMDAN) and empirical wavelet transform (EWT) for feature extraction in wind power data. Similarly, Fu *et al.* (2023) employed CEEMDAN and variational mode decomposition (VMD) for cascaded processing of wave heights, ultimately using long short-term memory (LSTM) to predict decomposition modes with satisfactory results. Wang *et al.* (2017a) also achieved successful electricity price predictions using Fast Ensemble EMD (FEEMD), VMD, and an improved BP algorithm.

Early research relied heavily on complex physical models to simulate battery degradation processes, which often required stringent parameters and experimental conditions (Depcik *et al.*, 2020; Pan *et al.*, 2019; Yao *et al.*, 2023). However, recent trends have shifted towards leveraging historical operational data and adopting statistical and machine learning methods, including linear regression and time series analysis (Eleftheroglou *et al.*, 2019; Sierra *et al.*, 2019). With the rapid advancements in machine learning and artificial intelligence, data-driven methods such as support vector machines (SVMs) (Xu *et al.*, 2023b) and neural networks (NNs) (Shibl *et al.*, 2023; Zhang *et al.*, 2021c) have gained prominence in battery life prediction (Li *et al.*, 2023d). These methods excel at learning complex patterns in battery data, leading to highly accurate predictions (Xu *et al.*, 2023a).

Despite these advancements, the fixed structure of deep learning models often struggles to handle the accumulating degradation data over the service life of UAV batteries. Traditional models face challenges in managing large volumes of degradation data in later stages, while constructing large predictive models may result in insufficient early-stage data for training. Emerging incremental random algorithms offer a practical solution to these challenges (Zhang *et al.*, 2024). These models dynamically adjust their hidden layers during battery RUL prediction, ensuring network flexibility and enhancing both accuracy and robustness. Additionally, the data dependency of random methods facilitates effective integration between the predictive network structure and service data, improving overall prediction performance.

Stochastic configuration networks (SCNs), introduced by Wang and Li (2017b), have demonstrated success in applications such as industrial equipment maintenance (Dai *et al.*, 2024; Wang *et al.*, 2022c), non-stationary industrial time series data (Lu *et al.*, 2020; Wang *et al.*, 2022a), and various time series predictions (Cao *et al.*, 2021; Zhang *et al.*, 2022b). However, implementing SCNs in UAV battery health management (BHM) presents several challenges. A primary issue is that increasing the number of hidden layer nodes over the service lifecycle raises the risk of model overfitting, which can compromise prediction accuracy and practicality. By integrating appropriate regularization strategies into the calculation of SCN output layer weights, it is possible to reduce model volatility in later prediction stages, thereby improving generalization and resistance to over-fitting (Ai and Wang, 2020; Liu *et al.*, 2024). Furthermore, in SCNs, the parameter range control factor $\lambda$ is typically set manually, influencing the distribution of input weights and bias parameters. Incremental adjustments to hidden layer parameters, even minor changes in $\lambda$, can cause significant performance fluctuations, impacting prediction accuracy and stability. An adaptive SCN framework incorporating small-scale meta-heuristic algorithms offers a practical solution to mitigate these instabilities (Wu *et al.*, 2022b; Zhang and Ding, 2021).

To address these challenges, we propose a multi-tier data processing approach that facilitates feature extraction and noise reduction in UAV battery data. Subsequently, we implement the decay regularized stochastic configuration network (DRSCN), a foundational technique that sparsifies the output weights of the network, effectively mitigating over-fitting risks. To further optimize the DRSCN model, we introduce the convex lens and dual-mechanism enhanced sand cat swarm optimization (CLDM-SCSO) algorithm. This advanced algorithm adaptively adjusts hidden layer weights within the DRSCN, significantly enhancing predictive performance. These refinements are applied during critical phases of the model's training process, particularly during population initialization and hunting phases, to ensure efficacy and accuracy.

To summarize, the key contributions of this chapter are as follows:

- We propose a novel multi-level signal enhancement framework (MLSEF), which integrates VMD and CEEMDAN with signal analysis and band-pass filtering, aiming to enhance signal quality and accurately extract key battery health indicators.
- We present an enhanced stochastic configuration network, which incorporates decay regularization and introduces the CLDM–SCSO algorithm for adaptive parameter tuning. These modifications are strategically designed to refine the model's structure, reduce the risk of over-fitting, and enhance prediction accuracy.
- Experiments on NASA High-Intensity Radiated Fields (HIRF) UAV battery dataset demonstrates the prediction performance of proposed model for predicting the remaining useful life (RUL) of UAV batteries.

## 2.2 Preliminaries

### 2.2.1 *Signal Processing*

The complex and non-linear nature of UAV battery signal data requires advanced signal processing techniques to accurately identify and predict battery health and degradation. These techniques encompass multilevel data processing methods, including variational mode decomposition (VMD), signal-to-noise ratio (SNR) analysis, complete ensemble empirical mode decomposition with adaptive noise (CEEMDAN), and bandpass filtering. VMD is highly effective in decomposing non-stationary signals, making it particularly useful for fault diagnosis and noise reduction. SNR analysis assesses signal quality by differentiating between useful signals and noise. CEEMDAN enhances signal decomposition precision by introducing adaptive noise, which helps reduce mode mixing. Bandpass filtering further improves signal relevance by allowing only signals within a specific frequency range to pass through. Together, these multi-level signal processing techniques form a comprehensive analytical framework that enables the extraction of key features from complex signals, ultimately enhancing the accuracy of battery health assessments and supporting the development of advanced predictive maintenance strategies for UAV batteries (Luo *et al.*, 2024; Ye and Yu, 2022).

### 2.2.2 *Sand Cat Swarm Optimization*

Sand cat swarm optimization (SCSO) is a meta-heuristic algorithm inspired by the natural behavior of sand cats, known for their efficient hunting strategies. This algorithm offers a simple yet effective approach to solve complex optimization problems by mimicking the processes of exploration, hunting, and capturing prey. SCSO is characterized by its computational simplicity, requiring minimal parameterization and offering ease of implementation (Kiani *et al.*, 2023; Niu *et al.*, 2024; Seyyedabbasi and Kiani, 2023)

The SCSO algorithm operates in three main phases: Initialization, searching, and capturing. Each member of the population represents a potential solution in a multi-dimensional search space, and the optimization process follows several key equations that model the behavior of sand cats in the wild.

The global sensitivity range, $r_G$, models the detection range of sand cats for prey, decreasing with the progress in search iterations as Eq. (2.1):

$$r_G = S_M - \left( \frac{2 \times S_M \times \text{iter}_c}{\text{iter}_{\max}} \right), \tag{2.1}$$

where $S_M$ denotes the auditory sensitivity range of sand cat; $\text{iter}_c$ is current iterations; $\text{iter}_{\max}$ indicates the maximum number of iterations.

The individual search sensitivity, $s$, adjusts the search intensity using $r_G$ and randomness as Eq. (2.2):

$$S = r_G \times \text{rand}(0, 1). \tag{2.2}$$

The algorithm dynamically alternates between exploration and exploitation based on the value of $R$, which is determined as Eq. (2.3):

$$R = 2 \times r_G \times \text{rand}(0, 1) - r_G. \tag{2.3}$$

In the exploration phase ($|R| > 1$), the position can be updated according to Eq. (2.4):

$$\text{Pos}(t + 1) = S \cdot (\text{Pos}_{bc}(t) - \text{rand}(0, 1) \cdot \text{Pos}_c(t)), \tag{2.4}$$

where $\text{Pos}_{bc}(t)$ represents the optimal solution, while $\text{Pos}_c(t)$ is the current locations of population.

During exploitation ($|R| \leq 1$), the update focuses on the vicinity of the best solution.

This mechanism effectively balances global exploration and local exploitation, enhancing the algorithm's ability to solve complex optimization problems by efficiently navigating the search space. SCSO's strength lies in its adaptability and robustness, making it a suitable algorithm for various optimization challenges. Its capability to dynamically adjust search parameters and alternate between exploration and exploitation enables it to achieve high quality solutions while maintaining computational efficiency.


## 2.3  Methodology

### 2.3.1  *Multi-Level Signal Enhancement Framework*

The primary challenge in analyzing UAV battery service data lies in effectively extracting key information from high-quality degradation signals while filtering out low-quality noise. The significant nonlinearity and non-stationarity of these signals further complicate the processing. Single-layer decomposition methods are often inadequate for reducing data complexity and eliminating the effects of high-frequency noise, which can hinder the performance of prediction models. To address these challenges, we propose a multi-level signal enhancement framework (MLSEF) to improve the extraction of crucial information from degradation signals. The framework comprises the following steps:

(1) **First-level VMD decomposition:** The original UAV battery signals are decomposed using variational mode decomposition (VMD), resulting in a series of variational mode functions (VMFs). These VMFs serve as the first layer of decomposition sequences.

(2) **Second-level SNR analysis and CEEMDAN decomposition:** Signal-to-noise ratio (SNR) analysis is performed on the VMFs to assess signal quality and identify the signals that require further decomposition. These identified signals undergo a second round of decomposition using complete ensemble empirical mode decomposition with adaptive noise (CEEMDAN) to enhance their clarity.

(3) **Third-level band-pass filtering and signal selection:** Based on the characteristics of the intrinsic mode functions (IMFs) from the second-level decomposition, bandpass filters are applied to remove unnecessary noise and retain the important degradation signals. This step effectively denoises the IMFs, improving signal quality.

(4) **Signal reconstruction and matrix stacking:** After filtering, the signals are reconstructed in reverse sequence to generate recombined signals. These signals are then stacked into a multi-dimensional degradation information matrix, which serves as the input for the predictive model.

The proposed multi-level signal enhancement framework (MLSEF) offers significant advancements over traditional methods for handling complex UAV battery signals. Existing techniques typically rely on single-layer decomposition approaches, such as VMD or EMD, which frequently experience noise interference and mode mixing. In contrast, our multi-layer decomposition strategy, which combines VMD with CEEMDAN, allows for the extraction of critical degradation signals across various frequency bands while reducing noise interference. Additionally, SNR analysis is uniquely integrated into our framework to evaluate the quality of the decomposed modes and determine which require further processing. This approach improves both the accuracy of signal processing and the reliability of the extracted data. By addressing the complexities of UAV battery degradation signals, this multi-level framework demonstrates enhanced adaptability and superior signal extraction performance compared to single- or dual-layer processing methods.

### 2.3.2　*Decay Regularized Stochastic Configuration Network with Adaptive Parameters*

Extensive studies of the SCNs have shown that control factors $\lambda$ and $r$ play a crucial role in determining the weights and biases of the hidden layers, directly impacting the model's overall performance. To address this issue, we introduce an innovative meta-heuristic algorithm named as convex lens and dual-mechanism enhanced sand cat swarm optimization (CLDM–SCSO) to adaptively adjust these control factors, which can optimize the performance of DRSCN model. This algorithm significantly enhances the efficiency and accuracy of RUL prediction by improving the optimization capability of the SCNs.

The core improvements focus on two main areas: First, during the initialization phase of SCSO, a convex lens imaging strategy is employed to increase the diversity of the population. Second, a unique dual-mechanism search strategy is introduced, integrating a natural adversarial mechanism that expands the population's search range. This mechanism improves both the accuracy and speed of the global search, facilitating a more efficient discovery of the optimal parameter configuration. The flowchart of proposed CLDM–SCSO–DRSCN is displayed in Fig. 2.1.

Drawing inspiration from optical principles, the convex lens imaging strategy treats each sand cat's position as a light source and generates symmetric positions in the solution space through simulated convex lens imaging. This broadens the search area and increases the probability of finding the global optimum. Additionally, a mirror strategy is incorporated to enhance the exploration process by creating mirror positions between the current and opposite positions, further expanding the search depth and breadth. This

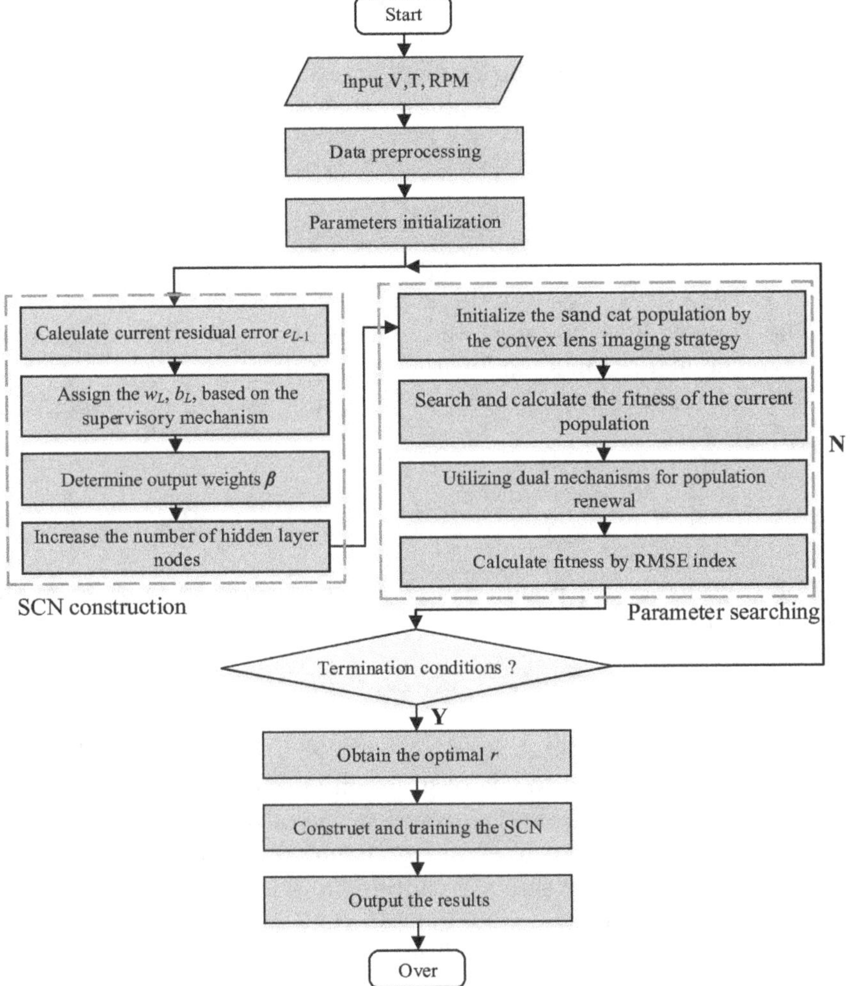


**Fig. 2.1.** Flowchart of CLDM–SCSO–DRSCN parameter selection.

method simulates light refraction between different media, allowing flexible switching between global and local searches by adjusting parameters, such as the refractive index, thereby increasing the likelihood of finding the optimal solution.

In the improved initialization process, an initial sand cat population is created, where each sand cat represents a potential solution.

The solution space exploration capability is enhanced through the convex lens imaging and mirror strategies:

Given a sand cat population, where each individual sand cat $s_i$ is represented in $D$ dimensional space as shown in Eq. (2.5):

$$s_i = [x_{i1}, x_{i2}, \ldots, x_{iD}], \tag{2.5}$$

where $x_{ij} \in [\text{lower}, \text{upper}]$ defines the position range of the $i$th sand cat in the $j$th dimension. The population size is set to $N_{\text{pop}}$, consisting of $i = 1, 2, \ldots, N_{\text{pop}}$ individuals.

The convex lens imaging and mirror strategies are adopted to enhance the algorithm's exploration capability:

For each sand cat position $s_i$, its opposite position $s_i^*$ is calculated using Eq. (2.6):

$$s_i^* = \frac{\text{upper} + \text{lower}}{2} - \left( s_i - \frac{\text{upper} + \text{lower}}{2} \right). \tag{2.6}$$

For each sand cat position $s_i$ and its opposite position $s_i^*$, the mirror position $s_i^{**}$ is calculated using Eq. (2.7):

$$s_i^{**} = s_i + \delta \cdot (s_i^* - s_i), \tag{2.7}$$

where $\delta$ is a tuning factor used to control the displacement of the mirror position relative to the original and opposite positions. In the convex lens imaging strategy, $\delta$ controls the offset of the mirror position, with a value range of $0 \leq \delta \leq 1$ and is dynamically adjusted according to the algorithm's requirements. Initially, $\delta$ is set close to 1, enhancing global exploration. As iterations progress, $\delta$ gradually decreases to approximately 0.1, improving local search accuracy. This adjustment mechanism ensures the algorithm balances between global search and local optimization.

**Evaluation and Selection:** The initial position $s_i$, opposite position $s_i^*$, and mirror position $s_i^{**}$ of each sand cat individual are evaluated for fitness; with the position with the highest fitness is selected as the new position for that individual.

An avoidance mechanism has been incorporated during the exploration phase, allowing sand cats to avoid predators passively while actively searching for prey. The parameters include a random value $M \in [0, 1], HT \in [0.5, 1]$, where $\alpha$ represents a random number in the range $(0, 1]$, and $Q$ denotes a random number following a standard normal distribution. $L$ is defined as a matrix of size $t \times d$, where all elements are 1. Specifically, agents are assigned a dynamic threshold $M$ and a distance to the predator $HT$. When $M < HT$, this condition signifies a safe search environment, enabling sand cats to perform extensive searches for optimal values. When $M \geq HT$, some sand cats face the threat of predation. Sand cats' positions are adjusted randomly following a normal distribution to evade predators. The improved search mechanism can be observed in Eqs. (2.8) and (2.9):

Development (when $|R| \leq 1$):

$$X(t+1) = \text{Pos}_b(t) - \text{Pos}_{\text{rnd}} \cdot \cos(\theta) \cdot S. \tag{2.8}$$

Exploration (when $|R| > 1$):

$$\vec{X}(t+1) = \begin{cases} S \cdot (\text{Pos}_{bc}(t) - \text{rand}(0,1) \cdot \text{Pos}_c(t)) & \text{if } M < HT; \\ \quad \cdot \exp\left(-\frac{t}{\alpha \cdot \text{iter}_{\max}}\right) \\ S \cdot (\text{Pos}_{bc}(t) - \text{rand}(0,1) \cdot \text{Pos}_c(t)) & \text{if } M \geq HT. \\ \quad + Q \cdot L \end{cases} \tag{2.9}$$

In SCN, the output weights $\beta$, calculated by the least squares method, are designed to minimize the error between predicted and actual battery RUL values. However, an exclusive focus on enhancing prediction accuracy, at the expense of the model's generalization ability, can inevitably lead to over-fitting in later prediction stages. To address this challenge, this study introduces the decay regularization (DR) technique to optimize the SCN output layer, focusing on achieving sparsity. This method significantly enhances the model's generalization capabilities and reduces the risk of over-fitting.

Within the SCN framework, all output weights $\beta$ are determined through the least squares method to ensure initial accuracy in battery RUL prediction. To enhance both the accuracy and generalization ability of the UAV battery RUL prediction model, a decay regularization mechanism has been incorporated in the computation of the SCN output layer, as shown in Eq. (2.10):

$$Y_L(x) = Y_{L-1}(x) + \sigma_L g_L \beta_L, \qquad (2.10)$$

where $\sigma_L$ is defined as $\frac{|g_L|^2 + \lambda_L}{|g_L|^2}$, where $\lambda_L$ denotes the decay regularization term. As layer $L$ approaches infinity, $\lambda_L$ converges to the form $le^{-L}$, with $l$ representing the regularization coefficient. At this point, the output weight matrix $\beta$ is expressed by the following decay-regularized least squares equation as Eq. (2.11):

$$\beta = \left(H^T H + \lambda_L I\right)^{-1} H^T E, \qquad (2.11)$$

where $E$ denotes the current residual matrix of the network. Introducing the decay regularization term promotes the sparsity of the output weights $\beta$ and enhances the model's generalization ability to new, unseen data, thus improving prediction accuracy and reducing the risk of over-fitting.

Decay regularization is a technique applied during model training that introduces a decay factor proportional to the weight size in the weight update formula, encouraging smaller weight scales. This method reduces the model's sensitivity to random fluctuations in the training data and, by adjusting the regularization parameter $\lambda$, improves the model's stability and adaptability. Additionally, decay regularization helps prevent the model from over-fitting to outlier data points, thereby improving its generalization ability. This strategy enables the model to demonstrate greater robustness and accuracy when handling unseen data.

By introducing decay regularization in the sparse SCN output layer, uncertainty from randomness can be effectively reduced, thereby improving the model's consistency and reliability across different training environments. Increasing the regularization parameter $\lambda$ enhances weight sparsity, reducing the risk of model over-fitting. Conversely, decreasing the value of $\lambda$ allows the model to adjust weights more freely to better accommodate complex data structures, enhancing adaptability to unseen data.


## 2.4   Experimental Results and Discussion

The experimental setup for this study was established on Windows 10 OS, utilizing a computer equipped with an Intel(R) Core(TM) i5-6300HQ CPU at 2.30 GHz and MATLAB R2022a.

### 2.4.1  *Experimental Settings*

#### 2.4.1.1  *Data Preprocessing*

The NASA high-intensity radiated fields (HIRF) UAV battery dataset serves as the primary dataset for this study. It provides detailed power data from a single lithium-ion battery pack used in the Edge 540 T UAV model. This dataset includes key parameters such as voltage, temperature, and revolutions per minute (RPM) recorded throughout various flight phases, including takeoff, cruising, and landing (Kulkarni *et al.*, 2020).

The UAV battery pack consists of two lithium battery modules, each containing five pouch cells with a total capacity of 7800 mAh. The battery supports propeller speeds of up to 6000 RPM. The dataset covers critical flight phases, making it ideal for predicting the RUL of UAV batteries. For instance, it captures the stable voltage during pre-takeoff, the voltage drop and temperature rise during takeoff and acceleration, the relatively stable voltage during cruising, and the gradual voltage recovery during landing. This variability in operating conditions makes the dataset particularly useful for modeling battery degradation.

In this study, signal decomposition and processing were applied to critical UAV battery parameters, resulting in the construction of an MLSEF. During the first layer of decomposition, substantial signal interference was encountered, indicating the initial layer's ineffectiveness in extracting degradation information. Consequently, CEEMDAN was employed for a second decomposition, successfully extracting more explicit signal features and eliminating most noise. Subsequently, a third-layer filter was applied to further optimize the signal. The signal was processed and reconstructed to obtain clear and stable data.

The specific information matrix, obtained after reconstruction and stacking, is depicted in Eq. (2.12):

$$
W_{\mathrm{MSEAF}} = \begin{pmatrix} V_1 & T_1 & \mathrm{RPM}_1 \\ V_2 & T_2 & \mathrm{RPM}_2 \\ \vdots & \vdots & \vdots \\ V_N & T_N & \mathrm{RPM}_N \end{pmatrix} \tag{2.12}
$$

where, $V_i, T_i$, and $\mathrm{RPM}_i$ represent the voltage, temperature, and speed of the $i$ sample, while $N$ signifies the total number of samples.

This matrix encapsulates all crucial information from the original UAV battery data, following multi-level cascaded decomposition, denoising, and reconstruction, thereby providing a rich foundation for subsequent model training.

### 2.4.1.2   *Evaluation Metrics*

Various performance metrics are utilized to quantitatively assess the model's predictive performance. The definitions and formulas for each metric are presented below, where $n$ represents the number of data points, $y_i$ denotes the actual RUL value at step $i$, and $\hat{y}_i$ signifies the predicted value at step $i$:

**Root mean squared error (RMSE):** It represents the error in the same units as the original data, providing an intuitive understanding of the error magnitude.

$$\text{RMSE} = \sqrt{\frac{1}{n}\sum_{i=1}^{n}(y_i - \hat{y}_i)^2}. \tag{2.13}$$

**Mean absolute error (MAE):** It calculates the average of the absolute differences between predicted and actual values.

$$\text{MAE} = \frac{1}{n}\sum_{i=1}^{n}|y_i - \hat{y}_i|. \tag{2.14}$$

$R^2$ (**$R$-squared**): It reflects the model's ability to explain the variation in actual values.

$$R^2 = 1 - \frac{\sum_{i=1}^{n}(y_i - \hat{y}_i)^2}{\sum_{i=1}^{n}(y_i - \bar{y})^2}. \tag{2.15}$$

**Response time:** It measures the time required for the predictive model to generate a prediction, which is crucial for applications requiring timely predictions, such as UAV BHM.

The performance improvement percentage metrics, PRMSE and PMAE, are introduced to further quantify improvement across models. Here, '1' refers to the error of the comparison model, and

'2' refers to the error of the proposed model.

$$\text{PRMSE} = \frac{\text{RMSE}_1 - \text{RMSE}_2}{\text{RMSE}_1} \times 100\%. \qquad (2.16)$$

$$\text{PMAE} = \frac{\text{MAE}_1 - \text{MAE}_2}{\text{MAE}_1} \times 100\%. \qquad (2.17)$$

### 2.4.2 *Main Results and Discussion*

This section presents a comprehensive evaluation of the performance of the proposed model and comparative models in predicting the RUL of UAV batteries. Given the expanding applications of UAVs in civilian and commercial domains, accurate prediction of battery health state is particularly critical, directly influencing operational efficiency and safety. This study explores the performance of various models through in-depth experimental analysis, aiming to identify an accurate and efficient prediction model.

This study incorporates two sets of experiments: comparative experiments involving a support vector machine (SVM, Model 1), Backpropagation (BP, Model 2), random vector functional link neural network (RVFLN, Model 3), and ablation experiments including Model 4 (SCN without preprocessing), alongside various composite models such as DRSCN (Model 5), MLSEF-SCN (Model 6), MLSEF-DRSCN (Model 7), and MLSEF-CLDMSCSO-SCN (Model 8). All models were evaluated on the same dataset, which comprised LLF, ULA, LRF, and URA, and analysis focused on each model's performance across multiple indicators (RMSE, MAE, $R^2$, and runtime).The parameter settings for each model are shown in Table 2.1.

In order to ensure a fair performance comparison, we optimized the parameters of each algorithm through cross-validation and grid search methods. For the BP algorithm, cross-validation was used to determine the optimal learning rate (0.5) and number of neurons (10), Adam was selected as the training algorithm, and Sigmoid function was used as the activation function. For SVM, we conducted a grid search for regularization parameters and kernel coefficient values to find the optimal combination. The regularization parameter value was set to 10, and the kernel coefficient was set to 1. The RVFL parameter settings follow standard practices in

**Table 2.1.** Revised and consolidated parameters for comparison algorithms.

| Algorithms | Parameters | Values |
|---|---|---|
| BP | Learning rate | 0.5 |
|  | Number of neurons | 10 |
|  | Training algorithm | Adam |
|  | Activation function | Sigmoid |
| SVM | Kernel type | RBF |
|  | Kernel coefficient | 1 |
|  | Regularization parameter | 10 |
| RVFL | Number of nodes | 20 |
|  | Random seed | 10 |
|  | Activation function | Sigmoid |
|  | Learning rate | 0.01 |
|  | Regularization parameter | 0.01 |
| SCN | Stopping condition | Tol $< 0.001$ or $L_{\max} \geq 100$ |
|  | $r$ | 0.9 to 1 |
|  | $\lambda$ | 0.5, 1, 3, 5, 10 |
| SCSO | Initial population | 50 |
|  | Number of iterations | 50 |

the literature, ensuring a robust baseline with 20 nodes, a learning rate of 0.01, regularization parameters of 0.01, and Sigmoid function as the activation function. SCN includes stopping conditions where the model error is less than 0.001, or the maximum number of nodes reaches $100(L_{\max})$, and the control parameter $r$ ranges from 0.9 to 1; the values of $\lambda$ are $0.5, 1, 3, 5,$ and $10$ . The parameters of decay regularization are finely adjusted, with the regularization parameter set to 0.01. The initial population size and number of iterations for SCSO are both set to 50. The parameter settings for each model are shown in Table 2.1. After 20 experiments, we take the average of all experimental results.

The primary objective of the comparative experiments involved evaluating the performance differences between the proposed model and existing techniques (Models 1–3). These models served as baselines to demonstrate the proposed model's advantages in predicting the RUL of UAV batteries. In the comparative experiments, all models were tested on the same dataset using identical data preprocessing

**Table 2.2.**  Error analysis in comparison experiments.

| Datasets | Metrics | Proposed | Model 1 | Model 2 | Model 3 |
|---|---|---|---|---|---|
| LLF | RMSE | 0.0496 | 0.0813 | 0.0687 | 0.8025 |
|  | MAE | 0.0433 | 0.0676 | 0.0620 | 0.0444 |
|  | $R^2$ | 0.8557 | 0.6578 | 0.7529 | 0.1951 |
|  | Time | 0.0092 | 0.0086 | 0.9102 | 0.0036 |
| ULA | RMSE | 0.0529 | 0.0960 | 0.0746 | 0.0926 |
|  | MAE | 0.0450 | 0.0784 | 0.0620 | 0.0760 |
|  | $R^2$ | 0.8300 | 0.4770 | 0.6832 | 0.5135 |
|  | Time | 0.0070 | 0.0089 | 0.9770 | 0.0023 |
| LRF | RMSE | 0.0567 | 0.1051 | 0.0722 | 0.7582 |
|  | MAE | 0.0487 | 0.0865 | 0.0615 | 0.0564 |
|  | $R^2$ | 0.8016 | 0.3751 | 0.6992 | 0.5785 |
|  | Time | 0.0089 | 0.0097 | 0.8540 | 0.0018 |
| URA | RMSE | 0.0471 | 0.1029 | 0.0754 | 0.2538 |
|  | MAE | 0.0378 | 0.0898 | 0.0651 | 0.1032 |
|  | $R^2$ | 0.8626 | 0.3269 | 0.6337 | 0.5948 |
|  | Time | 0.0085 | 0.0096 | 0.8884 | 0.0010 |

**Table 2.3.**  Performance comparison of models 1 to 4.

| | LLF | | ULA | | LRF | | URA | |
|---|---|---|---|---|---|---|---|---|
| Model | PRMSE (%) | PMAE (%) | PRMSE (%) | PMAE (%) | PRMSE (%) | PMAE (%) | PRMSE (%) | PMAE (%) |
|---|---|---|---|---|---|---|---|---|
| Model 1 | 38.99 | 35.95 | 44.90 | 42.60 | 46.05 | 43.70 | 54.23 | 57.91 |
| Model 2 | 27.80 | 30.16 | 29.09 | 27.42 | 21.47 | 20.81 | 37.53 | 41.94 |
| Model 3 | 93.82 | 2.48 | 42.87 | 40.79 | 92.52 | 13.65 | 81.44 | 63.37 |
| Model 4 | 77.33 | 77.51 | 57.30 | 58.41 | 64.56 | 65.82 | 69.69 | 71.85 |

methods, ensuring the fairness of the comparison and the validity of the results. Performance evaluation metrics, including RMSE, MAE, $R^2$, and prediction time, were selected to assess each model's accuracy, robustness, and efficiency comprehensively. Prediction results for datasets LLF, ULA, LRF, and URA are given in Table 2.2. The comparative analysis of the Proposed Model versus other models is provided in Table 2.3.

Based on these comparative experiment data, the following conclusions are drawn: The proposed model exhibited lower RMSE and MAE values across all datasets, signifying a substantial performance improvement over Models 1–3. This result underscores the proposed model's efficiency in processing complex data and accurately capturing battery degradation trends. The comparison of $R^2$ values demonstrated that the proposed model achieved a higher degree of fit, indicating a stronger correlation between predicted and actual values, affirming the model's robustness and reliability across diverse conditions.

While the BP neural network displayed high accuracy, ranking second to the proposed model, its time efficiency significantly lagged. In the context of UAV battery RUL prediction, where time efficiency is crucial, the BP model's lengthy training and prediction times limit its practicality. Despite the BP model's accuracy, its considerably longer runtime than other models necessitates recording its results in tables but excluding them from error charts to emphasize response speed in UAV battery RUL prediction applications.

In contrast, the RVFL network excelled in time efficiency, providing the quickest prediction response time. However, its lack of accuracy and prediction stability could lead to erroneous assessments of UAV battery states, escalating risk during flight operations. This drawback is particularly critical in safety-sensitive UAV applications and highlights the importance of balancing accuracy and response speed.

The proposed model showcased superior overall predictive performance in the comparative experiments, considering accuracy, stability, and time efficiency. It maintained a high level of prediction accuracy and optimized time efficiency, effectively balancing the crucial needs for predictive performance and response speed. Furthermore, the stability of the proposed model's predictions significantly enhances its practical applicability in UAV battery health monitoring and RUL prediction, establishing it as a leading solution among the evaluated models.

### 2.4.3  *Ablation Experiments*

The ablation study assessed how specific components contribute to the model's performance by systematically removing or replacing

**Table 2.4.** Error analysis in ablation experiments.

| Datasets | Metrics | Proposed | Model 4 | Model 5 | Model 6 | Model 7 | Model 8 |
|---|---|---|---|---|---|---|---|
| LLF | RMSE | 0.0496 | 0.2188 | 0.1246 | 0.0887 | 0.0760 | 0.0657 |
| | MAE | 0.0433 | 0.1925 | 0.1069 | 0.0807 | 0.0664 | 0.0571 |
| | $R^2$ | 0.8557 | $-2.8144$ | $-0.1522$ | 0.5038 | 0.6607 | 0.7489 |
| | Time | 0.0092 | 0.0281 | 0.0142 | 0.0061 | 0.0059 | 0.0071 |
| ULA | RMSE | 0.0529 | 0.1239 | 0.1162 | 0.0902 | 0.0732 | 0.0593 |
| | MAE | 0.0450 | 0.1082 | 0.1004 | 0.0825 | 0.0620 | 0.0501 |
| | $R^2$ | 0.8300 | $-0.3017$ | $-0.2425$ | 0.4229 | 0.6599 | 0.7729 |
| | Time | 0.0070 | 0.0240 | 0.0126 | 0.0049 | 0.0058 | 0.0085 |
| LRF | RMSE | 0.0567 | 0.1600 | 0.1040 | 0.0947 | 0.0801 | 0.0610 |
| | MAE | 0.0487 | 0.1425 | 0.0917 | 0.0866 | 0.0679 | 0.0528 |
| | $R^2$ | 0.8016 | $-1.1638$ | 0.2522 | 0.4032 | 0.6108 | 0.7656 |
| | Time | 0.0089 | 0.0211 | 0.0165 | 0.0071 | 0.0045 | 0.0083 |
| URA | RMSE | 0.0471 | 0.1554 | 0.0952 | 0.0879 | 0.0866 | 0.0811 |
| | MAE | 0.0378 | 0.1343 | 0.0818 | 0.0794 | 0.0780 | 0.0693 |
| | $R^2$ | 0.8626 | $-1.2921$ | 0.2724 | 0.4463 | 0.4823 | 0.5258 |
| | Time | 0.0085 | 0.0103 | 0.0109 | 0.0030 | 0.0033 | 0.0086 |

components within the proposed model. The components analyzed included SCN without preprocessing and composite models such as DRSCN, MLSEF–SCN, MLSEF–DRSCN, and MLSEF–CLDMSCSO–SCN. This method elucidates each component's contribution to overall performance by the incremental removal or replacement of specific model parts and observing their impact. Prediction results can be found in Table 2.4. The comparative analysis provided in Table 2.5.

Based on this ablation study data, the following conclusions were drawn:

Model 4, lacking any optimization techniques, demonstrated poor performance across all datasets. For example, on the LLF dataset, the RMSE of Model 4 was notably high, indicating significant deficiencies in explaining data variability and highlighting the limitations of the unoptimized SCN model in handling complex data.

Model 5, utilizing DR for optimization within the SCN framework, showed marked improvements. This underscores DR's effectiveness in reducing over-fitting and enhancing the model's generalization capabilities.

**Table 2.5.**　Performance comparison of models 5 to 8.

| Models | LLF | | ULA | | LRF | | URA | |
|---|---|---|---|---|---|---|---|---|
| | PRMSE (%) | PMAE (%) | PRMSE (%) | PMAE (%) | PRMSE (%) | PMAE (%) | PRMSE (%) | PMAE (%) |
| Model 5 | 60.19 | 59.49 | 54.48 | 55.18 | 45.48 | 46.89 | 50.53 | 53.79 |
| Model 6 | 44.08 | 46.34 | 41.35 | 45.45 | 40.13 | 43.76 | 46.42 | 52.39 |
| Model 7 | 34.74 | 34.79 | 27.73 | 27.42 | 29.21 | 28.28 | 45.61 | 51.54 |
| Model 8 | 24.51 | 24.17 | 10.79 | 10.18 | 7.05 | 7.77 | 41.92 | 45.45 |

Model 6, integrating MLSEF data preprocessing, significantly boosted the model's predictive performance, demonstrating the impact of high-quality preprocessing on model accuracy.

Model 7, combining MLSEF preprocessing and DR, exhibited further performance improvements, exceeding those of models employing MLSEF or DR alone. This result demonstrates the synergistic effect of these two techniques.

Model 8, which employs MLSEF preprocessing and the CLDM–SCSO algorithm, outperformed other models across all performance indicators, particularly in prediction accuracy and data interpretability. This highlights the efficiency of the CLDM–SCSO algorithm in hyperparameter optimization and Model 8's superior capability in RUL prediction for UAV batteries.

Upon comparing Models 4 to 8, Model 8 — combining MLSEF preprocessing, DR, and CLDM-SCSO — emerged as the superior performer in predicting UAV battery RUL. The integration of MLSEF preprocessing enhanced the initial quality of the data, DR effectively prevented over-fitting, and the CLDM–SCSO algorithm optimized the model's hyperparameter settings. Together, these components provide a comprehensive solution that significantly enhances predictive accuracy, interpretability, and efficiency, making Model 8 an optimal choice for UAV battery RUL prediction.

## 2.5　Summary

This study has successfully developed a predictive framework by integrating advanced data preprocessing with enhancements to the SCN model, significantly improving prediction accuracy and reliability for UAV battery RUL. The use of MLSEF enabled the extraction of valuable battery health indicators from complex data signals, effectively supporting accurate battery status predictions. The core contribution of this research resides in its innovative optimization of the SCN model, mainly through the introduction of decay regularization to sparsify the model's output layer weights and the use of the convex lens and dual-mechanism enhanced sand cat swarm optimization algorithm for precise hyper-parameter tuning. These optimization strategies significantly reduced the risk of over-fitting and markedly improved prediction accuracy and generalization ability.

A comprehensive analysis of the ablation experiments underscored the pivotal roles of the MLSEF data preprocessing method, decay regularization, and the CLDM–SCSO algorithm in enhancing predictive performance. Notably, the synergistic application of these techniques exhibited exceptional performance in processing complex UAV battery data, offering a novel and efficient solution for UAV battery health monitoring. In summary, this study's optimization of the SCN model has demonstrated its efficacy and reliability in UAV battery RUL prediction tasks. These optimization measures open new avenues for applying the SCN model in battery health monitoring, showcasing its significant potential in managing complex prediction tasks.

While this study has introduced significant improvements in UAV battery RUL prediction through multi-level signal processing and decay regularization in SCN models, future research could further enhance the model's robustness. Techniques such as kernel density estimation (KDE) could better handle input uncertainty by estimating the underlying data distribution more accurately, enabling the model to make more reliable predictions when faced with noisy or incomplete data. Additionally, applying the maximum correntropy criterion (MCC) could mitigate the impact of outliers by emphasizing the similarity between data points more robustly, thereby enhancing the model's resilience to anomalies. Integrating these techniques into the current framework could improve prediction accuracy and generalization ability, especially in the environments with high data uncertainty.

# Chapter 3

# Regularized Stochastic Configuration Network Based on Weighted Mean of Vectors

Stochastic configuration networks have demonstrated great potential for fast and efficient data modeling. However, the prediction accuracy and convergence rate of SCNs are frequently impacted by the parameter settings of the model. The weighted mean of vectors (INFO) is an innovative swarm intelligence optimization algorithm, with an optimization procedure consisting of three phases: updating rule, vector combining, and a local search. This chapter aims to establish a new regularized SCN based on the weighted mean of vectors algorithm (RSCN-INFO) to optimize its parameter selection and network structure. The regularization term that combines the ridge method with the residual error feedback is introduced into the objective function to dynamically adjust the training parameters. Meanwhile, INFO is employed to automatically explore an appropriate four-dimensional parameter vector for RSCN. The selected parameters may lead to a compact network architecture with a faster reduction of the network residual error. Simulation results over some benchmark datasets demonstrate that the proposed RSCN-INFO showed superior performance with respect to parameter setting, fast convergence, and network compactness compared with other contrast algorithms.

45

## 3.1  Introduction

Neural networks have shown superiority over data modeling because of their powerful representation learning ability to learn patterns with multiple levels of abstraction that make sense to the data (Bengio *et al.*, 2013). However, the gradient-based iterative training process of neural networks is time-consuming and computationally intensive (Wang and Li, 2017b). Feed-forward neural networks (FNNs) with random parameters have drawn widespread attention due to their faster training speed and lower computational cost (Scardapane and Wang, 2017). Igelnik and Pao (1995) found that any continuous function can be approximated by a random vector functional link (RVFL) with probability one under appropriate parameters. The hidden parameters of RVFL were assigned randomly in a preset scope and the output weights were calculated based on the least squares method (Cao *et al.*, 2021). However, determining the preset scope of randomized learning models is challenging, and the widely used scope of random parameters (e.g., $[-1, 1]$) is not always feasible (Li and Wang, 2017).

To resolve the infeasibility of using RVFL networks for data modeling with a fixed scope (i.e., $[-1, 1]$), Wang and Li (2017b) proposed a novel randomized learning framework, termed SCN. The hidden parameters (input weights and biases) of SCN are randomly assigned under a supervisory mechanism and adaptively select their ranges, which indicate prominent merits on human intervention of network structure, range adaptation of hidden layer parameters, and sound generalization (Dai *et al.*, 2019a).

However, SCN starts with a small-sized network structure and gradually adds new hidden nodes into the network until the residual error of SCN is smaller than the tolerance threshold. With the increasing number of hidden nodes, the constructive SCN model is prone to over-fitting and thus poor performance (Wang *et al.*, 2021). Meanwhile, the performance of SCN is frequently impacted by the parameter settings of the model, such as $\lambda$ (the scale factor of weights and bias) and $r$ (the contractive factor in the inequality). Seeking better model parameters is vital for SCN. It is well known that the $L_2$ regularization technique, which adds the "squared magnitude" of the coefficient to the loss function, can prevent the problem of over-fitting effectively. In the famous Residual Network (ResNet),

He *et al.* (2016) let the stacked nonlinear layers fit a residual mapping of $F(x) := H(x) - x$. Inspired by the idea of residual learning in ResNet, we used the current network residual error feedback to dynamically adjust the parameters of SCN.

Therefore, the objective of this section was to automatically obtain better parameters for SCN and get a more compact architecture. First, the $L_2$ regularization item combined with network residual error was introduced to improve the generalization performance of SCN. In addition, a regularized SCN based on INFO was developed to optimize the parameter selection of SCN. INFO is a relatively new swarm intelligence optimization method first published in 2022. Updating rule, vector combining, and a local search were the three core phases of INFO (Ahmadianfar *et al.*, 2022). It is a promising tool for parameter optimization of the regularized stochastic configuration network (RSCN). To summarize, the key contributions of this chapter are as follows:

- Introduce the regularization term that combines the ridge method with the network residual error into the objective function to dynamically adjust the training parameters of SCN.
- Optimize the scope setting of the input weights and biases $\lambda$, contractive factor $r$ in the inequality, regularization coefficient $\eta$, and positive scale factor $\gamma$ of feedback residual error of RSCN by INFO, which in turn achieves a better RSCN model with respect to fast convergence and structure compactness.
- Illustrate the merits of RSCN-INFO on one function approximation and three benchmark regression datasets. The evaluation results justify the effectiveness of the proposed RSCN-INFO.

## 3.2 Preliminaries

This section briefly reviews the newer weighted mean of vectors algorithm (INFO). INFO is a new population-based optimization algorithm that employs updating rule, vector combining, and local search to move the population's position in $D$-dimensional search domains. Given a population with $N_P$ vectors, $X_{l,j}^g = \{x_{l,1}^g, x_{l,2}^g, \ldots, x_{l,D}^g\}$, $l = 1, 2, \ldots, N_P$.

INFO randomly selected three differential vectors ($a1 \neq a2 \neq a3$) to calculate the weighted mean of vectors. To increase the diversity of the population, the best, better, and worst solutions were employed to define the MeanRule (mean-based rule) as:

$$\text{MeanRule} = k \times WM1_l^g + (1-k) \times WM2_l^g, \tag{3.1}$$

in which

$$WM1_l^g = \alpha \times \frac{w_1(x_{a1} - x_{a2}) + w_2(x_{a1} - x_{a3}) + w_3(x_{a2} - x_{a3})}{w_1 + w_2 + w_3 + \varepsilon}$$
$$+ \varepsilon \times \text{rand}, \tag{3.2}$$

$$w_1 = \cos((f(x_{a1}) - f(x_{a2})) + \pi) \times \exp\left(-\frac{f(x_{a1}) - f(x_{a2})}{\omega}\right), \tag{3.3}$$

$$w_2 = \cos((f(x_{a1}) - f(x_{a3})) + \pi) \times \exp\left(-\frac{f(x_{a1}) - f(x_{a3})}{\omega}\right), \tag{3.4}$$

$$w_3 = \cos((f(x_{a2}) - f(x_{a3})) + \pi) \times \exp\left(-\frac{f(x_{a2}) - f(x_{a3})}{\omega}\right), \tag{3.5}$$

$$\omega = \max(f(x_{a1}), f(x_{a2}), f(x_{a3})), \tag{3.6}$$

$$WM2_l^g = \alpha \times \frac{w_1(x_{\text{bs}} - x_{\text{bt}}) + w_2(x_{\text{bs}} - x_{ws}) + w_3(x_{\text{bt}} - x_{ws})}{w_1 + w_2 + w_3 + \varepsilon}$$
$$+ \varepsilon \times \text{rand}, \tag{3.7}$$

$$w_1 = \cos((f(x_{\text{bs}}) - f(x_{\text{bt}})) + \pi) \times \exp\left(-\frac{f(x_{\text{bs}}) - f(x_{\text{bt}})}{\omega}\right), \tag{3.8}$$

$$w_2 = \cos((f(x_{\text{bs}}) - f(x_{ws})) + \pi) \times \exp\left(-\frac{f(x_{\text{bs}}) - f(x_{ws})}{\omega}\right), \tag{3.9}$$

$$w_3 = \cos((f(x_{\text{bt}}) - f(x_{ws})) + \pi) \times \exp\left(-\frac{f(x_{\text{bt}}) - f(x_{ws})}{\omega}\right), \tag{3.10}$$

$$\omega = f(x_{ws}). \tag{3.11}$$

The weighted mean of vectors was used to generate two new vectors as follows:

$$\begin{cases} z1_l^g = x_l^g + \sigma \times \text{MeanRule} + \text{randn} \times \dfrac{(x_{\text{bs}} - x_{a1}^g)}{(f(x_{\text{bs}}) - f(x_{a1}^g) + 1)}, \\[2ex] z2_l^g = x_{\text{bs}} + \sigma \times \text{MeanRule} + \text{randn} \times \dfrac{(x_{a1}^g - x_{a2}^g)}{(f(x_{a1}^g) - f(x_{a2}^g) + 1)}, \end{cases}$$

$$\text{rand} < 0.5, \tag{3.12}$$

$$\begin{cases} z1_l^g = x_a^g + \sigma \times \text{MeanRule} + \text{randn} \times \dfrac{(x_{a2}^g - x_{a3}^g)}{(f(x_{a2}^g) - f(x_{a3}^g) + 1)}, \\[2ex] z2_l^g = x_{\text{bt}} + \sigma \times \text{MeanRule} + \text{randn} \times \dfrac{(x_{a1}^g - x_{a2}^g)}{(f(x_{a1}^g) - f(x_{a2}^g) + 1)}, \end{cases}$$

$$\text{rand} \geq 0.5, \tag{3.13}$$

where $f(x)$ is defined as the objective function, three different integers $(a1, a2, a3)$ are randomly chosen from $[1, N_P]$, $z1_l^g$ and $z2_l^g$ are two new vectors, and $\sigma$ is the scaling rate of a vector.

The two new vectors $z1_l^g$ and $z2_l^g$ are combined with vector $x_l^g$ to generate a new vector $\mu_l^g$ as:

$$\begin{cases} \begin{cases} \mu_l^g = z1_l^g + \mu.|z1_l^g - z2_l^g|, \text{rand} < 0.5, \\ \mu_l^g = z2_l^g + \mu.|z1_l^g - z2_l^g|, \text{rand} \geq 0.5, \end{cases} & \text{rand} < 0.5, \\[2ex] \mu_l^g = x_l^g, & \text{rand} \geq 0.5, \end{cases} \tag{3.14}$$

where $\mu_l^g$ is the composite vector of the $g$th generation.

The local search operator used the global position $(x_{\text{best}}^g)$ and the MeanRule to help INFO convergence to global optima as:

$$\begin{cases} \mu_l^g = x_{\text{bs}} + \text{randn} \times (\text{MeanRule} + \text{randn} \\ \qquad \times (x_{\text{bs}}^g - x_{a1}^g)), & \text{rand} < 0.5, \\[2ex] \mu_l^g = x_{\text{rnd}} + \text{randn} \times (\text{MeanRule} + \text{randn} \\ \qquad \times (v_1 \times x_{\text{bs}} - v_2 \times x_{\text{rnd}})), & \text{rand} \geq 0.5, \end{cases} \tag{3.15}$$

in which

$$x_{\text{rnd}} = \phi \times x_{\text{avg}} + (1 - \phi) \times (\phi \times x_{\text{bt}} + (1 - \phi) \times x_{\text{bs}}), \tag{3.16}$$

$$x_{\text{avg}} = \frac{(x_a + x_b + x_c)}{3}, \tag{3.17}$$

where rand and $\phi$ are two random values within $[0, 1]$ and $(0, 1)$, respectively. The random value $v_1$ and $v_2$ increased the best position's influence on the vector. INFO updated the best vector ($x_{\text{best}}$) and returned $x_{\text{best}}^{g}$ as the final solution. For more details about the INFO algorithm, refer to (Ahmadianfar *et al.*, 2022).

## 3.3  Methodology

### 3.3.1  *Regularized Stochastic Configuration Network*

Given a training dataset $(x_i, t_i)_{i=1}^{N}$, the objective function of the SCN with $L_2$ norm penalty term could be expressed as:

$$\min : J = \frac{1}{2}\|\beta\|^2 + \frac{\eta}{2}\sum_{i=1}^{N} E_i^2, \tag{3.18}$$

$$\text{s.t. } : h(x_i)\beta = t_i - E_i, \forall i,$$

where $h(x_i)$ stands for the hidden output for the input $x_i$, $\eta$ is a non-negative real number, and the regularization coefficient $\eta$ balances the residual error $(\sum_{i=1}^{N} E_i^2)$ and norm of the output weights $(\|\beta\|^2)$.

SCN added new hidden neuron $\beta_L, g_L$, incrementally leading to $f_L = f_{L-1} + g_L\beta_L$. After dynamically adjusting the output weights during the training process, the current residual error was added to the $L_2$ regularization term. After adding the $L$th new hidden node into an established SCN model with $L-1$ hidden nodes, a new objective function was introduced as:

$$f(\beta_L) = \frac{1}{2}\begin{bmatrix} \beta & \beta_L \end{bmatrix}\begin{bmatrix} \beta \\ \beta_L \end{bmatrix} + \frac{\eta}{2}\|E_L\|^2$$

$$= \frac{1}{2}\|\beta\|^2 + \frac{1}{2}\|\beta_L\|^2 + \frac{\eta}{2}\left\|E_{L-1} - \left(g_L + \frac{\|g_L\|^2}{\gamma}E_{L-1}\right)\beta_L\right\|^2. \tag{3.19}$$

where $\gamma$ is the positive scale factor of feedback residual error. The derivative of function of Eq. (3.19) with respect to $\beta_L$ can be denoted as:

$$\frac{\partial f(\beta_L)}{\partial \beta_L} = \beta_L - \eta\left\langle E_{L-1}, g_L + \frac{\|g_L\|^2}{\gamma}E_{L-1}\right\rangle + \eta\left\|g_L + \frac{\|g_L\|^2}{\gamma}E_{L-1}\right\|^2\beta_L. \tag{3.20}$$

Letting Eq. (3.20) be equal to 0, the output weights of the $L$th hidden node was obtained by:

$$\beta_L = \frac{\langle E_{L-1}, g_L + \frac{\|g_L\|^2}{\gamma} E_{L-1}\rangle}{\|g_L + \frac{\|g_L\|^2}{\gamma} E_{L-1}\|^2 + \frac{1}{\eta}}. \tag{3.21}$$

**Theorem 3.1.** *Assume that $span(\Gamma)$ is dense in $L_2$ space. Given $0 < r < 1$, $0 < \eta$, $0 < \gamma$, and a non-negative real number sequence $\mu_L$, with $\mu_L \geq 1 - r$ and $\lim_{L\to+\infty} \mu_L = 0$. $\forall g \in \Gamma$, $0 < \|g\| < b_g$ for some $b_g \in \mathbb{R}^+$. For $L = 1, 2, \ldots$ and $q = 1, 2, \ldots, m$, the random basis function $g_L$ is generated by Eq. (3.22), and the output weights of the $L$th hidden neuron are obtained by Eq. (3.23). Then, the SCN has $\lim_{L\to+\infty} \|f - f_L\| = 0$:*

$$\frac{\langle E_{L-1,q}, g_L + \frac{\|g_L\|^2}{\gamma} E_{L-1,q}\rangle^2}{(\|g_L + \frac{\|g_L\|^2}{\gamma} E_{L-1,q}\|^2 + \frac{1}{\eta})^2 / (\|g_L + \frac{\|g_L\|^2}{\gamma} E_{L-1,q}\|^2 + \frac{2}{\eta})} \tag{3.22}$$
$$\geq (1 - r - \mu_L)\|E_{L-1,q}\|^2, \quad q = 1, 2, \ldots, m,$$

$$\beta_{L,q} = \frac{\langle E_{L-1,q}, g_L + \frac{\|g_L\|^2}{\gamma} E_{L-1,q}\rangle}{\|g_L + \frac{\|g_L\|^2}{\gamma} E_{L-1,q}\|^2 + \frac{1}{\eta}}, \quad q = 1, 2, \ldots, m. \tag{3.23}$$

**Proof.** First, the monotonically decreasing property of $\|E_L\|$ will be proved.

$$\|E_L\|^2 - \|E_{L-1}\|^2$$

$$= \sum_{q=1}^{m}\left(\left\langle E_{L-1,q} - \left(g_L + \frac{\|g_L\|^2}{\gamma} E_{L-1,q}\right)\beta_L, E_{L-1,q}\right.\right.$$

$$\left.\left. - \left(g_L + \frac{\|g_L\|^2}{\gamma} E_{L-1,q}\right)\beta_L\right\rangle - \langle E_{L-1,q}, E_{L-1,q}\rangle\right)$$

$$= \sum_{q=1}^{m}\left(-2\left\langle E_{L-1,q}, \left(g_L + \frac{\|g_L\|^2}{\gamma} E_{L-1,q}\right)\beta_L\right\rangle\right.$$

$$\left. + \left\langle\left(g_L + \frac{\|g_L\|^2}{\gamma} E_{L-1,q}\right)\beta_L, \left(g_L + \frac{\|g_L\|^2}{\gamma} E_{L-1,q}\right)\beta_L\right\rangle\right)$$

$$= \sum_{q=1}^{m} \left( -2 \frac{\left\langle E_{L-1,q}, \left( g_L + \frac{\|g_L\|^2}{\gamma} E_{L-1,q} \right) \beta_L \right\rangle^2}{\left\| g_L + \frac{\|g_L\|^2}{\gamma} E_{L-1,q} \right\|^2 + \frac{1}{\eta}} \right.$$

$$\left. + \frac{\left\langle E_{L-1,q}, g_L + \frac{\|g_L\|^2}{\gamma} E_{L-1,q} \right\rangle^2 \left\| g_L + \frac{\|g_L\|^2}{\gamma} E_{L-1,q} \right\|^2}{\left( \left\| g_L + \frac{\|g_L\|^2}{\gamma} E_{L-1,q} \right\|^2 + \frac{1}{\eta} \right)^2} \right)$$

$$= -\sum_{q=1}^{m} \frac{\left( \left\| g_L + \frac{\|g_L\|^2}{\gamma} E_{L-1,q} \right\|^2 + \frac{2}{\eta} \right) \left\langle E_{L-1,q}, g_L + \frac{\|g_L\|^2}{\gamma} E_{L-1,q} \right\rangle^2}{\left( \left\| g_L + \frac{\|g_L\|^2}{\gamma} E_{L-1,q} \right\|^2 + \frac{1}{\eta} \right)^2}$$

$$= -\sum_{q=1}^{m} \frac{\langle E_{L-1,q}, g_L + \frac{\|g_L\|^2}{\gamma} E_{L-1,q} \rangle^2}{(\|g_L + \frac{\|g_L\|^2}{\gamma} E_{L-1,q}\|^2 + \frac{1}{\eta})^2 / (\|g_L + \frac{\|g_L\|^2}{\gamma} E_{L-1,q}\|^2 + \frac{2}{\eta})} \leq 0. \tag{3.24}$$

The monotonically decreasing property of $\|E_L\|$ has been proven. From Eqs. (3.22)–(3.24):

$$\|E_L\|^2 - (r + \mu_L)\|E_{L-1}\|^2$$

$$= \sum_{q=1}^{m} \left( \left\langle E_{L-1,q} - \left( g_L + \frac{\|g_L\|^2}{\gamma} E_{L-1,q} \right) \beta_L, E_{L-1,q} \right. \right.$$

$$\left. - \left( g_L + \frac{\|g_L\|^2}{\gamma} E_{L-1,q} \right) \beta_L \right\rangle$$

$$\left. - (r + \mu_L)\langle E_{L-1,q}, E_{L-1,q} \rangle \right). \tag{3.25}$$

According to Eq. (3.22),

$$\|E_L\|^2 - (r + \mu_L)\|E_{L-1}\|^2 \leq 0. \tag{3.26}$$

Therefore,

$$\|E_L\|^2 \leq r\|E_{L-1}\|^2 + \mu_L\|E_{L-1}\|^2. \tag{3.27}$$

Theorem 3.1 has given $\lim_{L\to+\infty}\mu_L = 0$, which means $\lim_{L\to+\infty}\mu_L\|E_{L-1}\|^2 = 0$. Based on Eq. (3.24), $\lim_{L\to+\infty}\|E_L\|^2 = 0$. Therefore, $\lim_{L\to+\infty}\|E_L\| = 0$. $\qquad\square$

**Remark 3.1.** In Theorem 3.1, the output weights are evaluated by Eq. (3.23) and kept fixed. This may cause a slow convergence rate. To cope with this problem, the output weights of all hidden neurons are updated by the least squares method after the new hidden node has been added. Let $[\beta_1^*, \beta_2^*, \ldots, \beta_L^*] = \arg\min_\beta \frac{\eta}{2}\|f - (G + \frac{\widetilde{G}}{\gamma} \circ E)\beta\|^2 + \frac{1}{2}\|\beta\|^2$, where $G = [g_1, g_2, \ldots, g_L]$, $\widetilde{G} = [\|g_1\|^2, \|g_2\|^2, \ldots, \|g_L\|^2]$, $E = [E_0^*, E_1^*, \ldots, E_{L-1}^*]$, 'o' denotes the Hadamard product (element-wise multiplication) and $E_L^* = f - \sum_{j=1}^L (g_j + \frac{\|g_L\|^2}{\gamma}E_{j-1}^*)\beta_j^*$.

The output weights are calculated by

$$[\beta_1^*, \beta_2^*, \ldots, \beta_L^*] = \arg\min_\beta \frac{\eta}{2}\left\|f - \left(G + \frac{\widetilde{G}}{\gamma} \circ E\right)\beta\right\|^2 + \frac{1}{2}\|\beta\|^2$$

$$= \left(\left(G + \frac{\widetilde{G}}{\gamma} \circ E\right)^T \left(G + \frac{\widetilde{G}}{\gamma} \circ E\right) + \frac{I}{\eta}\right)^{-1}\left(G + \frac{\widetilde{G}}{\gamma} \circ E\right)^T f.$$

$$(3.28)$$

The output weights are recalculated in accordance with Eq. (3.28) as the newly added hidden neuron is generated to satisfy Eq. (3.22). The inequality constraint guarantees the universal approximation capability of RSCN. The process of proof is similar to Theorem 3.1, so the detailed proof procedure is omitted.

**Remark 3.2.** In Eq. (3.19), the residual error $(\frac{\|g_L\|^2}{\gamma}E_{L-1})$ is added into the regularization term. The reason why $\frac{\|g_L\|^2}{\gamma}$ is used instead of $\gamma$ is that the value of the residual error is equal to the output of training samples before adding hidden neurons into the network $(E_0 = T)$. So, the residual error is relatively larger at the beginning of the construction process. It gradually decreases as the constructive process proceeds. Meanwhile, due to the randomness of SCN, $g_L$ is randomly generated under a set of inequality constraints. The scale factor $\frac{\|g_L\|^2}{\gamma}$ makes it possible for the feedback residual error

$\left(\frac{\|g_L\|^2}{\gamma} E_{L-1}\right)$ to adjust dynamically in pace with the change of the hidden output $(g_L)$.

### 3.3.2 *Regularized Stochastic Configuration Network with Weighted Mean of Vectors Algorithm*

INFO is a very competitive new optimization algorithm. In this section, INFO is applied to optimize the parameter $\lambda$, the contractive factor $r$, the regularization coefficient $\eta$, and the positive scale factor $\gamma$ for RSCN. The widely-used root mean square error (RMSE) is employed as the fitness function:

$$\mathrm{RMSE} = \sqrt{\frac{1}{N} \sum_{i=1}^{N} \left[\sum_{j=1}^{L} g_j(x_i w_j + b_j)\beta_j - t_i\right]^2}. \tag{3.29}$$

For convenience's sake, $\xi_{L,q}, q = 1, 2, \ldots, m$ is defined to describe the algorithm:

$$\xi_{L,q} = \frac{\left\langle E_{L-1,q}, g_L + \frac{\|g_L\|^2}{\gamma} E_{L-1,q}\right\rangle^2}{\zeta} - (1 - r - \mu_L)\|E_{L-1,q}\|^2, \tag{3.30}$$

where

$$\zeta = \frac{\left(\|g_L + \frac{\|g_L\|^2}{\gamma} E_{L-1,q}\|^2 + \frac{1}{\eta}\right)^2}{\|g_L + \frac{\|g_L\|^2}{\gamma} E_{L-1,q}\|^2 + \frac{2}{\eta}}. \tag{3.31}$$

### 3.3.3 *Computational Complexity*

The computational complexity of the INFO algorithm depends on the size of the population $N_P$, the times of iterations $G_{\max}$, and the dimensional search domain $D$. The complexity of INFO is $O(N_P \times G_{\max} \times D)$. For SCN, assume that a set of datasets with $N$ inputs $X = \{x_1, x_2, \ldots, x_N\}$, and the maximum number of hidden layer neurons of SCN is $L_{\max}$. The main cost of SCN is caused by computing Moore–Penrose pseudo-inverse $H_L^{\dagger} T$.

A rough estimate of the computational complexity of $H_L^\dagger$ can be expressed as $O(NL_{\max}^3 + N^2 L_{\max}^2 + L_{\max}^4)$(Li and Wang, 2017). Note that the cost of $H_L^\dagger T$ is calculated by the widely-used singular value decomposition. Hence, the total complexity of RSCN-INFO is $O(N_P \times G_{\max} \times D \times (NL_{\max}^3 + N^2 L_{\max}^2 + L_{\max}^4))$.

## 3.4 Experimental Results and Discussion

The effectiveness of RSCN-INFO was evaluated on a function approximation and three benchmark datasets from the Knowledge Extraction based on Evolutionary Learning (KEEL)[1] dataset repository supported by the Spanish Ministry of Science and Technology. The approximation function is a conventional high nonlinear compound function that is widely used to evaluate randomized neural networks. The KEEL dataset contains classification, regression, unsupervised, and time series datasets. To verify the effectiveness of RSCN-INFO, it was compared with classical IRVFL, SCN (Wang and Li, 2017b), RSCN (Wang *et al.*, 2021), and DASCN-II (Wang *et al.*, 2020c). All the experiments were implemented with MATLAB R2019b on a PC with AMD Ryzen 7 3.20 GHz CPU, NVIDIA GeForce MX450 GPU, and 16GB RAM.

### 3.4.1 *Function Approximation Problem*

Let the real-valued function $f(x)$ be defined as follows (Tyukin and Prokhorov, 2009):

$$y = 0.2e^{-(10x-4)^2} + 0.5e^{-(80x-40)^2} + 0.3e^{-(80x-20)^2}, \quad x \in [0, 1]. \tag{3.32}$$

We randomly generated 1,000 training samples and 300 test samples from the uniform distribution and a regularly spaced grid

---

[1]http://www.keel.es.

**Table 3.1.** Performance comparisons of different methods on function approximation problem.

| | Training results | |
|---|---|---|
| Methods | $L = 25$ | $L = 50$ |
| IRVFL | $0.08493 \pm 0.00548$ | $0.08389 \pm 0.00426$ |
| SCN | $0.02421 \pm 0.00479$ | $0.00535 \pm 0.00342$ |
| RSCN | $0.02090 \pm 0.00448$ | $0.00477 \pm 0.00222$ |
| DASCN-II | $0.02267 \pm 0.00345$ | $0.00512 \pm 0.00268$ |
| RSCN-INFO | $\mathbf{0.00179 \pm 0.00025}$ | $\mathbf{0.00015 \pm 0.00008}$ |

| | Test results | |
|---|---|---|
| Methods | $L = 25$ | $L = 50$ |
| IRVFL | $0.08405 \pm 0.00524$ | $0.06756 \pm 0.00559$ |
| SCN | $0.02681 \pm 0.00535$ | $0.00570 \pm 0.00364$ |
| RSCN | $0.02344 \pm 0.00499$ | $0.00506 \pm 0.00252$ |
| DASCN-II | $0.02523 \pm 0.00368$ | $0.00553 \pm 0.00285$ |
| RSCN-INFO | $\mathbf{0.00209 \pm 0.00031}$ | $\mathbf{0.00016 \pm 0.00009}$ |

over $[0, 1]$. Table 3.1 compares the function approximation performance of RSCN-INFO with IRVFL, SCN, RSCN, and DASCN-II. Since our proposed RSCN-INFO could achieve reliable and accurate performance with the lower number of hidden neurons, the value of $L_{\max}$ was set to 25. In the simulations, the value of RMSE remained virtually unchanged when the widely used setting $[-1, 1]$ was set for IRVFL. So, the scope of random parameters for IRVFL was set as $[-250, 250]$. For SCNs, the value of $T_{\max}$ was set to 100, $\lambda$ and $r$ were selected from the set $\{100 : 1 : 200\}$ and $\{0.9, 0.99, 0.999, 0.9999, 0.99999, 0.999999\}$. In RSCN-INFO, the population size $N_p$ and the maximum generations were set to 30 and 10, respectively. The lower bounds and upper bounds of $\lambda$, $r$, $\eta$, and $\gamma$ were set to $[100, 200]$, $[0.9, 0.999999]$, $[0, 2^{40}]$, and $[10^5, 10^9]$.

Moreover, Table 3.1 reports the average RMSE and standard deviation results of different models. It is evident that RSCN-INFO achieved more favorable results than the other algorithms. As seen in Table 3.1, the IRVFL showed far worse performance than that of

SCNs, while the performance of our proposed RSCN-INFO was the best.

### 3.4.2  *Benchmark Datasets*

Three real-world benchmark datasets for regression from KEEL were employed as experimental datasets. Specifications of these datasets are given in Table 3.2.

Each test's statistical results for the 20 run times and the average value of RMSE were selected to evaluate the performance of the different algorithms. The IRVFL could not reach the preset tolerance threshold, so it was omitted here. In this case, the scope of random parameters $\lambda$ in SCN was selected from the set $\{1 : 0.1 : 5\}$ and the lower and upper bounds of $\lambda$ in RSCN-INFO were set to $[1, 5]$. All the other parameters were set the same as the function approximation.

Table 3.3 shows similar performance between RSCN-INFO and the competitor algorithms on concrete. The reason for this phenomenon is that the concrete dataset contained smaller features and instances. For the Compactiv and Pole datasets, Tables 3.4 and 3.5 clearly show that RSCN-INFO can achieve lower RMSE in terms of both training and test results. Intuitively and obviously, the RMSE of RSCN was used as the fitness function of INFO. In essence, INFO explored a global optimum solution that minimizes the fitness function in a four-dimensional search domain $(\lambda, r, \gamma, \eta)$ over several successive generations.

To verify the effectiveness of RSCN-INFO, Table 3.6 lists the computational time among SCN, RSCN, DASCN-II, and RSCN-INFO on benchmark datasets. We found that the training time of RSCN-INFO was significantly shorter than the other methods on

**Table 3.2.**  Specifications of three benchmark regression datasets.

| Datasets | Attributes | | Instances |
|---|---|---|---|
| | Features | Output | |
| Concrete | 8 | 1 | 1,030 |
| Compactiv | 21 | 1 | 8,192 |
| Pole | 26 | 1 | 14,998 |

Table 3.3. Performance comparisons of different methods on Concrete.

| Methods | Training, test results | | | | |
|---|---|---|---|---|---|
| | $L = 20$ | $L = 30$ | $L = 40$ | $L = 50$ | $L = 60$ |
| SCN | $0.09842 \pm 0.10212$ | $0.09122 \pm 0.09786$ | $0.08626 \pm 0.09655$ | $0.08098 \pm 0.09381$ | $0.07566 \pm 0.09114$ |
| RSCN | $0.09912 \pm 0.10187$ | $0.09156 \pm 0.09831$ | $0.08613 \pm 0.09724$ | $0.08113 \pm 0.09438$ | $0.07594 \pm 0.09190$ |
| DASCN-II | $\mathbf{0.09840 \pm 0.10109}$ | $0.09175 \pm 0.09769$ | $0.08626 \pm 0.09613$ | $0.08066 \pm 0.09405$ | $0.07566 \pm 0.09239$ |
| RSCN-INFO | $0.09957 \pm 0.10391$ | $\mathbf{0.08933 \pm 0.09684}$ | $\mathbf{0.08097 \pm 0.09427}$ | $\mathbf{0.07545 \pm 0.09596}$ | $\mathbf{0.06944 \pm 0.09439}$ |

Table 3.4. Performance comparisons of different methods on Compactiv.

| Methods | Training, test results | | | | |
|---|---|---|---|---|---|
| | $L = 20$ | $L = 40$ | $L = 60$ | $L = 80$ | $L = 100$ |
| SCN | $0.08380 \pm 0.08076$ | $0.04963 \pm 0.05035$ | $0.03646 \pm 0.03823$ | $0.03090 \pm 0.03264$ | $0.02855 \pm 0.03032$ |
| RSCN | $0.08317 \pm 0.08091$ | $0.04902 \pm 0.04981$ | $0.03595 \pm 0.03752$ | $0.03093 \pm 0.03243$ | $0.02872 \pm 0.03049$ |
| DASCN-II | $0.08345 \pm 0.08081$ | $0.04972 \pm 0.05003$ | $0.03638 \pm 0.03781$ | $0.03096 \pm 0.03263$ | $0.02858 \pm 0.03028$ |
| RSCN-INFO | $\mathbf{0.05695 \pm 0.05613}$ | $\mathbf{0.03863 \pm 0.03856}$ | $\mathbf{0.03117 \pm 0.03211}$ | $\mathbf{0.02815 \pm 0.02932}$ | $\mathbf{0.02658 \pm 0.02839}$ |

Table 3.5. Performance comparisons of different methods on Pole.

| Methods | Training, test results | | | | |
|---|---|---|---|---|---|
| | $L = 30$ | $L = 60$ | $L = 90$ | $L = 120$ | $L = 150$ |
| SCN | $0.26345 \pm 0.26582$ | $0.22619 \pm 0.23069$ | $0.20756 \pm 0.21426$ | $0.19464 \pm 0.20406$ | $0.18507 \pm 0.19572$ |
| RSCN | $0.26411 \pm 0.26746$ | $0.22831 \pm 0.23278$ | $0.20871 \pm 0.21545$ | $0.19524 \pm 0.20409$ | $0.18542 \pm 0.19602$ |
| DASCN-II | $0.26462 \pm 0.26741$ | $0.22856 \pm 0.23264$ | $0.20895 \pm 0.21497$ | $0.1945 \pm 0.20299$ | $0.18478 \pm 0.19538$ |
| RSCN-INFO | $\mathbf{0.22182 \pm 0.22629}$ | $\mathbf{0.18604 \pm 0.18925}$ | $\mathbf{0.17349 \pm 0.17836}$ | $\mathbf{0.16272 \pm 0.16904}$ | $\mathbf{0.15479 \pm 0.16099}$ |

**Table 3.6.** The computational time of different algorithms on benchmark datasets.

| Datasets | Algorithms | Error tolerance $\tau$ | Training time (Mean $\pm$ STD) |
|---|---|---|---|
| Concrete | SCN | 0.08 | $0.1977 \pm 0.00379$ |
| | RSCN | | $0.2083 \pm 0.03008$ |
| | DASCN-II | | $0.2275 \pm 0.02442$ |
| | RSCN-INFO | | $\mathbf{0.1021 \pm 0.01095}$ |
| Compactiv | SCN | 0.03 | $2.1405 \pm 0.25356$ |
| | RSCN | | $2.1773 \pm 0.16212$ |
| | DASCN-II | | $2.5231 \pm 0.22985$ |
| | RSCN-INFO | | $\mathbf{1.2148 \pm 0.22618}$ |
| Pole | SCN | 0.20 | $6.5387 \pm 0.94180$ |
| | RSCN | | $6.2857 \pm 0.68270$ |
| | DASCN-II | | $7.9776 \pm 1.52610$ |
| | RSCN-INFO | | $\mathbf{1.7529 \pm 0.28892}$ |

the three benchmark datasets. Table 3.6 indicates that RSCN-INFO which employed optimized parameters and could achieve better efficiency. It should be noted that we did not take the parameter optimization process into account in this experiment. The optimization process may consume additional time. However, the improvement of regression accuracy and network structure may be worth the time that is spent on the parameter optimization.

To further illustrate the network compactness of RSCN-INFO, we investigated how many hidden nodes were required to meet a preset error tolerance. As shown in Fig. 3.1, RSCN-INFO requires fewer hidden nodes compared with other methods. It can be deduced that given a preset $\tau$, RSCN-INFO can reach the error tolerance using fewer hidden neurons. This is due to RSCN-INFO using optimized parameters that can achieve a higher residual error reduction. Therefore, the network structure is more compact. It should be pointed out that DASCN-II can also construct a relatively compact SCN. However, the tunable value $\gamma$ in DASCN-II is a fixed value. It is selected empirically and difficult to adjust. Moreover, an inappropriate $\gamma$ will seriously affect the accuracy of the model.

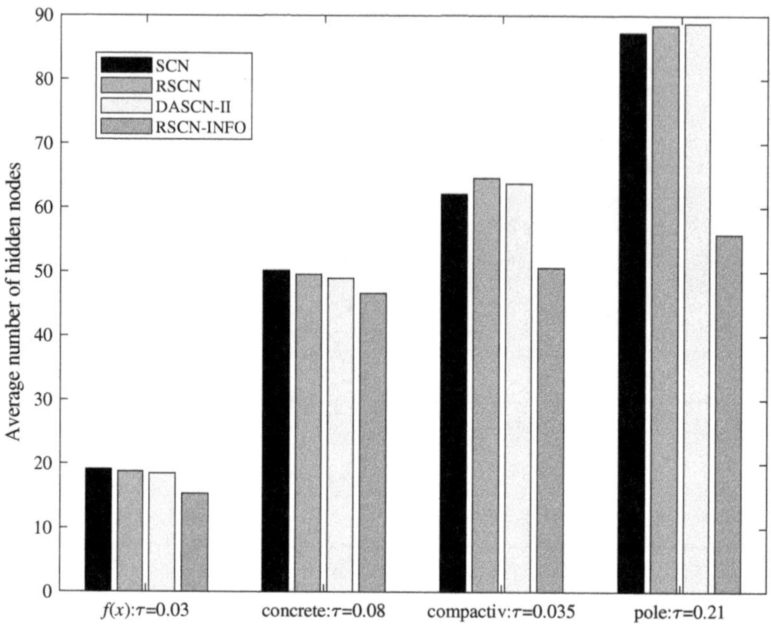



**Fig. 3.1.**　Average number of hidden nodes on $f(x)$ and benchmark datasets.

In classical SCN and its various variants, $\lambda$ tends to set a relatively larger value in complex problems. The parameter $r$ is unfixed and set based on an increasing sequence from 0.9 to 1. The other parameters are selected empirically in connection with practical applications. Therefore, the conclusion may be drawn that RSCN-INFO is not only helpful in adaptively selecting parameters of SCN but also beneficial for constructing a compact network.

## 3.5　Summary

This chapter developed a new regularized SCN based on the INFO optimization algorithm, named RSCN-INFO. On one hand, the added regularization term combines the ridge method with the residual error feedback, contributing to the balance of the structural (output weights) and empirical (network residual error) losses of SCN. On the other hand, RMSE was selected as the fitness function of INFO to assist SCN to locate up-and-coming areas in multi-dimensional search space. A higher residual error decreasing rate is impacted by the parameter selection of RSCN-INFO. The experimental results on a function approximation and three benchmark regression datasets from KEEL indicated that the proposed RSCN-INFO algorithm exhibits considerable advantages in parameter optimization and network structure compactness compared with other algorithms.

In almost all practical modeling tasks, the presence of noise and outliers is inevitable. This optimization strategy will accelerate the degradation of the learning performance of SCN that are subjected to noise or outliers. The robust skills used to weaken the negative influences of noise and outliers will be further discussed.

# Chapter 4

# Stochastic Configuration Networks with Group Lasso Regularization

Block-incremental SCNs (BSCN) extend the original SCNs with block increments to effectively reduce the number of iterations required during model building. Yet, two new issues emerge: the computationally expensive Moore–Penrose generalized inverse in inequality constraints, and some potential redundant hidden nodes. To address these limitations, this study presents efficient block-incremental SCNs (EBSCN) with group lasso regularization, termed EBSCNGL. The hidden block is treated as a specialized form of hidden node, and the output vector is directly replaced with the output matrix in the weights formula of SC-I (the first algorithmic implementation of SCNs) to evaluate the output weights of the newly added hidden block. Subsequently, a new set of inequalities without matrix generalized inverse is presented to ensure the universal approximation capability of EBSCN. Moreover, group lasso regularization is introduced to prune redundant nodes of the hidden layer. We further transform its regularized least-squares solution into an efficient form with proved convergence based on the Woodbury matrix identity. Empirical results on function approximation, benchmark classification, and a practical industrial application verify the efficiency and sparsity of our proposed method.


63

## 4.1 Introduction

Training neural networks (NNs) using randomization techniques has yielded remarkable success, as it can transform the highly nonconvex objective function optimization task into a tractable (often linear) optimization problem (Scardapane and Wang, 2017). SCNs adopt an incremental building approach where a hidden node and its corresponding weights and biases are added to the network under a supervision mechanism in a single iteration. The incremental learning strategy could be improved with some novel strategies to enhance the learning efficiency of SCNs. Wang and Cui (2017) has pointed out that the top several ranked candidate hidden nodes could be added into the network in each iteration to speed up the construction process of SCNs. Subsequently, Dai *et al.* (2019a) proposed a novel block version of SCNs (BSCN), which allows multiple hidden nodes to be added to the network simultaneously. Moreover,Dai *et al.* (2021) further designed hybrid parallel SCNs (HPSCN) by combining the point-incremental method of SCNs and the block-incremental method of BSCN. Qiao and Chen (2023) developed an extension of BSCN with chaotic maps (SCNCM) to dynamically adjust the size of the incremental block, thereby accelerating the construction process of the model. Zhu *et al.* (2019) established two new inequality constraints for SCNs to accelerate the learning process by reducing the reject rate of randomly assigned hidden parameters. The bidirectional SCNs proposed in Cao *et al.* (2021) consists of two alternative modes. The forward learning mode for odd nodes is the same as SCNs, and the backward learning mode for even nodes calculates the hidden parameters at one time according to the residual error feedback. Wu *et al.* (2022a) eliminated the incremental mechanism and directly set the number of hidden nodes for SCNs. They employed an improved sparrow search algorithm to retrain randomly assigned hidden parameters that failed to meet inequality constraints. Li *et al.* (2023c) provided a new inequality constraint and a node selection method based on the contribution degree and correlation of preselected hidden nodes. To enhance the computational efficiency of the pseudo-inverse for large-scale hidden output matrices, Li and Wang (2024b) developed a centralized distributed learning algorithm (ADMM–SCN) based on a divide-and-conquer approach and the alternating direction method of multipliers (ADMM) solver. Sun *et al.* (2024) integrated the generalized M-estimation and $L_2$ regularization into the SCNs model, respectively. The former was utilized to enhance the robustness of the model while the latter was employed to prevent over-fitting. SCNs have also been explored in various other research fields, such as robustness, ensemble learning, regularization technique, etc.

The incorporation of random learning method to train neural networks may lead to generate some low-quality hidden nodes. Thus, it is imperative to take appropriate measures to prune these redundant neurons and optimize the network structure. Lasso ($L_1$ regularization) is a classic approach renowned for reducing model complexity by dropping non-significant weights out of the model. It shrinks the coefficients toward zero by penalizing the sum of absolute values ($L_1$ norm penalty) of regression coefficients. Wang *et al.* (2022b) and Zhao *et al.* (2021) incorporated the lasso and elastic net regularization terms (Lasso and Ridge) into the objective function of SCNs, respectively. Both algorithms evaluated the output weights using the ADMM. However, these two methods are inadequate in eliminating redundant hidden nodes from the architecture as the lasso is designed for selecting individual variables rather than groups of variables. Typically, a neuron can only be removed from the network if all its connections (either incoming or outgoing) have been shrunk to zero during the training process.

Group lasso addresses this issue by simultaneously shrinking predefined groups of coefficients. It divides the coefficients into groups and penalize the sum of the $L_2$ norm of these groups. Group lasso induces sparsity at the node level by shrinking all outgoing connections from a hidden node towards zero (Scardapane *et al.*, 2017). Wang *et al.* (2017b) addressed numerical oscillations during the training process by incorporating smooth functions to approximate the group lasso penalty term. Zhang *et al.* (2019a) introduced four types of smooth functions (Sqrt Form, Quadratic Form, Quartic Form and Sextic Form) to feedforward NNs and elaborated on their convergence in detail. In Wang *et al.* (2020b), the group lasso penalty and the redundancy-control penalty were integrated into the objective function to select important features and control the redundancy level of these chosen features. Kang *et al.* (2022) applied the smoothing group $L_{1/2}$ penalty to prune sigma-pi-sigma NNs. To accelerate the training speed, an adaptive momentum term was employed to update the output weights. Li and Chu (2023) utilized the smoothing $L_{1/2}$ norm to remove redundant nodes in feedforward small-world NNs. Note that the $L_{1/2}$ regularization (Xu *et al.*, 2012) has demonstrated better performance than the $L_1$ norm in feature selection. The aforementioned group lasso and group $L_{1/2}$ regularization techniques have achieved satisfactory sparsity at the node level in various types of NNs. However, these methods primarily rely on the inefficient batch gradient descent algorithm to update the output weights iteratively. In this chapter, we focus on the $L_{2,1}$ norm as the group lasso penalty term to achieve sparsity at the node level. Furthermore, it is worth emphasizing that the proposed algorithm is also applicable to group $L_{1/2}$ regularization.

SCNs with block increments reported in Dai *et al.* (2019a) exhibit superior learning efficiency by reducing the number of iterations required during model construction. However, the improvement is somewhat constrained due to the additional computationally expensive Moore–Penrose generalized inverse operation in the block form of inequality constraints. In the first algorithmic implementation of SCNs (SC-I), a random basis function $g_L$ is generated when adding the $L$th hidden node to the model. Let $e_L$ represent the network residual error of SCNs. The output weights of the $L$th newly added hidden node can be obtained by

$$\beta_{L,q} = \frac{\langle e_{L-1,q}, g_L \rangle}{\|g_L\|^2}. \tag{4.1}$$

whereas in BSCN, let $\Delta_k$ be the hidden block size of the $k$th iteration. The intermediate values of the output weights for the $k$th hidden block are calculated by

$$\beta_{\Delta_k,q} = \left(H_{\Delta_k}^T H_{\Delta_k}\right)^+ H_{\Delta_k}^T e_{L-\Delta_k,q}. \tag{4.2}$$

where $H_{\Delta_k}$ represents the output matrix of the $k$th added hidden block, and $(H_{\Delta_k}^T H_{\Delta_k})^+$ is the Moore–Penrose pseudo-inverse of $H_{\Delta_k}^T H_{\Delta_k}$.

Unfortunately, the presence of $\beta_{\Delta_k,q}$ in the block form of inequality constraints necessitates the computation of the computationally expensive matrix generalized inverse at each iteration in BSCN. As pointed out by the author in Dai *et al.* (2019a), it counteracts the superiority of BSCN to a certain extent. Additionally, the coarse-grained block incremental mechanism and the inherent characteristics of randomized learning algorithms will inevitably generate some low-quality hidden nodes.

To accelerate the training speed and prune low-quality hidden nodes in BSCN, an efficient block incremental stochastic configuration network with group lasso regularization is presented in this chapter. EBSCN inherits the merits of BSCN and abandons its computationally expensive generalized inverse. In BSCN, the intermediate values of the output weights for the newly added hidden block are computed by taking the derivative of the cost function with respect to $\beta_{\Delta_k,q}$. In contrast, we treat $\beta_{\Delta_k,q}$ as a special form of $\beta_{L,q}$, with the only distinction being the replacement of the output vector $(g_L)$ of the $L$th hidden node by the output of the $k$th hidden block in matrix form $(H_{\Delta_k})$. EBSCN requires no computation of the matrix generalized inverse, while preserving the universal approximation capability of SCN. Furthermore, the group lasso regularization method is employed to prune redundant hidden nodes. The output weights formula derived from the regularized least-squares method is reformulated into another form with proved convergence based on the Woodbury matrix identity, and it can achieve convergence within a few number of iterations. Notably, our EBSCNGL eschews the commonly used gradient descent algorithm to update the output weights of the hidden layer. Overall, the primary contributions are as follows:

- Aimed at the problem of the computationally expensive generalized inverse in the block form of inequality in BSCN, a novel supervisory mechanism without the matrix generalized inverse is established to guarantee the universal approximation property of EBSCN.
- For the issue of some potential redundant hidden nodes in BSCN, group lasso regularization is integrated into the objective function to simplify the network architecture. The regularized least-squares solution of EBSCNGL is transformed into an efficient form with proved convergence based on the Woodbury matrix identity.
- Various simulations are carried out to illustrate the superiority of the proposed method. Experimental results on one-dimensional

and two-dimensional function approximation with outliers, as well as eight benchmark classification datasets, and a real-world industrial application demonstrate that EBSCNGL outperforms BSCN in terms of training efficiency and network compactness.


## 4.2  Preliminaries

Block incremental stochastic configuration networks are designed to allow more than one hidden node to be added to the network in each iteration, thereby effectively reducing the number of iterations during the learning process. The incremental construction process of BSCN is depicted in Fig. 4.1.

Suppose that a training dataset with $N$ samples is described as $\{x_i, t_i\}_{i=1}^N \subset \mathbb{R}^d \times \mathbb{R}^m$. $x_i$ and $t_i$ are the $i$th input and output instances, respectively. For a target function that needs to be approximated: $f : \mathbb{R}^d \to \mathbb{R}^m$. Assume a single hidden layer learner model with $L - 1$ hidden nodes has already been built. The network residual error can be represented as $e_{L-1} = f - f_{L-1}$. Given $0 < r < 1$ and a nonnegative real number sequence $\{\mu_L\}$, with $\mu_L \leq (1 - r)$ and

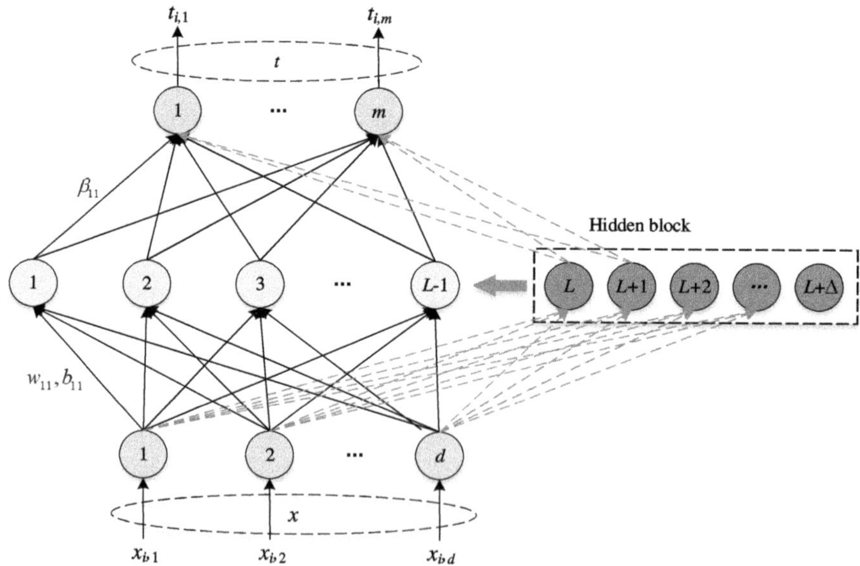

**Fig. 4.1.**  BSCN with block increments.

$\lim_{L\to+\infty}\mu_L = 0$. In BSCN, the randomly assigned parameters for the newly added hidden block need to be satisfied the following set of inequalities.

$$\langle e_{L-\Delta_k,q}(X), H_{\Delta_k}(X)\beta_{\Delta_k,q}\rangle \geqslant \delta_{L,q}, \quad q=1,2,\ldots,m \tag{4.3}$$

where $\delta_{L,q}$ is denoted as

$$\delta_{L,q} = (1-r-\mu_L)\|e_{L-\Delta_k,q}(X)\|^2, \quad q=1,2,\ldots,m \tag{4.4}$$

$H_{\Delta_k}$ and $\beta_{\Delta_k,q}$ in Eq. (4.3) represent the output and the output weights of the $k$th newly added hidden block, respectively. $H_{\Delta_k}$ is a matrix with $N$ rows and $\Delta_k$ columns.

$$H_{\Delta_k}(X) = [h_{L-\Delta_k+1}(X),\ldots,h_L(X)]_{N\times\Delta_k}. \tag{4.5}$$

One thing should be pointed out is that $\beta_{\Delta_k,q}$ is obtained by taking derivative of the network residual error with respect to the output weights. The network residual error is

$$\begin{aligned}
f(\beta) &= \|f-f_L\|^2 \\
&= \|e_{L-\Delta_k}\|^2 - \sum_{q=1}^{m}(2e_{L-\Delta_k,q}^T(H_{\Delta_k}\beta_{\Delta_k,q}) + (H_{\Delta_k}\beta_{\Delta_k,q})^T \\
&\quad \times (H_{\Delta_k}\beta_{\Delta_k,q})).
\end{aligned} \tag{4.6}$$

Differentiating Eq. (4.6) with respect to $\beta_{\Delta_k,q}$ yields that

$$\frac{\partial f(\beta)}{\partial\beta_{\Delta_k,q}} = -2H_{\Delta_k}^T e_{L-\Delta_k,q} + 2H_{\Delta_k}^T H_{\Delta_k}\beta_{\Delta_k,q}. \tag{4.7}$$

Let Eq. (4.7) be equal to zero. Then we get

$$\beta_{\Delta_k,q} = (H_{\Delta_k}^T H_{\Delta_k})^+ H_{\Delta_k}^T e_{L-\Delta_k,q}. \tag{4.8}$$

In the block form of the supervisory mechanism, $\beta_{\Delta_k,q}$ is utilized to constrain the randomly assigned $w_{\Delta_k}$ and $b_{\Delta_k}$ for the newly added hidden block. BSCN still computes the output weights of the hidden layer all together through the global least squares method after the residual error reaches a pre-set threshold value $\epsilon$. The interested reader is referred to Wang and Li (2017b) and Dai *et al.* (2019a) for technical details on SCNs and BSCN, respectively.

## 4.3   Methodology

The BSCN presented in Dai *et al.* (2019a) is capable of adding multiple hidden nodes into the network within a single iteration. However, the time saved by reducing the number of iterations is partially neutralized, as the Moore–Penrose generalized inverse of matrix in the block form of inequality adds additional overhead. Besides, the superposition of randomized learning techniques and coarse-grained block incremental mechanism is prone to generating some low-quality hidden parameters, especially in BSCN with fixed block method.

### 4.3.1   *Efficient Block Incremental Stochastic Configuration Networks*

SCNs can be viewed as a special case (when $\Delta_k = 1$) of BSCN. In turn, a hidden block can also be considered a special hidden node. The distinction lies in the output of the newly added hidden node ($g_L$ being a vector) and the hidden block ($H_{\Delta_k}$ being a matrix). To simplify the computationally expensive matrix generalized inverse in $\beta_{\Delta_k,q}$, we treat the hidden block as a special form of hidden node and directly replace $g_L$ with $H_{\Delta_k}$ in the formula of $\beta_{L,q}$. Therefore, according to $\beta_{L,q} = \langle e_{L-1,q}, g_L \rangle / \|g_L\|^2$, $\beta_{\Delta_k,q}$ can be obtained by

$$\beta_{\Delta_k,q} = \frac{\langle e_{L-\Delta_k,q}, H_{\Delta_k} \rangle}{\|H_{\Delta_k}\|^2}. \tag{4.9}$$

However, it is crucial to recognize that we adhere to the formula of $\beta_{L,q}$ mechanically to obtain Eq. (4.9). The $H_{\Delta_k}$ in Eq. (4.9) is a matrix with $N$ rows and $\Delta_k$ columns, so $\|H_{\Delta_k}\|^2 = tr(H_{\Delta_k}^T H_{\Delta_k})$. On the other hand, $e_{L-\Delta_k,q}$ is a vector with $N$ elements. The expression $\langle e_{L-1,q}, g_L \rangle$ represents the inner product of $e_{L-1,q}$ and $g_L$. In the case of $\beta_{\Delta_k,q}$, it can be treated as the inner product of $e_{L-\Delta_k,q}$ and each column vector of the matrix $H_{\Delta_k}$. Therefore, Eq. (4.9) can be formulated in the following form:

$$\beta_{\Delta_k,q} = \frac{H_{\Delta_k}^T e_{L-\Delta_k,q}}{tr(H_{\Delta_k}^T H_{\Delta_k})}. \tag{4.10}$$

Let us further analyze the structural form of Eq. (4.10). It can be expanded to Eq. (4.11).

$$\frac{H_{\Delta_k}^T e_{L-\Delta_k,q}}{\mathrm{tr}(H_{\Delta_k}^T H_{\Delta_k})}$$

$$= \begin{bmatrix} h_{L-\Delta_k+1}(x_1) & \cdots & h_{L-\Delta_k+1}(x_i) & \cdots & h_{L-\Delta_k+1}(x_N) \\ \vdots & \ddots & \vdots & \ddots & \vdots \\ h_{L-\Delta_k+j}(x_1) & \cdots & h_{L-\Delta_k+j}(x_i) & \cdots & h_{L-\Delta_k+j}(x_N) \\ \vdots & \ddots & \vdots & \ddots & \vdots \\ h_L(x_1) & \cdots & h_L(x_i) & \cdots & h_L(x_N) \end{bmatrix}_{\Delta_k \times N}$$

$$\times \begin{bmatrix} e_{L-\Delta_k,q}(x_1) \\ \vdots \\ e_{L-\Delta_k,q}(x_i) \\ \vdots \\ e_{L-\Delta_k,q}(x_N) \end{bmatrix}_{N \times 1} \Bigg/ \mathrm{tr}(H_{\Delta_k}^T H_{\Delta_k})$$

$$= \begin{bmatrix} \langle e_{L-\Delta_k,q}, h_{L-\Delta_k+1}^T \rangle / \mathrm{tr}(H_{\Delta_k}^T H_{\Delta_k}) \\ \vdots \\ \langle e_{L-\Delta_k,q}, h_{L-\Delta_k+j}^T \rangle / \mathrm{tr}(H_{\Delta_k}^T H_{\Delta_k}) \\ \vdots \\ \langle e_{L-\Delta_k,q}, h_L^T \rangle / \mathrm{tr}(H_{\Delta_k}^T H_{\Delta_k}) \end{bmatrix}_{\Delta_k \times 1}$$

$$= \begin{bmatrix} \beta_{L-\Delta_k+1,q} \\ \vdots \\ \beta_{L-\Delta_k+j,q} \\ \vdots \\ \beta_{L,q} \end{bmatrix}_{\Delta_k \times 1} = \beta_{\Delta_k,q}. \tag{4.11}$$

In the first algorithmic implementation of SCNs, the output weights of the newly added hidden node are evaluated by $\beta_{L,q} = \langle e_{L-1,q}, g_L \rangle / \|g_L\|^2$. While in Eq. (4.11), each row in $H_{\Delta_k}^T$ corresponds to the output of a node in the hidden block. Thus, $\langle e_{L-\Delta_k,q}, h^T_{L-\Delta_k+j}\rangle$ achieves the same effect as $\langle e_{L-1,q}, g_L\rangle$ and can be applied to evaluate the output weights of the $j$th hidden node in the block. Another difference between $\beta_{\Delta_k,q}$ and $\beta_{L,q}$ is the denominator of the fractional expression. In the sense of forms, $\beta_{\Delta_k,q}$ merely substitutes the output vector of the $L$th newly added hidden node with the output matrix of the $k$th newly added hidden block. From the structure of the formula, our new scheme to evaluate $\beta_{\Delta_k,q}$ is feasible.

Substitute Eq. (4.10) into $\langle e_{L-\Delta_k,q}(X), H_{\Delta_k}(X)\beta_{\Delta_k,q}\rangle \geqslant \delta_{L,q}$, we can easily derive the new supervisory mechanism of our proposed EBSCN.

$$\frac{e^T_{L-\Delta_k,q}H_{\Delta_k}H^T_{\Delta_k}e_{L-\Delta_k,q}}{\operatorname{tr}(H^T_{\Delta_k}H_{\Delta_k})} \geq (1-r-\mu_L)\|e_{L-\Delta_k,q}\|^2, \quad q=1,2,\ldots,m.$$

$$(4.12)$$

**Remark 4.1.** The essential difference between EBSCN and BSCN is that we use the trace of $H^T_{\Delta_k}H_{\Delta_k}$ $(1/\operatorname{tr}(H^T_{\Delta_k}H_{\Delta_k}))$ instead of its non-zero eigenvalue $(1/\sigma_1, 1/\sigma_2, \ldots, 1/\sigma_s)$ to get our new block form of inequalities. The detailed derivation can be obtained by singular value decomposition (SVD) of the positive semidefinite matrix $H^T_{\Delta_k}H_{\Delta_k}$.

Furthermore, we proceed to prove its universal approximation property. The proof process involves two steps: the monotonically decreasing and convergence property of the residual error sequence $\|e_L\|^2$. Since $H^T_{\Delta_k}H_{\Delta_k}$ is a positive semidefinite matrix, we have $\operatorname{tr}(H^T_{\Delta_k}H_{\Delta_k}) \geq 0$. From Eq. (4.10), we obtain

$$\|e_L\|^2 - \|e_{L-\Delta_k}\|^2$$

$$= \sum_{q=1}^{m}\left(-2\langle e_{L-\Delta_k,q}, H_{\Delta_k}\beta_{\Delta_k,q}\rangle + \langle H_{\Delta_k}\beta_{\Delta_k,q}, H_{\Delta_k}\beta_{\Delta_k,q}\rangle\right)$$

$$= \sum_{q=1}^{m}\left(-2\frac{e^T_{L-\Delta_k,q}H_{\Delta_k}H^T_{\Delta_k}e_{L-\Delta_k,q}}{\operatorname{tr}(H^T_{\Delta_k}H_{\Delta_k})} + \|H_{\Delta_k}\beta_{\Delta_k,q}\|^2\right)$$

$$\leq \sum_{q=1}^{m}\left(-2\frac{e^T_{L-\Delta_k,q}H_{\Delta_k}H^T_{\Delta_k}e_{L-\Delta_k,q}}{\operatorname{tr}(H^T_{\Delta_k}H_{\Delta_k})} + \|H_{\Delta_k}\|^2\|\beta_{\Delta_k,q}\|^2\right)$$

$$
= \sum_{q=1}^{m} \left( -2 \frac{e_{L-\Delta_k,q}^T H_{\Delta_k} H_{\Delta_k}^T e_{L-\Delta_k,q}}{\mathrm{tr}(H_{\Delta_k}^T H_{\Delta_k})} \right.
$$

$$
\left. + \frac{\|H_{\Delta_k}\|^2 e_{L-\Delta_k,q}^T H_{\Delta_k} H_{\Delta_k}^T e_{L-\Delta_k,q}}{(\mathrm{tr}(H_{\Delta_k}^T H_{\Delta_k}))^2} \right)
$$

$$
= -\sum_{q=1}^{m} \frac{e_{L-\Delta_k,q}^T H_{\Delta_k} H_{\Delta_k}^T e_{L-\Delta_k,q}}{\mathrm{tr}(H_{\Delta_k}^T H_{\Delta_k})} \leq 0. \tag{4.13}
$$

According to Eq. (4.10) and the inequality constraints of EBSCN, we have

$$
\|e_L\|^2 - (r + \mu_L)\|e_{L-\Delta_k}\|^2
$$

$$
= \sum_{q=1}^{m} ((1 - r - \mu_L)\|e_{L-\Delta_k,q}\|^2 - 2\langle e_{L-\Delta_k,q}, H_{\Delta_k}\beta_{\Delta_k,q}\rangle
$$

$$
+ \|H_{\Delta_k}\beta_{\Delta_k,q}\|^2)
$$

$$
\leq \sum_{q=1}^{m} \left( \delta_{L,q} - 2\frac{e_{L-\Delta_k,q}^T H_{\Delta_k} H_{\Delta_k}^T e_{L-\Delta_k,q}}{\mathrm{tr}(H_{\Delta_k}^T H_{\Delta_k})} + \|H_{\Delta_k}\|^2 \|\beta_{\Delta_k,q}\|^2 \right)
$$

$$
= \sum_{q=1}^{m} \left( \delta_{L,q} - \frac{e_{L-\Delta_k,q}^T H_{\Delta_k} H_{\Delta_k}^T e_{L-\Delta_k,q}}{\mathrm{tr}(H_{\Delta_k}^T H_{\Delta_k})} \right) \leq 0. \tag{4.14}
$$

where $\delta_{L,q} = (1 - r - \mu_L)\|e_{L-\Delta_k,q}\|^2$, $q = 1, 2, \ldots, m$.

Thus, we obtain

$$
\|e_L\|^2 \leq (r + \mu_L)\|e_{L-\Delta_k}\|^2. \tag{4.15}
$$

From Eqs. (4.13)–(4.15), we can easily get $\lim_{L\to\infty} \|e_L\| = 0$. Note that the step involving the definition of intermediate values to compare the values of $e_L^*$ and $e_L$ is omitted here. The value of $e_L^*$ is obtained through the output weights which are evaluated by the least squares method, whereas $e_L$ is acquired by our proposed $\beta_{\Delta_k,q}$. It is obviously that $e_L^* \leq e_L$.

The proposed EBSCN preserves the varied block size strategy based on simulated annealing (SA) algorithm utilized in BSCN.

The hidden block size $\Delta_k$ is dynamically adjusted by

$$\Delta_k = 1 + \text{round}((\Delta_1 - 1) \times (1 - \exp(dE/\gamma))), \qquad (4.16)$$

where $\text{round}(\cdot)$ is an integer function, and $\Delta_1$ represents the initial block size. $dE = \|e_L\| - \|e_{L-\Delta_k}\|$ represents the difference between the current and the previous network residual error, $\gamma$ is an adjustable parameter.

**Remark 4.2.** It is salutary to note that the output weights of the newly added bidden block $\beta_{\Delta_k,q} = H_{\Delta_k}^T e_{L-\Delta_k,q}/\text{tr}(H_{\Delta_k}^T H_{\Delta_k})$ is just used to deduce our new block form of inequality constraints and prove the universal approximation property of EBSCN. We still evaluate the output weights of the hidden layer all together using the global least squares method.

Our proposed EBSCN, in essence, builds upon the benefits of adding multiple hidden nodes to the network in each iteration while notably eliminating the computationally expensive matrix generalized inverse in the supervisory mechanism of BSCN.

### 4.3.2 *EBSCN with Group Lasso Regularization*

A reasonable architecture of NNs should strike a balance between being large enough to learn the training set and small enough to generalize well. However, the coarse-grained block incremental mechanism in BSCN may generate some potential redundant hidden nodes and deteriorate the performance of the model. Therefore, it is crucial to establish a more compact network structure for BSCN by pruning these low-quality hidden nodes. To resolve this issue, EBSCN with group lasso regularization (EBSCNGL) is introduced in this section. Group lasso penalizes variables at group level rather than individual elements. The $L_{2,1}$ norm has been effectively employed in group lasso and it is defined as

$$\|\beta\|_{2,1} = \sum_{i=1}^{L} \|\beta^i\|_2 = \sum_{i=1}^{L} \sqrt{\sum_{j=1}^{m} \beta_{i,j}^2}. \qquad (4.17)$$

We treat each row in $\beta$ as a group and utilize the $L_{2,1}$ norm to improve the network architecture of EBSCN. The output weights

$\beta$ can be partitioned into $L$ groups.

$$\beta = \begin{bmatrix} \beta_{1,1} & \beta_{1,2} & \cdots & \beta_{1,m} \\ \beta_{2,1} & \beta_{2,2} & \cdots & \beta_{2,m} \\ \vdots & \vdots & \vdots & \vdots \\ \beta_{L,1} & \beta_{L,2} & \cdots & \beta_{L,m} \end{bmatrix}_{L \times m} \quad \begin{array}{l} Group1 \\ Group2 \\ \vdots \\ GroupL \end{array} \tag{4.18}$$

The objective function of EBSCNGL with $L_{2,1}$ norm penalty is shown as

$$J(\beta) = \frac{1}{2}\|H\beta - T\|_F^2 + \alpha\|\beta\|_{2,1}, \tag{4.19}$$

where $H$ and $\beta$ represent the hidden layer output matrix and the output weights of the learner model, and $T$ is the target output. $H = [H_{\Delta_1}, H_{\Delta_2}, \ldots, H_{\Delta_k}]$ and $\beta = [\beta_1, \beta_2, \ldots, \beta_L]$. $\alpha$ is the regularization coefficient that balances the loss and the $L_{2,1}$ norm of the output weights. The parameter $\alpha$ controls the sparsity level of the output weights. There are many computational methods for determining the value of the regularization coefficient $\alpha$, such as generalized cross-validation, L-Curve, minimum mean square error, etc. In this study, we use the simple grid search approach to select the proper value of $\alpha$.

The output weights of feedforward NNs with group lasso regularization are typically obtained by initializing a random weight matrix around zero and then updating it iteratively via the gradient descent algorithm (Kang *et al.*, 2022; Li and Chu, 2023; Scardapane *et al.*, 2017; Wang *et al.*, 2017b, 2020b; Zhang *et al.*, 2019a). The weight updating formula based on back-propagation is

$$\beta_{i,j}^{n+1} = \beta_{i,j}^n - \eta\nabla\beta_{i,j}^n$$

$$= \beta_{i,j}^n - \eta\left(\frac{\partial\left(\frac{1}{2}\sum_{n=1}^N (H\beta - T)_{n*}^T (H\beta - T)_{n*} + \alpha\sum_{i=1}^L \sqrt{\sum_{j=1}^m \beta_{i,j}^2}\right)}{\partial\beta_{i,j}}\right)$$

$$= \beta_{i,j}^{n} - \eta \left( \sum_{n=1}^{N} H_{ni}(H_{n*}\beta_{*j} - T_{nj}) + \alpha \frac{\beta_{i,j}}{\sqrt{\sum_{j=1}^{m} \beta_{i,j}^{2}}} \right)$$

$$= \beta_{i,j}^{n} - \eta \left( \sum_{n=1}^{N} H_{ni}(H_{n*}\beta_{*j} - T_{nj}) + \alpha \frac{\beta_{i,j}}{\|\beta^{i}\|_{2}} \right), \qquad (4.20)$$

where $\eta$ is the learning rate, $\nabla \beta_{i,j}^{n}$ represents the gradient of $J(\beta^{n})$ with respect to $\beta_{i,j}^{n}$, $(H\beta - T)_{n*}$ and $H_{n*}$ correspond to the $n$th row vector of the matrix $(H\beta - T)$ and $H$, respectively. $\beta_{*j}$ is the $j$th column vector of the matrix $\beta$. It is generally recognized that the gradient descent method is not an efficient algorithm.

We employ a simple and efficient technique Nie *et al.* (2010) to update the output weights matrix and a diagonal matrix alternatively. Taking the derivative of Eq. (4.19) with respect to $\beta$, we get

$$\frac{\partial J(\beta)}{\partial \beta} = H^{T}(H\beta - T) + \alpha \frac{\partial(\sum_{i=1}^{L} \sqrt{\sum_{j=1}^{m} \beta_{i,j}^{2}})}{\partial(\beta_{i,j})} \qquad (4.21)$$

$$= H^{T}(H\beta - T) + \alpha \Sigma \beta,$$

where $\Sigma$ is

$$\Sigma = \begin{bmatrix} \frac{1}{\|\beta^{1}\|_{2}} & & & \\ & \frac{1}{\|\beta^{2}\|_{2}} & & \\ & & \ddots & \\ & & & \frac{1}{\|\beta^{L}\|_{2}} \end{bmatrix} \qquad (4.22)$$

$\beta^{i}$ represents the $i$th row vector of the output weights matrix, and $\|\beta^{i}\|_{2}$ is the $L_{2}$ norm of $\beta^{i}$.

Letting Eq. (4.21) be equal to 0, we have

$$\beta = (H^{T}H + \alpha \Sigma)^{-1} H^{T} T. \qquad (4.23)$$

Equation (4.23) can be transformed into an efficient form with proved convergence based on the Woodbury matrix identity (Gu *et al.*, 2011). The Woodbury matrix identity is

$$(A + UCV)^{-1} = A^{-1} - A^{-1}U(C^{-1} + VA^{-1}U)^{-1}VA^{-1}. \qquad (4.24)$$

From Eq. (4.24), $(H^T H + \alpha\Sigma)^{-1}$ in Eq. (4.23) is equal to

$$(H^T H + \alpha\Sigma)^{-1} = \frac{1}{\alpha}\Sigma^{-1} - \frac{1}{\alpha^2}\Sigma^{-1}H^T\left(I + \frac{1}{\alpha}H\Sigma^{-1}H^T\right)^{-1}H\Sigma^{-1}.$$

(4.25)

Therefore,

$$\begin{aligned}
\beta &= \frac{1}{\alpha}\Sigma^{-1}H^T T - \frac{1}{\alpha^2}\Sigma^{-1}H^T\left(I + \frac{1}{\alpha}H\Sigma^{-1}H^T\right)^{-1}H\Sigma^{-1}H^T T \\
&= \frac{1}{\alpha}\Sigma^{-1}H^T T - \frac{1}{\alpha}\Sigma^{-1}H^T\left(I + \frac{1}{\alpha}H\Sigma^{-1}H^T\right)^{-1}\left(\frac{1}{\alpha}H\Sigma^{-1}H^T\right)T \\
&= \frac{1}{\alpha}\Sigma^{-1}H^T T - \frac{1}{\alpha}\Sigma^{-1}H^T\left(I - \left(I + \frac{1}{\alpha}H\Sigma^{-1}H^T\right)^{-1}\right)T \\
&= \frac{1}{\alpha}\Sigma^{-1}H^T\left(I + \frac{1}{\alpha}H\Sigma^{-1}H^T\right)^{-1}T.
\end{aligned}$$

(4.26)

According to Eq. (4.26), $\beta$ and $\Sigma$ are updated alternatively until the algorithm converges and the convergence has been proved in Nie *et al.* (2010). EBSCNGL induces sparsity by shrinking all the elements within a group to zeros simultaneously. Consequently, the corresponding hidden nodes can be deemed nonessential neurons and should be eliminated from the network.

While for EBSCNGL, the $L_{2,1}$ norm regularization term is integrated to the cost function to prune redundant nodes of the hidden layer. The output weights matrix $\beta$ and the diagonal matrix $\Sigma$ are updated alternatively until the algorithm converges, achieving the same effect as the gradient descent algorithm. Theoretical analysis in Nie *et al.* (2010) has already proven that the method will converge to the global optimum. It can be concluded that EBSCNGL also possesses universal approximation capability. However, further research is still needed to provide rigorous mathematical proofs.

For the sake of simplicity, a set of variables $\xi_{L,q}, q = 1, 2, \ldots, m$ is introduced.

$$\xi_{L,q} = \frac{e_{L-\Delta_k,q}^T H_{\Delta_k} H_{\Delta_k}^T e_{L-\Delta_k,q}}{\mathrm{tr}(H_{\Delta_k}^T H_{\Delta_k})} - (1 - r - \mu_L)\|e_{L-\Delta_k,q}\|^2. \quad (4.27)$$

## 4.4   Experimental Results and Discussion

Numerous experiments from various perspectives are designed to evaluate and validate the effectiveness of our EBSCNGL. The primary objective of the first simulation is to examine the model's capability to approximate the target function with outliers. The second experiment involving benchmark classification datasets is intended to verify the efficiency and sparsity of the proposed EBSCNGL. The last simulations testify that EBSCNGL can achieve convergence within a few iterations. The benchmark classification datasets are sourced from the well-known KEEL (Knowledge Extraction based on Evolutionary Learning)[1] and UCI (University of California at Irvine)[2] machine learning repositories. The specific details of these benchmark datasets are listed in Table 4.1. We conducted a comparative analysis of five types of NNs, including SC-III in Wang and Li (2017b) (denoted as SCN), SCNs with fixed block increments (denoted as BSCN-I) and SCNs with varied block increments (denoted as BSCN-II) in Dai *et al.* (2019a), EBSCNGL with fixed block increments (denoted as EBSCNGL-I), EBSCNGL with varied block increments (denoted as EBSCNGL-II).

All the simulations are conducted within the MATLAB R2019b environment on a laptop with a 2.80 GHz Intel(R) Core(TM) i7-1165G7 CPU and 16.0 GB RAM. We employ mean absolute error (MAE), root mean square error (RMSE), mean square error (MSE), and determination coefficient ($R^2$) as evaluation indicators for different models on regression datasets. Accuracy, recall, precision, and F1-score are used as evaluation indicators for different algorithms on classification. The reported statistical results are the average values of 20 independent trials.

### 4.4.1   *Function Approximation Problem*

We consider two nonlinear functions, including a one-dimensional and a two-dimensional function, to assess the approximation capacity of the model. The $L_{2,1}$ norm possesses robustness in addition to its

---

[1]http://www.keel.es/.
[2]http://archive.ics.uci.edu/.

**Table 4.1.** Detailed information of benchmark classification datasets.

| Datasets | Instances | Training | Test | Features | Outputs | Classification | Source |
|---|---|---|---|---|---|---|---|
| Divorce predictors | 170 | 119 | 51 | 54 | 2 | Binary | UCI |
| Banknote authentication | 1372 | 960 | 412 | 4 | 2 | Binary | UCI |
| Rice (Cammeo and Osmancik) | 3810 | 2667 | 1143 | 7 | 2 | Binary | UCI |
| Iris | 150 | 105 | 45 | 4 | 3 | Multiclass | UCI |
| Vertebral column | 310 | 217 | 93 | 6 | 3 | Multiclass | UCI |
| Wireless indoor localization | 2000 | 1400 | 600 | 7 | 4 | Multiclass | UCI |
| Wine | 178 | 125 | 53 | 13 | 3 | Multiclass | KEEL |
| Vehicle | 846 | 592 | 254 | 18 | 4 | Multiclass | KEEL |

sparsity at the group level. Therefore, we artificially introduce some outliers into the training dataset. The two nonlinear functions used in this subsection can be expressed as

$$y = 8 + 2e^{1-x^2}\cos(2\pi x).$$
$$z = \sin(1 - (x^2 + y^2)). \tag{4.28}$$

For the one-dimensional function approximation task, both the training and test datasets consist of 600 samples. The training data is generated with 10% outliers, and the test data is noise-free. The input $x$ of the dataset is drawn from a uniform distribution in the range [–0.5,3.5]. Prior to the training process, the outliers in the dataset are pretreated using Eq. (4.29).

$$y = y + 3 * \text{rand}(0, 1) - 1.5. \tag{4.29}$$

In the two-dimensional function approximation experiment, we randomly pick 2500 samples from an equally spaced 50 * 50 grid with $-1 \leq x \leq 1$ and $-1 \leq y \leq 1$. The test patterns are chosen in a similar manner to the training data but without outliers. The noise data in the two-dimensional function is generated by applying the following transformation

$$z = z + 0.5 * (\text{rand}(0, 1) - 0.5). \tag{4.30}$$

The training samples and the target outputs with outliers of one-dimensional and two-dimensional function approximation datasets are plotted in Figs. 4.2 and 4.3 respectively.

In order to exhibit the merits of the algorithm more clearly, Table 4.2 reports the statistical results of the five algorithms on both the one-dimensional and the two-dimensional function approximation datasets. For clarity, we use 1D and 2D to denote the one-dimensional and two-dimensional functions in Table 4.2.

According to Table 4.2, our EBSCNGL offers a notable advantage: it requires significantly fewer hidden nodes compared to BSCN while maintaining similar performance. Additionally, it is observed that the training time for block incremental method is higher than SCN. This can be attributed to two main reasons: (1) The relatively small setting of the hidden block size $\Delta_k$ does not lead to a significant reduction in the number of iterations during model construction.

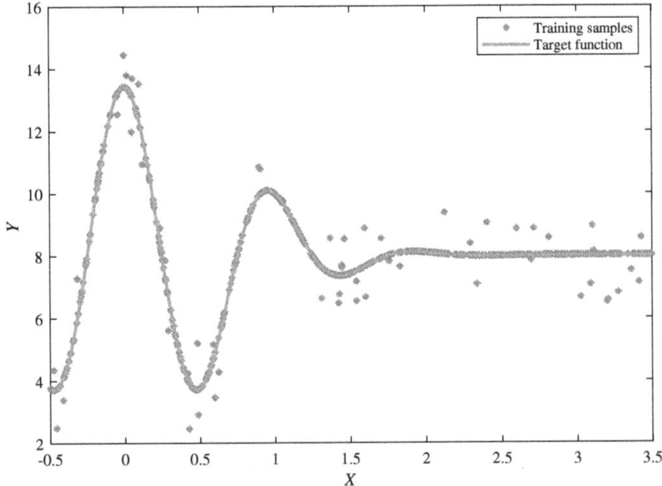

**Fig. 4.2.** Training samples and Target function.

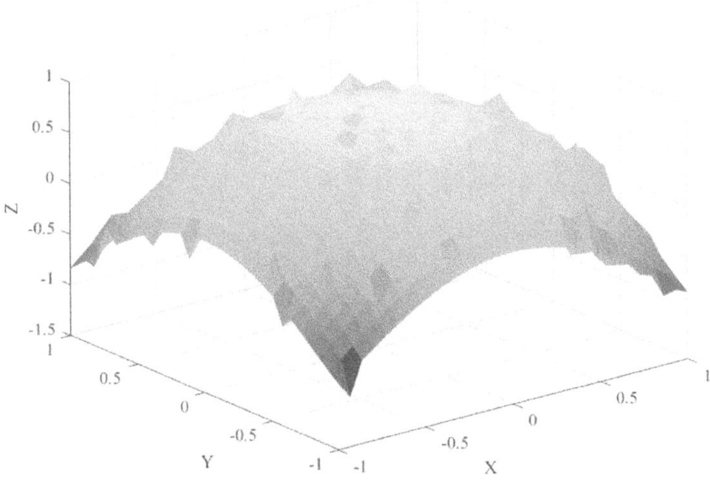

**Fig. 4.3.** Two-dimensional function with outliers.

Meanwhile, BSCN incurs additional computational overhead due to the matrix generalized inverse operation in the block form of inequalities. Simulation results indicate that when the hidden block size $\Delta_k$ is set to 1, the training efficiency of BSCN is lower than that of SCN.

**Table 4.2.** Test performance comparison among SCN, BSCN-I, EBSCNGL-I, BSCN-II and EBSCNGL-II on function approximate datasets.

| Function | Algorithms | Nodes | Time(s) | MAE | RMSE | MSE | $R^2$ | $(\Delta_k, T_{\max}, \alpha)$ |
|---|---|---|---|---|---|---|---|---|
| 1D | SCN | **52.4** | 0.0735 | 0.0729 | 0.1336 | 0.0184 | 0.9982 | 1,10,- |
| | BSCN-I | 94.2 | 0.1089 | 0.0778 | 0.1467 | 0.0218 | 0.9973 | 3,10,- |
| | EBSCNGL-I | 68.4 | **0.0704** | 0.0676 | 0.1045 | 0.0113 | 0.9967 | 3,10,0.5 |
| | BSCN-II | 65.8 | 0.1067 | 0.0678 | 0.1281 | 0.0165 | 0.9985 | 3,10,- |
| | EBSCNGL-II | 52.7 | 0.0869 | **0.0645** | **0.1011** | 0.0103 | **0.9988** | 3,10,0.5 |
| 2D | SCN | 148.6 | 0.6642 | 0.0192 | 0.0254 | 6.496e-04 | 0.8568 | 1,10,- |
| | BSCN-I | 182.5 | 0.3503 | 0.0184 | 0.0254 | 6.484e-04 | 0.8587 | 5,10,- |
| | EBSCNGL-I | 151.2 | **0.3116** | 0.0168 | **0.0216** | **4.677e-04** | 0.8598 | 5,10,0.1 |
| | BSCN-II | 147.3 | 0.8594 | 0.0191 | 0.0253 | 6.404e-04 | 0.8565 | 5,10,- |
| | EBSCNGL-II | **138.7** | 0.7895 | **0.0167** | 0.0223 | 4.945e-04 | **0.8599** | 5,10,0.1 |

(2) Another major reason lies in the application of simulated annealing to adjust the size of the hidden block during the learning process. Initially, the network residual error is $e_0 := [t_1, t_2, \ldots, t_N]^T$, and $dE = \|e_{\Delta_k}\| - \|e_0\|$ is typically relatively large. However, if the residual error difference $dE$ remains consistently small in subsequent iterations, the exponential function $\exp(dE/\eta)$ will maintain a smaller value. Consequently, the hidden block size $\Delta_k$ sharply decreases to 1, causing BSCN-II to degenerate into SCN. As a result, BSCN-II loses its ability to significantly reduce the number of iterations during model construction. But it still employs the block form of inequalities to constrain randomly assigned hidden parameters. As a comparison, our EBSCNGL-I and EBSCNGL-II outperform BSCN-I and BSCN-II with respect to both the training efficiency and the network architecture on the two datasets.

Specifically, EBSCN without group lasso regularization can also achieve comparable performance to BSCN. The only difference between BSCN and EBSCN is the block form of supervisory mechanism. The primary purpose of using the $L_{2,1}$ norm as the group lasso penalty term is to prune redundant hidden nodes generated by block incremental approach, it can also alleviate over-fitting to a certain extent.

### 4.4.2   *Benchmark Classification Datasets*

In this section, we choose eight benchmark classification datasets from KEEL and UCI to further evaluate the performance of our proposed EBSCNGL. We select 70% of the data points as the training data, while the remaining 30% are allocated for testing purposes on each dataset. To accelerate the convergence speed of the model, all datasets are normalized within the range of $[0, 1]$. The block size $\Delta_k$ is set to 10 for block incremental methods, and the value of the regularization coefficient $\alpha$ is 0.01 for EBSCNGL-I and EBSCNGL-II. The maximum value of random configuration $T_{\max}$ is set to 10 for all the algorithms. We utilize commonly used accuracy, precision, recall and F1 Score as evaluation indicators to assess the classification performance of different models.

To further demonstrate the efficiency and sparsity of our proposed EBSCNGL, Tables 4.3–4.6 lists the mean test accuracy, precision, recall and F1_score results for SCN, BSCN-I, BSCN-II,

EBSCNGL-I and EBSCNGL-II on 8 classification datasets. Since our EBSCNGL-I and EBSCNGL-II are the amelioration of BSCN-I and BSCN-II, it is prudent to compare the results of BSCN-I, EBSCNGL-I and BSCN-II, EBSCNGL-II separately. As illustrated in Tables 4.3-4.6, two outstanding merits of our proposed EBSCNGL-I and EBSCNGL-II become apparent: (1) fewer hidden nodes and (2) less training time. The former advantage can be chalked up to the group sparsity of the $L_{2,1}$ norm regularization term, while the latter superiority owes to the novel block form of inequality constraint without the Moore–Penrose generalized inverse of matrix. These results are consistent with our two main innovations.

We are noticing that the training time of BSCN-I and EBSCNGL-I is significantly lower than the other algorithms, primarily because SCN with fixed block increments can remarkably reduce the number of iterations. For instance, as illustrated in Tables 4.3–4.6, BSCN-I with $\Delta_k = 10$ can be established via only two iterations on the Vertebral classification dataset, whereas the original SCN necessitates nearly 17 times of iteration. The primary advantage of BSCN-I lies in its rapid training speed, but its deficiency is equally prominent. Moreover, BSCN-I consistently requires the maximum number of hidden neurons across all datasets, despite the fact that we have curtailed its growth by setting parameter values of $L_{\max}$ and $\epsilon$. The simulations underscore the necessity of the second contribution mentioned above. In addition, we found an abnormal phenomenon: the efficiency improvement of BSCN-II is not remarkable. The reason is mainly ascribed to the varied block size strategy which has already been discussed in Section 4.4.1. Notably, this issue is prevalent in datasets such as Rice (Cammeo and Osmancik), Iris, Wireless Indoor Localization, Wine and Vehicle datasets. It can potentially be solved by regulating the parameter $\eta$ dynamically during the training process. But the topic is beyond the scope of this article. By comparison, both the training time and the number of hidden nodes of EBSCNGL are invariably smaller than those of BSCN.

### 4.4.3  *Convergence Analysis*

In EBSCNGL, the output weights of the hidden layer and a diagonal matrix are updated alternatively until convergence, resulting

**Table 4.3.**    Average test results of SCN, BSCN-I, EBSCNGL-I, BSCN-II and EBSCNGL-II on Divorce and Banknote datasets.

| Datasets | Algorithms | Nodes | Time(s) | Accuracy $\pm$ STD | Precision $\pm$ STD | Recall $\pm$ STD | F1_Score $\pm$ STD |
|---|---|---|---|---|---|---|---|
| Divorce | SCN | 59.9 | 0.1458 | $0.9557 \pm 0.0154$ | $\mathbf{0.9519 \pm 0.0176}$ | $\mathbf{0.9501 \pm 0.0169}$ | $\mathbf{0.9509 \pm 0.0173}$ |
|  | BSCN-I | 74.5 | 0.0486 | $0.9451 \pm 0.0168$ | $0.9213 \pm 0.0372$ | $0.9192 \pm 0.0367$ | $0.9202 \pm 0.0369$ |
|  | EBSCNGL-I | 62.2 | $\mathbf{0.0346}$ | $\mathbf{0.9615 \pm 0.0212}$ | $0.9288 \pm 0.0295$ | $0.9259 \pm 0.0301$ | $0.9273 \pm 0.0297$ |
|  | BSCN-II | 59.8 | 0.1434 | $0.9538 \pm 0.0130$ | $0.9511 \pm 0.0171$ | $0.9481 \pm 0.0166$ | $0.9496 \pm 0.0168$ |
|  | EBSCNGL-II | $\mathbf{34.3}$ | 0.1371 | $0.9480 \pm 0.0234$ | $0.9512 \pm 0.0221$ | $0.9485 \pm 0.0262$ | $0.9496 \pm 0.0227$ |
| Banknote | SCN | 33.9 | 0.0776 | $\mathbf{0.9983 \pm 0.0013}$ | $0.9982 \pm 0.0014$ | $0.9984 \pm 0.0012$ | $0.9983 \pm 0.0013$ |
|  | BSCN-I | 39.5 | $\mathbf{0.0245}$ | $0.9973 \pm 0.0023$ | $0.9974 \pm 0.0025$ | $0.9976 \pm 0.0020$ | $0.9975 \pm 0.0022$ |
|  | EBSCNGL-I | 34.2 | 0.0286 | $0.9971 \pm 0.0019$ | $0.9970 \pm 0.0021$ | $0.9983 \pm 0.0016$ | $0.9982 \pm 0.0017$ |
|  | BSCN-II | 32.6 | 0.0521 | $0.9979 \pm 0.0020$ | $\mathbf{0.9984 \pm 0.0014}$ | $\mathbf{0.9985 \pm 0.0011}$ | $0.9985 \pm 0.0013$ |
|  | EBSCNGL-II | $\mathbf{27.9}$ | 0.0515 | $0.9978 \pm 0.0018$ | $0.9977 \pm 0.0023$ | $0.9981 \pm 0.0017$ | $\mathbf{0.9989 \pm 0.0018}$ |

**Table 4.4.** Average test results of SCN, BSCN-I, EBSCNGL-I, BSCN-II and EBSCNGL-II on Rice and Iris datasets.

| Datasets | Algorithms | Nodes | Time(s) | Accuracy $\pm$ STD | Precision $\pm$ STD | Recall $\pm$ STD | F1_Score $\pm$ STD |
|---|---|---|---|---|---|---|---|
| Rice | SCN | 43.9 | 0.6343 | $0.9238 \pm 0.0017$ | $0.9218 \pm 0.0021$ | $0.9237 \pm 0.0020$ | $0.9227 \pm 0.0021$ |
| | BSCN-I | 66.5 | 0.2198 | $\mathbf{0.9242 \pm 0.0026}$ | $\mathbf{0.9228 \pm 0.0025}$ | $0.9229 \pm 0.0022$ | $0.9226 \pm 0.0024$ |
| | EBSCNGL-I | 50.4 | **0.2077** | $0.9229 \pm 0.0021$ | $0.9215 \pm 0.0018$ | $0.9235 \pm 0.0020$ | $0.9224 \pm 0.0017$ |
| | BSCN-II | 48.1 | 0.6633 | $0.9241 \pm 0.0009$ | $0.9223 \pm 0.0014$ | $\mathbf{0.9238 \pm 0.0016}$ | $\mathbf{0.9231 \pm 0.0014}$ |
| | EBSCNGL-II | **37.2** | 0.4597 | $0.9236 \pm 0.0022$ | $0.9214 \pm 0.0019$ | $0.9234 \pm 0.0020$ | $0.9225 \pm 0.0019$ |
| Iris | SCN | 45.9 | 0.0416 | $0.9177 \pm 0.0271$ | $0.9049 \pm 0.0203$ | $0.8988 \pm 0.0233$ | $0.9019 \pm 0.0217$ |
| | BSCN-I | 58.4 | 0.0127 | $0.8667 \pm 0.0388$ | $0.8527 \pm 0.0357$ | $0.8433 \pm 0.0398$ | $0.8481 \pm 0.0377$ |
| | EBSCNGL-I | 43.9 | **0.0102** | $0.8978 \pm 0.0265$ | $0.8839 \pm 0.0338$ | $0.8744 \pm 0.0376$ | $0.8791 \pm 0.0356$ |
| | BSCN-II | 44.5 | 0.0446 | $\mathbf{0.9243 \pm 0.0301}$ | $\mathbf{0.9068 \pm 0.0278}$ | $\mathbf{0.9002 \pm 0.0318}$ | $\mathbf{0.9033 \pm 0.0297}$ |
| | EBSCNGL-II | **42.1** | 0.0335 | $0.9076 \pm 0.0253$ | $0.9044 \pm 0.0223$ | $0.8977 \pm 0.0253$ | $0.9011 \pm 0.0238$ |

**Table 4.5.** Average test results of SCN, BSCN-I, EBSCNGL-I, BSCN-II and EBSCNGL-II on Vertebral and Wireless datasets.

| Datasets | Algorithms | Nodes | Time(s) | Accuracy $\pm$ STD | Precision $\pm$ STD | Recall $\pm$ STD | F1_Score $\pm$ STD |
|---|---|---|---|---|---|---|---|
| Vertebral | SCN | **16.9** | 0.0162 | $0.8688 \pm 0.0158$ | $0.8325 \pm 0.0162$ | $0.8446 \pm 0.0204$ | $0.8385 \pm 0.0178$ |
| | BSCN-I | 20.0 | 0.0055 | $0.8731 \pm 0.0169$ | $\mathbf{0.8437 \pm 0.0186}$ | $0.8587 \pm 0.0205$ | $\mathbf{0.8511 \pm 0.0191}$ |
| | EBSCNGL-I | 17.3 | **0.0048** | $\mathbf{0.8736 \pm 0.0147}$ | $0.8352 \pm 0.0193$ | $0.8494 \pm 0.0215$ | $0.8423 \pm 0.0202$ |
| | BSCN-II | 17.9 | 0.0084 | $0.8623 \pm 0.0176$ | $0.8348 \pm 0.0123$ | $\mathbf{0.8507 \pm 0.0146}$ | $0.8426 \pm 0.0130$ |
| | EBSCNGL-II | 18.4 | 0.0064 | $0.8661 \pm 0.0153$ | $0.8357 \pm 0.0162$ | $0.8485 \pm 0.0189$ | $0.8420 \pm 0.0172$ |
| Wireless | SCN | 103.2 | 0.5811 | $0.9738 \pm 0.0035$ | $0.9758 \pm 0.0038$ | $0.9748 \pm 0.0042$ | $0.9753 \pm 0.0040$ |
| | BSCN-I | 184.5 | 0.2791 | $0.9691 \pm 0.0029$ | $0.9711 \pm 0.0028$ | $0.9692 \pm 0.0032$ | $0.9701 \pm 0.0033$ |
| | EBSCNGL-I | 109.2 | **0.1639** | $\mathbf{0.9771 \pm 0.0027}$ | $\mathbf{0.9776 \pm 0.0023}$ | $\mathbf{0.9765 \pm 0.0022}$ | $\mathbf{0.9772 \pm 0.0023}$ |
| | BSCN-II | 102.1 | 0.7044 | $0.9746 \pm 0.0036$ | $0.9757 \pm 0.0035$ | $0.9748 \pm 0.0034$ | $0.9753 \pm 0.0036$ |
| | EBSCNGL-II | **91.8** | 0.6120 | $0.9734 \pm 0.0038$ | $0.9742 \pm 0.0037$ | $0.9737 \pm 0.0038$ | $0.9738 \pm 0.0035$ |

**Table 4.6.**    Average test results of SCN, BSCN-I, EBSCNGL-I, BSCN-II and EBSCNGL-II on Wine and Vehicle datasets.

| Datasets | Algorithms | Nodes | Time(s) | Accuracy ± STD | Precision ± STD | Recall ± STD | F1_Score ± STD |
|---|---|---|---|---|---|---|---|
| Wine | SCN | 73.5 | 0.0809 | 0.9427 ± 0.0258 | 0.9385 ± 0.0259 | 0.9409 ± 0.0248 | 0.9397 ± 0.0251 |
| | BSCN-I | 91.4 | 0.0252 | 0.9172 ± 0.0346 | 0.9037 ± 0.0405 | 0.9088 ± 0.0417 | 0.9058 ± 0.0410 |
| | EBSCNGL-I | 79.1 | **0.0184** | **0.9618 ± 0.0242** | 0.9204 ± 0.0307 | 0.9262 ± 0.0314 | 0.9233 ± 0.0310 |
| | BSCN-II | 74.6 | 0.1043 | 0.9427 ± 0.0302 | 0.9401 ± 0.0264 | 0.9408 ± 0.0270 | 0.9404 ± 0.0264 |
| | EBSCNGL-II | **68.5** | 0.0873 | 0.9391 ± 0.0369 | **0.9428 ± 0.0335** | **0.9452 ± 0.0336** | **0.9440 ± 0.0334** |
| Vehicle | SCN | 152.2 | 0.7769 | 0.8023 ± 0.0147 | 0.8045 ± 0.0206 | 0.8028 ± 0.0182 | 0.8037 ± 0.0194 |
| | BSCN-I | 179.8 | 0.1707 | **0.8191 ± 0.0166** | **0.8232 ± 0.0132** | **0.8213 ± 0.0144** | **0.8221 ± 0.0138** |
| | EBSCNGL-I | 143.9 | **0.1701** | 0.7968 ± 0.0213 | 0.7906 ± 0.0157 | 0.7886 ± 0.0165 | 0.7896 ± 0.0161 |
| | BSCN-II | 153.3 | 0.9687 | 0.8011 ± 0.0280 | 0.8059 ± 0.0254 | 0.8017 ± 0.0262 | 0.8038 ± 0.0258 |
| | EBSCNGL-II | **138.3** | 0.8701 | 0.8062 ± 0.0191 | 0.8108 ± 0.0199 | 0.8078 ± 0.0187 | 0.8093 ± 0.0192 |

in the acquisition of a sparse output weights matrix. We utilize $J(\beta) = \|H\beta - T\|_F^2 + \alpha\|\beta\|_{2,1}$ as the objective function to illustrate the convergence property of the algorithm in this subsection. Fig. 4.4 presents the convergence curves of SCNGL (SCN with $L_{2,1}$ norm), EBSCNGL-I and EBSCNGL-II on 8 benchmark classification datasets. As depicted in Fig. 4.4, the objective functions of the three algorithms converge well on all the datasets. The experimental results confirm that our method can be successfully applied to network architecture optimization for SCN and BSCN. It is observed that the objective function $J(\beta)$ converges to different values on different datasets, but not zero. The reason for this is that we use $J(\beta) = \|H\beta - T\|_F^2 + \alpha\|\beta\|_{2,1}$ instead of RMSE to plot the convergence curve. The widely used RMSE is obtained by

$$\text{RMSE} = \sqrt{\frac{1}{N}\sum_{i=1}^{N}(t_i - f_i)^2}. \tag{4.31}$$

where $t_i$ and $f_i$ are the actual label and the model output for the $i$th sample, respectively. The relationship between the objective function $J(\beta)$ and RMSE is

$$J(\beta) = N * (\text{RMSE})^2 + \alpha\|\beta\|_{2,1}. \tag{4.32}$$

Assume, for instance, that the value of the objective function $J(\beta)$ on the Rice (Cammeo and Osmancik) dataset in Fig. 4.4(c) is 300, and the training set comprises 2667 samples. Then the training RMSE can be roughly calculated by $\sqrt{300/2667} \approx 0.3353$ by neglecting the $L_{2,1}$ regularization term. In fact, the training RMSE of SCN, EBSCNGL-I and EBSCNGL-II on the Rice (Cammeo and Osmancik) dataset is around 0.35, which is consistent with the convergence results in Fig. 4.4(c). Therefore, the simulation results depicted in Fig. 4.4 are entirely acceptable. Moreover, simulation results in Fig. 4.4 indicate that the algorithm can achieve convergence within a few number of iterations.

### 4.4.4 *Application in Electricity Prediction of the Horizontal-Axis Wind Turbine*

In this section, we deploy our proposed EBSCNGL in a practical industrial application to estimate electricity generated by the

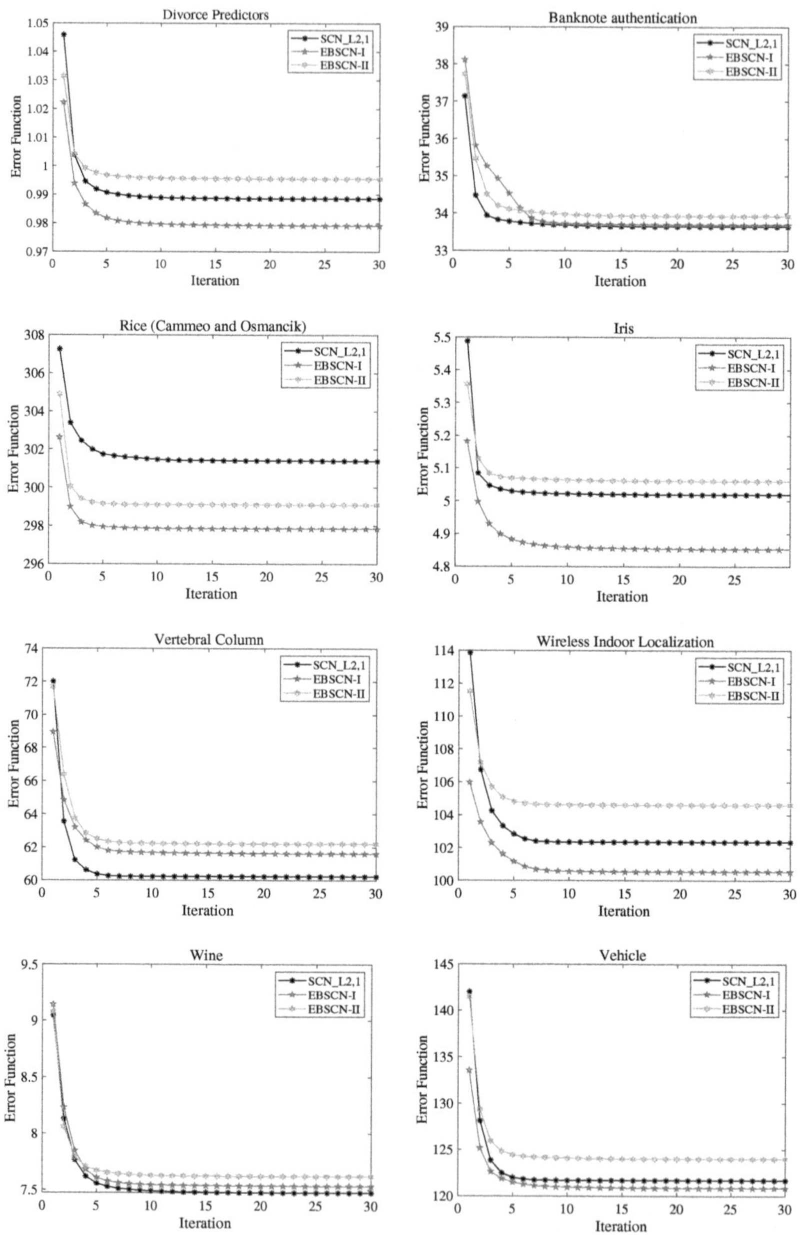

**Fig. 4.4.** Convergence comparisons among SCNGL, EBSCNGL-I and EBSCNGL-II on classification datasets.

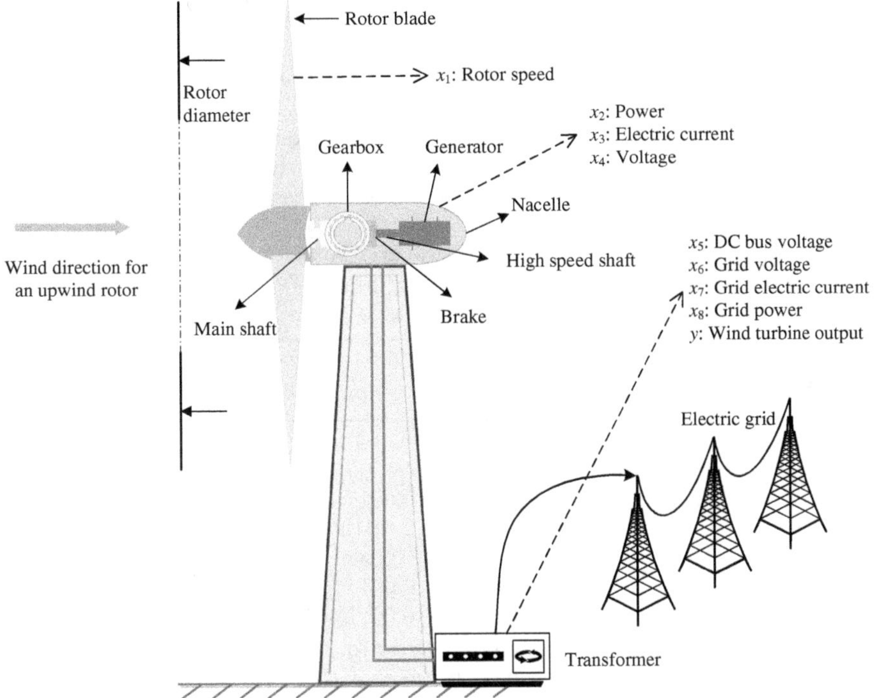


**Fig. 4.5.** A typical diagram of the horizontal-axis wind turbine.

horizontal-axis wind turbine (HAWT). The HAWT is a mechanical device that can convert the kinetic energy of wind into mechanical energy via the rotor blade initially, followed by the generation of electrical energy through the electric generator. The HAWT can serve as a distribution power supply to deliver electricity to the AC380V/AC220V electrical grid. Figure 4.5 shows a typical diagram of the horizontal-axis wind turbine. The amount of electricity generated by the HAWT is influenced by several key factors reported in Table 4.7. The HAWT model can be expressed as

$$y = \varphi(x_1, x_2, x_3, x_4, x_5, x_6, x_7, x_8) \tag{4.33}$$

where $y$ represents the electricity output of a horizontal-axis wind turbine, and $\varphi$ is an unknown nonlinear mapping function that needs to be learned.

The HAWT dataset contains 436 distinct instances collected from 16:45 to 24:00 on October 14, 2019. We partition the entire dataset

**Table 4.7.**  Related attributes of the HAWT.

| Notation | Attribute | Meaning | Units |
|---|---|---|---|
| $x_1$ | Wind_RS | Rotor speed | rpm |
| $x_2$ | Wind_W | Wind turbine power | W |
| $x_3$ | Wind_A | Wind turbine electric current | A |
| $x_4$ | Wind_V | Wind turbine voltage | V |
| $x_5$ | Wind_DC_V | DC bus voltage | V |
| $x_6$ | Grid_V | Electric grid voltage | V |
| $x_7$ | Grid_A | Electric grid electric current | A |
| $x_8$ | Grid_W | Electric grid power | W |

**Table 4.8.**  Average test performance comparisons on the HAWT dataset.

| Algorithms | $\Delta_k$ | Nodes | Time(s) | MAE | RMSE | MSE | $R_2$ |
|---|---|---|---|---|---|---|---|
| SCN | $\Delta_k = 1$ | 81.6 | **0.0927** | 0.0016 | 0.0045 | 2.154e-05 | 0.9988 |
| BSCN-I | | 81.8 | 0.1211 | **0.0015** | 0.0039 | 1.773e-05 | 0.9989 |
| EBSCNGL-I | | **64.5** | 0.1051 | 0.0018 | 0.0041 | 1.797e-05 | 0.9988 |
| BSCN-II | | 83.3 | 0.1270 | 0.0016 | 0.0039 | 1.787e-05 | 0.9991 |
| EBSCNGL-II | | 69.7 | 0.1092 | 0.0017 | **0.0038** | **1.765e-05** | **0.9992** |
| SCN | $\Delta_k = 5$ | 82.7 | 0.0945 | 0.0019 | 0.0058 | 3.944e-05 | **0.9991** |
| BSCN-I | | 118.2 | 0.0617 | 0.0026 | 0.0063 | 4.316e-05 | 0.9974 |
| EBSCNGL-I | | 87.3 | **0.0581** | 0.0019 | 0.0062 | 4.308e-05 | 0.9988 |
| BSCN-II | | 92.3 | 0.0874 | **0.0018** | 0.0059 | 4.091e-05 | 0.9977 |
| EBSCNGL-II | | **75.2** | 0.0781 | 0.0021 | **0.0054** | **3.368e-05** | 0.9989 |
| SCN | $\Delta_k = 10$ | 84.3 | 0.0908 | **0.0016** | 0.0056 | 3.944e-05 | 0.9994 |
| BSCN-I | | 129.2 | 0.0363 | 0.0026 | 0.0064 | 4.316e-05 | 0.9986 |
| EBSCNGL-I | | 91.7 | **0.0311** | 0.0021 | 0.0057 | 4.038e-05 | 0.9991 |
| BSCN-II | | 101.9 | 0.0494 | 0.0019 | 0.0061 | 4.145e-05 | 0.9993 |
| EBSCNGL-II | | 89.3 | 0.0439 | 0.0018 | **0.0051** | **3.871e-05** | **0.9995** |

into two segments: the size of the training dataset is 306, and the remaining 130 samples are used as the test set. Table 4.8 displays the average test performance of the five different algorithms on the HAWT dataset. When the hidden block size $\Delta_k = 1$ in Table 4.8, BSCN degrades to SCN and the number of hidden nodes between SCN and BSCN is similar. But the training time of BSCN-I and BSCN-II is higher than that of SCN. The findings reaffirm that unless the number of iterations can be significantly reduced, the training efficiency of BSCN will not witness any improvement. Moreover, the

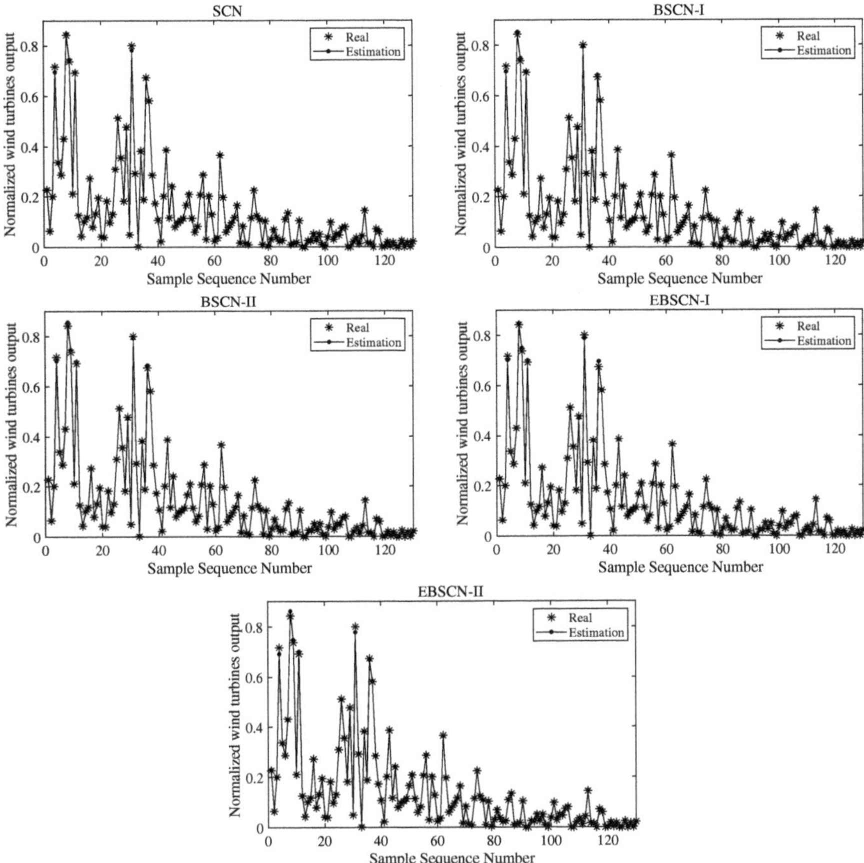

**Fig. 4.6.** Estimation results of SCN, BSCN-I, BSCN-II, EBSCNGL-I and EBSCNGL-II on the HAWT dataset.

additional computational overhead associated with the block form of supervisory mechanism may potentially lead to worse efficiency. As illustrated in Table 4.8, the value of $\Delta_k$ has a direct impact on the training time of BSCN. The training efficiency of BSCN is obviously better when $\Delta_k = 10$, but the number of hidden neurons increases along with the increase of $\Delta_k$. By contrast, both the training efficiency and the network architecture of our proposed EBSCNGL are better than the original BSCN.

Figure 4.6 further depicts the real and predictive values of electricity generated by the HAWT. As can be observed, all five algorithms can achieve satisfactory performance. However, from the test results reported in Table 4.8, both the training time and the number of hidden nodes of our EBSCNGL are lower than BSCN.

Prior to concluding this study, it is essential to reiterate that the foremost objective of block incremental approach is to accelerate convergence rate of SCN by reducing the number of iterations during the construction process. BSCN still uses the supervisory mechanism deduced by SCN to randomly assign the hidden parameters, and evaluate the output weights through the global least squares method. Basically speaking, the modeling technique of BSCN has no difference with the original SCN. In theory, a learner model based on the fine-grained point incremental method may achieve slightly better performance. Be different from SCN and BSCN, EBSCNGL computes the output weights through an efficient iterative method. The primary purpose of employing group lasso regularization is to eliminate hidden nodes whose output weights have been shrunk to zero during the iterative process. In other words, we strive to obtain comparable approximation performance to SCN and BSCN using a more compact network architecture, rather than aiming to improve the approximation performance of the model. Therefore, the performance of EBSCNGL does not stand out significantly compared with SCN and BSCN on the benchmark classification and HAWT datasets.

## 4.5  Summary

The primary focus of this study is to resolve two crucial technique issues associated with SCNs with block incremental approach. On the one hand, our proposed EBSCNGL is able to achieve similar or even superior performance compared to BSCN while circumventing the computationally expensive matrix generalized inverse in the block form of supervisory mechanism. On the other hand, EBSCNGL can effectively improve the sparsity of BSCN to get a more compact architecture. The output weights formula of the algorithm is transformed into an efficient form with proved convergence based on the Woodbury matrix identity, enabling convergence within a limited number of iterations. Simulation results on function approximation, various performance indices on benchmark classification datasets, and practical electricity prediction of the horizontal-axis wind turbine reveal the superiority of our EBSCNGL in terms of both efficiency and sparsity.

The varied block size strategy based on simulated annealing in the original BSCN exhibits poor dynamic adjustment ability on some classification datasets. It is recommended to explore more plausible methods without artificial hyper-parameter adjustment in the future studies. Apart from regularization methods, other strategies exist for optimizing the network architecture, such as low-rank matrix approximation, neural architecture search, knowledge distillation and so on. In the future, we will dedicate our efforts to more efficient and effective model compression techniques for stochastic configuration networks.

## Chapter 5

# Greedy Stochastic Configuration Networks for Ill-Posed Problems

The inequality constraint of stochastic configuration networks (SCNs) is the key to guarantee its universal approximation capability. SCNs add new units to neural networks incrementally under its supervisory mechanism. However, with the increasing number of hidden nodes, the output weights which are evaluated by the least squares method are frequently unstable. This unstable phenomenon (arbitrarily small perturbations may lead to large changes in the solutions) can be classified as ill-posed problems. One of the most important properties of ill-posed problems is instability and the widely used Tikhonov regularization method to deal with ill-posed problems is undesirable. This chapter studies the supervisory mechanism of SCNs and algebraic properties of the hidden output matrix. Then a new greedy stochastic configuration network (GSCN) for ill-posed problems is presented. Firstly, under the premise of ensuring the universal approximation capability, GSCN tries to optimize the randomly assigned input weights and biases based on hunter–prey optimization (HPO) algorithm. The optimized hidden parameters which can reduce the residual error most are selected for the newly added hidden node. Secondly, the singular value decomposition (SVD) and orthogonal-triangular (QR) decomposition with column pivoting are introduced to extract linearly independent subset of the hidden output matrix for ill-posed problems of SCNs. Finally, one function approximation, six benchmark regression, two classification datasets and bearing fault diagnosis are employed to evaluate the performance

97

of GSCN. Experimental results indicate that GSCN shows superior performance with respect to fast convergence, generalization and stability power than other contrast methods.


## 5.1 Introduction

It has been proven that random vector functional link (RVFL) networks can approximate any sufficiently smooth continuous function with probability one under appropriate random parameters (Igelnik and Pao, 1995). However, if the scope setting of random parameters is not set properly, the universal approximation capability of RVFL cannot be guaranteed (Tyukin and Prokhorov, 2009). Li and Wang (2017) provided some pitfalls and established a theoretical result on the infeasibility of RVFL networks. In recent years, an innovative randomized learning framework, termed stochastic configuration networks (SCNs), which is an incremental learning method with universal approximation property in the light of a supervisory mechanism has been developed by Wang and Li (2017b). SCNs randomly configure the parameters of hidden layer nodes under a set of inequality constraints and adaptively select their range, which indicate prominent merits on the subject of human intervention of network structure, range adaptation of hidden layer parameters and sound generalization (Dai *et al.*, 2019a). After the hidden layer node parameters are determined by stochastic configuration algorithm, SCNs can be considered as a linear system and the output weights can be analytically calculated based on pseudo-inverse theory. This mechanism makes SCNs train faster than traditional gradient-based iterative algorithms (Rumelhart *et al.*, 1995).

An ill-posed problem is unstable, as it depends on whether the problem satisfies the Hadamard criteria. It always occurs in various branches of science and engineering. Tikhonov regularization (also called $L_2$ regularization or ridge regression) is one of the most widely used methods for dealing with linear discrete ill-posed problems. Cui *et al.* (2020) designed an improved algorithm based on Tikhonov regularization matrix to address linear discrete ill-posed problems. Besides, they used the generalized cross validation function to determine a suitable parameter of the matrix. Park *et al.* (2018) extended the COSE (Hochstenbach *et al.*, 2015) method to optimize the regularization parameter which balances the fidelity term and regularization term for general-form Tikhonov regularization problems. In Reichel and Ugwu (2022), a large ill-posed problem was decomposed into several small sized problems by the t-product Golub–Kahan bidiagonalization process to get an orthonormal basis for t-Krylov subspace and then used the Tikhonov method to regularize the small-sized problem. Ill-posed problems also often arise in computer vision, such as image restoration, denoising, zooming, inpainting, demosaicing, super-resolution and so on. Zhang *et al.* (2021b) embedded different types of self-attention into the Siamese network to enhance its feature representation of ability. To tackle the ill-posed problems in image super-resolution, Liu *et al.* (2022) developed a self-attention negative feedback network to reconstruct high-quality image. Dai *et al.* (2022) combined sparse modeling with deep learning and they designed convolutional sparse coding layer to replace convolutional layer in ConvNets for handling input perturbations.

Although these SCNs variants have achieved better performance in respect of learning accuracy and generalization ability, most of the existing SCNs still suffer from the following weaknesses. The assignment mode of hidden layer parameters is related to the maximum times of random configuration $T_{\max}$, it selects $w_L$ and $b_L$ that maximize $\xi_L$ from the candidate hidden nodes pool $\Omega$. The variable $\xi_L$ is used to constrain the random assignment of the input weights and biases. However, there may exist some better $w_L$ and $b_L$ to reduce the residual error faster for SCNs. Moreover, the hidden layer output matrix of SCNs may be rank deficient or demonstrate multicollinearity. Intuitively, multicollinearity can compromise least squares as it leads to small singular values, thus the stability of SCNs would be significantly deteriorated. To resolve the above issues, we proposed a greedy stochastic configuration network with fast convergence rates for ill-posed problems in this chapter. Firstly, we select the optimized hidden parameters for each newly added hidden neuron based on greedy strategy. In addition, we conclude with a subset selection procedure of the hidden output matrix that combines the SVD and QR with column pivoting methods. This tends to produce a well-conditioned submatrix of the hidden output matrix. From a technical point of view, GSCN inherits the supervisory mechanism of original SCNs. And it further enlarges the probability of randomly assigned weights and biases to satisfy the inequality constraint based on greedy strategy. To put it another way, the strictness of the inequality constraint is weakened. The important difference between GSCN and SCNs is that GSCN explores in parameter space innovatively to get optimized parameters at each iteration, while SCNs and its variants configure the basis functions stochastically. PSCN (Zhang *et al.*, 2021a) and CSSA-SCN (Zhang and Ding, 2021) aim at obtaining better hyper-parameters for the model. SCN-AN and SCN-AL (Felicetti and Wang, 2022a) adopt different sampling strategies to get better hidden parameters. However, these variants still use the same random configuration strategy as SCNs. ISSA-FSCN (Wu *et al.*, 2022a) applies an improved sparrow search algorithm to generate the hidden parameters which maximize the variable $\xi_L$, but the number of hidden nodes is fixed in ISSA-FSCN. Strictly speaking, it can't be classified to the category of SCNs. Besides, the way of subset selection for the ill-posed problems of SCNs is different from SCN-$L_1$ (Wang *et al.*, 2022b) and SCN-$L_2$ (Wang *et al.*, 2021) regularization techniques. The existing methods for the ill-posed problems of SCNs mainly add penalty term to the loss function in terms of invertibility of the hidden output matrix. In contrast, our proposed GSCN is completely opposite with the widely used regularization method.

To summarize the above, the main contributions of the chapter are as follows:

- A new configuration strategy for hidden parameters based on greedy idea is proposed in this chapter. Hidden parameters for the newly added hidden node are optimized based on swarm-based optimization algorithm under the supervisory mechanism of SCNs. The optimized $w_L$ and $b_L$ can reduce the network residual error faster.
- The GSCN aims to minimize the network residual error at each iteration based on greedy idea. So the inequality constraint parameter $r$ is not necessary to keep varying and can be set a fixed value as closely as possible to 1 to enlarge the probability of constraint holding.
- The SVD and QR with column pivoting are combined to select a subset of columns from the hidden output matrix to address the ill-posed problem of SCNs. We are the first to integrate greedy strategy, SVD and QR with column pivoting into SCNs and enable

them to complement each other to improve the generalization ability and stability of SCNs.
- The merits of GSCN are illustrated on various benchmark datasets, including function approximation, classification, regression, and bearing fault diagnosis. The experimental results justify the effectiveness of the proposed GSCN.

## 5.2　Preliminaries

This section briefly reviews the newer swarm intelligence optimization algorithm, named hunter–prey optimization.

HPO is a new population-based optimization algorithm, which is inspired by the behavior of predator animals (Naruei *et al.*, 2022). In the process of HPO, the hunter moves its position to the distant prey, and the prey move its position to a safe place.

The initial population is randomly set to $x = \{x_1, x_2, \ldots, x_n\}$ and the objective function of the population is computed as $o = \{o_1, o_2, \ldots, o_n\}$. Equation (5.1) is used to generate the position of the initial population in $d$ dimensional search domain randomly.

$$x_i = \text{rand}(1, d). * (b_{\text{upper}} - b_{\text{lower}}) + b_{\text{lower}}, \tag{5.1}$$

where $x_i$ is the position of the hunter or prey, $b_{\text{lower}}$ and $b_{\text{upper}}$ are the minimum and maximum values of $x_i$.

HPO tends to explore promising areas through highly random behaviors in the search space. After finding promising areas, it exploits suitable solutions around promising areas by reducing random behaviors. The exploration and exploitation phases are balanced by parameter $C$, which is updated by Eq. (5.2)

$$C = 1 - it \left( \frac{0.98}{\text{MaxIt}} \right), \tag{5.2}$$

where $it$ and MaxIt represent the current and the maximum iteration value.

The adaptive parameter $Z$ which increases the population diversity is calculated by Eq. (5.3):

$$P = \vec{R}_1 < C; IDX = (P == 0);$$
$$Z = R_2 \otimes IDX + \vec{R}_3 \otimes (IDX); \tag{5.3}$$

where $\vec{R}_1$ and $\vec{R}_3$ are two random vectors over the range $[0,1]$, $P$ is a random vector with values 0 and 1, random number $R_2$ is within the range of $[0,1]$, $IDX$ is the index numbers of the vector $\vec{R}_1$ which satisfies the condition $(P == 0)$.

HPO selects the prey that is farthest from the population center as the attack target. However, in order to accelerate convergence, HPO considers a decreasing mechanism as Eq. (5.4):

$$\text{kbest} = \text{round}(C \times N_{\text{pop}}). \tag{5.4}$$

where $N_{\text{pop}}$ is the number of search agents.

The prey's position is calculated by Eq.(5.5), which means that the positions of prey are sorted in ascending order according to the distance to the population center.

$$\vec{P}_{\text{pos}} = \vec{x}_i| \; i \text{ is sorted } D_{\text{euc}}(\text{kbest}). \tag{5.5}$$

The average position is calculated by

$$\mu = \frac{1}{n} \sum_{i=1}^{n} x_i. \tag{5.6}$$

The Euclidean distance of each agent to the average position is

$$D_{\text{euc}(i)} = \left( \sum_{j=1}^{d} (x_{i,j} - \mu_j)^2) \right)^{\frac{1}{2}}. \tag{5.7}$$

The positions of hunter and prey are updated by Eqs. (5.8) and (5.9), respectively.

$$\begin{aligned} x_{i,j}(k+1) = x_{i,j}(k) + 0.5[(2CZP_{\text{pos}(j)} - x_{i,j}(k)) \\ + (2(1-C)Z\mu_j - x_{i,j}(k))], \end{aligned} \tag{5.8}$$

where $x(k)$ and $x(k+1)$ are the hunter's position at time $k$ and $k+1$, respectively. $P_{\text{pos}}$ is the prey's position, $\mu$ is the average position of hunter or prey.

$$x_{i,j}(k+1) = T_{\text{pos}(j)} + CZ\cos(2\pi R_4) \times (T_{\text{pos}(j)} - x_{i,j}(k)), \tag{5.9}$$

where $x(k)$ and $x(k+1)$ are the prey's position at time $k$ and $k+1$, respectively. $T_{\text{pos}}$ stands for the optimum global position, the value of random number $R_4 \in [-1, 1]$, and $\cos(2\pi R_4)$ is introduced to discover the area around $T_{\text{pos}}$ to improve the performance of exploitation.

In HPO, the random value $R_5 \in [0, 1]$ and the regulatory parameter $rp$ are used to select the hunter and prey. If $R_5 < rp$, the search agent is regarded as a hunter, and its position is updated by Eq. (5.8); otherwise the position of the search agent is updated by Eq. (5.9).For more details about HPO algorithm can refer to Naruei *et al.* (2022).

## 5.3  Methodology

### 5.3.1  *The Ill-Posed Problems of SCNs*

In SCNs, the hidden layer parameters are assigned randomly under a supervisory mechanism and the output weights are calculated by the least squares method. The output weights $\beta^*$ can be analytically determined by finding a least-squares solution of the linear system $H_L \beta = T$.

$$\beta^* = \arg \min_{\beta} \|H_L \beta - T\|_F^2 = H_L^{\dagger} T. \tag{5.10}$$

where $H_L$ is the hidden layer output matrix of SCNs.

Singular value decomposition is widely used for calculating the Moore–Penrose pseudo inverse. The SVD decomposition of $H_L^{\dagger}$ is given by

$$H_L^{\dagger} = V\Sigma^- U^T = \sum_{i=1}^{k} \frac{1}{\sigma_i} v_i u_i^T, \quad \Sigma^- = \begin{bmatrix} \Sigma_k^- & 0 \\ 0 & 0 \end{bmatrix}, \tag{5.11}$$

where $U$ and $V$ are two orthogonal columns matrices, $\Sigma_k^- = \text{diag}(\sigma_1^{-1} \ \sigma_2^{-1} \ ... \ \sigma_k^{-1})$ and $\sigma_1 \geqslant \sigma_2 \ ... \geqslant \sigma_k \geqslant 0$ are the singular values of $H_L$.

If the hidden output matrix $H_L$ is severely ill-posed, $\sigma_i$ may be close to 0 and $\sigma_i^{-1}$ will be very large. When those small singular values (and the corresponding singular vectors) which approach zero closely present in the calculation, the observed noise will be unreasonably amplified to destabilize the solution.

Moreover, the contractive factor $r$ in the inequality plays an important role in SCNs. The magnitude of $r$ determines the strictness of the inequality constraint and directly related to the rejection rate of random parameters. An improper setting of the hyper-parameters in SCNs such as the contractive factor $r$, the scope control set $\Upsilon := \{\lambda_1 : \Delta\lambda : \lambda_{\max}\}$ and the maximum times of random configuration $T_{\max}$ may reject lots of randomly assigned input weights and biases.

### 5.3.2 *GSCN Based on Greedy Idea*

In short, the core idea of SCNs theory is to find appropriate random parameters that satisfy the inequality constraint for the newly added node. It should be particularly noted that SCNs conduct $T_{\max}$ times of random configuration and finally select $w_L^*$ and $b_L^*$ from the candidate set with largest $\xi_L$. This is because a larger value of $\xi_L$ probably leads to a faster decrease in the current residual error. The constructive process of SCNs is equivalent to gradually decreasing the network residual error $e_L$ by incrementally adding a new hidden node.

$$f_L = f_{L-1} + g_L\beta_L,$$
$$e_{L-1} = f - f_{L-1}. \tag{5.12}$$

It is evident that the selection of $w_L^*$ and $b_L^*$ are closely connected with $T_{\max}$. Meanwhile, due to the inherent randomness of the algorithm, there may exist some better hidden parameters which can reduce the network residual error faster. Inspired by the way of selecting $w_L^*$ and $b_L^*$ that maximize $\xi_L$ in $\Omega$ and greedy idea, we proposed greedy stochastic configuration networks in this subsection. Our proposed GSCN aims at finding better $\tilde{w}_L$ and $\tilde{b}_L$ to minimize the network residual error at each iteration. In optimization problems, one or more objective functions are defined that should be minimized or maximized considering all the parameters. So GSCN and optimization algorithm share a common objective. In GSCN, the network residual error is defined as the fitness function of the hunter–prey optimization algorithm under the supervisory mechanism of SCNs. The optimization algorithm explore better $\tilde{w}_L$ and $\tilde{b}_L$ in search domain to minimize the network residual error. Intuitively and obviously, the optimized $\tilde{w}_L$ and $\tilde{b}_L$ can reduce the current residual error the most. Meanwhile, the universal approximation property can be guaranteed by the supervisory mechanism of SCNs.

Secondly, the parameter $r$ is flexible in SCNs. $r$ is set relatively smaller at the beginning of the construction process, which leads to a stricter inequality constraint and faster convergence. Then the randomly assigned input weights and biases under the inequality constraint produce a larger value of $\sum_{q=1}^{m} \langle e_{L-1,q}, g_L \rangle^2 / \|g_L\|^2$ which can reduce the current residual error faster. However, as the residual error of SCNs becomes smaller, it's very difficult to configure $w_L$ and $b_L$ stochastically. The GSCN aims to minimize the network residual error at each iteration, which is naturally consistent with the role of parameter $r$. So, $r$ is not necessary to keep varying and can be set a fixed value as closely as possible to 1 to enlarge the probability of feasible solutions (the randomly assigned input weights and biases).

Finally, $L_2$ regularization term is introduced to enhance the generalization performance of GSCN.

For a given objective function $f : \mathbb{R}^d \rightarrow \mathbb{R}^m$, assuming that a set of dataset with inputs $X = \{x_1, x_2, \ldots, x_N\}$ and its corresponding outputs $T = \{t_1, t_2, \ldots, t_N\}$, where $x_i = [x_{i,1}, x_{i,2}, \ldots, x_{i,d}] \in \mathbb{R}^d$ and $t_i = [t_{i,1}, t_{i,2}, \ldots, t_{i,m}] \in \mathbb{R}^m$. The current residual error with $L - 1$ hidden neurons is defined as

$$e_{L-1} = f - f_{L-1} = [e_{L-1,1}, \ldots, e_{L-1,q}, \ldots, e_{L-1,m}]. \tag{5.13}$$

The residual error sequence $\|e_L\|^2$ is monotonically decreasing and convergent which has been proven in Wang and Li (2017b). According to Eq. (5.12)

$$
\begin{aligned}
\|e_L\|^2 &= \|e_{L-1} - g_L \beta_L\|^2 \\
&= \sum_{q=1}^{m} \langle e_{L-1,q} - g_L \beta_{L,q}, e_{L-1,q} - g_L \beta_{L,q} \rangle. \\
&= \sum_{q=1}^{m} \left( \langle e_{L-1,q}, e_{L-1,q} \rangle - \frac{\langle e_{L-1,q}, g_L \rangle^2}{\|g_L\|^2} \right).
\end{aligned}
\tag{5.14}
$$

where $\beta_{L,q}$ is defined as $\langle e_{L-1,q}, g_L \rangle / \|g_L\|^2$.

To achieve higher decreasing rate of network residual error and improve the generalization ability of SCNs. The residual error of the network is selected as the fitness function of the hunter–prey optimization algorithm. The fitness function is defined as

$$
\phi_{L,q} = \begin{cases} +\infty, & \xi_{L,q} \leq 0 \\ e_{L-1,q}^T(X)e_{L-1,q}(X) - \frac{(e_{L-1,q}^T(X).h_L(X))^2}{h_L^T(X).h_L(X)} + \psi(L)(||w_L||^2 \\ +||b_L||^2), & \xi_{L,q} > 0 \end{cases}
$$

$$
fit(L) = \sum_{q=1}^{m} \phi_{L,q}, \quad q = 1, 2, \ldots, m, \tag{5.15}
$$

where $\psi(L)$ is a function of regularization parameter with positive real range, $h_L$ is the output of the $L$th hidden node which can be calculated by

$$
h_L = [g_L(x_1 w_L + b_L), \ldots, g_L(x_N w_L + b_L)]^T. \tag{5.16}
$$

In Eq. (5.15), the network residual error is chosen as the fitness function of HPO algorithm under the condition of $\xi_{L,q} > 0$. By minimizing the fitness function, the optimal solution for the parameters can reduce the residual error as much as possible at each iteration. Meanwhile, the supervisory mechanism guarantees the universal approximation ability of GSCN. As a matter of fact, HPO can be replaced with any other optimization algorithm in GSCN. The reason why we choose HPO as our optimization algorithm is that it is a relatively newer algorithm which is published in 2021 and the authors provided their source Matlab code for free. The HPO presented competitive results compared to the well-known and new optimization algorithms (including WOA, PSO, ALO, HHO, TSA LFD) (Naruei *et al.*, 2022).

### 5.3.3 *SVD with QR Factorization for Ill-Posed Problems*

If the hidden layer output matrix is rank deficient or multicollinearity, it may cause serious instability of the least squares solution. We resort to techniques that incorporate truncated SVD and QR with column pivoting to produce a well-conditioned submatrix of the hidden output.

In TSVD, the small singular values need to be truncated and we use Eq. (5.17) to determine a rank estimate $\tilde{r}$.

$$\tilde{r} = \sum_{i=1}^{k} (\sigma_i > (TT \times \sigma_1)), \tag{5.17}$$

where $TT$ represents the truncation threshold of singular values.

Suppose $U$, $\Sigma$ and $V$ are the computed SVD factors of the hidden output matrix and $\tilde{r}$ is accepted as its rank. The SVD can be expressed as

$$H_L = U \begin{bmatrix} \Sigma_{\tilde{r}} & 0 \\ 0 & 0 \end{bmatrix} V^T, \Sigma_{\tilde{r}} = \begin{bmatrix} \sigma_1 & 0 & \cdots & 0 \\ 0 & \sigma_2 & \cdots & 0 \\ \vdots & \vdots & \ddots & \vdots \\ 0 & 0 & \cdots & \sigma_{\tilde{r}} \end{bmatrix}, \tag{5.18}$$

where $\sigma_1 \geqslant \sigma_2 \geqslant \cdots \geqslant \sigma_{\tilde{r}} \geqslant 0$.

Then we can regard Eq. (5.19) as an approximation solution of the least squares method. The TSVD provides a low-rank matrix approximation of the hidden output matrix $H_L$.

$$\beta_{\tilde{r}} = \sum_{i=1}^{\tilde{r}} \frac{\tilde{u}_i^T T}{\sigma_i} \tilde{v}_i. \tag{5.19}$$

The truncated SVD can make a great deal of sense in those situations where $H_L$ is derived from noisy data. However, rank deficiency implies redundancy among the factors that comprise the underlying model. QR with column pivoting is one way to select columns of $H_L$ which factors in the model.

Suppose $H_L \in \mathbb{R}^{N \times L}$ has rank $\tilde{r}$. QR with column pivoting produces the factorization:

$$H_L \Pi = QR = [B_1 \mid B_2], \tag{5.20}$$

where

$$R = \begin{bmatrix} R_{11} & R_{12} \\ 0 & 0 \end{bmatrix} \begin{matrix} \tilde{r} \\ N - \tilde{r} \end{matrix}, \quad Q = \begin{matrix} [Q_1 \, Q_2] , \\ \tilde{r} \ \ L - \tilde{r} \end{matrix} \tag{5.21}$$

$\Pi$ is a permutation matrix, the first $\tilde{r}$ columns of $A\Pi$ are linearly independent. $Q$ is an orthogonal matrix and $R$ is an upper triangular matrix.

Unfortunately, the minimal $F$-norm solution obtained by the least squares method using the submatrix of $H_L$ may be unstable. Some subsets which involve independent columns may still render a larger residual. There is a trade-off between the independence of the chosen columns and the norm of the residual (Golub and Van Loan, 2013).

The Eckhart–Young Theorem gives the upper norm bound, Golub and Loan establish the lower norm bound of the rank-deficient matrix. Theorem 5.1 is stated as follows:

**Theorem 5.1.** Golub and Van Loan (2013) *Let the SVD of $A \in \mathbb{R}^{N \times L}$ be given by $U^T A V = \Sigma = \mathrm{diag}(\sigma_i)$ and define the matrix $B_1 \in \mathbb{R}^{L \times \tilde{r}}, \tilde{r} < rank(A)$, by*

$$A\Pi = \begin{matrix} \begin{bmatrix} B_1 \; B_2 \end{bmatrix}, \\ \tilde{r} \; L - \tilde{r} \end{matrix} \qquad (5.22)$$

*where $\Pi \in \mathbb{R}^{n \times n}$ is a permutation matrix. If*

$$\Pi^T V = \begin{matrix} \begin{bmatrix} \tilde{V}_{11} \; \tilde{V}_{12} \\ \tilde{V}_{21} \; \tilde{V}_{22} \end{bmatrix} & \begin{matrix} \tilde{r} \\ L - \tilde{r}, \end{matrix} \\ \tilde{r} \quad L - \tilde{r} \end{matrix} \qquad (5.23)$$

*and $\tilde{V}_{11}$ is nonsingular, then*

$$\frac{\sigma_{\tilde{r}}(A)}{\|\tilde{V}_{11}^{-1}\|_2} \leq \sigma_{\tilde{r}}(B_1) \leq \sigma_{\tilde{r}}(A). \qquad (5.24)$$

The useful bounds on $\sigma_{\tilde{r}}(B_1)$ indicate that an independent columns representative subset of $H_L$ can be get by choosing $\Pi$ which resulting the submatrix $\tilde{V}_{11}$ as well-conditioned as possible and hence $\|\tilde{V}_{11}^{-1}\|$ as small as possible. So we apply QR with column pivoting to compute $Q^T V(:, 1 : \tilde{r})^T \Pi = [R_{11} \mid R_{12}]$ and get the permutation matrix $\Pi$. Then we set $H_L \Pi = [B_1 \mid B_2]$. The submatrix $B_1$ is used to compute $\beta$ by the least squares method.

Since orthogonal transformations preserve norms, the least squares problem can be solved by

$$\begin{aligned} \|H_L \beta - T\|_F^2 &= \|Q^T (H_L \beta) - Q^T T\|_F^2 \\ &= \|(Q^T H_L \Pi)(\Pi^T \beta) - (Q^T T)\|_F^2, \end{aligned} \qquad (5.25)$$

where

$$Q^T T = \begin{bmatrix} Q_1^T \\ Q_2^T \end{bmatrix} T = \begin{bmatrix} D_1 \\ D_2 \end{bmatrix}, \tag{5.26}$$

Then, we have

$$\|H_L\beta - T\|_F^2 = \|(Q^T H_L \Pi)(\Pi^T \beta) - (Q^T T)\|_F^2$$

$$= \|(Q^T[B_1|B_2])(\Pi^T\beta) - (Q^T T)\|_F^2 = \| \begin{bmatrix} R_{11} & R_{12} \\ 0 & 0 \end{bmatrix} \begin{bmatrix} Y \\ Z \end{bmatrix} - \begin{bmatrix} D_1 \\ D_2 \end{bmatrix} \|_F^2$$

$$= \|R_{11}Y - (D_1 - R_{12}Z)\|_F^2 + \|D_2\|_F^2, \tag{5.27}$$

where

$$\Pi^T \beta = \begin{bmatrix} Y \\ Z \end{bmatrix} \begin{matrix} \tilde{r} \\ n - \tilde{r}. \end{matrix} \tag{5.28}$$

Thus, if $\beta$ is an LS minimizer, we have $R_{11}Y = D_1 - R_{12}Z$. $Z$ is set to zero matrix in GSCN, the output weights of GSCN is evaluated by:

$$\Pi^T \beta = \begin{bmatrix} R_{11}^{-1} D_1 \\ 0 \end{bmatrix}. \tag{5.29}$$

The overall process of SVD and QR with column pivoting for ill-posed problems in GSCN can be summarized as follows: First, SVD is used to estimate the rank of the hidden output matrix $H_L$. Second, QR with column pivoting is applied to obtain a permutation matrix $\Pi$ and a submatrix of the orthogonal matrix $V$ which is as much well-conditioned as possible. Third, a more independent set of columns of $H_L$ are picked based on the permutation matrix used in the second step. Finally, a well-conditioned submatrix of $H_L\Pi$ is used to get the minimum norm least squares solution.

The flowchart of GSCN is shown in Fig. 5.1.

**Step 1:** Initialize parameters of GSCN.

Initialization parameters of GSCN are reported in Table 5.1.

The parameter $r$ is set to a fixed value in GSCN. The maximum times of random configuration $T_{\max}$ is discarded in GSCN. It selects the optimal member from $N_{\text{pop}}$ size of the population. Then the

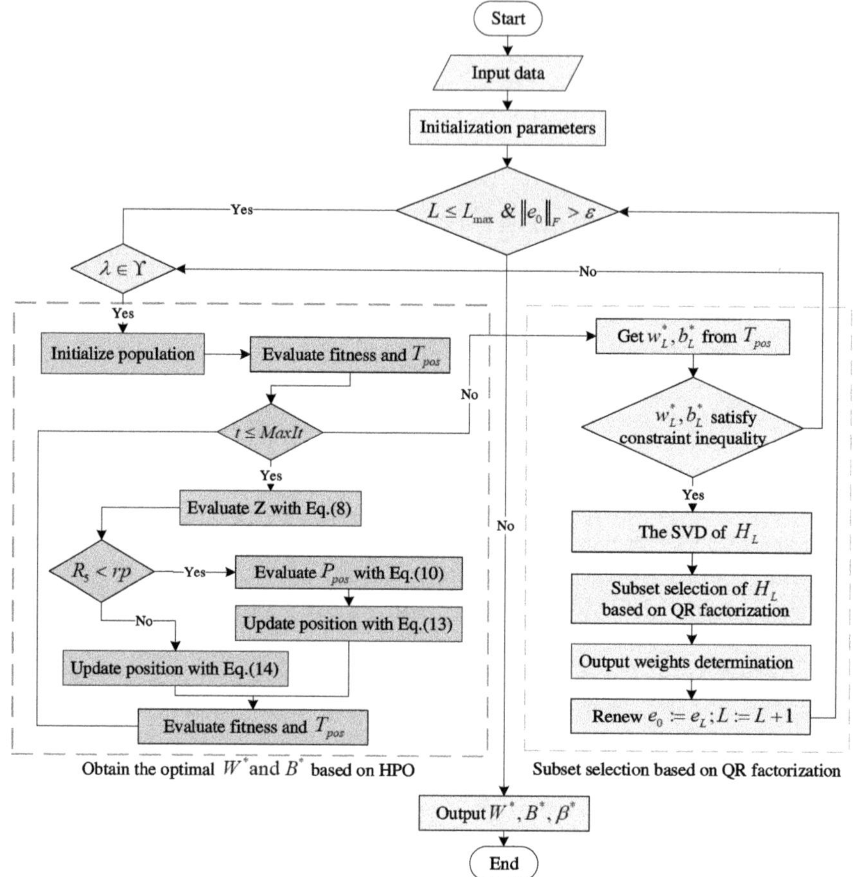


**Fig. 5.1.** The flowchart of GSCN.

**Table 5.1.** Initialization parameters of GSCN.

| Parameters | Description |
| --- | --- |
| $L_{\max}$ | Maximum number of hidden nodes |
| $\epsilon$ | Expected error tolerance |
| $\Upsilon = \{\lambda_{\min} : \Delta\lambda : \lambda_{\max}\}$ | A set of positive scalars |
| $N_{\mathrm{pop}}$ | Population size of HPO |
| MaxIt | Maximum iterations of HPO |
| $rp$ | Regulatory parameter of HPO |

selected $w$ and $b$ are optimized iteratively to find the optimal solution over MaxIt times of generation.

**Step 2:** Obtain the optimized $w$ and $b$ based on HPO algorithm.

Eq. (5.15) is chosen as the fitness function of HPO. The hunter and prey updates their position by Eqs. (5.8) and (5.9), respectively.

**Step 3:** Add a new hidden node into GSCN model.

The optimum global position $T_{\text{pos}}$ is obtained over MaxIt times of successive generation. Then the optimized $w_L^*$ and $b_L^*$ are chosen as the hidden parameters of the $L$th newly added hidden node.

**Step 4:** Output weights determination.

To resolve the ill-posed least squares problem and enhance the stability of GSCN, SVD and QR with column pivoting are used to select a linearly independent subset of $H_L = [h_1, h_2, \ldots, h_L]$. The well-conditioned submatrix of $H_L$ is used to calculate the output weights of GSCN.

GSCN involves several hyper-parameters, such as $\lambda$, $\Upsilon$, $\eta$, $N_{\text{pop}}$, etc. The scope setting of the input weights and biases $\lambda$, the contractive factor $r$ in the inequality, the scope control set $\Upsilon$, and the maximum number of hidden nodes $L_{\max}$ are defined in SCNs. The determination of these parameters can refer to SCNs. The maximum number of iterations MaxIt, the population size of HPO $N_{\text{pop}}$, and the regulatory parameter $rp$ belong to the HPO algorithm. GSCN utilizes similar parameters to the originated HPO. The truncation threshold of singular values $TT$ and the function of regularization parameter $\psi(L) = \frac{\eta}{L}$ are the newly added hyper-parameters of GSCN. The value of $TT$ in GSCN-II is equivalent to the threshold value in truncated singular value decomposition (TSVD). The values of $\alpha$ and $\eta$ are common regularization coefficient of $L_2$ regularization method and $\alpha$ is one of hyper-parameters of SCN-L2. Grid search is one of the most common approach to find proper value of regularization coefficient. On the basis of SCNs, GSCN only add a step to optimize the randomly assigned input weights and biases to accelerate decline rates of network residual error. In general, the parameter settings of GSCN is not different to determine and the model training process is not complex compared with other methods.

## 5.4    Experimental Results and Discussion

The effectiveness of GSCN is evaluated on a function approximation, six benchmark regression, two benchmark classification datasets from KEEL[1] and the bearing fault dataset from Bearing Data Center of Case Western Reserve University.[2] Our source Matlab code and all of experimental datasets are open-source, it is convenient for interesting readers to reproduce our experiments. The proposed GSCN is compared with IRVFLN, SCN-III (Wang and Li, 2017b), SCN-AN (Felicetti and Wang, 2022a) and SCN-AL (Felicetti and Wang, 2022a), where SCN-AN and SCN-AL represent SCN with adaptive normal distribution and SCN with adaptive logistic distribution, respectively. For simplicity and without loss of generality, SCN stands for SCN-III throughout the remainder of this chapter. It can be noted that GSCN-I only applies the HPO algorithm to optimize the randomly hidden parameters. The output weights of GSCN-I are directly evaluated by the Moore–Penrose generalized inverse of the hidden output matrix. On the basis of GSCN-I, GSCN-II introduces the SVD and QR factorization to extract linearly independent subset of the hidden layer output matrix for ill-posed problems of SCNs. It is evident that the performance of GSCN-II is more stable. Actually, GSCN-II can be regarded as an upgraded version of GSCN-I for ill-posed problems.

All the experiments are undertaken in Matlab R2021a on a PC with a Core i5, 3.1 GHz, and 8GB RAM. In the experiments, the activation function of all algorithms is set as sigmoid function. Each test's statistical results for 50 independent times and the average value is adopted to evaluate the performance of different algorithms. For SCN, $r$ is selected from the set {0.9, 0.99, 0.999, 0.9999, 0.99999, 0.999999, 0.9999999}. In GSCN, the regulatory parameter of HPO is set to 0.1. The maximum number of iterations and population size of HPO are 20 and 30, respectively. $r$ is set to 0.9999999. And we set the regularization coefficient $\psi(L) = \frac{\eta}{L}$ in the following experiments. The widely used root mean square error (RMSE), standard deviation (STD), classification accuracy, precision, recall, and

---

[1]KEEL: http://www.keel.es/.
[2]Bearing Data Center: https://engineering.case.edu/bearingdatacenter.

f1-score are employed to evaluate the performance of different algorithms.

### 5.4.1 *Function Approximation Problem*

We utilize the conventional high nonlinear compound function $f$ as our target (Tyukin and Prokhorov, 2009):

$$y = 0.2e^{-(10x-4)^2} + 0.5e^{-(80x-40)^2} + 0.3e^{-(80x-20)^2}, \quad x \in [0,1]. \tag{5.30}$$

In this experiment, 600 training samples are randomly generated from the uniform distribution [0,1], while the test dataset also contains 600 test samples from a regularly spaced grid over $[0,1]$. To verify the generalization ability of the proposed algorithm, we randomly take 10% of training samples and pretreat the target output of the selected samples via Eq. (5.31), while the test dataset remains unchanged.

$$y_{i,\text{Outlier}} = y_i + 0.4 \times \text{rnd} - 0.2, \tag{5.31}$$

where $y_i$ is the target output of the selected sample, $y_{i,\text{Outlier}}$ represents the outlier, and rnd is a random number in the range $(0,1)$.

For SCN, $\lambda$ is selected from the scope control set $\Upsilon := \{250 : 1 : 300\}$ and the maximum times of random configuration $T_{\max}$ is set to 100. For IRVFLN, the input weights and biases are randomly assigned from the uniform distribution over $[-250, 250]$. For the proposed GSCN, $\Upsilon$ is set the same as SCN, $\eta$ and $r$ are set to 0 and 0.9999999, respectively. The value of $TT$ is set to $10^{-6}$.

Table 5.2 lists the average RMSE values and standard deviations (STD) of different models. The last column in Table 5.2 corresponds to evaluating indicator in best value. From Table 5.2, it is obvious that GSCN can achieve lower RMSE value than the other algorithms. GSCN-I and GSCN-II show similar performance. This is because the hidden output is a well-conditioned matrix on function approximation. The SVD with QR factorization for ill-posed problem in GSCN-II hardly fulfill its functions in this experiment.

### 5.4.2 *Benchmark Datasets*

Six real-world benchmark regression and two classification datasets from the KEEL dataset repository are employed to verify the

**Table 5.2.** Average performance on function approximate problem.

| Algorithms | Average test performance at different $L$ (RMSE$\pm$STD) | | | | | Optimal |
| --- | --- | --- | --- | --- | --- | --- |
| | $L=10$ | $L=20$ | $L=30$ | $L=40$ | $L=50$ | |
| IRVFLN | $0.1705\pm0.0112$ | $0.0160\pm0.0109$ | $0.1530\pm0.0104$ | $0.1484\pm0.0103$ | $0.1451\pm0.0110$ | $0.1451\pm0.0110$ |
| SCN | $0.0675\pm0.0133$ | $0.0380\pm0.0114$ | $0.0268\pm0.0089$ | $0.0217\pm0.0052$ | $0.0181\pm0.0035$ | $0.0181\pm0.0035$ |
| SCN-AN | $0.0661\pm0.0123$ | $0.0381\pm0.0095$ | $0.0289\pm0.0079$ | $0.0226\pm0.0052$ | $0.0193\pm0.0048$ | $0.0193\pm0.0048$ |
| SCN-AL | $0.0649\pm0.0133$ | $0.0373\pm0.0105$ | $0.0265\pm0.0058$ | $0.0224\pm0.0058$ | $0.0211\pm0.0052$ | $0.0211\pm0.0052$ |
| GSCN-I | $\mathbf{0.0534\pm0.0054}$ | $\mathbf{0.0277\pm0.0076}$ | $0.0189\pm0.0039$ | $0.0164\pm0.0027$ | $0.0158\pm0.0022$ | $0.0158\pm0.0022$ |
| GSCN-II | $0.0545\pm0.0049$ | $0.0292\pm0.0099$ | $\mathbf{0.0172\pm0.0031}$ | $\mathbf{0.0153\pm0.0029}$ | $\mathbf{0.0149\pm0.0026}$ | $\mathbf{0.0149\pm0.0026}$ |

**Table 5.3.** Specifications of benchmark datasets.

| Datasets | Type | Attributes | Outputs | Instances | TT of values singular values |
|---|---|---|---|---|---|
| Dee | Regression | 6 | 1 | 365 | $\{10^{-5}, 10^{-6}, 10^{-7}\}$ |
| Laser | Regression | 4 | 1 | 993 | $\{10^{-5}, 10^{-6}, 10^{-7}\}$ |
| ANACALT | Regression | 7 | 1 | 4052 | $\{10^{-5}\}$ |
| Friedman | Regression | 5 | 1 | 1200 | $\{10^{-6}\}$ |
| Concrete | Regression | 8 | 1 | 1030 | $\{10^{-5}\}$ |
| Compactiv | Regression | 21 | 1 | 8192 | $\{10^{-6}\}$ |
| MV | Regression | 10 | 1 | 40768 | $10^{-5}$ |
| Pole | Regression | 26 | 1 | 13750 | $10^{-7}$ |
| Iris | Classification | 4 | 3 | 150 | $\{10^{-5}\}$ |
| Vehicle | Classification | 18 | 4 | 846 | $\{10^{-5}\}$ |

performance of GSCN. Specifications of these datasets are given in Table 5.3. We randomly pick out 70% instances as the training data from total instances, while the rest of data are chosen as test dataset.

To illustrate the preferable generalization performance of GSCN, it is compared with IRVFLN, SCN, SCN-AN,SCN-AL and SCN-L2 on benchmark datasets. For SCN-L2, the output weights are evaluated by

$$\beta^* = \operatorname*{argmin}_{\beta} \|H_L\beta_L - T\|_F^2 + \frac{\alpha}{2} \|\beta\|_F^2 = \left(H_L^T H_L + \alpha I\right)^{-1} H_L T,$$

$$(5.32)$$

where $\alpha$ is set to 0.0001. For IRVFLN, the input weights and biases of hidden layer are randomly assigned in the range $[-1, 1]$. The scope control set $\Upsilon$ is $\{0.5, 1, 5, 10, 30, 50,100,150, 200, 250\}$ in SCN and its variants. $\eta$ is set to 0.1 and 0 for

To further demonstrate the advantages of GSCN, Tables 5.4 and 5.5 rcport the statistical results on the regression and classification datasets. We can clearly see that the GSCN-II has the best performance on ANACALT and Iris datasets. Tables 5.4 and 5.5 indicate that GSCN has considerable advantages over the other methods. SCN-AN and SCN-AL perform better in most of the benchmark datasets than SCN. However, their performance are inferior to GSCN on both regression and classification datasets. This means that the performance improvement by different sampling strategies is limited.

**Table 5.4.** Average performance on regression datasets ($L_{max} = 150$).

| Datasets | Algorithms | Average test performance at different $L$ (RMSE $\pm$ STD) | | | |
| --- | --- | --- | --- | --- | --- |
| | | $L = 50$ | $L = 100$ | $L = 150$ | Optimal |
| ANACALT | IRVFLN | $0.2471 \pm 0.0209$ | $0.2206 \pm 0.0133$ | $0.2088 \pm 0.0096$ | $0.2088 \pm 0.0096$ |
| | SCN | $0.1066 \pm 0.0128$ | $0.2040 \pm 0.0972$ | $0.8266 \pm 0.3864$ | $0.1028 \pm 0.0189$ |
| | **SCN-AN** | $0.0910 \pm 0.0133$ | $0.2350 \pm 0.1837$ | $0.4944 \pm 0.2690$ | $0.0874 \pm 0.0190$ |
| | **SCN-AL** | $0.0840 \pm 0.0079$ | $0.1546 \pm 0.0915$ | $0.7307 \pm 1.8582$ | $0.0806 \pm 0.0143$ |
| | SCN-L2 | $0.1033 \pm 0.0045$ | $\mathbf{0.0816 \pm 0.0137}$ | $\mathbf{0.1027 \pm 0.0377}$ | $0.0782 \pm 0.0064$ |
| | GSCN-I | $\mathbf{0.0556 \pm 0.0064}$ | $0.0822 \pm 0.0268$ | $0.4601 \pm 0.2094$ | $\mathbf{0.0456 \pm 0.0084}$ |
| | GSCN-II | $0.0677 \pm 0.0051$ | $0.0830 \pm 0.0228$ | $0.1086 \pm 0.0307$ | $0.0677 \pm 0.0051$ |
| Friedman | IRVFLN | $0.1699 \pm 0.0278$ | $0.1368 \pm 0.0184$ | $0.1167 \pm 0.0109$ | $0.1167 \pm 0.0109$ |
| | SCN | $0.0442 \pm 0.0007$ | $0.0462 \pm 0.0013$ | $0.0496 \pm 0.0026$ | $0.0439 \pm 0.0007$ |
| | **SCN-AN** | $0.4339 \pm 0.0010$ | $\mathbf{0.0426 \pm 0.0009}$ | $0.0479 \pm 0.0020$ | $0.0422 \pm 0.0008$ |
| | **SCN-AL** | $0.0451 \pm 0.0014$ | $0.0430 \pm 0.0011$ | $0.0459 \pm 0.0014$ | $0.0427 \pm 0.0011$ |
| | SCN-L2 | $0.0463 \pm 0.0011$ | $0.0445 \pm 0.0007$ | $0.0461 \pm 0.0011$ | $0.0440 \pm 0.0008$ |
| | GSCN-I | $0.0423 \pm 0.0004$ | $0.0436 \pm 0.0005$ | $0.0464 \pm 0.0007$ | $\mathbf{0.0418 \pm 0.0005}$ |
| | GSCN-II | $\mathbf{0.0422 \pm 0.0004}$ | $0.0436 \pm 0.0006$ | $\mathbf{0.0461 \pm 0.0009}$ | $0.0420 \pm 0.0005$ |

**Table 5.5.** Average performance on classification datasets ($L_{max} = 100$).

| Datasets | Algorithm | Accuracy $\pm$ STD | Precision $\pm$ STD | Recall $\pm$ STD | F1-Score $\pm$ STD |
|---|---|---|---|---|---|
| Iris | IRVFLN | $0.7849 \pm 0.0237$ | $0.8516 \pm 0.0186$ | $0.7849 \pm 0.0237$ | $0.8156 \pm 0.0159$ |
| | SCN | $0.9551 \pm 0.0201$ | $0.9575 \pm 0.0192$ | $0.9551 \pm 0.0201$ | $0.9563 \pm 0.0196$ |
| | SCN-AN | $0.9528 \pm 0.0202$ | $0.9549 \pm 0.0193$ | $0.9528 \pm 0.0202$ | $0.9539 \pm 0.0195$ |
| | SCN-AL | $0.9493 \pm 0.0186$ | $0.9537 \pm 0.0181$ | $0.9493 \pm 0.0186$ | $0.9511 \pm 0.0184$ |
| | SCN-L2 | $0.9609 \pm 0.0151$ | $0.9624 \pm 0.0147$ | $0.9609 \pm 0.0151$ | $0.9616 \pm 0.0149$ |
| | GSCN-I | $\mathbf{0.9729 \pm 0.0092}$ | $\mathbf{0.9751 \pm 0.0076}$ | $\mathbf{0.9729 \pm 0.0092}$ | $\mathbf{0.9740 \pm 0.0084}$ |
| | GSCN-II | $0.9729 \pm 0.0111$ | $0.9750 \pm 0.0096$ | $0.9729 \pm 0.0111$ | $0.9739 \pm 0.0104$ |
| Vehicle | IRVFLN | $0.5320 \pm 0.0269$ | $0.5443 \pm 0.0315$ | $0.5377 \pm 0.0272$ | $0.5541 \pm 0.0288$ |
| | SCN | $0.8341 \pm 0.0160$ | $0.8322 \pm 0.0165$ | $0.8365 \pm 0.0157$ | $0.8344 \pm 0.0162$ |
| | SCN-AN | $0.8328 \pm 0.0167$ | $0.3820 \pm 0.0169$ | $0.8352 \pm 0.0164$ | $0.8332 \pm 0.0160$ |
| | SCN-AL | $0.8363 \pm 0.0164$ | $0.8359 \pm 0.0178$ | $0.8384 \pm 0.0162$ | $0.8371 \pm 0.0176$ |
| | SCN-L2 | $0.8329 \pm 0.0156$ | $0.8318 \pm 0.0181$ | $0.8353 \pm 0.0154$ | $0.8334 \pm 0.0145$ |
| | GSCN-I | $0.8543 \pm 0.0103$ | $0.8539 \pm 0.0104$ | $0.8565 \pm 0.0101$ | $0.8552 \pm 0.0103$ |
| | GSCN-II | $\mathbf{0.8543 \pm 0.0095}$ | $\mathbf{0.8542 \pm 0.0097}$ | $\mathbf{0.8565 \pm 0.0094}$ | $\mathbf{0.8552 \pm 0.0096}$ |

**Table 5.6.**  Efficiency comparison on regression datasets.

| Datasets | Algorithms | $\epsilon$ | Training time(s) | $L_{\text{hidden}} \pm$ STD |
|---|---|---|---|---|
| ANACALT | SCN | 0.08 | 0.6483 | $52.30 \pm 3.0254$ |
| | SCN-AN | | 0.4306 | $45.56 \pm 3.0651$ |
| | SCN-AL | | 0.3373 | $42.56 \pm 4.8411$ |
| | GSCN-I | | **0.3228** | $\mathbf{38.02 \pm 3.5427}$ |
| | GSCN-II | | 0.4061 | $43.48 \pm 4.8665$ |
| Friedman | SCN | 0.04 | 0.1768 | $41.52 \pm 3.1052$ |
| | SCN-AN | | **0.1502** | $43.24 \pm 3.8149$ |
| | SCN-AL | | 0.1624 | $50.54 \pm 4.6432$ |
| | GSCN-I | | 0.1952 | $\mathbf{36.84 \pm 3.0663}$ |
| | GSCN-II | | 0.1933 | $37.26 \pm 2.8271$ |

**Table 5.7.**  Efficiency comparison on classification datasets.

| Datasets | Algorithms | $\epsilon$ | Training time(s) | $L_{\text{hidden}} \pm$ STD |
|---|---|---|---|---|
| Iris | SCN | 0.25 | 0.0615 | $14.20 \pm 1.4254$ |
| | SCN-AN | | 0.0579 | $14.84 \pm 1.2675$ |
| | SCN-AL | | **0.0418** | $\mathbf{13.61 \pm 1.7379}$ |
| | GSCN-I | | 0.0459 | $14.92 \pm 1.0850$ |
| | GSCN-II | | 0.0487 | $14.91 \pm 1.0926$ |
| Vehicle | SCN | 0.4 | 1.8313 | $142.60 \pm 4.0254$ |
| | SCN-AN | | 1.5661 | $145.42 \pm 4.2861$ |
| | SCN-AL | | 1.1965 | $143.94 \pm 3.7384$ |
| | GSCN-I | | **0.8231** | $\mathbf{128.02 \pm 3.5254}$ |
| | GSCN-II | | 0.9297 | $128.61 \pm 2.7405$ |

To illustrate the effectiveness of GSCN, Tables 5.6 and 5.7 compare the computational time among GSCN and other SCN variants on benchmark datasets. In this experiment, MaxIt and $L_{\max}$ are set to 4 and 300, respectively. For SCN, SCN-AN, and SCN-AL, $T_{\max}$ is set to $T_{\max} = \text{MaxIt} \times N\text{pop} = 120$, while the other parameters remain unchanged. From Tables 5.6 and 5.7, we can observe an obvious phenomenon that the computational time and the network complexity of GSCN are similar to the other contrast methods. However, the training time of GSCN is significantly less than that of SCN when the number of hidden nodes is larger (on MV, Pole, and Vehicle datasets). GSCN achieves better efficiency and a more

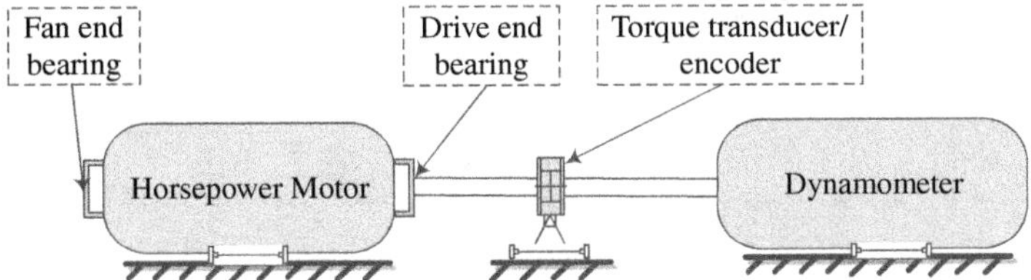


**Fig. 5.2.** Bearing test bed of Case Western Reserve University.

compact network structure, especially in building large-scale neural networks.

### 5.4.3 *Bearing Fault Diagnosis*

The above benchmark regression and classification tasks have demonstrated the merits of GSCN. In this subsection, a practical industrial application dataset from Bearing Data Center of Case Western Reserve University is utilized to verify the performance of GSCN. The SCN model is small and easy to deploy, it is very suitable for bearing fault diagnosis. The test stand consists of a 2 hp motor, a torque transducer/encoder, and a dynamometer and control electronics. The test bearings with single point faults have fault diameters of 7, 14 and 21 mils. Vibration data was collected by accelerometers. Vibration signals were collected using a 16 channel DAT recorder. Numerical drive end bearing faults data was collected at 12000 and 48000 samples per second. Speed and horsepower data were collected using the torque transducer/encoder. Bearing test bed of Case Western Reserve University is shown in Fig. 5.2.

We select the normal and the drive end bearing fault data with the motor load of 3 HP, the approximate speed of 1730 and the sampling rate of 48KHZ as the test dataset. For outer raceway faults, load zone centered at 6:00 is used in the experiment. The sample frame size is equal to the sliding frame size, which implies that there is no overlap between frames. The detailed specifications are listed in Table 5.8.

For vibration data, five parameters including crest factor, kurtosis factor, impulse factor, clearance factor and form factor are extracted from the vibration signals. In addition, we use the db3 wavelet to decompose the 3-layer wavelet packet to obtain the energy characteristics of each frequency band in the third layer. The bearing features are shown in Table 5.9.

**Table 5.8.**    Specifications of bearing fault diagnosis dataset.

|  |  | Sample frame | |
| --- | --- | --- | --- |
| Data type | Number of samples | Size | Sliding size |
| Normal | 480 | 1000 | 1000 |
| Inner race fault | 480 | 1000 | 1000 |
| Ball fault | 480 | 1000 | 1000 |
| Outer race fault at center | 480 | 1000 | 1000 |

**Table 5.9.**    Features of the bearing vibration dataset.

| Feature type | Feature name | | | | | | | |
| --- | --- | --- | --- | --- | --- | --- | --- | --- |
| Time domain | Crest | Kurtosis | Impluse | Clearance | Form | - | - | - |
| Energy | E1 | E2 | E3 | E4 | E5 | E6 | E7 | E8 |

The scope control set $\Upsilon$ is important for SCN to adaptively determine the scope setting of the random parameters $w$ and $b$. $\lambda \in \Upsilon$ varies during the process of adding new hidden layer nodes. In this section, a special experiment is designed to test the influence of $\Upsilon$ on SCN. Two $\Upsilon$ are employed to train SCN and its variants. $\Upsilon_1$ and $\Upsilon_2$ are set to $\{0.5, 1, 5, 10, 30, 50, 100\}$ and $\{0.2 : 0.2 : 1\}$, respectively. For GSCN, $\eta$ is set to 0. To evaluate the capacity of GSCN for constructing large-scale neural networks, the expected error tolerance $\epsilon$ is set to $10^{-6}$. The input weights and biases are randomly assigned from $[-1, 1]$ in IRVFLN.

Table 5.10 displays average test performance on bearing fault diagnosis dataset under $\Upsilon_1$. The average test results are obtained by 50 independent trials. According to Table 5.10, all the algorithms can achieve acceptable results except for the IRVFL. However, our proposed GSCN achieves the best performance with respect to different types of evaluating indicators.

To further evaluate and confirm the efficiency of GSCN, SCN with $T_{\max} = 100$, $T_{\max} = 500$, and $T_{\max} = 1000$ are compared with GSCN-I under $\Upsilon_2$. In Table 5.11, the number following SCN represents the corresponding $T_{\max}$.

When the scope range is relatively small ($\Upsilon_2 = \{0.2 : 0.2 : 1\}$) in Table 5.11, SCN suffers from early stopping. Although $T_{\max}$ is set

Table 5.10. Average test performance under $\Upsilon_1$.

| Algorithms | Accuracy $\pm$ STD | Precision $\pm$ STD | Recall $\pm$ STD | F1-Score $\pm$ STD | $L$(MEAN $\pm$ STD) |
|---|---|---|---|---|---|
| IRVFLN | $0.7163 \pm 0.0107$ | $0.7196 \pm 0.0103$ | $0.7163 \pm 0.0107$ | $0.7179 \pm 0.0104$ | $300 \pm 0$ |
| SCN | $0.9417 \pm 0.0061$ | $0.9423 \pm 0.0059$ | $0.9417 \pm 0.0061$ | $0.9420 \pm 0.0060$ | $300 \pm 0$ |
| SCN-AN | $0.9430 \pm 0.0055$ | $0.9434 \pm 0.0055$ | $0.9430 \pm 0.0055$ | $0.9432 \pm 0.0055$ | $300 \pm 0$ |
| SCN-AL | $0.9423 \pm 0.0067$ | $0.9430 \pm 0.0065$ | $0.9423 \pm 0.0067$ | $0.9426 \pm 0.0066$ | $300 \pm 0$ |
| SCN-L2 | $0.9439 \pm 0.0044$ | $0.9445 \pm 0.0044$ | $0.9439 \pm 0.0044$ | $0.9442 \pm 0.0044$ | $300 \pm 0$ |
| GSCN-I | $\mathbf{0.9604 \pm 0.0047}$ | $\mathbf{0.9609 \pm 0.0054}$ | $\mathbf{0.9604 \pm 0.0047}$ | $\mathbf{0.9606 \pm 0.0055}$ | $300 \pm 0$ |
| GSCN-II | $\mathbf{0.9606 \pm 0.0042}$ | $\mathbf{0.9611 \pm 0.0043}$ | $\mathbf{0.9606 \pm 0.0042}$ | $\mathbf{0.9609 \pm 0.0043}$ | $300 \pm 0$ |

Table 5.11.　Average test performance with different $T_{\max}$ under $\Upsilon_2$.

| Algorithms | Accuracy $\pm$ STD | Precision $\pm$ STD | Recall $\pm$ STD | F1-Score $\pm$ STD | $L$(MEAN $\pm$ STD) |
|---|---|---|---|---|---|
| SCN-100 | $0.9180 \pm 0.0091$ | $0.9181 \pm 0.0093$ | $0.9180 \pm 0.0091$ | $0.9181 \pm 0.0092$ | $37.58 \pm 3.9429$ |
| SCN-500 | $0.9347 \pm 0.0068$ | $0.9350 \pm 0.0069$ | $0.9347 \pm 0.0068$ | $0.9349 \pm 0.0069$ | $48.82 \pm 3.6617$ |
| SCN-1000 | $0.9367 \pm 0.0052$ | $0.9370 \pm 0.0054$ | $0.9367 \pm 0.0052$ | $0.9369 \pm 0.0053$ | $51.80 \pm 2.9829$ |
| GSCN-I | $\mathbf{0.9679 \pm 0.0035}$ | $\mathbf{0.9683 \pm 0.0034}$ | $\mathbf{0.9679 \pm 0.0035}$ | $\mathbf{0.9681 \pm 0.0034}$ | $\mathbf{300 \pm 0}$ |

from 100 to 1000, the performance improvement of SCN is still not ideal. It is difficult for SCN to find appropriate random parameters when $\Upsilon_2$ is set small even though $T_{\max}$ is large enough. The number of hidden nodes of SCN model is between 49 and 55 in most trials when $\Upsilon_2 = \{0.2 : 0.2 : 1\}$ and $T_{\max} = 1000$. In contrast, GSCN can build a large-scale network with 300 hidden neurons and achieve more than 95% accuracy on bearing faults diagnosis. In essence, the parameter $r$ is set to 0.999999 in GSCN, so the randomly assigned parameters are easy to satisfy the inequality constraint. Meanwhile, even if the randomly assigned $w$ and $b$ are not satisfied with the inequality constraint, the hunter–prey optimization algorithm can assist GSCN in obtaining appropriate $w$ and $b$ which satisfy the constraint condition. Based on the above analysis, it is evident that the GSCN can build a large-scale network easily even if the scope setting $\Upsilon$ of the model is set improperly. It may be concluded that GSCN has a reliable and accurate efficiency compared to SCN.

## 5.5  Summary

To improve the training efficiency, generalization, and stability performance of SCNs, we proposed a new GSCN framework in this chapter. The randomly assigned $w$ and $b$ are optimized based on the hunter–prey optimization algorithm, this way of assigning the random parameters based on greedy idea can effectively accelerate the convergence speed of GSCN. For the ill-conditioned hidden output matrix of SCNs, we are the first to introduce the SVD and QR with column pivoting into SCN to pick principal columns of the hidden output matrix. A heuristic solution to this problem can be obtained by the generated well-conditioned submatrix. The experimental results on function approximation, regression, classification, and bearing fault diagnosis have indicated that the proposed GSCN exhibits considerable advantages in terms of convergence rate, generalization, and stability compared with other algorithms.

GSCN has a strong ability to search appropriate random parameters which can satisfy the inequality constraint. Meanwhile, it also brings some negative effects. GSCN usually selects hidden parameters from a small fixed range. That is to say, the small scope may lead to the hidden layer output matrix being not full rank. In addition,

GSCN has advantages of building compact neural networks. Despite the fact that the GSCN shows significant speedups on large-scale networks, it does not significantly contribute to small-sized networks.

As deep neural network is more effective than the shallow model in data representation. So in future work, we will extend our work to the deep version of SCNs. In addition, it is inevitable to produce redundant hidden nodes due to the inherent feature of randomized algorithm. Therefore, another future research will focus on efficient sparse learning representation methods for deep stochastic configuration networks.

Part 2

# Robust Data Analysis

# Chapter 6

# Intuitionistic Fuzzy Stochastic Configuration Networks

Stochastic configuration network (SCN) is an emerging type of random neural network that allocates node parameters via supervised mechanisms to ensure universal approximation capability.However, outliers and noise in real-world data can adversely affect SCN's classification performance. Fuzzy theory has emerged as a powerful tool for addressing uncertainties in data, with intuitionistic fuzzy numbers (IFNs) playing a pivotal role in characterizing fuzzy information. By leveraging IFNs to measure data reliability, noise and outliers can be effectively identified and distinguished, thereby mitigating their adverse effects on the model learning process. To enhance the precision and robustness of SCN in classification tasks and enable them to effectively utilize fuzzy information, this chapter introduces IFNs as penalty weights for samples, assigning appropriate weights based on their reliability. Subsequently, the supervisory mechanism of SCN is employed to allocate hidden layer node parameters, and the output weights of these nodes are computed by solving a weighted least squares problem, culminating in the development of an intuitionistic fuzzy stochastic configuration network (IFSCN). Furthermore, to better harness deep abstract features and deep fuzzy information within the data, this chapter extends the IFSCN to a deeper architecture, aiming to improve the model's classification accuracy and robustness.

## 6.1  Introduction

In practical industrial process, the acquired data may be contaminated by various levels of noise because of the sensor failure, environmental implication and human error (Dai *et al.*, 2015; Gribonval *et al.*, 2015). The standard SCN model uses the least squares method to update hidden layer weights, treating all samples equally, which makes it sensitive to noisy data and outliers, reducing the model's generalization and classification performance. Therefore, ensuring SCN's robustness and generalization under noisy and outlier conditions is a critical issue.To enhance the robustness of neural networks with random weights based on $L_2$ norm loss functions, SCNs with cost-sensitive based least squares loss function have been presented to solve the data with outliers (Li *et al.*, 2019b; Wang and Li, 2017a).

Among them, intuitionistic fuzzy sets (IFS) Atanassov (1986), introduced in 1983, allow data samples to belong to multiple categories with both membership and non-membership degrees, helping classification algorithms handle uncertainty and fuzziness more effectively, improving accuracy and robustness. This technique uses the membership function to quantify the nearness of training samples to the class center, while the non-membership function examines the correlations between inconsistent samples and their neighboring data instances (Rezvani *et al.*, 2019; Rezvani and Wu, 2023). By weighting samples with IFS, the influence of noisy data on the least squares method can be reduced, improving SCN's classification performance and robustness. Additionally, IFS quantifies the uncertainty of sample points, providing richer information and enhancing the algorithm's interpretability. Subsequently, IFS theory has been effectively employed to mitigate the adverse effects of noise and outliers on the performance of machine learning models, various IFS based-models have been demonstrated for binary classification task, such as intuitionistic fuzzy twin support vector machine (IFTWSVM) (Rezvani *et al.*, 2019; Rezvani and Wu, 2023), intuitionistic fuzzy kernel ridge regression (IFKRR) (Hazarika *et al.*, 2021), intuitionistic fuzzy random forest (IFRF) (Ren *et al.*, 2022). In addition, IFS based-cost sensitive $L_2$ norm loss functions have been used in neural networks with random weights, such as intuitionistic fuzzy random vector functional link nets (IFRVFL) (Ganaie *et al.*, 2024; Hazarika *et al.*, 2023; Malik *et al.*, 2024; Mishra *et al.*, 2023).

Therefore, to improve the performance of SCN in solving binary classification problems containing outliers and noise, this chapter combines the concepts related to IFNs with SCN for the first time. It constructs a new supervisory mechanism for assigning hidden layer node parameters and weighting the output weights, and proposes an intuitionistic fuzzy SCN (IFSCN). Furthermore, DSCN with multi-layers usually has better feature representation, which can improve the performance of classification and regression problems, a deep version of IFSCN, named IFDSCN, is conceptualized, demonstrating a layered approach to feature extraction and network design.

Overall, the primary contributions are as follows:

- Introducing the concept of intuitionistic fuzzy sets (IFSs), defining newmembership and non-membership functions, and constructing a new score function.
- Constructing an innovative supervisory mechanism for hidden layer node parameter assignment based on weighted samples using an intuitionistic fuzzy score function, pioneering the proposal of IFSCN and IFDSCN. Thus, injecting fresh ideas into this field.
- Numerous experiments indicate IFSCN and IFDSCN have higher classification accuracy compared to other involved models on eight benchmark binary classification datasets.

## 6.2 Preliminaries

The classical SCN models usually employ the least squares method to update the output weights, making it sensitive to the noise in sample data. Based on the intuitionistic fuzzy membership degree and non-membership degree, this chapter introduces intuitionistic fuzzy numbers $\alpha$ and $\alpha^*$ for each training sample. These are calculated based on the intuitionistic fuzzy set theory to evaluate abnormalities in the data set and ensure model robustness.

The membership degree, non-membership degree, and the scoring function are defined as follows:

(1) **Membership degree:** The membership degree considers the distance between each sample and its corresponding class center in the high-dimensional feature space.

For a training sample $x_i$, the membership degree is defined as

$$\alpha(x_i) = \begin{cases} 1 - \frac{\|\phi(x_i) - D_+\|}{r^+ + \xi}, & y_i = +1 \\ 1 - \frac{\|\phi(x_i) - D_-\|}{r^- + \xi}, & y_i = -1, \end{cases} \tag{6.1}$$

where $D_+$ and $D_-$ are the centers of positive and negative classes, respectively, and $r^+$ and $r^-$ represent the radii of the classes. $\xi$ is an adjustable parameter, and $\|\phi(x_i) - D\|$ represents the distance between the sample and its class center.

The centers $D_+$ and $D_-$ are defined as

$$D_+ = \frac{1}{n_+} \sum_{y_i = +1} \phi(x_i), \tag{6.2}$$

$$D_- = \frac{1}{n_-} \sum_{y_i = -1} \phi(x_i), \tag{6.3}$$

and the radii of the classes are given by

$$r^+ = \max_{y_i = +1} \|\phi(x_i) - \phi(x_j)\|, \quad r^- = \max_{y_i = -1} \|\phi(x_i) - \phi(x_j)\|. \tag{6.4}$$

(2) **Non-membership degree:** The non-membership degree allocates a value for each sample, quantifying its abnormality based on its neighborhood's density and dissimilarity.

The non-membership degree is defined as

$$\alpha^*(x_i) = (1 - \alpha(x_i))\Phi(x_i), \quad \text{s.t. } 0 \leq \alpha(x_i) + \alpha^*(x_i) \leq 1, \tag{6.5}$$

where

$$\Phi(x_i) = \begin{cases} \{x_j : \|\phi(x_i) - \phi(x_j)\| \leq \eta, y_j \neq y_i\}, & \text{if } y_j \neq y_i \\ \{x_j : \|\phi(x_i) - \phi(x_j)\| \leq \eta\}, & \text{otherwise.} \end{cases} \tag{6.6}$$

Here, $\eta$ is an adjustable parameter, and $|\cdot|$ represents the cardinality of the set.

Using the kernel trick, the distance can be computed as

$$\|\phi(x) - \phi(y)\| = \sqrt{K(x, x) + K(y, y) - 2K(x, y)}, \tag{6.7}$$

where $K(x, y)$ is the kernel function.

(3) **Scoring function:** The scoring function quantifies the difference between the membership and non-membership degrees, providing a way to measure the degree of belonging of a sample to a set.

Assuming the training set is $X = \{(x_1, y_1, \alpha_1, \alpha_1^*), \ldots, (x_N, y_N, \alpha_N, \alpha_N^*)\}$, where $\alpha_i$ and $\alpha_i^*$ represent the membership and non-membership degrees of sample $x_i$, the scoring function is defined as

$$s_i = \begin{cases} \alpha_i, & \alpha_i^* = 0, \\ 0, & \alpha_i \leq \alpha_i^*, \\ \frac{1-\alpha_i^*}{2-\alpha_i-\alpha_i^*}, & \text{otherwise.} \end{cases} \tag{6.8}$$

Based on the definitions and calculations of intuitionistic fuzzy numbers in this chapter, the scoring function can be used as a penalty weight for updating the output weights of the stochastic configured networks.

## 6.3 Methodology

### 6.3.1 *Intuitionistic Fuzzy Stochastic Configuration Network*

Different from the traditional SCN, the intuitionistic fuzzy stochastic configuration network (IFSCN) proposed in this section can assign intuitionistic fuzzy hesitant weights to each sample in the dataset, which evaluates the reliability of the data samples.

Therefore, the objective function of IFSCN is defined as Eq. (6.9):

$$\min_{\beta} \frac{1}{2}\|\beta\|^2 + \frac{C}{2}\sum_{i=1}^{N} s_i \left\| \sum_{j=1}^{L} g(w_j, b_j, x_i)\beta_j - y_i \right\|^2, \tag{6.9}$$

where $s_i$ is the intuitionistic fuzzy hesitant weight of sample $i$, representing the importance of the sample in the objective function Eq. (6.9). $L$ denotes the number of hidden layer nodes; $\beta_j$ and $b_j$ are the weight and bias of the hidden layer nodes, respectively; $g(\cdot)$ is the activation function; and $C$ is the regularization coefficient.

Assume that span($\Gamma$) is dense in $L_2$ space, and for $\forall h \in \Gamma$ and some $b_g$, we have $0 < \|g\| < b_g$. Given $0 < r < 1$ and a non-negative real-valued sequence $\{\mu_L\}$, where $\{\mu_L\}$ satisfies $\lim_{L\to\infty} \mu_L = 0$ and $\mu_L \leq (1-r)$. For $L = 1, 2, \ldots$, let:

$$\delta_L^* = 7\sum_{q=1}^{m} \delta_{L,q}^*, \quad \delta_{L,q} = (1 - r - \mu_L)\|\tilde{e}_{L-1,q}\|^2. \tag{6.10}$$

$$\xi = \lim_{L\to\infty} (1 - \varepsilon)^L < 1. \tag{6.11}$$

If the randomly generated basis function $g_L$ satisfies Eq. (6.12):

$$\langle \tilde{e}_{L-1,q}, g_L \rangle^2 \geq \left( \frac{b_g^2 + \frac{1}{C}}{b_g^2 + \frac{2}{C}} \right)^2 \delta_{L,q}. \tag{6.12}$$

And if the output weights $\beta$ be calculated as

$$\beta^* = \arg\min \left\{ \frac{C}{2} \left\| f - \sum_{j=1}^{L} g_j \beta_j \right\|^2 + \frac{1}{2}\|\beta\|^2 \right\}. \tag{6.13}$$

Thus, we have

$$\sqrt{\xi}\|f\| \leq \lim_{L\to\infty} \|e_L^*\| \leq \sqrt{r}\frac{1}{\sqrt{\|f\|}}. \tag{6.14}$$

Therefore, the supervisory mechanism of SCN with $L_2$ regularization and intuitionistic fuzzy hesitant weighting can be rewritten as Eq. (6.15):

$$\xi_{L,q} = \frac{\left( \tilde{e}_{L-1,q}(X) \cdot \tilde{h}_L(X) \right)^2}{\gamma} - (1 - r - \mu_L)\tilde{e}_{L-1,q}^T(X)\tilde{e}_{L-1,q}(X), \tag{6.15}$$

where

$$\gamma = \frac{\left( \tilde{h}_L^T(X) \cdot \tilde{h}_L(X) + \frac{1}{C} \right)^2}{\tilde{h}_L^T(X) \cdot \tilde{h}_L(X) + \frac{2}{C}}. \tag{6.16}$$

Through the proof provided above, we can ensure the global convergence of the intuitionistic fuzzy stochastic configuration network proposed in this section.

Meanwhile, due to the introduction of the $L_2$ regularization term, the generalization ability of IFSCN has been further improved. By solving Eq. (6.9), the output weights can be calculated as

$$\beta = \begin{cases} H^T \left(\frac{I}{C} + SHH^T\right)^{-1} SY, & N < L \\ \left(\frac{I}{C} + H^T SH\right)^{-1} H^T SY, & N \geq L, \end{cases} \tag{6.17}$$

where $S = \mathrm{diag}(s_1, s_2, \ldots, s_N)$.

It is worth noting that the hesitant weight matrix $S$ in Eq. (6.17) may be a non-singular matrix. Without the $L_2$ regularization term, solving for the output weights $\beta$ could result in an ill-conditioned problem. This demonstrates that the introduction of the $L_2$ regularization term simultaneously resolves mathematical computational issues.

The time complexity for configuring hidden layer nodes is $O(N \times L_{\max} \times T_{\max})$. According to the data scale, the complexity for output weight calculation is either $O(L_{\max}^3)$ or $O(N^3)$. Therefore, the overall time complexity of IFSCN is either: $O(N \times L_{\max} \times T_{\max}) + O(L_{\max}^3) + O(N)$ or $O(N \times L_{\max} \times T_{\max}) + O(N^3) + O(N)$.

Under normal circumstances, similar to the standard SCN algorithm, the most time-consuming part of IFSCN typically lies in solving the inverse of the hidden layer output matrix. In general, IFSCN only incurs additional computational overhead in the weight-determination phase.

### 6.3.2 *Intuitionistic Fuzzy Deep Stochastic Configuration Network*

In the previous section, this chapter successfully integrated intuitionistic fuzzy sets with stochastic configuration networks, proposing a novel algorithmic model IFSCN. This model not only ensures powerful function approximation capability but also enhances classification accuracy and robustness. Meanwhile, due to the introduction of intuitionistic fuzzy sets, this approach has also strengthened the model's interpretability.

However, similar to SCN, IFSCN as a data-driven algorithmic model faces certain challenges in processing data due to network layer limitations, particularly in extracting high-level abstract features from data. This limitation somewhat weakens the model's ability to capture complex data patterns and deep kernel information. To further enhance IFSCN's performance, enabling it to more effectively learn and express features from low-level to high-level, and capture more refined kernel information, it is necessary to deepen and expand the IFSCN model.

Based on these considerations, this section will focus on describing IFSCN's depth expansion method, constructing an Intuitionistic Fuzzy Deep Stochastic Configuration Network (IFDSCN). Through increasing network depth and complexity, IFDSCN will be able to better capture high-level features and deep kernel information from data, thereby further improving model performance. The network structure and training algorithm of IFDSCN will be detailed below.

The network structure of IFDSCN is identical to DeepSCN, which will not be elaborated here. For each sample point, IFDSCN assigns a score value to evaluate the reliability of the sample point, with its objective function defined by

$$\min_{\beta} \frac{1}{2}\|\beta\|_2^2 + \frac{C}{2}\sum_{i=1}^{N} s_i \left\|\sum_{k=1}^{n}\sum_{j=1}^{L_k} g_{k,j}\beta_j^{(k)} - y_i\right\|^2, \qquad (6.18)$$

where $s_i$ is the evaluation weight of sample $i$, representing the sample's contribution; $g_{k,j} = g_{k,j}(w_{k,j}, b_{k,j}, x)$ represents the activation function; $w_{k,j}$ and $b_{k,j}$ represent the weight and bias of the $j$th node in the $k$th hidden layer respectively; $\beta_j^{(k)}$ represents the output weight of the $j$th node in the $k$th layer.

Given training sample input $X = \{x_1, x_2, \ldots, x_N\}$, $x_i = [x_{i,1}, \ldots, x_{i,d}]$, output $Y = \{y_1, y_2, \ldots, y_N\}$, $y_i = [y_{i,1}, y_{i,2}, \ldots, y_{i,m}]$, the network residual is calculated by:

$$e_{L_n-1}^{(n)} = [e_{L_n-1}^{(n)}(x_1), \ldots, e_{L_n-1}^{(n)}(x_N)], \quad q = 1, 2, \ldots, m. \qquad (6.19)$$

After adding the $L_n$th node to the $n$th hidden layer, the hidden layer output can be expressed as

$$h_{L_n}^{(n)} := h_{L_n}^{(n)}(X) = [g^{n,1}(x^{(n-1)}), \ldots, g^{n,L_n}(x^{(n-1)})]^T. \qquad (6.20)$$

Due to sample processing, the residual $e_{L_n-1}^{(n)}$ and hidden layer output $h_{L_n}^{(n)}$ are redefined by

$$\tilde{e}_{L_n-1}^{(n)} = \Theta e_{L_n-1}^{(n)}(X), \tag{6.21}$$

$$\tilde{h}_{L_n}^{(n)} = \Theta h_{L_n}^{(n)}(X), \tag{6.22}$$

where $\Theta = \mathrm{diag}\{\sqrt{s_1}, \sqrt{s_2}, \ldots, \sqrt{s_N}\}$. For convenience of presentation and understanding, we will continue to use $e_{L_n-1}^{(n)}$ and $h_{L_n}^{(n)}$ to represent network residual and hidden layer output.

Referring to the content discussed in IFSCN, we redefine IFD-SCN's supervisory control as below, and the model's global approximation capability can be easily proven:

$$\xi_{L_n,q}^{(n)} = \frac{\langle e_{L_n-1}^{(n)}, h_{L_n}^{(n)}\rangle}{\gamma} - (1-r)\langle e_{L_n-1,q}^{(n)}(X), e_{L_n-1,q}^{(n)}(X)\rangle, \tag{6.23}$$

where

$$\gamma = \frac{(\langle h_{L_n}^{(n)}, h_{L_n}^{(n)}\rangle + \frac{1}{C})^2}{\langle h_{L_n}^{(n)}, h_{L_n}^{(n)}\rangle + \frac{2}{C}}. \tag{6.24}$$

The optimization problem in Eq. (6.18) is a convex quadratic optimization problem. Therefore, this problem has a unique global optimal solution. The solution is:

$$\beta = \begin{cases} H^T \left(\frac{I}{C} + SHH^T\right)^{-1} SY, & N < L \\ \left(\frac{I}{C} + H^T SH\right)^{-1} H^T SY, & N \geq L, \end{cases} \tag{6.25}$$

where $S = \mathrm{diag}\{s_1, s_2, \ldots, s_N\}$.

According to the above algorithm description, assume the number of samples in the dataset is $n$. Using Big-$O$ notation to evaluate the time complexity of IFDSCN, the time complexity for calculating the membership and non-membership degrees for each data sample is $O(N)$. The construction of the algorithm model comprises two key phases: first, configuring parameters for each hidden layer node; second, calculating the output weights of hidden layer nodes. Assuming the maximum number of nodes in each hidden layer is identical, the time complexity for hidden layer node parameter configuration is $O(N \times M \times L_{\max} \times T_{\max})$. Based on different data scales, the time complexity for output weight calculation is either $O((M \times L_{\max})^3)$ or $O(M \times N^3)$. Therefore, the overall time complexity of IFDSCN is either $O(N \times M \times L_{\max} \times T_{\max}) + O((M \times L_{\max})^3) + O(N)$ or $O(N \times M \times L_{\max} \times T_{\max}) + O(M \times N^3) + O(N)$.

Similar to IFSCN, under normal circumstances, the time complexity of IFDSCN still primarily depends on solving the inverse of the hidden layer output matrix.

## 6.4  Experimental Results and Discussion

### 6.4.1  *Experimental Settings*

All experiments were conducted on a platform with MATLAB R2022b, Intel® Core® CPU 12900H 2.50 GHz, 32GB RAM, and Windows 11 operating system. The Gaussian kernel function was adopted in the experiments:

$$K(x_1, x_2) = \exp(-\|x_1 - x_2\|^2/\mu^2), \tag{6.26}$$

where $\mu$ is the kernel parameter.

To comprehensively evaluate the performance of IFSCN and IFD-SCN algorithms, two types of models were selected for comparison. The first type includes classical machine learning models, namely KRR (Saunders *et al.*, 1998) and RVFL (Pao *et al.*, 1994). The second type comprises newer intuitionistic fuzzy machine learning algorithms, including IFTSVM (Rezvani *et al.*, 2019) and IFKRR (Hazarika *et al.*, 2021). Through comparison with these two types of models, we can more thoroughly understand the performance of IFSCN and IFDSCN in different types of algorithms.

The experimental datasets cover both UCI and KEEL, two well-known machine learning databases, comprising eight benchmark datasets in total. These datasets come from different domain application scenarios, possessing certain diversity and representativeness. To ensure experimental validity, we adopted random partitioning to

**Table 6.1.** Details of datasets.

| Dataset | Samples | Negative samples | Positive samples | Features |
|---|---|---|---|---|
| ecoli2 | 335 | 283 | 52 | 7 |
| ecoli-0-1-4-7_vs_2-3-5-6 | 336 | 308 | 28 | 7 |
| ecoli3 | 335 | 300 | 35 | 7 |
| wpbc | 198 | 151 | 98 | 33 |
| heart | 270 | 150 | 120 | 14 |
| pima | 768 | 268 | 500 | 8 |
| vehicle1 | 845 | 628 | 217 | 18 |
| abalone918 | 730 | 688 | 42 | 8 |

*Note*: Table contains UCI and KEEL benchmark datasets.

divide each dataset according to a 7:3 ratio into training and test sets. The training set is used for model learning and parameter tuning, while the test set is used to evaluate the model's generalization capability. Detailed information about the datasets, such as sample sizes, positive/negative sample numbers, and feature dimensions, is listed in Table 6.1.

The other experimental settings and procedures are explained as follows:

(1) **Parameter settings:** The parameters $C$ and $\mu$ are selected from $\{10^{-5}, \ldots, 10^5\}$ and $\{2^{-6}, \ldots, 2^6\}$ respectively. Specifically, for IFTSVM model, we set $C_1 = C_2 = C_3 = C_4 = C$; for RVFL model, the number of hidden layer nodes is selected from $\{10, 20, 50, 100, 200, 500\}$; for the proposed IFSCN and IFD-SCN, the maximum number of nodes $L_{\max}$ will be selected from $\{10, 20, 50, 100, 200, 500\}$; IFDSCN's maximum number of layers $M$ is set to 3; both models' maximum number of candidate nodes $T_{\max}$ is set to 100.

(2) **Hyperparameter optimization:** Grid search method is employed to optimize hyperparameters for various models. Grid search is a strategy that exhaustively evaluates all given parameter combinations to find the optimal parameter configuration. In this method, each set of hyperparameter configurations is evaluated and compared to assess their impact on model performance. To accurately evaluate the performance of each parameter configuration, this chapter employed five-fold cross-validation for model evaluation and

verification. During the five-fold cross-validation process, the dataset is randomly divided into five equal-sized subsets, ensuring that each subset fairly represents the overall data. Each subset serves as the test set in turn, while the remaining four subsets are combined as the training set for model training. This way, each subset gets to serve as the test set, ensuring comprehensive and fair evaluation.

(3) **Evaluation metrics:** In this experiment, accuracy and average ranking are used as indicators to evaluate model performance. However, since a model may perform exceptionally well on one dataset but poorly on others, a single accuracy indicator cannot fully reflect the model's performance. Therefore, in this experiment, independent evaluations and rankings are conducted on the model's performance for each dataset to comprehensively measure its performance. Specifically, we rank each model's performance on different datasets separately. In the ranking process, the following principle is followed: a lower rank indicates better model performance on that dataset; conversely, a higher rank suggests relatively poor performance. Through this ranking method, we can clearly identify the model with the best comprehensive performance across all datasets, i.e., the model with the lowest total rank across all datasets. The average ranking for the $j$th model is calculated using:

$$R_j = (1/N) \sum_{i=1}^{N} r_j^i, \tag{6.27}$$

where $N$ is the number of datasets, and $r_j^i$ is the rank of the $j$th model on the $i$th dataset.

### 6.4.2   *Main Results and Discussion*

Based on these experimental data in Table 6.2, we can draw the following conclusions:

(1) SCN demonstrates significant performance advantages in classification tasks compared to RVFL, and its performance is superior to other classical algorithms on multiple datasets. This highlights SCN's effective supervisory control mechanism in configuring node parameters, endowing the model with strong generalization capability.

**Table 6.2.** Performance comparison of different models on classification datasets.

| Dataset | IFTSVM | KRR | IFKRR | RVFL | SCN | IFSCN | IFDSCN |
|---|---|---|---|---|---|---|---|
| ecoli2 | 0.857 | 0.697 | 0.809 | 0.807 | 0.943 | <u>0.946</u> | **0.950** |
| ecoli-0-1-4-7_vs_2-3-5-6 | 0.917 | 0.900 | 0.839 | 0.800 | 0.959 | <u>0.969</u> | **0.973** |
| ecoli3 | 0.857 | 0.721 | 0.809 | 0.807 | 0.926 | <u>0.932</u> | **0.936** |
| wpbc | 0.564 | 0.494 | 0.520 | 0.672 | 0.757 | <u>0.780</u> | **0.782** |
| heart | 0.840 | **0.872** | 0.787 | <u>0.857</u> | 0.804 | 0.819 | 0.821 |
| pima | 0.758 | 0.761 | 0.689 | 0.745 | 0.758 | <u>0.771</u> | **0.780** |
| vehicle1 | 0.786 | 0.777 | 0.737 | 0.768 | 0.803 | <u>0.823</u> | **0.834** |
| abalone918 | 0.750 | 0.696 | 0.702 | 0.704 | 0.949 | <u>0.953</u> | **0.964** |
| Average Accuracy | 0.791 | 0.740 | 0.736 | 0.770 | 0.862 | <u>0.874</u> | **0.886** |
| Average Rank | 4.00 | 5.250 | 6.125 | 5.250 | 3.625 | <u>2.375</u> | **1.375** |

*Note*: Best results are shown in **bold**, second best results are <u>underlined</u>.

(2) IFSCN effectively utilizes the intuitionistic fuzzy information in the dataset, improving SCN's classification accuracy. This reasonably demonstrates that considering and utilizing the model's intuitionistic fuzzy information is beneficial for enhancing algorithm classification performance. By introducing intuitionistic fuzzy sets, IFSCN can more comprehensively and precisely capture data features, thereby making more accurate classification decisions.

(3) As a deep extension of IFSCN, IFDSCN further improves classification accuracy across all datasets, indicating the importance of high-level data features and deep kernel information for classification decisions. Through increasing network depth and complexity, IFDSCN can learn and extract hierarchical features from data and capture more refined kernel information.

### 6.4.3 *Statistical Testing*

For a more precise statistical analysis of model performance, this chapter adopts the T paired win-tie-loss sign test. This method evaluates overall performance by counting the number of wins, ties, and losses for each classifier pair across different datasets. Under the win-tie-loss sign test framework, the null hypothesis assumes no performance difference between two models across all datasets, specifically that each model's wins are theoretically equal to half

**Table 6.3.** Win-tie-loss test results.

|        | IFTWSM    | KRR       | IFKRR     | RVFL      | SCN       | IFSCN     |
|--------|-----------|-----------|-----------|-----------|-----------|-----------|
| KRR    | [2, 0, 6] |           |           |           |           |           |
| IFKRR  | [0, 0, 8] | [4, 0, 4] |           |           |           |           |
| RVFL   | [2, 0, 6] | [4, 0, 4] | [5, 0, 3] |           |           |           |
| SCN    | [7, 1, 0] | [6, 0, 2] | [8, 0, 0] | [7, 0, 1] |           |           |
| IFSCN  | [7, 0, 1] | [7, 0, 1] | [8, 0, 0] | [7, 0, 1] | [8, 0, 0] |           |
| IFDSCN | [7, 0, 1] | [7, 0, 1] | [8, 0, 0] | [7, 0, 1] | [8, 0, 0] | [8, 0, 0] |

of their total comparisons. When the difference in wins between two models reaches statistical significance, meaning one model's wins significantly exceed the other's, we consider there to be a significant performance difference between these models. For ties, the two models' performances are considered equal and their win counts are evenly split. When a model's win count is at least $N/2 + 1.96\sqrt{N}/2$ (in this experiment, when a model wins on more than 5.96 datasets), we can determine that this model shows significant performance differences.

Combining the above theoretical introduction to the win-tie-loss sign test, analysis of Table 6.3 reveals that IFDSCN's accuracy shows significant differences compared to all other algorithmic models, indicating clear advantages over other models. Meanwhile, IFSCN shows significant accuracy differences compared to all models except IFDSCN, demonstrating IFSCN's effectiveness in handling classification problems and proving the importance of introducing intuitionistic fuzzy sets for improving classification performance.

### 6.4.4 *Robustness Performance Analysis*

To deeply explore and verify the robustness of the IFSCN and IFDSCN models when facing noise, this section specifically designed a series of robustness evaluation experiments based on the Circle-in-the-Square problem. Circle-in-the-Square is a classic binary classification problem that requires the classifier to accurately determine whether sample points within a square region lie inside or outside a circular region. In this problem, the circular region is located at the center of the square, with an area equal to half that of the square. In the experimental design, a total of 10,000 sample points were selected to ensure statistical significance and reliability of the experimental results. To simulate real-world data uncertainty and complexity, Gaussian noise was introduced to these samples at three different ratios: 0%, 5%, and 10%. By controlling the noise ratio, we can systematically evaluate the robustness performance of IFSCN and IFDSCN models under different noise levels, examining their anti-interference ability and generalization capability.

As shown in Table 6.4 and Fig. 6.1, the performance trends of different models as noise ratio increases are clearly displayed. Through in-depth analysis of the experimental data, it can be seen that the IFDSCN model proposed in this research demonstrates better performance on noisy datasets. At any noise level, IFDSCN maintains the

**Table 6.4.** Accuracy of the CIRCLE-IN-THE-SQUARE problem with noise.

| Noise (%) | IFTSVM | RVFL | SCN | IFSCN | IFDSCN |
|---|---|---|---|---|---|
| 0 | 0.994 | 0.979 | 0.995 | <u>0.996</u> | **0.998** |
| 5 | 0.985 | 0.964 | 0.984 | <u>0.991</u> | **0.994** |
| 10 | 0.980 | 0.959 | 0.973 | <u>0.987</u> | **0.992** |

*Note*: Best results are shown in **bold**, second best results are <u>underlined</u>.

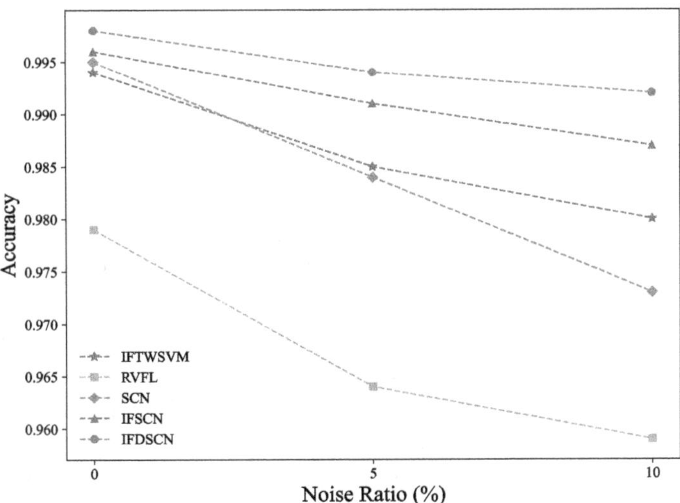


**Fig. 6.1.** Performance trends of different models under varying noise ratios.

highest classification accuracy, exhibiting powerful noise processing capability and generalization ability. These results fully demonstrate the effectiveness of combining intuitionistic fuzzy theory with Deep-SCN, showing that IFDSCN can utilize the deep kernel information contained in the data to enhance model robustness. Following closely is the intuitionistic fuzzy stochastic configuration network IFSCN model, which also shows excellent performance at various noise levels, second only to IFDSCN. IFSCN effectively handles the uncertainty in the data through introducing intuitionistic fuzzy sets, improving the model's noise resistance capability. Although its performance is slightly inferior to IFDSCN, compared to traditional SCN and other baseline models, IFSCN still demonstrates significant advantages.

Notably, as the noise ratio gradually increases, while both IFSCN and IFDSCN show some decline in classification accuracy, their decline amplitude is relatively small compared to other models. This phenomenon fully demonstrates the superior robustness of these two algorithms when facing noise challenges. Benefiting from the introduction of intuitionistic fuzzy sets, IFSCN and IFDSCN can effectively evaluate sample reliability, reducing the impact of noise on classification decisions. At the same time, by utilizing the kernel information contained in the data, these two models can more comprehensively and precisely capture the internal structure and relationships of the data, thereby maintaining relatively high classification accuracy even in noisy environments.

## 6.5  Summary

This chapter addresses the challenges of classification accuracy and robustness faced by SCN when dealing with noise and outliers by proposing improvements. By introducing intuitionistic fuzzy membership functions to weight the samples and effectively evaluating sample reliability, the embedded kernel information in the data is leveraged to construct the IFSCN model, which is further extended to IFDSCN. The improved IFSCN achieves higher classification accuracy and robustness compared to SCN, and its global approximation capability is theoretically proven. Through deep extension, IFDSCN successfully utilizes the deep kernel information and high-level abstract features in the data, achieving further improvement in classification accuracy and robustness, with its global approximation capability also proven. The proposed IFSCN and IFDSCN demonstrate superior model accuracy in classification tasks compared to not only traditional SCN but also other classical algorithms.

# Chapter 7

# Weighted Deep Stochastic Configuration Networks Based on M-Estimator Functions

Deep stochastic configuration network (DSCN) is an randomized incremental learning model, it can start from a small structure, increase the nodes and hidden layers gradually. As the input weights and biases of nodes are assigned according to supervisory mechanism, meantime, all the nodes in hidden layer are fully connected to the outputs, the output weights of DSCN are determined through the least square method. Therefore, DSCN has the advantages of less manual intervention, high learning efficiency, strong generalization ability. However, although the randomized feedforward learning process of DSCN has faster efficiency, the feature learning ability is still insufficient. In the meantime, with the increase of nodes and hidden layers, it is easy to lead to over-fitting phenomenon. When solving regression problems with noise, the performance of original DSCN is easily affected by outliers, which reduces the generalization ability of the model. Therefore, to improve the regression performance and robustness of DSCN, weighted deep stochastic configuration networks (WDSCN) based on M-Estimator functions are proposed. First of all, we adopt two common M-Estimator functions (i.e., Huber and Bisquare) to acquire the sample weights for reducing the negative impact of outliers. When the sample has a smaller training error, give this sample a larger weight, while when the training error of sample is larger, it is determined to be outlier data and give this sample a smaller weight. The sample weight decreases monotonically with the increase of the absolute value of the error, thus reducing the influence of noisy data onto the model and improving the generalization of the algorithm. Meanwhile, the weighted least square method and $L_2$ regularization strategy are introduced to calculate output weight vector replace the least square method. It can not only solve the noisy data regression problems and avoid over-fitting problem of DSCN. In the second place, the model based on $L_1$ regularization is helpful to extract sparse features and improve the accuracy of supervised learning, for further improve the representation ability of WDSCN, a stochastic configuration sparse autoencoder (SC-SAE) is designed, SC-SAE use the supervision mechanism of DSCN to assign input parameters, at the same time, we adopt the $L_1$ regularization technique to objective function for getting sparse features, alternating direction method of multipliers (ADMM) approach is utilized to solve the objective function for determining the output weights of SC-SAE. And then, as the randomness encoding process of SC-SAE, we can obtain the diversity of features of different SC-SAE models, consequently effective feature representation can be acquired through fusion features from multiple SC-SAE for the training of WDSCN. Finally, experimental results on real-world datasets show that the proposed WDSCN-Huber and WDSCN-Bisquare have higher generalization performances and regression accuracies than DSCN, SCN, and other weighted models (e.g., RSC-KDE, RSC-Huber, RSC-IQR, RDSCN-KDE, WBLS-KDE and RBLS-Huber). But in the meantime, the results of ablation experiment show that WDSCN with fusion sparse features which exacted from multiple different SC-SAE models are superior to those models with fusion sparse feature. Therefore, it is verified that SC-SAE can extract effective sparse features and improve the learning ability of weighted models.

## 7.1 Introduction

Deep neural networks (DNNs) can extract high-level features, and has stronger feature representation ability than shallow models, showing great potential in machine vision, pattern recognition, natural language processing and some other fields (LeCun *et al.*, 2015). To enhance the representation learning capacity of SCNs and construct a lightweight deep learning architecture, Wang and Li (2018) extended SCN to deep stochastic configuration network (DSCN), showing potential in the field of intelligent information processing. Subsequently, to enhance the performance of DSCN, Felicetti and Wang (2022b) used symmetric zero-mean distribution to construct DSCN, Felicetti and Wang (2022a) also employed Monte Carlo tree search and random search strategies to find hyper-parameters of DSCN. As ensemble learning can significantly improve the accuracy and generalization performance of neural networks, Zhang *et al.* (2022a) proposed a ensemble DSCN model based on AdaBoost algorithm, which improves the regression performance of DSCN.

In practical applications, due to sensor failure, human interference, environmental impact and other problems, there are different proportions of noise and outliers in the collected data (Gribonval *et al.*, 2015), which seriously affects the accuracy and generalization performance of deep stochastic configuration networks (DSCNs). To improve the abnormal data processing capability and robustness of SCN, RSC-KDE based on kernel density estimation (Wang and Li, 2017a; Xie and Zhou, 2020), RSC-MCC based on maximum correlation entropy criterion (Xie and Zhou, 2020), RSC-Huber and RSC-IQR based on M-estimator functions, and RSC-NKDE based on non-parametric kernel density estimation (NKDE) (Dai *et al.*, 2019b) were proposed for robust regression tasks, robust SCNs can use different weighting functions to assign penalty weights to noise samples, and update the output weights based on weighted least squares methods, reducing the negative impact of noise data or outliers on the model. Moreover, Dai *et al.* (2019b) proved the universal approximation property of robust SCNs. In addition, to utilize high-level features, RSC-KDE was extended to a deep version of RDSCN-KDE based on DSCN (Guo and Yan, 2021). However, as the number of nodes and hidden layers increase, DSCN is prone to over-fitting problems, and as a randomized neural networks model, it still exist insufficient feature learning capabilities.

To explore the potential of DSCN in noisy data analysis, effectively eliminate the impact of noise, and improve the robustness and generalization of the model, this chapter proposes weighted deep stochastic configuration networks (WDSCNs) based on the M-estimator functions. Firstly, a stochastic configuration sparse autoencoder (SC-SAE) was designed in order to improve the representation ability of the WDSCN model and multiple SC-SAEs were used for feature learning and fused for WDSCN unsupervised feature learning. Secondly, two commonly used M-estimator functions (Huber and Bisquare) were employed to calculate the weights of each training samples, then weighted least squares method based on $L_2$ regularization strategy were adopted to update output weights of WDSCNs for reducing the negative impact of outliers on modeling. Finally, experimental results on real-world datasets demonstrated that WDSCN-Huber and WDSCN-Bisquare have higher robust performance and regression accuracy than DSCN, SCN, and robust models such as RSC-KDE, RSC-Huber, RSC-IQR, RDSCN-KDE, WBLS-KDE and RBLS-Huber.

Overall, the primary contributions are as follows:

- We present weighted deep stochastic configuration networks (WDSCNs) based on the M-estimator functions, weighted least squares with $L_2$ regularization strategies to update the output weights of WDSCNs, thereby reducing the negative impact of outliers on WDSCNs.
- We propose a novel stochastic configuration sparse Autoencoder (SC-SAE), which using supervised mechanism of SCN to assign input parameters randomly, and alternating direction method of multipliers (ADMM) is used to compute the output weights of SC-SAE.
- To obtain effective feature representations, leverage the randomness and diversity of features generated by SC-SAE. We adopt multiple SC-SAE models for feature learning and fusion, which are then used for WDSCN model training.
- Experimental results on KEEL regression datasets with different outlier ratios demonstrate that WDSCN exhibits stronger robustness and generalization compared to DSCN. Moreover, it outperforms other robust models such as RSC-KDE, RSC-Huber, RSC-IQR, RDSCN-KDE, WBLS-KDE, and RBLS-Huber.

## 7.2   Methodology

### 7.2.1   *Stochastic Configuration Sparse Autoencoder*

SCN adopts an incremental learning method, using inequality constraints to randomly configure the parameters of hidden layer nodes. The network structure gradually increases from one hidden layer node to the completion of the network construction, and has sound universal approximation characteristics (Wang and Li, 2017b). Therefore, using the universal approximation characteristics of SCN, a stochastic configuration sparse autoencoder (SC-SAE) is designed to extract the sparse features of the original data.

Among them, the architecture of stochastic configuration sparse autoencoder (SC-SAE) is shown in Fig. 7.1. In which, the supervision mechanism of SCN is used to randomly assign input parameters of SC-SAE, and the objective function based on the $L_1$ regularization is used to reconstruct features for obtaining sparse features.

In brief, the construction process of SC-SAE can be described as follows: Given training data $\{X, Y\}$, where $X = \{X_1, X_2, \ldots, X_N\}$ represents sample features, $x_i = [x_{i,1}, x_{i,2}, \ldots, x_{i,d}] \in \mathbb{R}^d$; $i = 1, 2, \ldots, N$, $N$ represents the number of samples.

Given the objective function $f : \mathbb{R}^d \to \mathbb{R}^{d'}$, $d'$ represents the reconstructed feature dimension, assuming that the $L - 1$ hidden layer

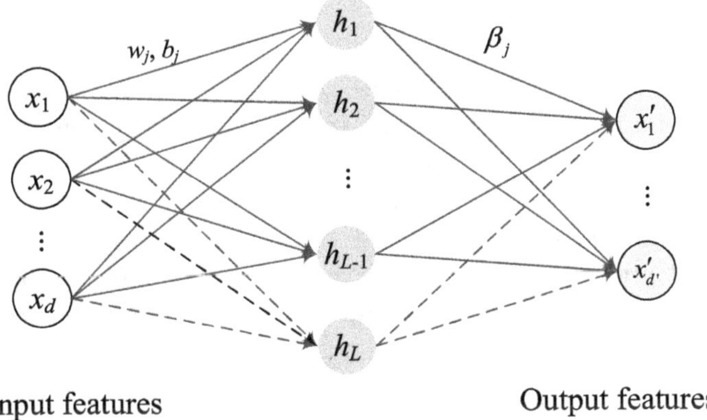


**Fig. 7.1.**   The architecture of stochastic configuration sparse autoencoder.

nodes of SC-SAE have been configured, the current network outputs $f_{L-1}(X)$ of SC-SAE can be calculated by Eq. (7.1):

$$f_{L-1}(X) = \sum_{j=1}^{L-1} g_j\left(Xw_j + b_j\right)\beta_j \ (L = 1, 2, \ldots, f_0 = 0), \qquad (7.1)$$

where $\beta_j$ represents the output weights of node $j$ ; $g_j$ is the activation function; $w_j$ and $b_j$ indicate the input weight and bias of node $j$, respectively, and their ranges are $[-\lambda, \lambda]^d$ and $[-\lambda, \lambda]$, $\lambda$ denotes the parameter range; $j = 1, 2, \ldots, L_{\max}$ .

The current network residual vector can be calculated by Eq. (7.2):

$$e_{L-1} = f - f_{L-1}(X) = \left[e_{L-1,1}(X), e_{L-1,2}(X), \ldots, e_{L-1,d'}(X)\right].$$
$$(7.2)$$

According to the preset error $\varepsilon$ or the maximum number of nodes $L_{\max}$ , determine whether the preset conditions are met. If the preset conditions are not met, adaptively increase the number of nodes $L$, and configure the node parameters according to Eq. (7.4), the candidate node parameter that satisfies the maximum value of $\xi_L = \sum_{q=1}^{m} \xi_{L,q}$ will be selected as the parameter of node $L$.

$$h_L = [g_L(x_1 w_L + b_L), \ldots, g_L(x_N w_L + b_L)]^T , \qquad (7.3)$$

$$\xi_{L,q} = \frac{\langle e_{L-1,q}, h_L \rangle^2}{\| h_L \|^2} - (1 - r - \mu_L) \| e_{L-1,q} \|^2, \qquad (7.4)$$

where $q = 1, 2, \ldots, d'$ represents the output dimension; $h_L$ is the output of node $L$, which calculated by (7.3); $w_L$ and $b_L$ are the parameters of node $L$ respectively; $T_{\max}$ indicates the number of candidate parameters; $r \in (0, 1)$; $\{\mu_L\}$ expresses a non-negative real number sequence, where $\mu_L \leq 1 - r, \lim_{L \to +\infty} \mu_L = 0$.

The output weights $\beta$ of SC-SAE can be determined based on the objective function as Eq. (7.5), and we can obtain the reconstructed features and output $f$ through Eqs. (7.6) and (7.7) respectively,

$$\beta = \arg\min_{\beta} \|H\beta - X\|^2 + C_1\|\beta\|_1, \qquad (7.5)$$

where $\beta = [\beta_1, \beta_2, \ldots, \beta_L]$; $H = [h_1, h_2, \ldots, h_L]$.

$$X' = X\beta, \qquad (7.6)$$

$$f = X'\beta^+, \tag{7.7}$$

where $\beta^+$ represents the Moore–Penrose inverse of $\beta$.

To solve the objective function of Eq. (7.5), ADMM methods is employed as follows.

We first convert Eq. (7.5) into the ADMM form as Eq. (7.8):

$$\arg\min_{\beta} u(\beta) + v(o), \text{ s.t. } \beta - o = 0, \tag{7.8}$$

where $u(\beta) = \|H\beta - X\|^2$, $v(o) = C_1\|\beta\|_1$.

Then Eq. (7.8) can be solved by the following iterative process:

$$\begin{cases} \beta_{k+1} = (H^T H + \rho I)^{-1} \left(H^T X + \rho(o^k - z^k)\right) \\ o_{k+1} = S_{\underline{C_1}}(\beta_{k+1} + z_k) \\ z_{k+1} = z_k + (\beta_{k+1} - o_{k+1}), \end{cases} \tag{7.9}$$

where $\rho > 0$; $S$ represents a soft threshold operator as Eq. (7.10).

$$S_\kappa(a) = \begin{cases} a - \kappa, a > \kappa \\ 0, \quad |a| \le \kappa \\ a + \kappa, a < \kappa. \end{cases} \tag{7.10}$$

### 7.2.2 *Framework of Weighted Deep Stochastic Configuration Networks*

The learning process of weighted deep stochastic configuration networks (WDSCNs) mainly divided into two stages: Unsupervised feature learning and supervised learning. Unsupervised learning uses multiple SC-SAEs to learn the input data in parallel. Through multiple unsupervised learning, the input data is converted into a random feature space, overcoming the shortcomings of insufficient feature learning ability of a single SC-SAE, which helps to extract more effective high-level features and hidden information from the original data. In the supervised learning stage, when DSCN is adopted and noise-oriented data analysis is introduced, the traditional least squares method is used to calculate the training error, which is easy to reduce the generalization of the model due to serious outliers and over-fitting problems. In order to reduce the impact of outliers on the generalization of the model, this section introduces

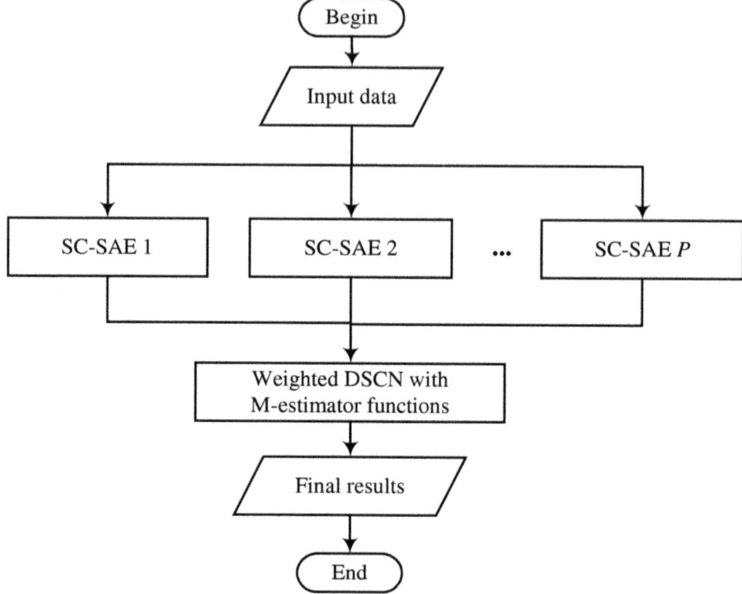


**Fig. 7.2.** The framework of weighted deep stochastic configuration networks.

weighted least squares and regularization strategies as the objective function of WDSCNs, and uses a weighting function based on the M-estimator function to calculate the sample weights and update the output weights.

The framework of weighted deep stochastic configuration networks is shown in Fig. 7.2.

To analyze regression problem with noise, in addition to sparse feature learning based on SC-SAE, the weighting process of WDSCN is described as follows:

Given training data $\{X, Y\}$, where $X = \{x_1, x_2, \ldots, X_N\}$ represents sample features, $x_i = [x_{i,1}, x_{i,2}, \ldots, x_{i,d}] \in \mathbb{R}^d$; $Y = \{y_1, y_2, \ldots, y_N\}$ represents sample labels, $y_i = [y_{i,1}, y_{i,2}, \ldots, y_{i,m}] \in \mathbb{R}^m$; $i = 1, 2, \ldots, N$, $N$ represents the number of samples.

### 7.2.2.1 *Unsupervised Feature Learning*

To obtain effective feature representation, the randomness and diversity of features generated by SC-SAE are utilized to adopt multiple SC-SAEs for feature learning and feature embedding. Among them,

$P$ represents the number of SC-SAE models, $Q$ is the feature dimension extracted by each SC-SAE, and for better feature learning, $P$ and $p$ need to be set according to the dataset.

### 7.2.2.2 *Supervised Learning Process*

To simplify the description, the number of hidden layers of DSCN is set to $M$, and the number of nodes in each hidden layer is uniformly set to $L_{\max}$. Then the construction of weighting process can be described as follows:

Given the objective function $f : \mathbb{R}^d \to \mathbb{R}^m$, suppose that the current training errors are calculated through Eq. (7.11), and weighting matrix $\theta = \mathrm{diag}\,(\theta_1, \theta_2, \ldots, \theta_N)$ which is calculated by M-estimator functions, we can get weighted training errors as Eq. (7.12):

$$e^M_{L-1} = f - f^M_{L-1}(X) = \left[ e^M_{L-1,1}(X), e^M_{L-1,2}(X), \ldots, e^M_{L-1,m}(X), \right] \tag{7.11}$$

$$e^M_{L-1}{}' = \theta e^M_{L-1}(X), \tag{7.12}$$

where $e^M_{L-1,q}{}'(X) = [e^M_{L-1,q}{}'(x_1), e^M_{L-1,q}{}'(x_2), \ldots, e^M_{L-1,q}{}'(x_N)] \in \mathbb{R}^N$, $q = 1, 2, \ldots, m$.

If $\|e^M_{L-1}\|^2$ does not meet the preset error $\varepsilon$ or does not reach the maximum number of nodes in this layer $L_{\max}$, randomly assign node $L$ candidate parameters, then we calculate outputs $h^M_L$ of node $L$ according to Eq. (7.13), and define the weighted outputs $h^{M'}_L$ as Eq. (7.15):

$$\begin{aligned} X^{(M)} &= \Phi(X^{(M-1)}; W^{(M-1)}, B^{(M-1)}) \\ &= \left[ \phi_{M,1}(X^{(M-1)}), \phi_{M,2}(X^{(M-1)}), \ldots, \phi_{M,L}(X^{(M-1)}) \right], \quad M \geq 1, \end{aligned} \tag{7.13}$$

$$h^M_L = \left[ \phi_{M,L}(x^{M-1}_1 w^{M-1}_L + b^{M-1}_L), \ldots, \phi_{M,L}(x^{M-1}_N w^{M-1}_L + b^{M-1}_L) \right]^T, \tag{7.14}$$

$$h^{M'}_L = \theta h^M_L, \tag{7.15}$$

where $w^{M-1}_L$ and $b^{M-1}_L$ are the input weight and bias of node $L$ in the $M$ layer; $\phi_{M,L}(\cdot)$ represents the activation function.

The candidate parameter that satisfies the maximum value of $\xi_L^{M'} = \sum_{q=1}^{m} \xi_{L,q}^{M'} \geq 0$ is selected as the parameter of the $M$ layer node $L$, in which $\xi_{L,q}^{M'}$ is determined as Eq. (7.16):

$$\xi_{L,q}^{M'} = \frac{\langle e_{L-1,q}^{M}{}', h_L^{M'}\rangle^2}{\langle h_L^{M'}, h_L^{M'}\rangle} - (1-r)\langle e_{L-1,q}^{M}{}', e_{L-1,q}^{M}{}'\rangle, \tag{7.16}$$

where $q = 1, 2, \ldots, m; r \in (0,1)$.

Finally, the output weights of WDSCNs are calculated by using Eq. (7.17),

$$\beta = \arg\min_{\beta} \|\theta H\beta - \theta Y\|_2^2 = \left(H^T\theta^2 H\right)^{-1} H^T\theta^2 Y, \tag{7.17}$$

where $H = [H_L^1, H_L^2, \ldots, H_L^M]$ is the output of all hidden layers, and $H_L^M = [h_1^M, h_2^M, \ldots, h_L^M]$ represents the outputs of node $L$ in $M$ layer.

In addition, the randomized modeling method of the feed-forward neural network with random weights will cause the model to over-fitting problem as the number of layers and nodes increase. To keep the generalization performance of the model, $L_2$ regularization term is employed in the objective function based on the ridge regression theory. Therefore, Eq. (7.17) can be modified as follows:

$$J(\beta) = \arg\min_{\beta} \|\theta H\beta - \theta Y\|_2^2 + C_2\|\beta\|_2^2. \tag{7.18}$$

By taking the partial derivative of Eq. (7.18) and setting it to 0, we can get Eq. (7.20):

$$\frac{\partial J}{\partial \beta} = 2H^T\theta^2 H\beta - 2H^T\theta^2 Y + 2C_2\beta = 0, \tag{7.19}$$

$$\beta = \left(H^T\theta^2 H + C_2 I\right)^{-1} H^T\theta^2 Y, \tag{7.20}$$

where $C_2$ indicates the regularization parameter, $I$ denotes the identity matrix.

### 7.2.3    *M-Estimator Functions*

To ensure the robustness of WDSCNs, the selection of weighting functions needs to ensure that the weight coefficient can monotonically

**Table 7.1.**　M-estimator functions.

| Function | Weighting function $\theta(e_i)$ | Default tuning |
|---|---|---|
| Huber | $\min\left(1, \frac{k}{|e_i|}\right)$ | 1.345 |
| Bisquare | $\left(1 - \left(\frac{e_i}{k}\right)^2\right)^2, \mid e_i \mid \le k$ | 4.685 |

decrease with the increase of training error. When the model training error is too large, a smaller weight coefficient is assigned to reduce the sensitivity of the learning model to outliers. Therefore, this section selects two commonly M-estimator functions, Huber and Bisquare as weighting functions of WDSCNs, as shown in Table 7.1.

The relevant function curves are shown in Fig. 7.3, among them, (a) introduces the curve of Huber function, and (b) illustrates the curve of Bisquare function. When the sample training error is small, the sample can be given a larger weight; when the sample training error is large, it is judged as an outlier data with a smaller weighting coefficient. The sample weight decreases monotonically with the increase of the absolute value of the error, thereby reducing the impact of abnormal data on the model and improving the generalization of the algorithm.

At the same time, to ensure that the model can be fully trained and improve the regression performance of noise data, the threshold $k$ is usually calculated using Eq. (7.21):

$$k = \text{tuning} \times \sigma, \tag{7.21}$$

where *tuning* represents the default tuning parameter of the weighting function; $\sigma$ express the standard deviation of the training error $e$.

In the case of abnormal values, $\sigma$ can be expressed by Eq. (7.22):

$$\sigma = \text{med}(|e|)/0.6745, \tag{7.22}$$

where $\text{med}(\cdot)$ represents the median of the error value, and the constant is introduced to ensure the unbiasedness of $\sigma$ under Gaussian error conditions.

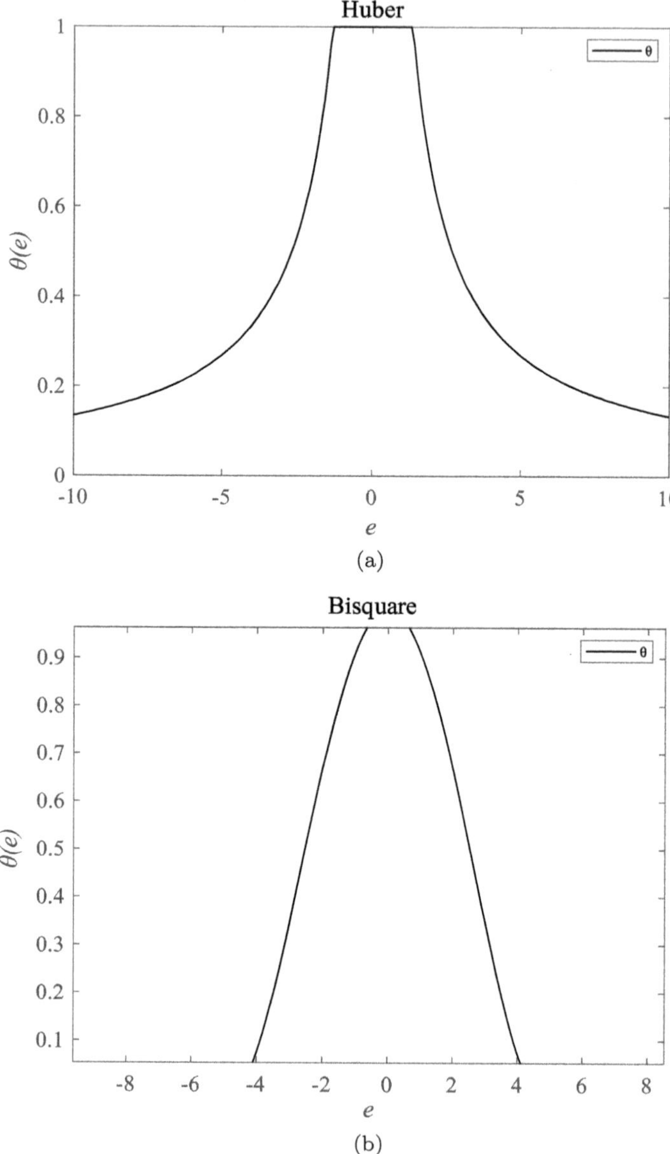



**Fig. 7.3.** Curves of M-estimator functions. (a) Presents the curve of Huber function; (b) presents the curve of Bisquare function.

## 7.3 Experimental Results and Discussion

### 7.3.1 *Experimental Settings*

All experiments were conducted in MATLAB R2019b under a PC with Intel (R) Core (TM) i7-9750H CPU@2.60GHz, 64.00GB RAM, Windows 10 64-bit operating system. We compared WDSCN-Huber and WDSCN-Bisquare with DSCN (Wang and Li, 2018), SCN (Wang and Li, 2017b), RSC-KDE (Wang and Li, 2017a), RSC-Huber (Dai *et al.*, 2019b), RSC-IQR (Dai *et al.*, 2019b), RDSCN-KDE (Guo and Yan, 2021), RBLS-Huber (Guo and Xu, 2023) and WBLS-KDE (Chu *et al.*, 2019).

To demonstrate the performance of WDSCN for the noisy data regression problem, 5 KEEL benchmark datasets[1] were selected for the experiments. The descriptions of benchmark datasets are shown in Table 7.2. For reducing the impact of different feature ranges on the model, first, the input and output vectors of the original data are normalized to $[0, 1]$, of which 75% of the samples are randomly used as training data and the rest are used as test data. Secondly, 10%, 20%, 30%, and 40% uniform distributed outliers are randomly added to the output values of the training data, ranging from $[-0.5, 0.5]$. Therefore, the output value range of the noisy training data is transformed into $[-0.5, 1.5]$.

To ensure the fairness of experiments, all 10 models use the activation function shown in (7.23).

$$S(x) = \frac{1}{1 + e^{-x}}. \tag{7.23}$$

**Table 7.2.** Attributes of KEEL benchmark datasets.

| Datasets | Number of features | Number of samples |
|---|---|---|
| Abalone | 8 | 4177 |
| Wizmir | 9 | 1461 |
| Concrete | 8 | 1030 |
| Stock | 9 | 950 |
| Mortgage | 15 | 1049 |

---

[1]Knowledge Extraction based on Evolutionary Learning, http://www.keel.es/.

All experiments are run independently 20 times, and the average root mean square error (RMSE) in (7.24) is used as the evaluation index to evaluate the models.

$$\text{RMSE} = \sqrt{\frac{1}{N} \sum_{i=1}^{N} (y_i - f_i)^2}, \tag{7.24}$$

where $y_i$ represents the actual value of sample $i$; $f_i$ is the regression result of sample $i$; $N$ denotes the total number of samples.

The parameter settings of all compared models are given as follows:

The number of hidden layer nodes in each layer of all models are selected from $\{25, 50, 75, 100\}$; DSCN, RDSCN-KDE, WDSCN-Huber and WDSCN-Bisquare models adopt two hidden layers; the parameter $r$ and the control factor $\lambda$ are determined by the set $\{0.9, 0.99, 0.999, 0.9999, 0.99999, 0.999999\}$ and $\{0.5, 1, 5, 10, 30, 50, 100, 150, 200, 250\}$ respectively; the size of maximum candidate pool is set to 100; the preset error is set to 0.001.

Different from the DSCN and RDSCN-KDE, WDSCN-Huber and WDSCN-Bisquare empoly sparse feature learning embedding based on SC-SAE. In the feature learning stage, the number of SC-SAE models and the nodes of each SC-SAE are selected from the range of $\{1, 2, 3, \ldots, 20\}$. To accelerate the efficiency of feature learning based on SC-SAE At the same time, the number of feature mapping nodes and the number of mappings of WBLS-KDE and RBLS-Huber are selected within the range of $\{1, 2, 3, \ldots, 20\}$.

It should be noted that, to avoid over-fitting problems, DSCN, RDSCN-KDE, WDSCN-Huber and WDSCN-Bisquare, WBLS-KDE and RBLS-Huber use regularization parameters with a range of $\{2^{-30}, 2^{-25}, 2^{-20}, 2^{-15}, 2^{-10}, 2^{-5}, 2^{0}\}$, determined by grid search, and the other models keep the same settings as the references.

To distinguish the differences between the comparison models, Table 7.3 analyzes the differences of each model.

### 7.3.2  *Main Results and Discussion*

The test performance of WDSCN-Huber and WDSCN-Bisquare on 5 datasets, including Abalone, Wizmir, Concrete, Stock and Mortgage.

**Table 7.3.** Differential analysis of each model.

| Comparison models | Regularization | Features embedding | Supervision mechanism |
|---|---|---|---|
| SCN | × | × | ✓ |
| RSC-IQR | × | × | ✓ |
| RSC-Huber | × | × | ✓ |
| RSC-KDE | × | × | ✓ |
| DSCN | ✓ | × | ✓ |
| RDSCN-KDE | ✓ | × | ✓ |
| WBLS-KDE | ✓ | ✓(R-SAE) | × |
| RBLS-Huber | ✓ | ✓(R-SAE) | × |
| WDSCN-Bisquare | ✓ | ✓(SC-SAE) | ✓ |
| WDSCN-Huber | ✓ | ✓(SC-SAE) | ✓ |

Among them, each dataset has 5 different noise ratios as 0%, 10%, 20%, 30% and 40%.

For numerical analysis, the average test errors of WDSCN-Huber, WDSCN-Bisquare and related comparison algorithms on five real data sets are shown in Tables 7.4–7.8. It can be seen from Tables 7.4–7.8 that with the increase of noise ratio, the test errors of WDSCN-Huber and WDSCN-Bisquare gradually increase, and the overall performance shows a downward trend, but the downward trend is relatively gentle, without large fluctuations, and has good robustness. Moreover, when the noise ratio is 0%, the WDSCN proposed in this chapter has achieved the best results on 5 datasets including Abalone, Wizmir, Concrete and Mortgage. In the Stock dataset, the test performance of WDSCN-Bisquare is the same as DeepSCN, both of which are the best, indicating that WDSCN based on sparse feature fusion is suitable for original regression datasets without outliers.

As the noise ratio in the training data set increases, the test performance of SCN and DSCN decreases significantly, indicating that the generalization performance of the model is easily affected by outliers. However, the two WDSCN models proposed in this chapter achieved the best results in the five datasets with different noise ratios. As the noise ratio increases, the increase in the test error is effectively reduced, the downward trend is alleviated, and the robustness and generalization of the model are improved.

**Table 7.4.** Performance comparison of 10 models on Abalone dataset.

| Algorithm | Test performance (RMSE) ↓ | | | | |
|---|---|---|---|---|---|
| | 0% | 10% | 20% | 30% | 40% |
| SCN | 0.0762 | 0.078 | 0.0785 | 0.0783 | 0.0808 |
| RSC-IQR | 0.078 | 0.0773 | 0.0776 | 0.0779 | 0.0778 |
| RSC-Huber | 0.0768 | 0.0772 | 0.0763 | 0.0761 | 0.0783 |
| RSC-KDE | 0.0783 | 0.0779 | 0.0782 | 0.0775 | 0.0775 |
| DeepSCN | 0.0754 | 0.0762 | 0.0769 | 0.076 | 0.0773 |
| RDSCN-KDE | 0.0759 | 0.075 | 0.0764 | 0.0765 | 0.0771 |
| WBLS-KDE | 0.0756 | 0.0751 | 0.0759 | 0.076 | 0.0764 |
| RBLS-Huber | 0.0752 | 0.0747 | 0.0754 | 0.0754 | 0.0758 |
| WDSCN-Bisquare | **0.0736** | **0.074** | **0.0743** | **0.0744** | 0.0754 |
| WDSCN-Huber | **0.0736** | 0.0741 | 0.0744 | **0.0744** | **0.0746** |

**Table 7.5.** Performance comparison of 10 models on Wizmir dataset.

| Algorithm | Test performance (RMSE) ↓ | | | | |
|---|---|---|---|---|---|
| | 0% | 10% | 20% | 30% | 40% |
| SCN | 0.0193 | 0.0295 | 0.035 | 0.0452 | 0.0507 |
| RSC-IQR | 0.0185 | 0.0194 | 0.0204 | 0.021 | 0.0228 |
| RSC-Huber | 0.0194 | 0.0202 | 0.021 | 0.0222 | 0.0255 |
| RSC-KDE | 0.0185 | 0.0195 | 0.0203 | 0.0223 | 0.0231 |
| DSCN | 0.0185 | 0.0226 | 0.024 | 0.0254 | 0.0268 |
| RDSCN-KDE | 0.018 | 0.0182 | 0.019 | 0.0196 | 0.0212 |
| WBLS-KDE | 0.0178 | 0.0188 | 0.0191 | 0.02 | 0.0219 |
| RBLS-Huber | 0.0177 | 0.0183 | 0.0189 | 0.0205 | 0.0241 |
| WDSCN-Bisquare | **0.0172** | **0.0172** | **0.0178** | 0.0183 | **0.0196** |
| WDSCN-Huber | 0.0173 | 0.0173 | 0.0179 | 0.0184 | **0.0196** |

At the same time, by comparing WDSCN based on different M-estimator functions, the two models of WDSCN-Huber and WDSCN-Bisquare can improve the robustness of the DSCN model and achieve the best results in the test data with different noise ratios. Among them, WDSCN-Bisquare achieved 17 best results (including tied best results) and WDSCN-Huber achieved 13 best results (including tied best results). According to the above experimental results, when the noise ratio is 30% and 40%, WDSCN-Bisquare obtains four best results (including tied best results), and

**Table 7.6.**  Performance comparison of 10 models on Concrete dataset.

| Algorithm | Test performance (RMSE) ↓ | | | | |
|---|---|---|---|---|---|
| | 0% | 10% | 20% | 30% | 40% |
| SCN | 0.0882 | 0.0982 | 0.1039 | 0.1051 | 0.108 |
| RSC-IQR | 0.0923 | 0.0923 | 0.0996 | 0.1057 | 0.1115 |
| RSC-Huber | 0.0875 | 0.0939 | 0.0995 | 0.1036 | 0.11 |
| RSC-KDE | 0.0909 | 0.0946 | 0.0987 | 0.1007 | 0.1066 |
| DSCN | 0.0805 | 0.0927 | 0.0967 | 0.0999 | 0.1006 |
| RDSCN-KDE | 0.0788 | 0.0833 | 0.0889 | 0.093 | 0.0948 |
| WBLS-KDE | 0.0829 | 0.0873 | 0.0921 | 0.0958 | 0.0996 |
| RBLS-Huber | 0.0827 | 0.0861 | 0.0909 | 0.0954 | 0.1001 |
| WDSCN-Bisquare | 0.075 | **0.0788** | 0.0838 | 0.0909 | 0.0953 |
| WDSCN-Huber | **0.0748** | 0.0799 | **0.0835** | **0.089** | **0.0941** |

**Table 7.7.**  Performance comparison of 10 models on Stock dataset.

| Algorithm | Test performance (RMSE) ↓ | | | | |
|---|---|---|---|---|---|
| | 0% | 10% | 20% | 30% | 40% |
| SCN | 0.0318 | 0.0483 | 0.0518 | 0.0554 | 0.0618 |
| RSC-IQR | 0.0349 | 0.0361 | 0.0398 | 0.0462 | 0.0557 |
| RSC-Huber | 0.034 | 0.0391 | 0.0436 | 0.0478 | 0.0544 |
| RSC-KDE | 0.0352 | 0.0386 | 0.0417 | 0.0479 | 0.0513 |
| DSCN | 0.029 | 0.0437 | 0.0477 | 0.0517 | 0.0559 |
| RDSCN-KDE | 0.0297 | 0.034 | 0.037 | 0.0409 | 0.0447 |
| WBLS-KDE | 0.0321 | 0.0369 | 0.0395 | 0.0417 | 0.0458 |
| RBLS-Huber | 0.032 | 0.0351 | 0.0388 | 0.043 | 0.0485 |
| WDSCN-Bisquare | **0.029** | **0.0314** | **0.0348** | 0.0396 | 0.0448 |
| WDSCN-Huber | 0.0293 | 0.0317 | 0.0349 | **0.0385** | **0.0425** |

WDSCN-Huber obtains eight best results (including tied best results). It can be seen that compared with the Bisquare function, the Huber function can weight samples with large errors, and effectively improve the robustness of the model as the noise ratio increases.

### 7.3.3  *Ablation Experiments*

To illustrate the effectiveness of the proposed model, this section conducts an ablation experiment, in which WDSCN-Bisquare and WDSCN-Huber represent the final models; DSCN-Bisquare* and

**Table 7.8.** Performance comparison of 10 models on Mortgage dataset.

| Algorithm | Test performance (RMSE) ↓ | | | | |
| --- | --- | --- | --- | --- | --- |
| | 0% | 10% | 20% | 30% | 40% |
| SCN | 0.0053 | 0.0229 | 0.0292 | 0.0379 | 0.0436 |
| RSC-IQR | 0.0055 | 0.0072 | 0.0085 | 0.0105 | 0.0152 |
| RSC-Huber | 0.0054 | 0.0092 | 0.0104 | 0.0136 | 0.0194 |
| RSC-KDE | 0.0055 | 0.0081 | 0.0095 | 0.0122 | 0.0164 |
| DSCN | 0.0048 | 0.0156 | 0.0185 | 0.0198 | 0.0222 |
| RDSCN-KDE | 0.0048 | 0.006 | 0.0077 | 0.0094 | 0.012 |
| WBLS-KDE | 0.0049 | 0.0063 | 0.0074 | 0.0094 | 0.0111 |
| RBLS-Huber | 0.0049 | 0.0064 | 0.0081 | 0.0113 | 0.0156 |
| WDSCN-Bisquare | **0.0047** | **0.0059** | **0.0073** | **0.0088** | 0.011 |
| WDSCN-Huber | **0.0047** | 0.0061 | 0.0074 | 0.0089 | **0.0109** |

**Table 7.9.** Performance comparison of different models on Abalone dataset.

| Algorithm | Test performance (RMSE) ↓ | | | | |
| --- | --- | --- | --- | --- | --- |
| | 0% | 10% | 20% | 30% | 40% |
| DSCN-Bisquare* | 0.075 | 0.0753 | 0.0753 | 0.0756 | 0.0766 |
| DSCN-Huber* | 0.0746 | 0.0751 | 0.0762 | 0.0756 | 0.076 |
| DSCN-Bisquare | 0.0753 | 0.0757 | 0.0759 | 0.0761 | 0.0766 |
| DSCN-Huber | 0.0747 | 0.075 | 0.0761 | 0.075 | 0.0762 |
| WDSCN-Bisquare | **0.0736** | **0.074** | **0.0743** | **0.0744** | 0.0754 |
| WDSCN-Huber | **0.0736** | 0.0741 | 0.0744 | **0.0744** | **0.0746** |

DSCN-Huber* adopt the weighted least squares as Dai *et al.* (2019b); Guo and Yan (2021); Wang and Li (2017a); DSCN-Bisquare and DSCN-Huber employ the same weighting methods as WDSCN-Bisquare and WDSCN-Huber. DSCN-Bisquare*, DSCN-Huber*, DSCN-Bisquare, and DSCN-Huber do not adopt SC-SAE sparse feature learning.

The specific experimental results are shown in Tables 7.9–7.13.

It can be seen from Tables 7.9–7.13 that WDSCN-Bisquare and WDSCN-Huber achieve the best results in Abalone, Wizmir, Concrete and Stock; in the Mortgage dataset, when the noise ratio is 0,

**Table 7.10.** Performance comparison of different models on Wizmir dataset.

| Algorithm | Test performance (RMSE) $\downarrow$ | | | | |
| --- | --- | --- | --- | --- | --- |
| | 0% | 10% | 20% | 30% | 40% |
| DSCN-Bisquare* | 0.018 | 0.0182 | 0.0189 | 0.0198 | 0.0208 |
| DSCN-Huber* | 0.0179 | 0.019 | 0.0196 | 0.0205 | 0.0215 |
| DSCN-Bisquare | 0.0179 | 0.0185 | 0.0191 | 0.0194 | 0.0206 |
| DSCN-Huber | 0.0182 | 0.0185 | 0.0189 | 0.0196 | 0.0203 |
| WDSCN-Bisquare | **0.0172** | **0.0172** | **0.0178** | **0.0183** | **0.0196** |
| WDSCN-Huber | 0.0173 | 0.0173 | 0.0179 | 0.0184 | **0.0196** |

**Table 7.11.** Performance comparison of different models on Concrete dataset.

| Algorithm | Test performance (RMSE) $\downarrow$ | | | | |
| --- | --- | --- | --- | --- | --- |
| | 0% | 10% | 20% | 30% | 40% |
| DSCN-Bisquare* | 0.0784 | 0.0831 | 0.0915 | 0.0942 | 0.1005 |
| DSCN-Huber* | 0.0767 | 0.0828 | 0.0868 | 0.0937 | 0.0948 |
| DSCN-Bisquare | 0.0772 | 0.0826 | 0.0876 | 0.0916 | 0.0996 |
| DSCN-Huber | 0.079 | 0.0833 | 0.0876 | 0.0919 | 0.0967 |
| WDSCN-Bisquare | 0.075 | **0.0788** | 0.0838 | 0.0909 | 0.0953 |
| WDSCN-Huber | **0.0748** | 0.0799 | **0.0835** | **0.089** | **0.0941** |

DeepSCN-Huber* is the best, and when the noise ratio is 40%, DeepSCN-Huber and WDSCN-Huber are the best.

At the same time, DSCN-Bisquare and DSCN-Huber have the best overall performance compared to DSCN-Bisquare* and DSCN-Huber*. In the comparison of the two types of models, DSCN-Bisquare and DSCN-Huber achieved 16 best results (including tied best results), and DSCN-Bisquare* and DSCN-Huber* achieved 11 best results (including tied best results), which shows that the weighted coefficient used in this chapter can better reduce the negative impact of high-proportion noise.

In summary, the weighted method and its sparse feature extraction and fusion method based on SC-SAE in this chapter can better process noisy data and improve the robustness of the model.

**Table 7.12.** Performance comparison of different models on Stock dataset.

| | Test performance (RMSE) ↓ | | | | |
|---|---|---|---|---|---|
| Algorithm | 0% | 10% | 20% | 30% | 40% |
| DSCN-Bisquare* | 0.0294 | 0.0328 | 0.0379 | 0.0432 | 0.0492 |
| DSCN-Huber* | 0.0291 | 0.0349 | 0.0397 | 0.0433 | 0.0483 |
| DSCN-Bisquare | 0.0305 | 0.0324 | 0.0366 | 0.0417 | 0.0472 |
| DSCN-Huber | 0.0307 | 0.0333 | 0.0362 | 0.0412 | 0.0447 |
| WDSCN-Bisquare | **0.029** | **0.0314** | **0.0348** | 0.0396 | 0.0448 |
| WDSCN-Huber | 0.0293 | 0.0317 | 0.0349 | **0.0385** | **0.0425** |

**Table 7.13.** Performance comparison of different models on the Mortgage dataset.

| | Test performance (RMSE) ↓ | | | | |
|---|---|---|---|---|---|
| Algorithm | 0% | 10% | 20% | 30% | 40% |
| DSCN-Bisquare* | 0.0047 | 0.0062 | 0.0078 | 0.0098 | 0.0113 |
| DSCN-Huber* | **0.0045** | 0.0073 | 0.0093 | 0.0110 | 0.0134 |
| DSCN-Bisquare | 0.0047 | 0.0060 | 0.0076 | 0.0088 | 0.0111 |
| DSCN-Huber | 0.0049 | 0.0063 | 0.0078 | 0.0089 | **0.0109** |
| WDSCN-Bisquare | 0.0047 | **0.0059** | **0.0073** | **0.0088** | 0.0110 |
| WDSCN-Huber | 0.0047 | 0.0061 | 0.0074 | 0.0089 | **0.0109** |

### 7.3.4 *Significance Testing*

In order to show the significant differences between the proposed WDSCN-Bisquare and WDSCN-Huber models and other related models, the test errors of the 10 models in Tables 7.4–7.8 under five datasets with different noise ratios are selected for Friedman and The significance testing results of the post hoc Nemenyi test (Demšar, 2006; Reyes *et al.*, 2018), except for RDSCN-KDE, the statistical test results of WDSCN-Bisquare and WDSCN-Huber models and other algorithms are all less than 0.05, which proves that the proposed model has significant differences with other models at the 5% significance level.

It should be pointed out that in the experiment, in order to avoid over-fitting of RDSCN-KDE, a regularization parameter was added to it. At the same time, although there is no significant difference between the WDSCN-Bisquare and WDSCN-Huber models and the RDSCN-KDE model, the experimental results are better than those of RDSCN-KDE.

In summary, WDSCN can be effectively applied to normal data and abnormal data processing, and the introduction of weighted and regularized strategies based on the M-estimator function improves the generalization and robustness of the model.

## 7.4 Summary

In practical applications, sensor-collected data are vulnerable to multiple interference factors including device malfunctions, environmental variations, and human interventions, which significantly reduce model generalization capabilities. Current robust stochastic configuration networks (SCN) face dual challenges: conventional SCN models exhibit limited feature learning capacity, while their deep counterparts (DSCN) tend to suffer from over-fitting risks when handling outlier-contaminated data. To address these limitations in uncertain data regression tasks, this chapter proposes a weighted deep stochastic configuration network (WDSCN) integrated with M-estimator functions. The methodological innovations are threefold: (1) A multi-branch sparse feature extraction mechanism employing stochastic configuration sparse autoencoder (SC-SAE) to adaptively capture and fuse discriminative sparse representations; (2) A hybrid robust learning framework combining Huber/Bisquare weighting functions with $L_2$ regularization to enhance model robustness while controlling over-fitting; (3) A stacked architecture inheriting the universal approximation properties of SCN while improving feature hierarchy learning.

Comprehensive experiments demonstrate that WDSCN based on Huber and Bisquare functions and regularized strategies can effectively handle the regression problem of uncertain data with different noise ratios, overcome the problems of low generalization performance and over-fitting of DSCN, and has higher regression performance than SCN, DSCN and robust models such as RSC-KDE, RSC-IQR, RSC-Huber, RDSCN-KDE, BLS-Huber and BLS-Bisquare. At the same time, ablation experimental results illustrate that WDSCN with sparse features has higher regression accuracy than DSCN model based on M-estimator function without SC-SAE feature extraction, which verifies the effectiveness of extracting and fusing features based on SC-SAE.

Future work will focus on three directions: (1) Developing theoretical guidelines for regularization parameter selection via stability analysis; (2) Extending the weighting mechanism to handle non-convex loss functions; (3) Implementing hardware-aware architecture optimization for edge computing deployments. These enhancements aim to strengthen WDSCN's applicability in real-world industrial sensing systems where data uncertainty and resource constraints coexist.

# Chapter 8

# Noise Robust Regularized Deep Stochastic Configuration Networks

Deep stochastic configuration network (DSCN) is an efficient tool for intelligent analysis of industrial data, but the outliers in the data may reduce the robustness of the model. Aiming at enhancing industrial noise data regression accuracy and robustness of DSCN, a novel robust deep random neural network model, robust regularized deep stochastic configuration network is proposed, termed as RDSCN. Unlike other robust stochastic configuration network (RSCN) models with weighted methods, RDSCN adopts $L_1$ norm loss function to process outliers with sparse characteristics. Meanwhile, $L_2$ regularization technique is employed to alleviate over-fitting problems of RDSCN. Furthermore, slime mould algorithm (SMA) is applied to choose more appropriate parameter scale of weights and biases for enhancing the robustness of the RDSCN. Experiments on some real-world regression datasets with different contamination rates show that RDSCN with $L_1$ norm loss function and $L_2$ regularization technique has higher regression accuracy for addressing outlier data with uniform distributed noises, RDSCN optimized by SMA can further improve robustness performance of RDSCN.


## 8.1 Introduction

Neural networks have been rapidly developed because of their strong feature learning capability and nonlinear approximation properties

167

(Chen and Chen, 1995). Nowadays, deep learning models have achieved breakthrough success in the fields of feature representation, image classification and pattern recognition by learning multi-level features from high-dimensional large-scale data (Deng *et al.*, 2014; LeCun *et al.*, 2015). However, deep belief networks (DBNs), deep Boltzmann machines (DBMs) and convolutional neural networks (CNNs) usually adopt back propagation (BP) algorithm to update the parameters, which have complex network structures and large number of network parameters (Hinton and Salakhutdinov, 2012; Hinton *et al.*, 2006; Krizhevsky *et al.*, 2012). However, industrial data analysis has higher requirements for real-time performance of the system, how to analyze industrial data quickly and efficiently is still worth studying.

Nowadays, random neural networks generate network parameters in a random manner, which are more suitable for industrial data analysis scenarios with high real-time performance. Stochastic configuration network (SCN) is different from classical random vector functional link neural network (RVFLN) (Li and Wang, 2017; Wang *et al.*, 2017a), which uses inequality constraints to assign parameters and calculates the output weights by the least square method, ensures the universal approximation of the model. To solve the uncertain data regression problems effectively, Wang and Li (2017a) firstly proposed a robust stochastic configuration network (RSC-KDE), which use kernel density estimation (KDE) to calculate the penalty weights of training samples, and the weighted least square approach is applied to determine the output weights for reducing the negative impact of noise data or outliers. Then, Xie and Zhou (2020) proposed an improved multi-output version of RSC-KDE for the molten iron quality prediction in blast furnace ironmaking. Subsequently, maximum correntropy criterion was applied for the calculation of the penalty weights, Li *et al.* (2019b) proposed a robust stochastic configuration network based on maximum correntropy criterion (RSC-MCC). Dai *et al.* (2019b) introduced M-estimation with Huber loss function, M-estimation with interquartile range and nonparametric kernel density estimation into SCN, and RSC-Huber, RSC-IQR, RSC-NKDE are proposed respectively. In addition, Wu *et al.* (2022b) proposed Bayesian stochastic configuration network (BSCN) for processing uncertain data by introducing Bayesian inference (BI) to calculate the output weights of SCN which provide a new solution for processing noisy data. Lu *et al.* (2020) designed a robust SCN based on a mixture of the Gaussian and Laplace distributions, termed as MoGL-SCN, meanwhile, bootstrap ensemble strategy was introduced into MoGL-SCN for reducing uncertainties caused by the model and outliers in the training data.

Meanwhile, to further improve the feature learning ability of SCN, deep stochastic configuration network (DSCN) has been proposed which can use inequality constraint to assign parameters and construct deep random model (Wang and Li, 2018). The proposal of DSCN can provide a new solution for noise data analysis. However, the weighted-based robust stochastic configuration networks need to calculate the weighted output matrix, which have higher computational complexity. DSCN with weighted methods will affect the real-time nature of the industrial data modeling. As the noises occupy a small part of training data usually, which can be considered as outliers with sparse characteristics. Some studies have shown that $L_1$ norm is more robust to process sparse data (Cai *et al.*, 2016; Cao *et al.*, 2015). Meanwhile, the supervisory mechanism of DSCN guarantees its universal approximation performance, with the increase of nodes and layers, it is easy to face the risk of over-fitting, $L_2$ regularization technique can reduce the risk of model over-fitting (Li *et al.*, 2019c). Thus, we propose a novel robust regularized deep stochastic configuration (RDSCN) which uses $L_1$ norm loss function and $L_2$ regularization technique, Augmented Lagrange multiplier algorithm (ALM) is adopted to determine the output weights of RDSCN.

Moreover, although the supervision mechanism of DSCN reduces the degree of human intervention in the process of parameter configuration, some parameters of DSCN still need to be set manually to improve the modeling accuracy. To optimize the hyper-parameters of SCN and DSCN, Li *et al.* (2018) used genetic algorithm (GA) to select the control factor array of input weights and biases and proposed GA-SCN. Zhang *et al.* (2021c) designed a novel chaotic sparrow search algorithm (CSSA) for choosing optimal parameter control factor and contraction factor of SCN. Wu *et al.* (2022a) canceled the incremental learning mode of SCN, then generated input weights and biases of all nodes through the improved sparrow search algorithm (ISSA) under the supervision mechanism of SCN.

Chen *et al.* (2022) adopted the VMD to extract the features of non-stationary time series, the improved whale optimization algorithm (IWOA) was applied to select the number of input nodes, the maximum number of hidden layer nodes and the maximum number of candidate parameters of nodes. Besides, Niu *et al.* (2020) discussed the heavy-tailed distribution such as Lévy distribution, Cauchy distribution and Weibull distribution to initialize the input parameters of SCN nodes which verified the effectiveness of heavy-tailed distribution for node parameters configuration. Zhu *et al.* (2019) presented two new inequality constraints, which improved the training efficiency of SCN. For the parameter optimization of DSCN, Felicetti and Wang (2022a) introduced Monte-Carlo tree search (MCTS) and random search strategy into DSCN, meanwhile, the superiority of normal distribution and Logistic distribution for the parameter initialization was proved (Felicetti and Wang, 2022b). Moreover, to solve the prediction intervals problem of for carbon residual of crude oil, Lu and Ding (2019a) combined lower-upper bound estimation (LUBE) method with DSCN, the modified backtracking search optimization algorithm (MBSA) was designed to optimize the output weights for achieving the optimal prediction intervals.

Different ranges of node parameter candidates have different effects on algorithm performance. Hence, how to choose the optimal node parameters under the supervision mechanism is still the key to improve the generalization and universal approximation of RDSCN. Recently, swarm intelligent optimization algorithm has been widely used in the field of parameter optimization of neural networks. Among them, slime mould algorithm (SMA) proposed in 2020, which has advantages of fewer parameters, faster optimization efficiency (Li *et al.*, 2020). Therefore, we use SMA to select the optimal ranges of node parameter candidates for RDSCN to enhance the robustness of the model. In a word, the significant contributions of our chapter are given as follows:

- As the sparsity characteristic of outliers, RDSCN is proposed for solving uncertain data regression problems through introduce $L_1$ norm loss function and $L_2$ regularization technique to DSCN. Meanwhile, we use ALM algorithm to calculate the output weights of RDSCN for keeping the effectiveness and efficiency.
- To select the optimal ranges of node parameter candidates and enhance the effectiveness of RDSCN, an optimized RDSCN based

on SMA is designed. To distinguish from the RDSCN with fixed-parameters, the optimized version termed as SMA-RDSCN.

- Numerous experiments indicate that SMA-RDSCN and RDSCN have higher regression accuracy compared with involved models in solving uncertain data with uniform distributed noises.

## 8.2   Preliminaries

Slime mould algorithm (SMA) is a newer optimization method, which mainly simulates the foraging behavior and morphological changes of slime mould. The mathematical model of SMA includes three stages: approaching food, surrounding food, and grabbing food (Li *et al.*, 2020).

**Parameters initialization:** Population size (Pop), maximum iterations $(T)$, initial location $(X)$, upper bound $(Ub)$ and lower bound $(Lb)$ of the search space, fitness function $S$.

### Stage 1: Approaching food

Slime mould approach food through smell in the air, and their approach behavior can be expressed by Eq. (8.1):

$$X(t + 1) = X(t) + vb \cdot (W \cdot X_A(t) - X_B(t)), \qquad (8.1)$$

where $X(t)$ and $X(t + 1)$ are denoted as the location of population at the $t$ and $t + 1$ iteration respectively; $X_b(t)$ indicates the optimal location at $t$ iteration; $X_A(t)$ and $X_B(t)$ are two slime individuals which are selected randomly; $vb$ with the range of $[-a, a]$, among them, $a = \mathrm{arctanh}(1 - t/T)$; $vc$ decreases linearly from 1 to 0; $R$ expresses a random value with the range of $[0, 1]$; $P = \tanh(|S(i) - DF|)$, in which $i = 1, 2, \ldots, N$, $S(i)$ is denoted as the fitness value of the $i$th individual, $DF$ is the global optimal fitness value; $W$ is the weight of the slime mould which can be calculated through Eq. (8.2):

$$W(\text{condition}) = 1 + r \cdot \log\left(\frac{bF - S(i)}{bF - wF} + 1\right), \qquad (8.2)$$

where condition refers to the individuals whose fitness value ranks in the top half of the population; $bF$ and $wF$ are denoted as the current optimal fitness and worst fitness respectively. SortIndex represents the sorted fitness value sequence.

## Stage 2: Surrounding food

The higher the concentration of food exposed to the vein, the stronger the propagation wave produced by the biological oscillator, the faster the cytoplasm flow, and the thicker the vein. The higher the food concentration, the greater the weight of the slime mould near the area. If the food concentration is low, the slime molds will turn to other areas where they are lighter. Based on the above principles, update the location of population based on Eq. (8.3):

$$X(t+1) = X(t) + vb \cdot (W \cdot X_A(t) - X_B(t)) + vc \cdot (X_b(t) - X(t)),$$

$$(8.3)$$

where rand represent random values in the range of $[0, 1]$; $Z = 0.03$ is a parameter used to weigh the search and development stages.

## Stage 3: Grabbing food

At this stage, the cytoplasmic flow in the vein is changed by the propagation wave generated by the biological oscillator, and the change of vein width and oscillation frequency of myxomycetes were simulated by $vb$, $vc$, and $W$, so that the myxomycetes could approach the food more slowly when the food concentration was low, and approach to grab the food faster when they found high-quality food.

## 8.3   Methodology

This part aims at developing robust deep models based on DSCN for solving uncertain data regression problems with outliers. In the first place, a faster robust regularized deep model, SMA-RDSCN with $L_1$ norm loss function is presented which uses ALM to update the output weights of RDSCN effectively and efficiently. In the second place, SMA to select the control factor array of input weights and biases for further improving the generalization and robustness of the RDSCN.

### 8.3.1   *Robust Regularized Deep Stochastic Configuration Network*

Due to the universal approximation ability of DSCN depends on training samples, although the addition of nodes and layers can further minimize the training error, however, the risk of over-fitting increases which will reduce the test accuracy. Therefore, feed-forward neural networks with stronger generalization performance have better tradeoff between the training error and norm of output weight. Meanwhile, as the noises usually occupy a small part of training data usually, it can be considered as outliers with sparse characteristics, $L_1$ norm is more robust to guarantee the sparsity characteristic (Cai et al., 2016; Cao et al., 2015).

Hence, to enhance the generalization performance and process outliers, the objective function can be modified as Eq. (8.4) by introducing $L_1$ norm loss function, then we propose a robust regularized deep stochastic configuration network (RDSCN) for uncertain data regression.

$$\min_{\beta} \left( \|e\|_1 + C\|\beta\|_2^2 \right), \tag{8.4}$$

where $e$ denotes the training error vector; $C$ is denoted as the $L_2$ regularization parameter.

As Eq. (8.4) can be described as a constrained convex optimization problem, we can use augmented Lagrange multiplier method (ALM) to solve this question as Eq. (8.5):

$$L_\mu(e, \beta, \gamma) = \|e\|_1 + \frac{1}{C}\|\beta\|_2^2 + \upsilon^T(Y - H\beta - e)$$

$$+ \frac{\mu}{2}\|Y - H\beta - e\|_2^2, \tag{8.5}$$

where $\upsilon$ demonstrates the vector of Lagrange multiplier.

In the chapter, we use ALM approach to estimate the optimal $(e, \beta)$ and the Lagrange multiplier $\upsilon$ iteratively according to Eq. (8.6):

$$\begin{cases} (e_{\rho+1}, \beta_{\rho+1}) = \arg\min_{e,\beta} L_\mu(e, \beta, \upsilon_\rho) \\ \upsilon_{\rho+1} = \upsilon_\rho + \mu(Y - H\beta_{\rho+1} - e_{\rho+1}). \end{cases} \tag{8.6}$$

Furthermore, the problem of Eq. (8.6) can be transformed as Eq. (8.7):

$$\begin{cases} \beta_{\rho+1} = \arg\min_{\beta} L_\mu(e_\rho, \beta, \upsilon_\rho) \\ e_{\rho+1} = \arg\min_{e} L_\mu(e, \beta_{\rho+1}, \upsilon_\rho) \\ \upsilon_{\rho+1} = \upsilon_\rho + \mu(Y - H\beta_{\rho+1} - e_{\rho+1}), \end{cases} \tag{8.7}$$

Among them, $\beta_{\rho+1}$ and $e_{\rho+1}$ can be explicitly expressed as Eqs. (8.8) and (8.9):

$$\beta_{\rho+1} = (H^T H + 2/C\mu I)^{-1} H^T (Y - e_\rho + v_\rho/\mu), \qquad (8.8)$$

$$\begin{aligned} e_{\rho+1} &= \mathrm{shrink}(Y - H\beta_{\rho+1} + v_\rho/\mu, 1/\mu) \\ &\triangleq \max\{|Y - H\beta_{\rho+1} + v_\rho/\mu - 1/\mu, 0|\} \circ \mathrm{sign}(Y - H\beta_{\rho+1} + v_\rho/\mu) \end{aligned}, \qquad (8.9)$$

where "$\circ$" indicates the element-wise multiplication.

### 8.3.2  *Parameter Optimization of RDSCN*

In the RDSCN model, the parameter range control factor $\lambda$ can determine the input weights and bias parameter assignments, which are closely related to the model performance. Usually, the set of $\lambda$ parameters is set by human. In order to improve the accuracy of RDSCN model, this section proposes a SMA-RDSCN model by using SMA on the selection of input weights and bias parameter range control factor $\lambda$. The SMA-RDSCN mainly includes two aspects of RDSCN construction and SMA parameter search, and the specific algorithm is described as follows:

### Step 1: SMA-RDSCN Parameter Initialization

Initialize population size $(N)$, maximum iterations $(T)$, initial location $(X)$, upper bound $(Ub)$ and lower bound $(Lb)$ of the search space, fitness function $S$, the $\lambda$ parameter set dimension $(D)$, the maximum number of hidden layers $n$, the maximum number of hidden layers $L_{\max}$, the prediction error $\epsilon$, the maximum candidate nodes number $N_{\max}$.

Given the need to select the set of $\lambda$ parameters, the initialized population location is: $X_i = (X_{i1}, X_{i2}, \ldots, X_{iD})$ $(i = 1, 2, \ldots, N)$, and the SMA-RDSCN test error is used as the SMA objective function.

### Step 2: Construction of SMA-RDSCN Model

Using initialization parameters according to Step 1 and constructing and training the SMA-RDSCN model to output the adaptation values when the SMA-RDSCN satisfies the preset parameters.

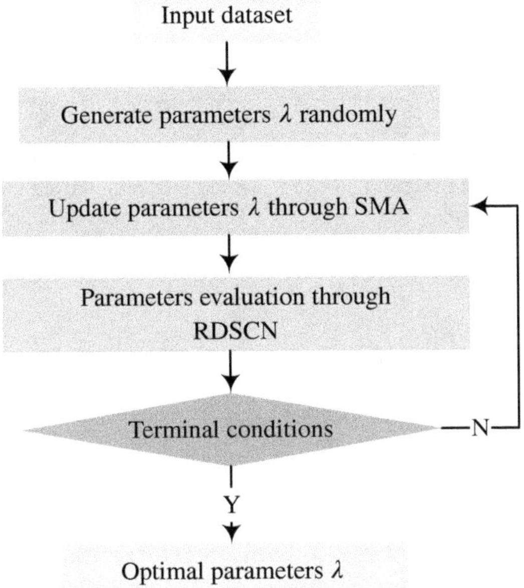


**Fig. 8.1.** The flowchart of SMA-RDSCN.

## Step 3: Update the Parameter Range Control Factor $\lambda$

Updating the parameter range control factor $\lambda$ according to the Eqs. (8.1),(8.2), and (8.3), respectively.

## Step 4: Iterative Training to Obtain the Optimal Parameters

Repeat Step 2 and Step 3 until the termination condition is satisfied to obtain the global optimal parameter $G_{\text{best}}$ of SMA-RDSCN.

## Step 5: Output SMA-RDSCN Results

To verify the validity of the parameters, construct and train SMA-RDSCN using the $\lambda$ selected in Step 4, and output the training results and test results.

The flowchart of SMA-RDSCN is listed as Fig. 8.1.

## 8.4  Experimental Results and Discussion

The related experimental codes are programmed based on MATLAB 2019b.

**Table 8.1.** The attributes of five experimental datasets.

| Datasets | Input features | Instances |
| --- | --- | --- |
| **Stock** | 9 | 950 |
| **Treasury** | 15 | 1049 |
| **Mortgage** | 15 | 1049 |
| **Laser** | 4 | 993 |
| **Ailerons** | 40 | 13750 |

### 8.4.1 *Benchmark Datasets*

To evaluate the industrial noise data regression accuracy of RDSCN and SMA-RDSCN, we select five benchmark regression datasets (Stock, Treasury, Mortgage, Laser, Ailerons) from KEEL (Knowledge Extraction based on Evolutionary Learning, http://www.keel. es/) as experimental datasets. Table 8.1 introduces the descriptions of experimental datasets.

To demonstrate the robustness of RDSCN and SMA-RDSCN, the benchmark datasets should be contaminated by adding outliers. Firstly, we normalize the input and output of these datasets into the range of $[0, 1]$. Then we choose 75% of the data samples randomly as the training dataset, while the rest of the data samples are selected as the test dataset. Thirdly, 10%, 20%, 30%, and 40% outliers with uniform distribution in the range of $[-0.5, 0.5]$ are randomly added into the output values of the training dataset, and the output range of the contaminated training dataset is transformed into $[-0.5, 1.5]$.

### 8.4.2 *Experimental Settings*

#### 8.4.2.1 *Evaluation Indicator*

To demonstrate the performance of SMA-RDSCN and RDSCN, we choose SCN (Wang *et al.*, 2017a), DSCN (Wang and Li, 2018), RSC-IQR (Dai *et al.*, 2019b), RSC-Huber (Dai *et al.*, 2019b), and RSC-NKDE (Dai *et al.*, 2019b) as the contrast algorithms. Then we run each algorithm 100 times, and the mean values of root mean square error (RMSE) are recorded as the final results. The RMSE is defined as:

$$\text{RMSE} = \sqrt{\frac{1}{N}\sum_{i=1}^{N}(y_i - \hat{y}_i)^2}, \tag{8.10}$$

where $y_i$ expresses the real value of point $i$, $\hat{y}_i$ represents the predictive value of point $i$, and $N$ is denoted as the number of data points.

### 8.4.2.2 *Parameters Settings*

To guarantee the fairness of the experiments, some important parameters of compared models are given as follows:

All the algorithms use the sigmoidal function as the activation function:

$$f(x) = \frac{1}{1 + e^{-x}}. \tag{8.11}$$

The number of nodes in each layer is set to 50 uniformly for all the single or multi-layer models. The maximum number of iterations for all the models is set as 100, and the tolerance error $\epsilon$ of all the models is set to 0.001.

The contraction factor $r$ of the inequality constraint is selected from the set $\{0.9, 0.99, 0.9999, 0.99999, 0.999999\}$ adaptively. Except for the SMA-RDSCN, the $\lambda$ of other models is chosen from $\{0.5, 1, 5, 10, 30, 50, 100, 150, 200, 250\}$ adaptively.

The hidden layer of SMA-RDSCN, RDSCN, and DSCN is set to 2. SMA-RDSCN, RDSCN, and DSCN adopt $L_2$ regularization technique, and the regularization parameter $C$ is selected from $\{2^{-10}, 2^{-5}, 0, \ldots, 2^{15}, 2^{20}\}$ through grid search. The maximum iterations of ALM in SMA-RDSCN and RDSCN are set as 50. The population size is set as 20, and the maximum iterations of SMA is set as 10.

Except for the parameters given above, other key parameters of IQR, Huber, and NKDE loss function keep the same as RSC-IQR, RSC-Huber, and RSC-NKDE in the chapter (Dai *et al.*, 2019b).

**Table 8.2.** Performance comparison of different models on Stock with uniform distributed outliers.

| Models | 10% | 20% | 30% | 40% |
|---|---|---|---|---|
| SCN | 5.0066e-02 | 5.9971e-02 | 6.9163e-02 | 7.8050e-02 |
| RSC-IQR | 4.0678e-02 | 4.2375e-02 | 4.5533e-02 | 5.4179e-02 |
| RSC-Huber | 4.1241e-02 | 4.2696e-02 | 4.5031e-02 | 5.1328e-02 |
| RSC-NKDE | 4.3064e-02 | 4.4613e-02 | 4.5888e-02 | <u>4.7833e-02</u> |
| DSCN | 4.4333e-02 | 5.1553e-02 | 5.7690e-02 | 6.2992e-02 |
| **RDSCN** | <u>3.6848e-02</u> | <u>3.9684e-02</u> | <u>4.2985e-02</u> | 4.9632e-02 |
| **SMA-RDSCN** | **3.6583e-02** | **3.7326e-02** | **3.9943e-02** | **4.2603e-02** |

**Table 8.3.** Performance comparison of different models on Treasury with uniform distributed outliers.

| Models | 10% | 20% | 30% | 40% |
|---|---|---|---|---|
| SCN | 3.5408e-02 | 4.8824e-02 | 5.9609e-02 | 7.0072e-02 |
| RSC-IQR | 1.2393e-02 | 1.3277e-02 | 1.8021e-02 | 2.6211e-02 |
| RSC-Huber | 1.2393e-02 | 1.4680e-02 | 1.8090e-02 | 2.6212e-02 |
| RSC-NKDE | 1.2743e-02 | 1.3862e-02 | 1.6498e-02 | 2.0562e-02 |
| DSCN | 2.2045e-02 | 2.9413e-02 | 3.5985e-02 | 3.9415e-02 |
| **RDSCN** | <u>1.1946e-02</u> | <u>1.3395e-02</u> | <u>1.4670e-02</u> | <u>1.8727e-02</u> |
| **SMA-RDSCN** | **1.0788e-02** | **1.0886e-02** | **1.2425e-02** | **1.2665e-02** |

### 8.4.3  *Main Results and Discussion*

In this section, we give the performance evaluation of SMA-RDSCN and RDSCN. Tables 8.2–8.6 show the average test RMSE results of SMA-RDSCN and RDSCN compared with different models on four regression problems with uniform distributed outliers. Among them, the optimal experimental results are displayed in bold, and the suboptimal experimental results are underlined.

From Tables 8.2–8.6, we can conclude that RDSCN achieves better performance on five datasets compared with SCN, DSCN, RSC-IQR, RSC-Huber, and RSC-NKDE, which indicates the strong robustness of RDSCN at different levels of outliers. Moreover, because RDSCN uses fixed learning parameters, the algorithm performance is not optimal. SMA-RDSCN can search for the best range of parameters based on different datasets, and the optimized version of SMA-RDSCN is superior to RDSCN in terms of all test results on

**Table 8.4.** Performance comparison of different models on Mortgage with uniform distributed outliers.

| Models | 10% | 20% | 30% | 40% |
| --- | --- | --- | --- | --- |
| SCN | 3.4221e-02 | 4.7901e-02 | 5.6524e-02 | 6.5410e-02 |
| RSC-IQR | 7.4764e-03 | 9.8509e-03 | 1.5192e-02 | 2.8681e-02 |
| RSC-Huber | 7.7288e-03 | 1.0121e-02 | 1.5360e-02 | 2.6521e-02 |
| RSC-NKDE | 7.9566e-03 | 8.8572e-03 | 1.2890e-02 | 1.8352e-02 |
| DSCN | 1.9435e-02 | 2.7586e-02 | 3.4146e-02 | 3.7074e-02 |
| **RDSCN** | 6.1977e-03 | 7.0041e-03 | 8.4777e-03 | 1.2827e-02 |
| **SMA-RDSCN** | **5.8974e-03** | **5.7979e-03** | **6.7366e-03** | **7.8766e-03** |

**Table 8.5.** Performance comparison of different models on Laser with uniform distributed outliers.

| Models | 10% | 20% | 30% | 40% |
| --- | --- | --- | --- | --- |
| SCN | 5.7872e-02 | 8.1678e-02 | 9.3918e-02 | 1.1977e-01 |
| RSC-IQR | 3.0424e-02 | 3.1904e-02 | 3.7289e-02 | 4.2800e-02 |
| RSC-Huber | 3.0160e-02 | 3.4132e-02 | 3.5738e-02 | 3.7825e-02 |
| RSC-NKDE | 3.2191e-02 | 3.4972e-02 | 3.8216e-02 | 4.1147e-02 |
| DSCN | 4.0862e-02 | 3.9174e-02 | 4.0605e-02 | 4.1708e-02 |
| **RDSCN** | 2.9916e-02 | 3.0257e-02 | 3.2636e-02 | 3.4908e-02 |
| **SMA-RDSCN** | **2.2645e-02** | **2.8643e-02** | **2.8667e-02** | **3.3302e-02** |

**Table 8.6.** Performance comparison of different models on Ailerons with uniform distributed outliers.

| Models | 10% | 20% | 30% | 40% |
| --- | --- | --- | --- | --- |
| SCN | 4.7837e-02 | 4.9933e-02 | 5.4090e-02 | 5.4865e-02 |
| RSC-IQR | 4.6191e-02 | 4.6655e-02 | 4.6474e-02 | 4.6697e-02 |
| RSC-Huber | 4.6111e-02 | 4.6465e-02 | 4.6575e-02 | 4.7205e-02 |
| RSC-NKDE | 4.6811e-02 | 4.7313e-02 | 4.6666e-02 | 4.7063e-02 |
| DSCN | 4.5712e-02 | 4.7124e-02 | 4.7816e-02 | 4.8535e-02 |
| **RDSCN** | 4.5843e-02 | 4.6343e-02 | 4.6523e-02 | 4.6536e-02 |
| **SMA-RDSCN** | **4.3285e-02** | **4.3619e-02** | **4.4652c-02** | **4.5957e-02** |

those regression datasets. In particular, it needs to be pointed out that the introduction of SMA can reduce the parameter influence of the model.

In summary, RDSCN with $L_1$ norm loss function can solve uncertain data regression with uniform distributed outliers effectively, and the SMA method is helpful to enhance the robustness and stability of RDSCN well.

## 8.5 Summary

This chapter presents noise robust regularized deep stochastic configuration networks for solving uncertain regression problems. Firstly, RDSCN based on $L_1$ norm loss function was designed to solve outliers with sparse characteristics. Thereafter, for reducing the influence of parameters, SMA-based optimization technique was introduced to enhance the uncertain regression accuracy of SMA-RDSCN. Finally, the performance evaluation on some regression datasets with uniform noises, DSCN model, with $L_1$ regularization method and parameter optimization, has outstanding performance superior to SCN, DSCN, RSC-IQR, RSC-Huber and RSC-NKDE.

## Chapter 9

# Robust Semi-Supervised Stochastic Configuration Network

In real-world pattern analysis scenarios, data is prone to problems such as labels missing and noise, the generalization performance and robustness of stochastic configuration network (SCN) significantly decrease with limited labeled data and noise interference. To improve SCN's regression performance in these scenarios, we propose a novel robust semi-supervised stochastic configuration network (RS$^3$CN). RS$^3$CN uses kernel density estimation (KDE) to evaluate the density of labeled training samples, reducing the influence of noise or outliers. Additionally, manifold regularization is employed to learn the features of unlabeled data. The combination of these two techniques improves the SCN's generalization performance in such scenarios. Furthermore, we introduce an $l_2$ regularization term to manage outliers in sparse features, reducing over-fitting. Finally, we demonstrate its universal approximation property within an improved robust semi-supervised optimization framework. Simulation experiments on benchmark datasets show a significant improvement in both semi-supervised learning and robustness for the proposed RS$^3$CN compared to the original algorithm.

## 9.1 Introduction

Nowadays, SCNs have been widely applied to classification and regression tasks in supervised learning. However, in real-world pattern analysis scenarios, collecting labeled data is often time-consuming, challenging, and expensive, thus only a small portion of the data is labeled, with the majority remaining unlabeled in practical settings (Belkin *et al.*, 2006). Semi-supervised learning leverages information from unlabeled data, combined with labeled data, to improve model performance. Many semi-supervised learning methods are not directly applicable to regression tasks due to the continuous nature of labels (Van Engelen and Hoos, 2020). While most research has focused on classification, graph-based methods, especially manifold learning theory, have shown significant promise in both classification and regression (Liu *et al.*, 2015). To enhance the generalization of SCNs with limited labeled data, Zhao *et al.* (2023) proposed the locality preserving stochastic configuration network (LPSCN), a semi-supervised method that incorporates manifold regularization, specifically designed for regression tasks.

In addition, factors such as sensor malfunctions, environmental conditions, and human errors may introduce noise and outliers into collected data samples, adversely affecting model training (Zhang *et al.*, 2024). To enhance the model's robustness in the face of uncertainty, the design of the loss function becomes crucial.Robust SCN is achieved by incorporating additional constraints into the original loss function, enhancing SCN's ability to address broader challenges of robustness in regression and classification tasks. Wang and Li (2017a) proposed the RSC-KDE based on kernel density estimation, which enhances resilience in regression tasks with uncertain data. Dai *et al.* (2019b) proposed three methods to enhance the robustness of SCN, namely Huber-RSCN, IQR-RSCN, and NKDE-RSCN, each employing penalty weights based on the Huber loss function, interquartile range (IQR), and non-parametric kernel density estimation (NKDE), respectively. Lu and Ding (2019b) proposed a robust SCN based on a Bayesian framework with a mixture of Gaussian and Laplace distributions (MoGL-SCN), which effectively characterizes the complex distributions of real-world data and enhances robustness. Wu's Bayesian SCN incorporates uncertainty directly into the model through a Bayesian framework, making it more capable of handling noisy and incomplete data (Wu *et al.*, 2022b). Lu *et al.* (2021) introduced the Bayesian-learning-based sparse SCN (BSSCN) to address the uncertainty caused by noise and model mismatch in real-world data. The comprehensive application of these methods enables SCN to better adapt and handle challenges in noisy data environments, improving the network's widespread applicability.

When robust SCNs are employed for regression tasks with a limited amount of labeled data, there is a significant risk of over-fitting to the restricted labeled samples, which can considerably compromise their robustness. Firstly, the existing LPSCN method faces challenges when processing labeled data that contains outliers. Although the manifold regularization term integrated into LPSCN alleviates this issue to some extent and improves generalization, it is not sufficient to handle noise or outlier data effectively. To address this, Deng *et al.* (2024b) introduced the global and local constraints SCN (GLSCN), which incorporates consistency regularization based on LPSCN and shows significant robustness in the presence of noisy unlabeled data. In addition, both LPSCN and GLSCN are only effective when the number of labeled training samples exceeds the number of hidden neurons. However, in many semi-supervised learning scenarios, the amount of labeled data is often limited, making it challenging to maintain fewer hidden neurons than labeled samples. Moreover, the updated supervision mechanisms in both LPSCN and GLSCN increase training time compared to the original SCN's supervision mechanism, especially when dealing with large-scale datasets. Furthermore, while GLSCN is designed to handle noise in unlabeled data, it does not perform any optimization with noisy labeled data. Building upon these considerations, this chapter proposes a novel robust semi-supervised stochastic configuration network ($RS^3CN$) to enhance the robustness of SCN against noisy or outlier-prone limited labeled data in regression tasks.

The main contributions of this section are as follows:

- We present a novel $RS^3CN$ algorithm designed to address noise and outliers in limited labeled data for regression tasks. It also introduces the comparative algorithms we proposed, including $S^3CN$, $RS^3CN$-Huber, and $RS^3CN$-IQR.
- We simultaneously incorporated a manifold regularization term and kernel density estimation into $RS^3CN$, enhancing its generalization performance in regression tasks with noisy limited labeled data.

- We optimize the calculation of hidden layer output weights, eliminating the limitation on the number of labeled samples, thereby enhancing the applicability of semi-supervised learning.
- We demonstrate the universal approximation property of $\mathrm{RS^3CN}$ while maintaining the original supervision mechanism of SCN.

## 9.2    Preliminaries

### 9.2.1    *Robust Stochastic Configuration Networks*

The RSCN model is built upon a robust learning framework, progressively refining its modeling through the introduction of a novel supervisory mechanism and addressing the weighted least squares (WLS) problem. In the realm of robust data regression, it seeks a potent learning model capable of successfully capturing the true distribution from uncertain data samples. Different from traditional SCN, RSCN is established by addressing the weighted least squares problem, with the following objective function:

$$\min_{\beta,\theta} \sum_{i=1}^{N} \theta_i \left\| \sum_{j=1}^{L} g_j(x_i w_j + b_j)\beta_j - y_i \right\|^2, \qquad (9.1)$$

where $\theta_i > 0(i = 1, 2, \ldots, N)$ represents the penalty weight for the $i$ sample, representing the contribution of the corresponding sample to the objective function. All other elements are the same as in SCN.

For a more efficient configuration of input parameters $w_j$ and $b_j$ for the hidden layer nodes, The weighted values of variables $e_{L-1}(X)$ and $h_L(X)$ are denoted as $\hat{e}_{L-1}(X) = \hat{\Theta}e_{L-1}(X)$ and $\hat{h}_L(X) = \hat{\Theta}h_{L-1}(X)$ respectively, where $\hat{\Theta} = \mathrm{diag}\left\{ \sqrt{\theta_1}, \ldots, \sqrt{\theta_N} \right\} \in \mathbf{R}^{N \times N}$. Let $\tilde{\xi}_L = \sum_{q=1}^{m} \tilde{\xi}_{L,q}$ and the new supervisory mechanism is defined as:

$$\xi_{L,q} = \frac{\left\langle \hat{e}_{L-1,q}(X) \cdot \hat{h}_L(X) \right\rangle^2}{\left\| \hat{h}_L(X) \right\|^2} - (1 - r - \mu_L)\|e_{L-1,q}(X)\|^2 > 0,$$

$$\times (q = 1, 2, \ldots, m). \qquad (9.2)$$

The parameters of hidden node $L$ will be adopted from the candidate node that satisfies the maximum value of $\hat{\xi}_L = (\sum_{q=1}^{m} \hat{\xi}_{L,q}) \geq 0$. Additionally, according to Eq. (9.1), the output weights $\beta''$ can be computed by solving the following Weighted Least Squares (WLS) problem:

$$\beta'' = \arg\min_{\beta} (H\beta - Y)^T \Theta (H\beta - Y) = (H^T \Theta H)^+ H^T \Theta, \qquad (9.3)$$

where $\Theta = \text{diag}\{\theta_1, \theta_2, \ldots, \theta_N\}$. $Y$ and $\beta$ share the same elements as in SCN. Update $L = L + 1$ and iterate through the steps above until specific termination criteria are met. For detailed performance results, refer to Wang and Li (2017a).

### 9.2.2 *Manifold Regularization*

Manifold Regularization (MR) is a machine learning approach that revolves around the core idea of locally introducing additional prior knowledge during the training process, thereby strengthening the exploration of the overall data distribution. In semi-supervised learning, the common scenario involves only a small portion of data being labeled, with the majority being unlabeled (Belkin *et al.*, 2006). MR offers an effective approach for semi-supervised learning by leveraging local correlations and manifold structure among unlabeled data samples, thereby enhancing algorithm performance and generalization capabilities.

The realization of semi-supervised learning through MR relies on the satisfaction of the following two assumptions:

(1) **Distributional Consistency Assumption**:
Both the $l$ labeled datasets $(X_l)$ and the $u$ unlabeled datasets $(X_u)$ should exhibit consistency in terms of probability distribution, indicating that they originate from a common marginal distribution $P_X$;

(2) **Smoothness Assumption**:
The conditional probabilities $P(y|x_1)$ and $P(y|x_2)$ should be similar when $x_1$ and $x_2$ are close to each other.

The objective function of the manifold regularization framework is as follows:

$$\min \frac{1}{2} \sum_{i,j} w_{i,j} \| P(y|x_i) - P(y|x_j) \|^2, \qquad (9.4)$$

furthermore, it can equivalently be expressed as

$$\min \frac{1}{2}\sum_{i,j} w_{i,j} \left\| \hat{y}_i - \hat{y}_j \right\|^2 = \min \mathrm{Tr}(\hat{Y}^T L_p \hat{Y}), \tag{9.5}$$

where $\hat{y}_i$ and $\hat{y}_j$ correspond to the predicted values of $x_i$ and $x_j$, respectively. $w_{i,j}$ denotes the pair-wise similarity between two patterns $x_i$ and $x_j$. When $x_i$ and $x_j$ are connected, $w_{i,j}$ can be represented as

$$w_{i,j} = \exp\left(-\left\| x_i - x_j \right\|^2 \Big/ 2\sigma^2\right), \tag{9.6}$$

where $\sigma$ is set as the average edge length in the local adjacency. otherwise, $w_{i,j}$ can be zero. The Laplacian matrix $L_p \in \mathbf{R}^{(l+u)\times(l+u)}$ can be obtained using the following mathematical expression:

$$L_p = D - W, \tag{9.7}$$

where $W = [w_{i,j}]_{i,j=l+u}$ is similarity matrix, typically sparse, and $D$ is a diagonal matrix calculated as

$$D_{ii} = \sum_{j=1}^{l+u} w_{i,j}. \tag{9.8}$$

## 9.3   Methodology

In this section, we elucidate our algorithm, encompassing the process of constructing the RS$^3$CN network and providing proof of its general approximation property.

### 9.3.1   *Robust Semi-Supervised Stochastic Configuration Network*

In a semi-supervised context, we possess a limited amount of labeled data accompanied by an abundance of unlabeled data. Given the training set includes both labeled data $\{X_l, Y_l\} = \{x_i, y_i\}_{i=1}^{l}$ and unlabeled data $\{X_u\} = \{x_i\}_{i=1}^{u}$, where $l$ and $u$ respectively represent the counts of labeled and unlabeled instances. Given the specified limits, tolerance error $\varepsilon$, and maximum hidden nodes $L_{\max}$.

RS$^3$CN integrates methods such as manifold regularization and density estimation to enhance classification accuracy in situations where labeled data is scarce and noise is present. Based on SCN, the objective function for RS$^3$CN with $L$ hidden nodes is derived by adjusting its original objective function:

$$\min_{\beta} \frac{1}{2}\|\beta\|^2 + \frac{c}{2}\left\|\tilde{\Theta}^{\frac{1}{2}}e_L\right\|^2 + \frac{\lambda}{2}\mathrm{Tr}\left((H\beta)^T L_p(H\beta)\right), \qquad (9.9)$$

$$\text{s.t.} \quad e_L = Y_l - \tilde{H}\beta, \quad i = 1, 2, \ldots, l$$
$$\tilde{H} \in \mathbf{R}^{l \times L} = [\tilde{h}_1(X), \ldots, \tilde{h}_L(X)]$$
$$\tilde{h}_i(\boldsymbol{X}) = [g_i(x_1 w_i + b_i), \ldots, g_i(x_l w_i + b_i)]^T$$
$$(i = 1, 2, \ldots, L),$$

where $e_L$ represents the algorithm error computed from labeled data. $H \in \mathbf{R}^{(l+u) \times L}$ denotes the hidden layer output matrix for the entire input dataset, and $h_L^T(X) \in \mathbf{R}^{l+u}$ represents the last column of $H$, indicating the outputs of labeled and unlabeled data at the hidden layer node of $L$. $\tilde{h}_L(X)$ and $\tilde{H} \in \mathbf{R}^{l \times L}$ correspond to the first $l$ rows of $H$ and $h_L(X)$, respectively. Adding the regularization term represented by $\lambda \mathrm{Tr}\left((H\beta)^T L_p(H\beta)\right)/2$ aims to enable semi-supervised learning. The parameters $c$ and $\lambda$ balance the algorithm's fitting on the training data and its generalization performance on new data. $\tilde{\Theta} \in \mathbf{R}^{l \times l}$ is a diagonal matrix with dimensions $l \times l$, representing the density value for the error of each sample.

Under typical circumstances, the sample errors of anomalous values tend to deviate from the central distribution of errors in normal data samples. Therefore, we employ the kernel density estimation (KDE) method to calculate the probability density values of each sample error. Different density values, corresponding to various sample densities within the entire data distribution, allow us to enhance the fitting of samples in regions with higher density. This emphasizes the significance of high-density areas in the data distribution while mitigating the impact of samples in sparse regions by assigning smaller penalty weights. Throughout network training, these weights are utilized to adjust the fitting of each sample, enabling the network to concentrate more on high-density regions and thus improving fitting accuracy and robustness.

$\theta_i$ is the $i$th diagonal element of matrix $\tilde{\Theta}$. Specifically, the density value for every $\theta_i$ equal to $\Phi(e_L(x_i))$, representing the probability density function of each residual error $e_L(x_i)(i = 1, 2, \ldots, N)$, can be assigned as:

$$\theta_i = \Phi(e_L(x_i)) = \frac{1}{\tau N} \sum_{k=1}^{N} K\left(\frac{\|e_L(x_i) - e_L(x_k)\|}{\tau}\right), \qquad (9.10)$$

where $\tau = 1.06\hat{\sigma}N^{-1/5}$ is an estimation window width, $\hat{\sigma}$ is the standard deviation of the residual errors, $K$ is a Gaussian function defined by:

$$K(t) = \frac{1}{\sqrt{2\pi}} \exp\left(\frac{t^2}{2}\right). \qquad (9.11)$$

We substitute constraints into the objective function, rewriting the formula in matrix form:

$$\min_{\beta} \frac{1}{2}\|\beta\|^2 + \frac{c}{2}\|\Theta\left(Y - H\beta\right)\|^2 + \frac{\lambda}{2}\mathrm{Tr}((H\beta)^T L_p\left(H\beta\right)), \qquad (9.12)$$

where $Y \in \mathbf{R}^{(l+u) \times m}$ represents the target output for the entire training set, with its first $l$ rows are equal to $Y_l$ and the remaining $u$ rows are equal to 0. $\Theta \in \mathbf{R}^{(l+u) \times (l+u)}$ denotes a diagonal matrix of dimension $(l + u) \times (l + u)$, with its first $l$ rows are equal to $\tilde{\Theta}$, and the remaining $u$ rows are equal to 0.

The values of $\beta$ can be obtained through the global least squares method:

$$\beta^* = \arg\min_{\beta} \frac{1}{2}\|\beta\|^2 + \frac{c}{2}\|\Theta\left(Y - H\beta\right)\|^2 + \frac{\lambda}{2}\mathrm{Tr}\left((H\beta)^T L_p\left(H\beta\right)\right).$$

$$(9.13)$$

specifically, taking the derivative of Eq. (9.12) or (9.13) for $\beta$ and setting it equal to zero, we get

$$\nabla = \beta + H^T\Theta(Y - H\beta) + \lambda H^T L_p H\beta = 0. \qquad (9.14)$$

Based on the gradient being zero, we can derive the hidden layer output weights $\beta$ for RS$^3$CN:

$$\beta^* = \begin{cases} \left(I_L + cH^T\Theta H + \lambda H^T L_p H\right)^{-1} cH^T\Theta Y, l + u > L \\ H^T\left(I_{l+u} + c\Theta HH^T + \lambda L_p HH^T\right)^{-1} c\Theta Y, l + u \leq L. \end{cases} \qquad (9.15)$$

In Eq. (9.15), we provide two solutions for $\beta$, which are commonly encountered in semi-supervised learning. The algorithm can operate smoothly even when the quantity of labeled data is less than the number of hidden neurons. The final algorithm output can be calculated using Eq. (9.16), while its labeled output can be computed by Eq. (9.17).

$$f_L = H\beta^*, \tag{9.16}$$

$$\tilde{f}_L = \tilde{H}\beta. \tag{9.17}$$

New hidden layer nodes are added in RS$^3$CN when the specified limits are not satisfied, namely $e_L^* \leq \varepsilon$ and $L + 1 > L_{\max}$. Otherwise, the construction of RS$^3$CN is complete. During the addition process, set $L = L + 1$; then, the random basis function $h_L(X)(w_L$ and $b_L)$ needs to satisfy the following inequality constraint, which is equivalent to the one in the initial SCN.

$$\xi_{L,q} = \frac{\langle e_{L-1,q}(X) \cdot \tilde{h}_L(X) \rangle^2}{\tilde{h}_L^T(X) \cdot \tilde{h}_L(X)} - (1 - r - \mu_L)\|e_{L-1,q}(X)\|^2 > 0,$$

$$\times (q = 1, 2, \dots, m). \tag{9.18}$$

The addition of new nodes will generate multiple sets of candidate values ($w_L$ and $b_L$). We select the set of candidate values that satisfy the constraint and correspond to the maximum $\xi_{L,q}$ as the input weights ($w_L$) and bias ($b_L$) for the new node. Repeat the above process until the specified limits are satisfied.

### 9.3.2 *Universal Approximation Property*

When modifying the objective function of the original SCN, for instance, by introducing new regularization terms or adding a penalty term to the objective function, it results in alterations to the computation of hidden layer output weights. This is evident when comparing Eqs. (9.2) and (9.18) with the original SCN's supervision mechanism, highlighting the differences in output weights resulting from the modified objective function in the original SCN. Even with the sustained use of the inequality constraints from the original SCN, equivalent to Eq. (9.18), does the RS$^3$CN error, represented by $\|e_L\|$, still maintain its convergence? This crucially prompts the question of whether the algorithm can still uphold its universal approximation property, making it a topic worthy of investigation.

The least squares method can obtain globally optimal network output weights, and thus, we can conclude:

$$\|e_L^*\|^2 \leq \|\tilde{e}_L\|^2 = \left\|e_{L-1}^* - \tilde{h}_L(X)\tilde{\beta}_L\right\|^2 \leq \|e_{L-1}^*\|^2 \leq \|\tilde{e}_{L-1}\|^2,$$

(9.19)

where the error $\tilde{e}_L$ represents the localized update of algorithmic error when adding the $L$th hidden layer node, while the calculation of $e_L^*$ utilizes the global least squares method for an update, as follows:

$$e_L^* = Y_l - \tilde{H}\beta^*,$$

(9.20)

where $\tilde{\beta}_L$ denotes the output weight of the $L$th hidden node, obtained through the inequality constraint specified in Eq. (9.18) as follows:

$$\tilde{\beta}_{L,q} = \frac{\langle e_{L-1,q}, \tilde{h}_L(X)\rangle}{\|\tilde{h}_L(X)\|^2}, \quad (q = 1, 2, \ldots, m).$$

(9.21)

According to Eq. (9.19), the residual error sequence $\|e_L^*\|$ (corresponding to $\|e_L\|$) monotonically decreases with an increase in the number of hidden nodes $L$. If we identify suitable penalty coefficients $c$ and $\lambda$, this will also lead to

$$\|e_L^*\| \leq \|e_L\| \leq \|\tilde{e}_L\|.$$

(9.22)

When there are a sufficient number of nodes in the hidden layer, the selection of random basis functions is constrained, leading to the algorithm's error converging towards a non-zero constant. To ensure that the algorithm possesses a universal approximation property, we set the error sequence convergence rate of RS$^3$CN to satisfy the following inequality:

$$\|e_L\|^2 - (r + \mu_L)\|e_{L-1}\|^2 \leq 0.$$

(9.23)

Expanding $\|e_L\|^2 - (r + \mu_L)\|e_{L-1}\|^2$, we obtain

$$\|e_L\|^2 - (r + \mu_L)\|e_{L-1}\|^2 \leq \|\tilde{e}_L\| - (r + \mu_L)\|e_{L-1}\|^2$$

$$= \|e_{L-1} - \tilde{h}_L\tilde{\beta}_L\| - (r + \mu_L)\|e_L\|^2$$

$$= \sum_{q=1}^{m} \left(\delta_{L-1,q} - 2\langle e_{L-1,q}, \tilde{h}_L\tilde{\beta}_{L,q}\rangle + \langle \tilde{h}_L\tilde{\beta}_{L,q}, \tilde{h}_L\tilde{\beta}_{L,q}\rangle\right)$$

$$= \sum_{q=1}^{m} \left( \delta_{L-1,q} - 2\langle e_{L-1,q}, \tilde{h}_L \rangle \cdot \tilde{\beta}_{L,q} + \|\tilde{h}_L\|^2 \cdot \|\tilde{\beta}_{L,q}\|^2 \right)$$

$$= \sum_{q=1}^{m} \left( \delta_{L-1,q} - \frac{\langle e_{L-1,q}, \tilde{h}_L \rangle^2}{\|\tilde{h}_L\|^2} \right),$$

$$\delta_{L-1,q} = (1 - r - \mu_L) \langle e_{L-1,q}, e_{L-1,q} \rangle . \tag{9.24}$$

When the algorithm satisfies Eq. (9.18) during the generation process, Eq. (9.24) holds consistently. As a result, the sequence $\|e_L\|$ of the algorithm converges with an increase of $L$. Let $\gamma_L = \mu_L \|e_{L-1}\|^2 \geq 0$ and then, based on Eq. (9.23), we can obtain:

$$\|e_L\|^2 \leq r\|e_{L-1}\|^2 + \gamma_L. \tag{9.25}$$

It is known that $\lim_{L\to+\infty}\gamma_L = 0$. Taking limits on both sides of Eq. (9.25), we have $\lim_{L\to+\infty}\|e_L\|^2 = 0$, that indicates $\lim_{L\to+\infty}\|e_L^*\| = 0$. Therefore, the sequence $\|e_L^*\|$ of the RS$^3$CN algorithm monotonically decreases and converges to 0 as the node count $L$ increases.

### 9.3.2.1 *Computational Complexity Analysis*

In this section, we will analyze the computational complexity of the proposed algorithm. The computational complexity primarily arises from the calculation of the output weights. Specifically, based on Eq. (9.15), the computational complexity per node is $O(N^2L + NL^2 + L^3)$ when $l + u \geq L$, and $O(N^3 + N^2L)$ when $l + u < L$. Therefore, for RS$^3$CN with $L$ ($L \leq l + u$) nodes, the computational complexity is $O\left(N^2L^2 + NL^3 + L^4\right)$; for RS$^3$CN with $L$ ($L > l + u$) nodes, the computational complexity is $O(N^3L + N^2L^2 + NL^3)$.

It can be seen that the computational complexity of this algorithm is directly related to the data volume and the number of hidden nodes. When handling large-scale semi-supervised robust data modeling tasks, the computational complexity increases significantly as the data volume and number of hidden nodes grow, which may result in a sharp rise in computational burden. Therefore, the algorithm is more suitable for small to medium-sized datasets, as it ensures high computational accuracy while maintaining fast processing speed. However, when dealing with large-scale datasets, optimizing the computational complexity and reducing unnecessary calculations remains a significant challenge for the algorithm's application.

## 9.4   Experimental Results and Discussion

In this section, we will demonstrate the effectiveness of our proposed RS$^3$CN algorithm by testing it on seven benchmark regression datasets. All experiments were conducted on the Matlab R2022b platform. We use the Root Mean Square Error (RMSE) as the evaluation metric to assess the algorithm's performance, and the expression for RMSE is

$$\text{RMSE} = \sqrt{\frac{\sum_{i=1}^{n} (y_i - f_i)^2}{n}}. \tag{9.26}$$

where $y_i$ represents the label value of the $i$th sample. $f_i$ is the true output of sample $i$. $N$ denotes the number of samples.

### 9.4.1   *Experimental Settings*

#### 9.4.1.1   *Benchmark Datasets*

To evaluate the performance of RS$^3$CN in regression tasks, we conducted experiments using seven benchmark datasets obtained from KEEL, including Laser, Electrical-Maintenance, Abalone, Stock, Prices, Weather Izmir, Mortgage, and Computer Activity. Detailed information for these datasets is provided in the Table 9.1. In the experiments, we will assess RS$^3$CN's performance on these datasets to determine its applicability and effectiveness in various regression problems.

#### 9.4.1.2   *Comparative Algorithm*

Conducting comparative experiments is crucial to highlight the differences among various algorithms in the same environment. Therefore, we selected eight comparative experiments: classical SCN (Wang and Li, 2017b), robust SCN (RSC-KDE) (Wang and Li, 2017a),

**Table 9.1.** Standard dataset information.

| Datasets | Features | Instances |
| --- | --- | --- |
| Laser | 4 | 993 |
| Electrical-maintenance | 4 | 1056 |
| Abalone | 8 | 4177 |
| Stock prices | 9 | 950 |
| Weather Izmir | 9 | 1461 |
| Mortgage | 15 | 1049 |
| Computer activity | 21 | 8192 |

Huber-RSCN (Dai *et al.*, 2019b), IQR-RSCN (Dai *et al.*, 2019b), semi-supervised SCNs (LPSCN) (Zhao *et al.*, 2023) and S$^3$CN), and our proposed robust semi-supervised SCNs (RS$^3$CN-Huber and RS$^3$CN-IQR).

The objective function of S$^3$CN, is as follows:

$$\min_{\beta} \frac{1}{2}\|\beta\|^2 + \frac{c}{2}\|(Y - H\beta)\|^2 + \frac{\lambda}{2}\mathrm{Tr}\left((H\beta)^T L_p (H\beta)\right), \qquad (9.27)$$

where all elements are identical to those in Eq. (9.12). We set the supervision mechanism of S$^3$CN to be the same as that of the original SCN. Even when there are changes in the objective function, the inequality constraints of the original SCN can ensure the algorithm's universal approximation, as demonstrated in Section 3.2. Moreover, the original inequality constraints help significantly reduce the algorithm's time complexity. The output weights of the hidden layer are

$$\beta''' = \begin{cases} \left(I_L + cH^T H + \lambda H^T L_p H\right)^{-1} cH^T Y, & l + u > L \\ H^T \left(I_{l+u} + cHH^T + \lambda L_p HH^T\right)^{-1} cY, & l + u \leq L. \end{cases} \qquad (9.28)$$

The objective functions of RS$^3$CN-Huber and RS$^3$CN-IQR are the same as in Eq. (9.12), and the outputs are the same as in Eq. (9.15), with the difference lying in the method used to obtain the weights $\Theta$. RS$^3$CN-Huber's weights are solved as follows:

$$\theta_{i,q}^{\mathrm{Huber}} = p(u_{i,q}) = \begin{cases} 1, & \text{if } |u_{i,q}| \leq c \qquad q = 1, 2, \ldots m, \\ \frac{c}{|u_{i,q}|}, & \text{if } |u_{i,q}| > c, \qquad i = 1, 2, \ldots, l \end{cases} \qquad (9.29)$$

where c is a positive adjustable parameter and is typically set to 1.345. $u_{i,q} = e_{L,q}/\hat{z}$ represents the standardized residuals of $i$th sample corresponding to the $q$th output node. $\hat{z}$ is the robust scale estimator and is set as $\hat{z} = \text{MAR}/0.6745$, where $\text{MAR} = \text{Med}(|e_{L,q} - \text{Med}(e_{L,q})|)$, and $\text{Med}(\cdot)$ is Median function.

RS$^3$CN-IQR's weights are solved as follows:

$$\theta_{i,q}^{\text{IQR}} = p'(u_{i,q}) = \begin{cases} 1, & |u_{i,q}| \leq c_1 \\ \frac{c_2 - u_{i,q}}{c_2 - c_1}, & c_1 \leq |u_{i,q}| \leq c_2, \\ 10^{-4}, & |u_{i,q}| \geq c_2 \end{cases} \quad \begin{array}{l} q = 1, 2, \ldots, m, \\ i = 1, 2, \ldots, l \end{array}$$

$$(9.30)$$

where $c_1{=}2.5$ and $c_2{=}3$. The computation method for $u_{i,q}$ is the same as above, and $\hat{z}$ is modified to $\hat{z} = \frac{\text{IQR}}{2 \times 0.6745}$. Here, IQR denotes the difference between the 75th and 25th percentiles.

### 9.4.1.3 *Parameter Settings*

To ensure the fairness and reliability of the experiments, we will provide the selection range for key parameters of the relevant models along with specific experimental procedures.

All comparative experiments, including RS$^3$CN, utilized a single hidden layer feedforward neural network. Therefore, we defined the range for the number of hidden nodes as 2 to 1502, with a step size of 25. The maximum number of candidate nodes generated in each iteration, denoted as $T_{\max}$, was set to 50. The tolerance error $\varepsilon$ was specified as 0.001. During input parameter generation for hidden nodes, both $\lambda$ (selected from $\{0.5, 1, 5, 10, 30, 50, 100\}$) and the adaptive contraction factor $r$ (chosen from $0.99, 0.999, 0.9999, 0.99999, 0.999999\}$) were included in the supervisory mechanism across all five models. For the regularization parameters $c$ and $\lambda$ in LPSCN, RS$^3$CN, and S$^3$CN, we performed grid searches and selected values from the set $\{2^{-18}, 2^{-15}, \ldots, 2^{15}, 2^{18}\}$.

To ensure the fairness of experimental results, we designated 75% of the dataset as the training set, leaving the remaining 25% as the test set. Subsequently, 10% of the training set was randomly chosen as labeled data, with the remaining portion considered as unlabeled data. To illustrate the algorithm's robustness to noise, we introduced varying proportions of Gaussian distribution noise to the labels of the labeled data, such as 10%, 20%, and 30% outliers. In different datasets and with diverse algorithms, aiming to showcase their optimal performance fully, we repeated the parameter selection process five times (beginning with reselection from the training and test sets each time). We then computed the average of the results from these five tests and selected the parameters with the highest average. Lastly, leveraging the selected parameters, we replicated the experiment 100 times and derived the final result as the average of these 100 experiments. This experimental design helps ensure the reliability and stability of the results.

## 9.4.2 *Main Results and Discussion*

### 9.4.2.1 *Parameter analysis*

We randomly selected stock price data with 30% noise from seven datasets to analyze the model parameters. The model includes two random parameters, $c$ and $\lambda$. To assess the impact of parameter changes on model performance, we employed the method of controlling variables. First, under this noise condition, we determined the optimal parameters ($c = 2^{12}$, $\lambda = 2^{9}$). Then, we analyzed the effect of other parameters near the optimal values on model performance. Specifically, we fixed $c$ and varied $\lambda$, with the results shown in Table 9.2; next, we fixed $\lambda$ and varied $c$, with the results shown in Table 9.3. To visualize these results more clearly, Figs. 9.1 and 9.2 illustrate the trend of how parameter changes affect

**Table 9.2.** RMSE for different parameter settings.

| $c$ | $\lambda$ | RMSE |
|---|---|---|
| $2^{12}$ | $2^{-3}$ | $0.0823 \pm 0.0156$ |
| $2^{12}$ | $2^{0}$ | $0.0807 \pm 0.0164$ |
| $2^{12}$ | $2^{3}$ | $0.0804 \pm 0.0149$ |
| $2^{12}$ | $2^{6}$ | $0.0781 \pm 0.0149$ |
| $2^{12}$ | $2^{8}$ | $0.0712 \pm 0.0130$ |
| $\mathbf{2^{12}}$ | $\mathbf{2^{9}}$ | $\mathbf{0.0685 \pm 0.0105}$ |
| $2^{12}$ | $2^{10}$ | $0.0807 \pm 0.0164$ |
| $2^{12}$ | $2^{12}$ | $0.0979 \pm 0.0172$ |
| $2^{12}$ | $2^{15}$ | $0.2213 \pm 0.0233$ |
| $2^{12}$ | $2^{18}$ | $0.4035 \pm 0.0180$ |

**Table 9.3.** RMSE for different parameter settings.

| $c$ | $\lambda$ | RMSE |
|---|---|---|
| $2^3$ | $2^9$ | $0.4735 \pm 0.0146$ |
| $2^6$ | $2^9$ | $0.2860 \pm 0.0275$ |
| $2^8$ | $2^9$ | $0.1510 \pm 0.0211$ |
| $2^9$ | $2^9$ | $0.1088 \pm 0.0205$ |
| $2^{11}$ | $2^9$ | $0.0710 \pm 0.0123$ |
| $\mathbf{2^{12}}$ | $\mathbf{2^9}$ | $\mathbf{0.0685 \pm 0.0105}$ |
| $2^{13}$ | $2^9$ | $0.0730 \pm 0.0136$ |
| $2^{15}$ | $2^9$ | $0.0937 \pm 0.0172$ |
| $2^{16}$ | $2^9$ | $0.1121 \pm 0.0201$ |
| $2^{18}$ | $2^9$ | $0.1486 \pm 0.0267$ |

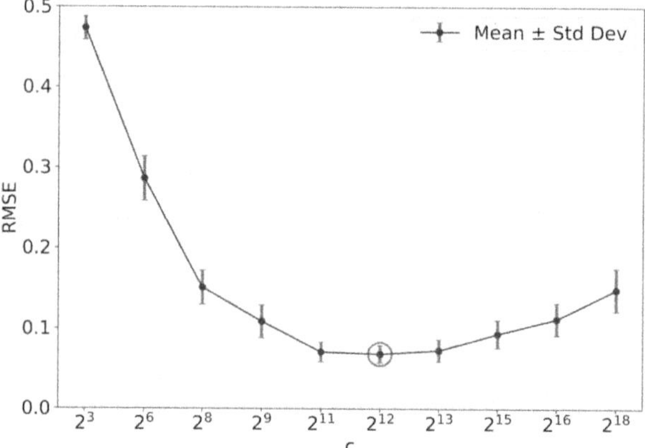


**Fig. 9.1.** RMSE vs. $c$ for Constant $\lambda$.

model performance (RMSE) through line charts, helping to better understand how variations around the optimal parameters influence model performance.

As shown in Fig. 9.1 and Table 9.2, when $\lambda$ varies within a small range around $2^9$, the impact on model performance (RMSE) is minimal, particularly when $\lambda$ is close to $2^9$, where the model performs best. As $\lambda$ increases or decreases, the RMSE gradually increases, indicating that both excessively large and small values of $\lambda$ reduce the model's predictive performance. Based on Table 9.5 and Fig. 9.2,

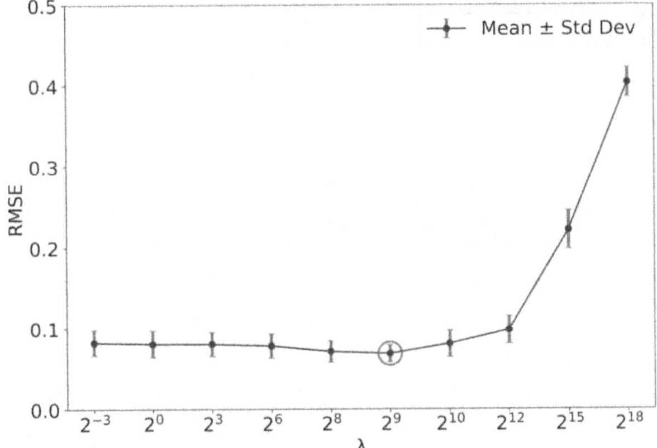

**Fig. 9.2.** RMSE vs. $\lambda$ for Constant $c$.

we observe that the variation trend of the $c$ value around $2^{11}$ is similar to the change in $\lambda$. More importantly, we identify a common characteristic: when $\lambda$ exceeds $c$, the RMSE increases dramatically, and when $\lambda$ is much larger than $c$, the increase in RMSE is even more pronounced. This indicates that in this model, the manifold regularization corresponding to the parameter $c$ has a significant impact on model performance. This phenomenon arises because, in our dataset, the majority of the data is unlabeled, and manifold regularization works particularly well on unlabeled data. We have confirmed this pattern through extensive experimentation, which is crucial for selecting the optimal parameters and has significantly reduced the time spent on parameter selection in subsequent experiments.

### 9.4.2.2 *Result Analysis*

In this section, we present the experimental results of RS$^3$CN and eight comparative algorithms (SCN, RSC-KDE, Huber-RSCN, IQR-RSCN, LPSCN, S$^3$CN, RS$^3$CN-Huber and RS$^3$CN-IQR) on various benchmark datasets, with varying proportions of noise or outlier values in the labels of labeled data (0%, 10%, 20%, and 30%). These experiments aim to evaluate the robustness and performance of RS3CN under limited labeled data with varying proportions of outlier values. Additionally, in this experiment, our focus is on evaluating the performance of our proposed model in regression tasks.

We primarily use RMSE and standard deviation (std) as the key metrics. The goal is to minimize RMSE on the test set, ensuring that the model's predictions on actual data are as accurate and The detailed results and trends are shown in Tables 9.4–9.10 and Figs. 9.3–9.9.

Upon examining Tables 9.4–9.10, we found that when the Gaussian noise occupies 10%, 20%, and 30% of labeled data across various datasets, $RS^3CN$ exhibited the smallest RMSE values compared to the other four algorithms. This further validates the exceptional robustness of $RS^3CN$ in regression tasks with limited labeled data, highlighting its outstanding ability to handle outliers and adapt to the true data distribution. When the Gaussian noise ratio is 0%, $RS^3CN$ may not achieve the optimal RMSE on Laser, Electrical-Maintenance, Stock Prices, Mortgage, and Computer Activity datasets. However, compared to the original SCN algorithms such as LPSCN, RSCN, and SCN, $RS^3CN$ still exhibits the smallest RMSE values, highlighting its outstanding generalization performance.

The left side of Figs. 9.3–9.9 shows that, except for the Computer Activity dataset, RSC-KDE exhibits the smallest RMSE across all datasets with different noise distributions, indicating its relatively best generalization performance in noisy environments. This is one of the reasons why we chose the KDE method. Meanwhile, the Huber and IQR methods also show relatively good performance, which is why we extend them for use in robust semi-supervised scenarios. Although RSC-KDE does not perform as well on the Computer Activity dataset, its robust semi-supervised algorithm $RS^3CN$ performs the best on this dataset.

From the right-hand side of Figs. 9.3–9.9, it is clearly evident that our proposed $RS^3CN$ achieves the lowest RMSE across all noisy datasets. Its variants, $RS^3CN$-Huber and $RS^3CN$-IQR, also demonstrate comparable performance. In contrast, LPSCN and $RS^3CN$ show significantly poorer results. This highlights the crucial role of our robust methods (KDE, Huber, and IQR) in enhancing the performance of $RS^3CN$, with this improvement achieved under the same manifold regularization optimization.

Based on the observations from Figs. 9.3–9.9, we found that the algorithms on the right, which incorporate manifold regularization, consistently show lower overall RMSE compared to those on the

**Table 9.4.** RMSE $\pm$ STD at different noise levels on the Laser dataset.

| Algorithms \ Noise levels | 0% | 10% | 20% | 30% |
|---|---|---|---|---|
| SCN | $0.0959 \pm 0.0765$ | $0.1101 \pm 0.0145$ | $0.1124 \pm 0.0170$ | $0.1146 \pm 0.0162$ |
| RSC-KDE | $0.0806 \pm 0.0446$ | $0.1126 \pm 0.0167$ | $0.1122 \pm 0.0173$ | $0.1121 \pm 0.0177$ |
| Huber-RSCN | $0.0805 \pm 0.0506$ | $0.1124 \pm 0.0165$ | $0.1128 \pm 0.0168$ | $0.1129 \pm 0.0177$ |
| IQR-RSCN | $0.0835 \pm 0.0423$ | $0.1125 \pm 0.0159$ | $0.1126 \pm 0.0176$ | $0.1126 \pm 0.0165$ |
| LPSCN | $0.0562 \pm 0.0267$ | $0.0667 \pm 0.0142$ | $0.0782 \pm 0.0155$ | $0.0812 \pm 0.0126$ |
| S$^3$CN | $\mathbf{0.0516 \pm 0.0225}$ | $0.0647 \pm 0.0138$ | $0.0750 \pm 0.0144$ | $0.0825 \pm 0.0159$ |
| RS$^3$CN-Huber | $0.0592 \pm 0.0128$ | $0.0618 \pm 0.0139$ | $0.0643 \pm 0.0149$ | $0.0722 \pm 0.0162$ |
| RS$^3$CN-IQR | $0.0613 \pm 0.0126$ | $0.0613 \pm 0.0144$ | $0.0654 \pm 0.0168$ | $0.0715 \pm 0.0196$ |
| RS$^3$CN | $0.0572 \pm 0.0153$ | $\mathbf{0.0590 \pm 0.0149}$ | $\mathbf{0.0594 \pm 0.0143}$ | $\mathbf{0.0666 \pm 0.0164}$ |

**Table 9.5.** RMSE $\pm$ STD at different noise levels on the Electrical-Maintenance dataset.

| Algorithms | Noise levels 0% | 10% | 20% | 30% |
|---|---|---|---|---|
| SCN | $0.0527 \pm 0.0419$ | $0.0579 \pm 0.0105$ | $0.0590 \pm 0.0098$ | $0.0616 \pm 0.0098$ |
| RSC-KDE | $0.0559 \pm 0.0116$ | $0.0554 \pm 0.0107$ | $0.0565 \pm 0.0082$ | $0.0566 \pm 0.0105$ |
| Huber-RSCN | $0.0561 \pm 0.0100$ | $0.0564 \pm 0.0102$ | $0.0570 \pm 0.0102$ | $0.0578 \pm 0.0097$ |
| IQR-RSCN | $0.0558 \pm 0.0101$ | $0.0566 \pm 0.0114$ | $0.0567 \pm 0.0111$ | $0.0569 \pm 0.0113$ |
| LPSCN | $0.0216 \pm 0.0041$ | $0.0402 \pm 0.0137$ | $0.0476 \pm 0.0128$ | $0.0579 \pm 0.0141$ |
| S$^3$CN | $\mathbf{0.0190 \pm 0.0036}$ | $0.0302 \pm 0.0072$ | $0.0357 \pm 0.0088$ | $0.0436 \pm 0.0110$ |
| RS$^3$CN-Huber | $0.0217 \pm 0.0021$ | $0.0221 \pm 0.0024$ | $0.0248 \pm 0.0049$ | $0.0295 \pm 0.0070$ |
| RS$^3$CN-IQR | $0.0204 \pm 0.0016$ | $0.0211 \pm 0.0022$ | $0.0226 \pm 0.0048$ | $0.0263 \pm 0.0074$ |
| RS$^3$CN | $0.0205 \pm 0.0012$ | $\mathbf{0.0207 \pm 0.0018}$ | $\mathbf{0.0223 \pm 0.0028}$ | $\mathbf{0.0262 \pm 0.0059}$ |

**Table 9.6.** RMSE $\pm$ STD at different noise levels on the Abalone datasets.

| Algorithms / Noise levels | 0% | 10% | 20% | 30% |
|---|---|---|---|---|
| SCN | 0.0896 $\pm$ 0.0093 | 0.0958 $\pm$ 0.0037 | 0.0961 $\pm$ 0.0035 | 0.0963 $\pm$ 0.0040 |
| RSC-KDE | 0.0826 $\pm$ 0.0037 | 0.0830 $\pm$ 0.0045 | 0.0858 $\pm$ 0.0042 | 0.0893 $\pm$ 0.0077 |
| Huber-RSCN | 0.0820 $\pm$ 0.0033 | 0.0851 $\pm$ 0.0045 | 0.0884 $\pm$ 0.0071 | 0.0943 $\pm$ 0.0080 |
| IQR-RSCN | 0.0827 $\pm$ 0.0039 | 0.0841 $\pm$ 0.0048 | 0.0875 $\pm$ 0.0058 | 0.0927 $\pm$ 0.0087 |
| LPSCN | 0.0819 $\pm$ 0.0064 | 0.0821 $\pm$ 0.0038 | 0.0829 $\pm$ 0.0033 | 0.0915 $\pm$ 0.0057 |
| S$^3$CN | **0.0786 $\pm$ 0.0031** | 0.0799 $\pm$ 0.0030 | 0.0824 $\pm$ 0.0034 | 0.0820 $\pm$ 0.0034 |
| RS$^3$CN-Huber | 0.0789 $\pm$ 0.0025 | 0.0796 $\pm$ 0.0030 | 0.0813 $\pm$ 0.0035 | 0.0817 $\pm$ 0.0035 |
| RS$^3$CN-IQR | 0.0790 $\pm$ 0.0031 | 0.0803 $\pm$ 0.0032 | 0.0807 $\pm$ 0.0025 | 0.0825 $\pm$ 0.0045 |
| RS$^3$CN | 0.0796 $\pm$ 0.0027 | **0.0794 $\pm$ 0.0028** | **0.0804 $\pm$ 0.0028** | **0.0810 $\pm$ 0.0032** |

**Table 9.7.** RMSE $\pm$ STD at different noise levels on the Stock Prices dataset.

| Algorithms | Noise levels 0% | 10% | 20% | 30% |
|---|---|---|---|---|
| SCN | $0.0641 \pm 0.0102$ | $0.1147 \pm 0.0245$ | $0.1471 \pm 0.0354$ | $0.1611 \pm 0.0209$ |
| RSC-KDE | $0.0679 \pm 0.0087$ | $0.0792 \pm 0.0142$ | $0.0969 \pm 0.0218$ | $0.1239 \pm 0.0273$ |
| Huber-RSCN | $0.0650 \pm 0.0084$ | $0.0854 \pm 0.0167$ | $0.1101 \pm 0.0255$ | $0.1342 \pm 0.0290$ |
| IQR-RSCN | $0.0639 \pm 0.0082$ | $0.0818 \pm 0.0174$ | $0.1110 \pm 0.0265$ | $0.1422 \pm 0.0380$ |
| LPSCN | $0.0596 \pm 0.0054$ | $0.0744 \pm 0.0096$ | $0.0888 \pm 0.0127$ | $0.0927 \pm 0.0132$ |
| S$^3$CN | $0.0534 \pm 0.0057$ | $0.0722 \pm 0.0101$ | $0.0849 \pm 0.0124$ | $0.0861 \pm 0.0123$ |
| RS$^3$CN-Huber | $0.0555 \pm 0.0042$ | $0.0603 \pm 0.0074$ | $0.0683 \pm 0.0088$ | $0.0731 \pm 0.0110$ |
| RS$^3$CN-IQR | $0.0572 \pm 0.0075$ | $0.0596 \pm 0.0067$ | $0.0644 \pm 0.0087$ | $0.0776 \pm 0.0138$ |
| RS$^3$CN | $\mathbf{0.0529 \pm 0.0048}$ | $\mathbf{0.0569 \pm 0.0064}$ | $\mathbf{0.0621 \pm 0.0086}$ | $\mathbf{0.0685 \pm 0.0105}$ |

**Table 9.8.** RMSE $\pm$ STD at different noise levels on the Weather Izmir dataset.

| Algorithms \ Noise levels | 0% | 10% | 20% | 30% |
|---|---|---|---|---|
| SCN | $0.0289 \pm 0.0067$ | $0.0730 \pm 0.0156$ | $0.0773 \pm 0.0185$ | $0.0790 \pm 0.0178$ |
| RSC-KDE | $0.0243 \pm 0.0027$ | $0.0357 \pm 0.0126$ | $0.0530 \pm 0.0166$ | $0.0748 \pm 0.0192$ |
| Huber-RSCN | $0.0240 \pm 0.0026$ | $0.0421 \pm 0.0127$ | $0.0688 \pm 0.0192$ | $0.0749 \pm 0.0168$ |
| IQR-RSCN | $0.0240 \pm 0.0027$ | $0.0356 \pm 0.0117$ | $0.0595 \pm 0.0211$ | $0.0742 \pm 0.0176$ |
| LPSCN | $0.0229 \pm 0.0024$ | $0.0390 \pm 0.0064$ | $0.0500 \pm 0.0093$ | $0.0540 \pm 0.0094$ |
| $S^3CN$ | $\mathbf{0.0214 \pm 0.0017}$ | $0.0346 \pm 0.0065$ | $0.0400 \pm 0.0072$ | $0.0459 \pm 0.0092$ |
| $RS^3CN$-Huber | $0.0220 \pm 0.0014$ | $0.0235 \pm 0.0021$ | $0.0278 \pm 0.0057$ | $0.0317 \pm 0.0063$ |
| $RS^3CN$-IQR | $0.0221 \pm 0.0016$ | $0.0231 \pm 0.0020$ | $0.0243 \pm 0.0027$ | $0.0283 \pm 0.0055$ |
| $RS^3CN$ | $0.0215 \pm 0.0014$ | $\mathbf{0.0231 \pm 0.0015}$ | $\mathbf{0.0238 \pm 0.0021}$ | $\mathbf{0.0268 \pm 0.0034}$ |

**Table 9.9.** RMSE $\pm$ STD at different noise levels on the Mortgage dataset.

| Algorithms \ Noise levels | 0% | 10% | 20% | 30% |
|---|---|---|---|---|
| SCN | $0.0118 \pm 0.0024$ | $0.0878 \pm 0.0160$ | $0.0890 \pm 0.0159$ | $0.0897 \pm 0.0176$ |
| RSC-KDE | $0.0112 \pm 0.0023$ | $0.0323 \pm 0.0154$ | $0.0658 \pm 0.0276$ | $0.0871 \pm 0.0180$ |
| Huber-RSCN | $0.0115 \pm 0.0017$ | $0.0452 \pm 0.0181$ | $0.0860 \pm 0.0160$ | $0.0875 \pm 0.0163$ |
| IQR-RSCN | $0.0113 \pm 0.0022$ | $0.0334 \pm 0.0214$ | $0.0787 \pm 0.0293$ | $0.0883 \pm 0.0181$ |
| LPSCN | $0.0117 \pm 0.0022$ | $0.0501 \pm 0.0089$ | $0.0633 \pm 0.0131$ | $0.0511 \pm 0.0123$ |
| $S^3CN$ | $0.0101 \pm 0.0018$ | $0.0297 \pm 0.0077$ | $0.0362 \pm 0.0082$ | $0.0427 \pm 0.0108$ |
| $RS^3CN$-Huber | $0.0113 \pm 0.0017$ | $0.0162 \pm 0.0034$ | $0.0207 \pm 0.0044$ | $0.0267 \pm 0.0068$ |
| $RS^3CN$-IQR | $0.0102 \pm 0.0019$ | $0.0149 \pm 0.0019$ | $0.0178 \pm 0.0046$ | $0.0251 \pm 0.0093$ |
| $RS^3CN$ | $\mathbf{0.0100 \pm 0.0016}$ | $\mathbf{0.0143 \pm 0.0033}$ | $\mathbf{0.0173 \pm 0.0023}$ | $\mathbf{0.0217 \pm 0.0049}$ |

**Table 9.10.** RMSE $\pm$ STD at different noise levels on the Computer Activity dataset.

| Algorithms \ Noise levels | 0% | 10% | 20% | 30% |
|---|---|---|---|---|
| SCN | $0.0678 \pm 0.0202$ | $0.0982 \pm 0.0334$ | $0.1026 \pm 0.0127$ | $0.1051 \pm 0.0164$ |
| RSC-KDE | $0.0862 \pm 0.0194$ | $0.0960 \pm 0.0178$ | $0.1004 \pm 0.0201$ | $0.1083 \pm 0.0244$ |
| Huber-RSCN | $0.0879 \pm 0.0231$ | $0.1026 \pm 0.0211$ | $0.1047 \pm 0.0181$ | $0.1106 \pm 0.0204$ |
| IQR-RSCN | $0.0812 \pm 0.0151$ | $0.0933 \pm 0.0351$ | $0.0993 \pm 0.0183$ | $0.1086 \pm 0.0207$ |
| LPSCN | $0.0545 \pm 0.0094$ | $0.0653 \pm 0.0084$ | $0.0667 \pm 0.0084$ | $0.0734 \pm 0.0091$ |
| $S^3CN$ | $0.0453 \pm 0.0048$ | $0.0522 \pm 0.0053$ | $0.0551 \pm 0.0057$ | $0.0563 \pm 0.0056$ |
| $RS^3CN$-Huber | $\mathbf{0.0406 \pm 0.0039}$ | $0.0451 \pm 0.0052$ | $0.0468 \pm 0.0059$ | $0.0527 \pm 0.0059$ |
| $RS^3CN$-IQR | $0.0408 \pm 0.0041$ | $0.0438 \pm 0.0052$ | $0.0442 \pm 0.0053$ | $0.0503 \pm 0.0043$ |
| $RS^3CN$ | $0.0438 \pm 0.0054$ | $\mathbf{0.0424 \pm 0.0060}$ | $\mathbf{0.0435 \pm 0.0048}$ | $\mathbf{0.0482 \pm 0.0047}$ |

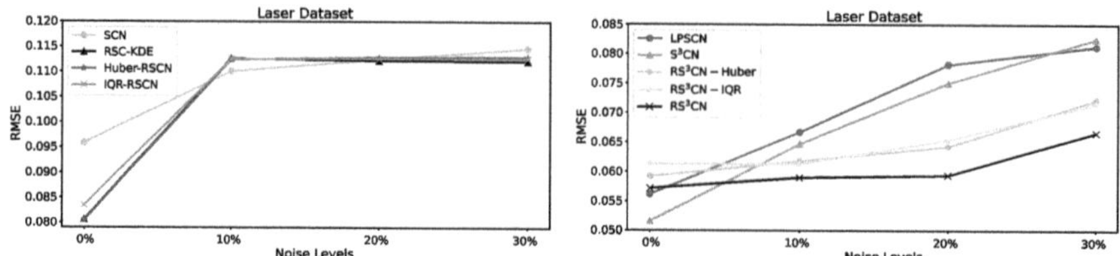

**Fig. 9.3.** RMSE of algorithms on Laser dataset with varying noise levels.

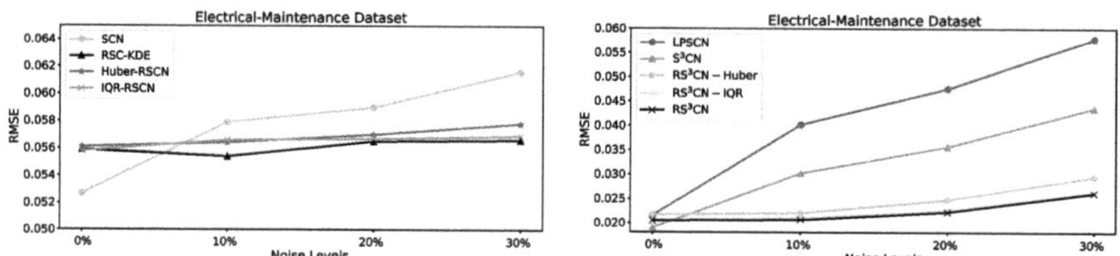

**Fig. 9.4.** RMSE of algorithms on Electrical-Maintenance dataset with varying noise levels.

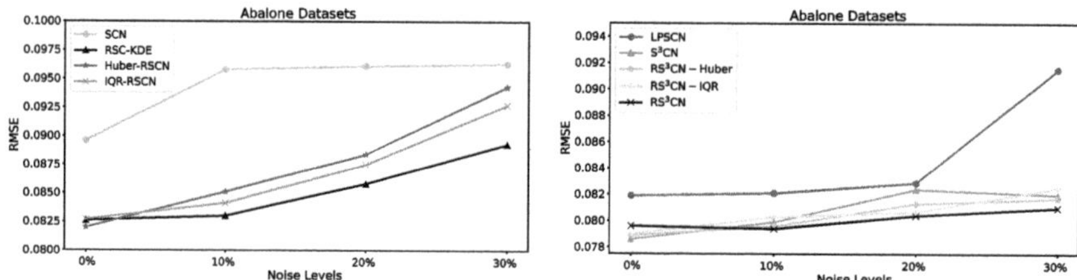

**Fig. 9.5.** RMSE of algorithms on Abalone dataset with varying noise levels.

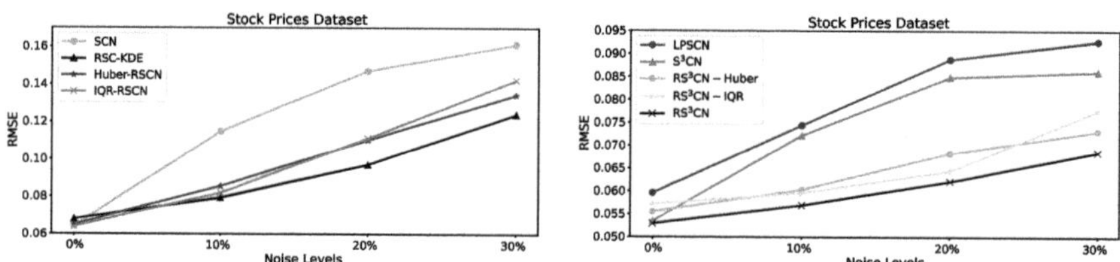

**Fig. 9.6.** RMSE of algorithms on Stock Prices dataset with varying noise levels.

left without manifold regularization. In the semi-supervised learning scenario, manifold regularization effectively facilitates feature learning from unlabeled data. Therefore, it is evident that manifold regularization plays a significant role in enhancing the optimization performance of the RS$^3$CN algorithm when labeled data is limited.

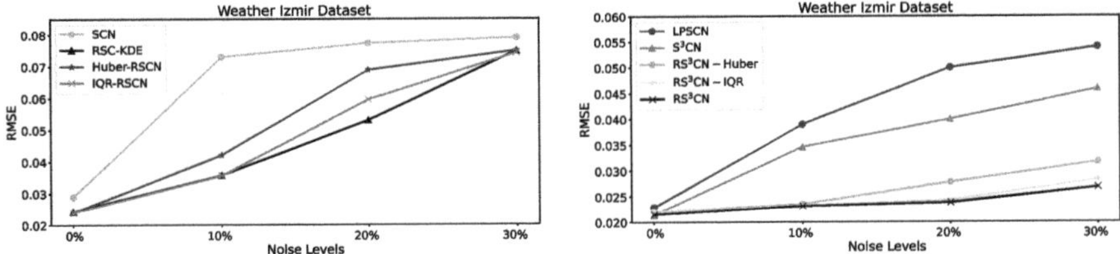

**Fig. 9.7.** RMSE of algorithms on Weather Izmir dataset with varying noise levels.

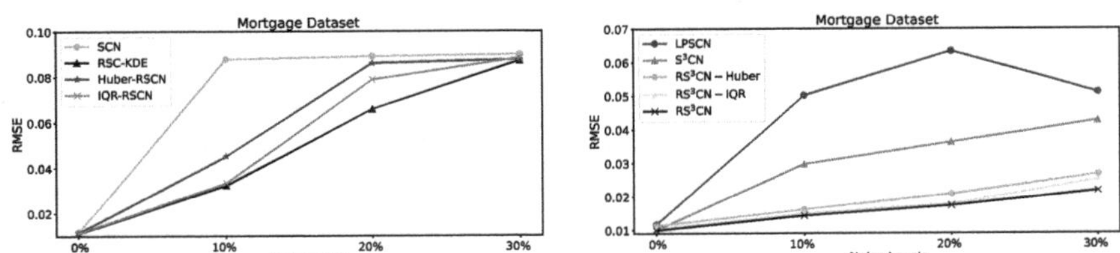

**Fig. 9.8.** RMSE of algorithms on Mortgage dataset with varying noise levels.

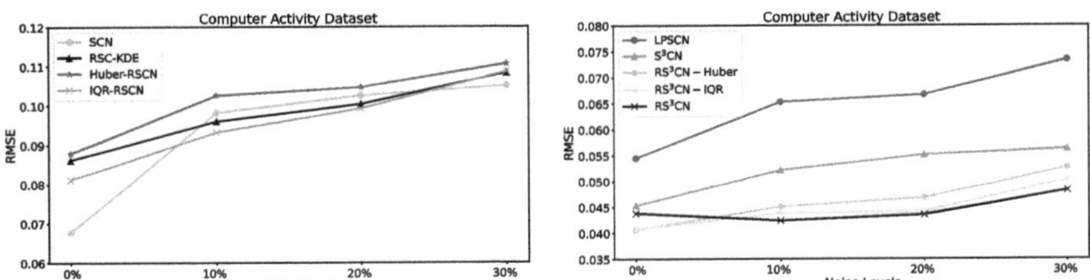

**Fig. 9.9.** RMSE of algorithms on Computer Activity dataset with varying noise levels.

Additionally, we also demonstrated the stability of RMSE by incorporating the standard deviation. In summary, RS$^3$CN, by introducing manifold regularization and robust methods (with a focus on KDE in this chapter), demonstrates outstanding performance in handling regression tasks with noisy and limited labeled data. This further validates the effectiveness of our approach in addressing regression problems and provides a reliable foundation for future applications and improvements.

## 9.5 Summary

To address the issue of reduced generalization performance of traditional SCN in semi-supervised settings, especially in the presence of anomalous label values, this chapter introduces RS$^3$CN to enhance its generalization capability for regression tasks in such scenarios.

However, several research directions remain worth exploring. For instance, this chapter does not investigate the impact of different types of noise on algorithm performance. Future work could examine the robustness of the algorithm under various noise conditions, such as Gaussian noise, quantization noise, data missingness, and salt-and-pepper noise, in order to enhance its adaptability across multiple scenarios. Furthermore, while this chapter primarily focuses on regression tasks, future research could extend RS$^3$CN to classification tasks. As the data scale increases, the computational complexity of the algorithm also grows, which may lead to significant computational burdens when handling large-scale robust data modeling tasks. Therefore, optimizing RS$^3$CN in combination with distributed learning methods is a promising direction for future exploration. Given that RS$^3$CN is an incremental learning algorithm, it can also be further extended to handle streaming data, particularly in industrial real-time processing scenarios, where it holds vast potential for application.

Part 3

# Deep Fusion Learning

Chapter 10

# Deep Stochastic Configuration Networks Ensemble via Hyper-Parameter Optimization

Deep Stochastic configuration network (DSCN), as a novel incremental generation model with supervisory mechanism, has an excellent superiority in solving large-scale data regression and classification problems. However, the accuracy of DSCN is affected by the assignation and selection of some network parameters significantly. To select scale of node parameters adaptively and improve the generalization of multi-model ensemble based on DSCN, this chapter proposes a deep stochastic configuration network ensemble model based on chaotic sparrow search algorithm. In the first place, chaotic sparrow search algorithm is designed which mainly utilizes logistic mapping, self-adaptive hyper-parameters, mutation operator to enhance the global optimization capability. In the second place, as the performance of DSCN is related to regularization parameter $r$ and scale factor $\lambda$ of weights and biases, the chaotic sparrow search algorithm is used to optimize the hyper-parameter of DSCN, then we use optimal hyper-parameter to training the base models and construct the adaptive boosting model, which reduces the model generalization error and improves the ensemble model regression accuracy. Finally, several datasets are used to evaluate the performance of CSSA-DSCN and CSSA-DSCNE respectively. Experimental results demonstrate the feasibility and validity of CSSA-DSCN and CSSA-DSCNE compared with SCN and other contrast algorithms.

211

## 10.1   Introduction

In recent years, as data size gradually increases with the development of information technology, it is necessary to develop a faster deep neural networks model with higher computational efficiency for large-scale data analytics. For this purpose, Wang and Li (2018) first expanded SCN to a deep version which is named deep stochastic configuration network (DSCN) in 2018. The introduction of supervisory mechanism has advantages of less human interference in the SCN and DSCN size setting, faster learning and preferable generalization performances. However, the performance of SCN and DSCN are sensitive to its parameters including the parameter selection of $r$ (regularization parameter) and $\lambda$ (scale factor of weights and biases). For any SCN and DSCN model, the parameter selection of $r$ and $\lambda$ are given in two sets respectively. Different parameter settings probably lead to distinct SCN and DSCN with different generalization ability. Seeking some better parameters to maximize network performance and minimize network architecture is vital for enhancing the effectiveness of SCN and DSCN. As meta-heuristic approaches have been widely used for selecting the optimal parameters of neural networks, at the same time, too little research has been devoted to optimizing random parameter selection of SCN and DSCN.

Meta-heuristic algorithms, including particle swarm optimization (PSO) (Shi and Eberhart, 1999), grey wolf optimizer (GWO) (Mirjalili *et al.*, 2014), sine cosine algorithm (SCA) (Mirjalili, 2016), multi-verse optimizer (MVO) (Mirjalili *et al.*, 2016), moth-flame optimization (MFO) (Mirjalili, 2015), parasitism predation algorithm (PPA) (Mohamed *et al.*, 2020), whale optimization algorithm (WOA) (Mirjalili and Lewis, 2016), lightning attachment procedure optimization (LAPO) (Nematollahi *et al.*, 2017), perform well in various parameter selection problems of machine learning and deep learning models. PSO was employed to the parameter optimization of support vector machine (SVM) for fault identification of rolling bearing in Yan and Jia (2018). Zhang *et al.* (2020) proposed a chaotic krill herd algorithm (CKH) to select the optimal parameters of support vector regression (SVR).Gao *et al.* (2020b) presented a twin support vector machine (TWSVM) based on artificial fish swarm algorithm (AFSA). Besides this, hyper-parameters tuning of deep learning and neural networks have been a hot research topic. As random single-hidden layer feedforward neural network (RSLFN) has faster learning speed, but the performance of RSLFN is related to randomly initialized input weights and other parameters, Han *et al.* made a comprehensive survey on RSLFN optimized by meta-heuristic algorithms (Han *et al.*, 2019). Gao *et al.* (2019b) proposed a new dendritic neuron model (DNM) by considering the nonlinearity of synapses and using meta-heuristic algorithms to train it for solving classification, approximation and prediction problems. The parameters of artificial neural network (ANN) were chosen by ALO and WOA in Ansal (2020); Haghnegahdar and Wang (2020). Otherwise, these algorithms can also be used for optimizing parameters of deep learning models, such as deep convolutional neural network (DCNN), deep stacking network (DSN) and deep belief network (DBN) (Goluguri *et al.*, 2021; Li *et al.*, 2019a; Tang *et al.*, 2017).

Sparrow search algorithm (SSA), as a novel meta-heuristic algorithm proposed in 2020, is mainly inspired by foraging and anti-predation behavior of sparrow population. SSA has a stronger optimization ability and faster efficiency compared with PSO, GWO, LAPO and other learning algorithms on benchmark functions (Xue and Shen, 2020). However, SSA is the same as other intelligence algorithms, the population diversity of SSA will decrease in the later iteration and it is easy to fall into local optimum. To avoid converging on local optimum of meta-heuristic algorithms and improve the global optimization ability, different improvement strategies have been put forward. Ibrahim *et al.* (2018) used chaotic logistic mapping and opposition-based learning (OBL) to generate initial solutions in the improved version of grey wolf optimizer (GWO). To increase the diversity of population, chaotic local search (CLS) mechanisms under a selection mechanism with the combination of 12 different chaotic maps are employed to JADE Gao *et al.* (2019a). Lei *et al.* (2020) proposed an aggregative learning gravitational search algorithm (ALGSA) by introducing self-adaptive gravitational constants. Wang *et al.* (2020d) constructed a population interaction network (PIN) to discover population interaction in the evolutionary process. In addition, different mutation strategies are utilized to firefly algorithm (FA) and moth-flame optimizer (MFO) respectively (chuan Wang *et al.*, 2020; Xu *et al.*, 2019). These tactics are beneficial to improve the performance of meta-heuristic algorithms.

Therefore, for seeking the most preferred solutions, we first propose a chaotic sparrow search algorithm (CSSA) by introducing logistic mapping, self-adaptive hyper-parameters and mutation operator to increase global searching ability of the algorithm, then an optimized deep stochastic configuration networkbased on chaotic sparrow search algorithm are presented, termed CSSA-DSCN. In addition, as a single DSCN model is prone to lack performance stability due to parameter randomization, multi-model ensemble using bagging, boosting and stacking can improve the generalization ability of the DSCN model. Among them, AdaBoost can train multiple base models, adaptively adjust sample weights according to their training errors, and generate a strong learner, which is conducive to reducing the impact of random parameters on network performance and improving model regression accuracy (Gao *et al.*, 2010; Solomatine and Shrestha, 2004; Zhang *et al.*, 2022a). Therefore, we propose a CSSA-DeepSCN ensembel model based on AdaBoost. Finally, the performance of CSSA-DeepSCN and its ensemble model are verified by experiments on function approximation problems and KEEL benchmark datasets.

In a nutshell, the significant characteristics of this chapter are listed as:

- Logistic mapping, self-adaptive hyper-parameters and mutation operator are adopted to enhance the global optimization ability of SSA.
- The regularization parameter $r$ and scale factor $\lambda$ of weights and biases of DSCN are optimized by CSSA, named as CSSA-DSCN.
- The ensemble version of CSSA-DSCN is demonstrated as CSSA-DSCNE, which is an deep stochastic configuration networks ensemble model via hyper-parameter optimization.
- Numerous experiments demonstrate that CSSA-DSCNE can get satisfactory regression results.

## 10.2 Preliminaries

Sparrow search algorithm (SSA) is one of swarm intelligence optimization algorithms with a stronger optimization ability and faster efficiency. It is mainly inspired by foraging and anti-predation behavior of sparrow population in 2020 (Xue and Shen, 2020). As sparrow is a smart social creature which has a good memory, the sparrow population has some biological characteristics in the foraging process:

(1) Sparrow population is usually divided into two types, termed as producer and scrounger. Producers have a larger searching space to seek food sources while scroungers find food according to the producers.
(2) Sparrows have a stronger anti-predation capability and some sparrows are selected as scouters to avoid predators in the foraging process.
(3) Producers and scroungers can be transformed dynamically in order to obtain a better food source.
(4) Scroungers can always find a better food source provided by producers and some scroungers even monitor producers to get more food.

Therefore, the mathematical model of SSA can be summarized as follows (Xue and Shen, 2020):

**Step 1:** Parameters initialization, including the population size of sparrows (pop); the number of producers $(PN)$; the number of scroungers $(\text{pop} - PN)$; the number of scouters $(SN)$; the maximum iterations $(g_{\max})$; the dimension of searching space $(D)$; the upper bound $(ub)$ and lower bound $(lb)$ of domain. The initial location of sparrows can be defined as $x_i = (x_{i1}, x_{i2}, \ldots, x_{iD})\,(i = 1, 2, \ldots, \text{pop})$ which are generated randomly, $f(x_i)$ indicates the fitness value of sparrow $i$.

**Step 2:** The locations of producers are updated by Eq. (10.1):

$$x_i^{g+1} = \begin{cases} x_i^g \cdot \exp\left(\frac{-i}{\alpha \cdot g_{\max}}\right) & R < ST \\ x_i^g + Q \cdot L & R \geq ST, \end{cases} \tag{10.1}$$

where $i = 1, 2, \ldots, PN$; $g$ represents the current iteration; $\alpha$ is a random value in the range of $(0, 1]$; $Q$ indicates a random number that follows a normal distribution; $L$ denotes a $1 \times D$ matrix with each element value is 1; $R \in [0, 1]$ and $ST \in [0.5, 1]$ are shown as alarm value and safety threshold respectively. $R < ST$ is defined that producers are able to continue an extensive search with no predators around while $R \geq ST$ means sparrows have been discovered by the predator, all sparrows should fly to other safe areas quickly.

**Step 3:** Calculate the scroungers' locations according to Eq. (10.2):

$$
x_i^{g+1} = \begin{cases} Q \cdot \exp\left(\frac{G_{\text{worst}} - x_i^g}{i^2}\right) & i > \text{pop}/2 \\ S_{\text{best}} + |x_i^g - S_{\text{best}}| \cdot A^+ \cdot L & \text{else ,} \end{cases}
\tag{10.2}
$$

where $i = PN+1, PN+2, \ldots, \text{pop}$; $G_{\text{worst}}$ represents the worst location of sparrows; $S_{\text{best}}$ expresses the current best location of producers; $A$ shows a $1 \times D$ matrix with each element value is assigned 1 or $-1$ randomly and $A^+ = A^T \left(A^T\right)^{-1}$. When $i > \text{pop}/2$, it indicates that the scrounger $i$ does not get food and it needs to fly to other places for obtaining higher energy; when $i \leq \text{pop}/2$, the scrounger $i$ will foraging around $S_{\text{best}}$.

**Step 4:** To be aware of the danger, $10-20\%$ of the sparrow population are chosen as scouters randomly and renew the locations of scouters according to Eq. (10.3):

$$
x_i^{g+1} = \begin{cases} G_{\text{best}} + \eta \cdot |x_i^g - G_{\text{best}}| & f(x_i^g) > f(G_{\text{best}}) \\ x_i^g + K \cdot \left(\frac{|x_i^g - G_{\text{worst}}|}{(f(x_i^g) - f(G_{\text{worst}})) + \sigma}\right) & f(x_i^g) = f(G_{\text{best}}), \end{cases}
\tag{10.3}
$$

where $G_{\text{best}}$ indicates the current optimal location of the population; $\eta$ denotes a random number that follows a normal distribution with a mean value of 0 and a variance of 1; $K \in [-1, 1]$ expresses as a direction and step size control factor which is a random number; $\sigma$ is a smaller constant. $f(x_i^g) > f(G_{\text{best}})$ demonstrates that sparrow $i$ is at the edge of the group where it is easier to encounter predators; $f(x_i^g) = f(G_{\text{best}})$ means that sparrow $i$ is in the center of populations which needs to approach the other sparrows so as to anti-predation.

**Step 5:** Achieve the current locations of sparrow population and update the best fitness value.

**Step 6:** Repeat the Step 2 to Step 5 until meet the tolerance error $\varepsilon$ or the maximum iterations $g_{\max}$, output the optimal location $x_{\text{best}}$ and best fitness value $f_{\text{best}}$.

## 10.3  Methodology

### 10.3.1  *Chaotic Sparrow Search Algorithm*

Although SSA has a stronger global searching ability and faster convergence speed in high-dimensional optimization problems, it is easy to fall into the local optimum at the later stage of iteration. To increase the global optimization ability and avoid converging on local optimum of SSA, a chaotic sparrow search algorithm (CSSA) is presented by introducing logistic mapping, self-adaptive hyper-parameters, mutation operator to enhance the global searching ability of the algorithm.

The improvement strategies of CSSA mainly come from three aspects. Firstly, SSA is the same as other swarm intelligence algorithms. The initialization of the population location is generated randomly, using chaotic mapping to initialize the population location is beneficial to improve the quality of initial solutions. Secondly, to accelerate the convergence and efficiency of SSA, two self-adaptive hyper-parameters are adopted to update locations of producers and number of scouters. Thirdly, as the population diversity will decrease in the iteration process, to get the global optimum value and overcome the local optimum of SSA, mutation operator is beneficial to increase the population diversity of SSA. The detailed improvement strategies of CSSA are summarized as follows.

#### 10.3.1.1  *Logistic Mapping*

Logistic mapping (Ibrahim *et al.*, 2018) is a typical chaotic system which can be described as Eq. (10.4):

$$x(k+1) = \mu x(k)(1 - x(k)), \tag{10.4}$$

where $x(k) \in (0, 1)$; $\mu \in (0, 4]$ is denoted as control parameter, when $3.5699 < \mu \leq 4$, the system is in chaos.

As can be seen in Fig. 10.1, when $\mu$ is closer to 4, the generated chaotic sequence is almost evenly distributed between 0 and 1 and it is not convergent and non-periodic. Therefore, the control parameter $\mu$ should be set closer to 4.

According to the properties of the logistic mapping, the initial population location of CSSA can be achieved as follows:

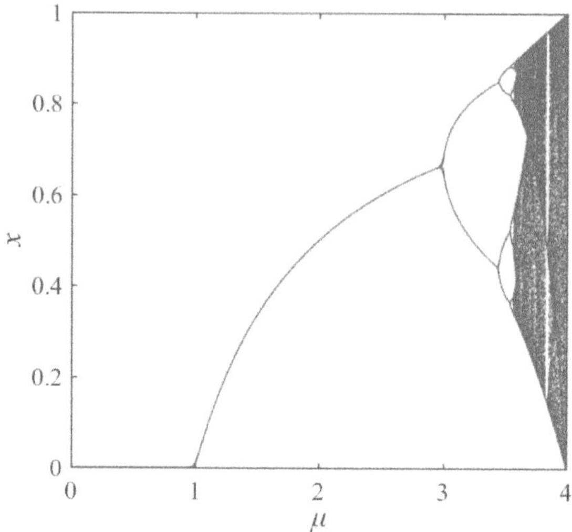

**Fig. 10.1.**   Feigenbaum bifurcation diagram of Logistic mapping.

Normalize the initial location of sparrow $x_{ij}(i = 1, 2, \ldots, N; j = 1, 2, \ldots, D)$ into $x_{ij}(0)(i = 1, 2, \ldots, N; j = 1, 2, \ldots, D)$ to satisfy the chaotic form using Eq. (10.5):

$$x_{ij}(0) = (x_{ij} - lb) / (ub - lb),  \tag{10.5}$$

where $ub$ and $lb$ represent the upper bound and lower bound of $x_{ij}$, respectively.

Logistic mapping is employed to obtain the $x_{ij}(k + 1)$ by Eq. (10.6):

$$x_{ij}(k + 1) = \mu x_{ij}(k) \left(1 - x_{ij}(k)\right).  \tag{10.6}$$

$x_{ij}(k + 1)$ is transformed into original domain from $[0, 1]$ to a new $x_{ij}(i = 1, 2, \ldots, N; j = 1, 2, \ldots, D)$ according to Eq. (10.7):

$$x_{ij} = lb + x_{ij}(k + 1) \times (ub - lb).  \tag{10.7}$$

### 10.3.1.2   *Self-Adaptive Hyper-parameters*

As sparrow population is divided into producers and scroungers, producers need a larger searching space to seek food sources while scroungers find food according to the producers, So the optimization ability of SSA is mainly related to the searching scope of producers.

In Eq. (10.1), the update of producers' locations influenced by $\exp\left(\frac{-g}{\alpha \cdot g_{\max}}\right)$ which the value range may gradually decreases from $(0, 1)$ to approximately $(0, 0.4)$ as $i$ gets larger when $\alpha$ has a bigger random value. Therefore, we introduce the adaptive control factor (Eq. (10.7)) to expand the searching scope of producers as Eq. (10.8):

$$w = w_0 \times c^g, \tag{10.8}$$

where $w_0 = 1$ is initial weight, $c$ is an adaptive factor of $w$ and it can be set according to the practical problems, $g$ is the current iteration number. Among them, $c$ is set to 0.9 to keep $w$ has a smaller value to expand the searching scope of producers for increasing global searching capability.

$$x_i^{g+1} = \begin{cases} x_i^g \cdot \exp\left(\frac{-i}{w \cdot \alpha \cdot g_{\max}}\right) & R < ST \\ x_i^g + Q \cdot L & R \geq ST \end{cases} \quad (i = 1, 2, \ldots, PN). \tag{10.9}$$

In addition, to avoid predators in the foraging process, $10\%-20\%$ of sparrows are selected as scouters. The existence of scouters can help the sparrow population get better solutions to SSA. When the number of scouters $(SN)$ is bigger, it is beneficial to improve the global optimization ability of the sparrows. However, when $SN$ is smaller, it is helpful to accelerate the convergence of SSA algorithm. Therefore, a self-adaptive updating formula of scouter's number is proposed as shown in Eq. (10.9), which can decrease nonlinearly during iteration.

$$SN = SN_{\max} - \text{round}\left[(SN_{\max} - SN_{\min}) \times \frac{g}{g_{\max}}\right], \tag{10.10}$$

where $SN_{\max}$ is the maximum value of scouter's number; $SN_{\min}$ expresses the minimum value of scouter's number; round function is used to round numbers; $g$ represents the current iteration; $g_{\max}$ indicates the maximum iterations.

### 10.3.1.3 *Mutation Operator*

During the searching process of the SSA, the diversity of the sparrow population will be reduced, which may cause premature convergence of the algorithm. To overcome the local optimum of SSA, mutation operation is introduced to increase the population diversity which is beneficial to jump out of the local optimum. In particular, only one individual is mutated randomly in each iteration, it has little effect on algorithm convergence.

$$x_r = lb + (ub - lb) \cdot \mathrm{rand}(1, D), \qquad (10.11)$$

where $r$ expresses one random individual in each iteration, and the location of sparrow $r$ will be initialized by using mutation.

### 10.3.2  *Deep Stochastic Configuration Network via Chaotic Sparrow Search Algorithm*

In the DSCN model, the regularization parameter $r$ and the scale factor $\lambda$ of input weights and biases which are extremely important for the performance of DSCN, however, the parameter $r$ and $\lambda$ are limited by the preset range. To improve the efficiency and accuracy of the DSCN, the proposed CSSA is utilized to optimize the regularization parameter $r$ and the scale factor $\lambda$ of input weights and biases, named as CSSA-DSCN. The CSSA-DSCN is described in detail as follows, which mainly includes two aspects: DSCN construction and parameter searching.

**Step 1:** CSSA-DSCN initialization.

Initialize the population size (pop), producers' number $(PN)$, scroungers' number (pop $- PN$), maximum scouter's number $(SN_{\max})$; minimum scouter's number $(SN_{\min})$; initial scouters' number $(SN)$, maximum iterations ( $g_{\max}$ ), dimension $(D)$, upper bound $(ub)$ and lower bound $(lb)$ of $r$ and $\lambda$, control parameter $(\mu)$, maximum number of hidden layer nodes ( $L_{\max}$ ), maximum number of candidate nodes $(T_{\max})$, tolerance error $(\varepsilon)$.

As the regularization parameter $r$ and the scale factor $\lambda$ are need to be selected, we generate initial $x_i = (x_{i,r}, x_{i,\lambda})\,(i = 1, 2, \ldots, \mathrm{pop})$ randomly, where $x_{i,r}$ and $x_{i,\lambda}$ represent $r, \lambda$, respectively.

**Step 2:** Logistic mapping and transform. Logistic mapping and transform of initial $x_i = (x_{i,r}, x_{i,\lambda})\,(i = 1, 2, \ldots, \mathrm{pop})$ by using Eqs. (10.5)–(10.7).

**Step 3:** Construct and training DSCN model. Using the $r$ and $\lambda$ of Eq. (10.7) as the initialization parameters to construct and training DSCN.

**Step 4:** Update regularization parameter $r$ and the scale factor $\lambda$.

The regularization parameter $r$ and the scale factor $\lambda$ can be updated by Eqs. (10.2),(10.3) and (10.9).

**Step 5:** Calculate fitness value. Root mean square error (RMSE) is chosen as the fitness function to evaluate the CSSA-DSCN, the fitness value of each individual can be computed by Eq. (10.12):

$$f\left(x_i^t\right) = \sqrt{\sum_{n=1}^{N}\left(y_n - \hat{y}_n\right)^2 / N}, \tag{10.12}$$

where $y_n$ expresses the actual value of sample $n$; $\hat{y}_n$ is denoted as the output value of sample $n$; $N$ defines the total number of sample points.

**Step 6:** Mutation operation by using Eq. (10.11):

**Step 7:** Terminal conditions and get the final parameters.

When CSSA-DSCN reaches the maximum iterations $g_{\max}$ or meets the preset tolerance error, then obtains the best fitness value and achieves the optimal $r, \lambda$ by using Eqs. (10.13) and (10.14), respectively:

$$f_{\text{best}} = \min f\left(x_i^t\right), \tag{10.13}$$

$$x_{\text{best}}^t = \left(x_{\text{best},r}^t, x_{\text{best},\lambda}^t\right). \tag{10.14}$$

Otherwise, repeat Step 2 to Step 7 until meet the terminal conditions.

**Step 8:** Output the results of DSCN. The global optimal parameters $x_{\text{best},r}, x_{\text{best},\lambda}$ of DSCN which selected in Step 7 are used to construct and training the DSCN, then output the training and test results.

### 10.3.3 *Deep Stochastic Configuration Networks Ensemble via Chaotic Sparrow Search Algorithm*

As shown in Fig. 10.2, the AdaBoost-based CSSA-DeepSCN ensemble process can be described as follows (Zhang *et al.*, 2022a):

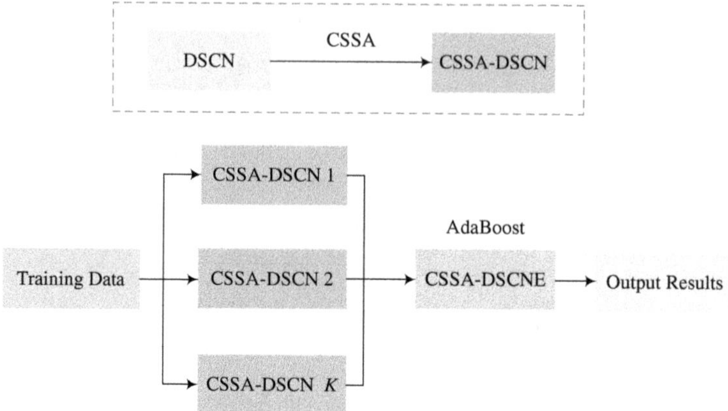

**Fig. 10.2.**  CSSA-DeepSCN ensemble process based on AdaBoost.

First, initialize the weights of each training sample by using Eq. (10.15):

$$w_i = \frac{1}{N}, \quad i = 1, 2, \ldots, N,$$ (10.15)

where $N$ represents the number of training samples.

Calculate the weight distribution according to Eq. (10.16):

$$D_t(i) = \frac{w_i}{\sum_{j=1}^{N} w_j}.$$ (10.16)

Training $K$ CSSA-DSCN models with the optimal parameters, and calculate the errors of each sample according to Eq. (10.17):

$$\epsilon_k = \sum_{i=1}^{N} D_t(i) \cdot \mathbb{I}(y_i \neq h_k(x_i)),$$ (10.17)

where $h_k(x_i)$ represents the training result of the $k$th CSSA-DSCN model, and $y_i$ is the true label of the sample.

Calculate the weighted loss and weighted coefficient of $h_k(x_i)$ according to Eqs. (10.18) and (10.19), respectively,

$$L_k = \frac{1}{2} \ln \left( \frac{1 - \epsilon_k}{\epsilon_k} \right).$$ (10.18)

$$\alpha_k = \frac{L_k}{\sum_{j=1}^{K} L_j}.$$ (10.19)

Update the weights of the training samples according to Eq. (10.20):

$$w_i = w_i \cdot \exp(-\alpha_k \cdot y_i \cdot h_k(x_i)), \tag{10.20}$$

where $\epsilon_{th}$ represents the error threshold for training samples, used to determine abnormal sample values.

Finally, weighting each model according to Eq. (10.21) to construct the CSSA-DSCN ensemble model:

$$f(x) = \sum_{k=1}^{K} \alpha_k \cdot h_k(x), \tag{10.21}$$

where $f(x)$ represents the output of the CSSA-DSCN ensemble model.

## 10.4 Experimental Results and Discussion

The experiments are implemented with MATLAB 2019b running on a PC with Intel (R) Core (TM) i7-9750H 2.60 GHz CPU, NVIDIA GPU GTX1650 and 64 GB RAM.

### 10.4.1 *Benchmark Datasets*

One function approximation problem and three real-world datasets of KEEL (Knowledge Extraction based on Evolutionary Learning, http://www.keel.es/) are chosen as experimental datasets to demonstrate the performance of CSSA-SCN. The descriptions of experimental datasets are given as Table 10.1.

Real-valued function $f(x)$:

$$f(x) = 0.2e^{-(10x-4)^2} + 0.5e^{-(80x-40)^2} + 0.3e^{-(80x-20)^2}, x \in [0, 1]. \tag{10.22}$$

The training dataset consists of 1000 samples, all the points of $x$ are generated from the uniform distribution on $[0, 1]$, while the test dataset with 300 samples which is generated from a regularly spaced grid over $[0, 1]$.

**Stock:** The dataset gives daily stock prices of ten aerospace companies from January 1988 through October 1991. It is used for

**Table 10.1.**   The attributes of four benchmark datasets.

| Datasets | Input Features | Output Variable | Instances |
| --- | --- | --- | --- |
| $f(x)$ | 1 | 1 | 1300 |
| Stock | 9 | 1 | 950 |
| Concrete | 8 | 1 | 1030 |
| Compactiv | 21 | 1 | 8192 |

estimating the stock price of the 10th company by using the prices of the other nine companies. The whole dataset contains 950 samples, each sample has nine input features and one output.

**Concrete:** This dataset is employed to predict concrete compressive strength. Concrete, as the most important material in civil engineering, its compressive strength is related to the ingredients, such as cement, blast furnace slag, fly ash, water, superplasticizer, coarse aggregate, fine aggregate and age. The whole dataset involves 1020 instances, each instance has 8 input vectors and one output vector.

**Computer Activity:** The computer activity dataset is a collection of computer systems activity measures which are used for prediction of the portion of time that CPUs run in user-mode.

The 8192 computer activities were collected from a computer workstation with 128 MB of memory running in a multi-user university department. Each data point has 21 input variables to evaluate computer activity.

To decrease the effects of difference scales of the features on model, normalization preprocessing method is applied to the input and output vectors. The original values can be converted into $[0, 1]$.

### 10.4.2   *Parameters and Evaluation Indicator*

The parameter settings of the CSSA-DSCN and CSSA-DSCNE are as follows. The population size (pop) is set to 20; producers' number $(PN)$ is set 4; scroungers' number $(pop - PN)$ is set to 16; maximum scouter's number $(SN_{\max})$ and minimum scouter's number $(SN_{\min})$ are set to 4 and 1 respectively; maximum iterations $(g_{\max})$ is set to 10; dimension $(D)$ is set to 2; the maximum number of candidate nodes $(T_{\max})$ is set to 200; tolerance error $(\varepsilon)$ is set to $1e - 3$; the maximum of hidden layers is set as 2; the number of CSSA-DSCN in CSSA-DSCNE model is set as 5; Some other parameters will be specified later, such as maximum number of hidden layer nodes ($L_{\max}$), the upper bound ($ub$) and lower bound ($lb$) of $r$ and $\lambda$. Otherwise, the sigmoidal function $S(x) = \frac{1}{1+e^{-x}}$ is selected as the activation function of CSSA-DSCN and CSSA-DSCNE.

To evaluate the accuracy of the proposed model, 75% instances of all three real-world datasets are chosen randomly as training data while the rest samples of datasets are selected as test set, root mean square error (RMSE) (10.23) is introduced as evaluation indicator, the smaller value of RMSE, the better regression accuracy the model.

$$\text{RMSE} = \sqrt{\frac{1}{N} \sum_{i=1}^{N} (y_i - p_i)^2}, \tag{10.23}$$

where $y_i$ describes the actual value of sample $i$ while $p_i$ indicates the predictive results of sample $i$; $N$ is the number of sample data, $p$ expresses the number of features.

### 10.4.3  *Main Results and Discussion*

To demonstrate the validity of optimized stochastic configuration network by chaotic sparrow search algorithm, we compare CSSA-DSCNE and CSSA-DSCN to modified quickprop (MQ) (Kwok and Yeung, 1997), incremental RVFL networks (IRVFL) (Li and Wang, 2017), SCN (Wang and Li, 2017b), each model runs 100 times independently and the average values and standard deviations of RMSE (10.23) are adopted to evaluate performance of the models.

Among them, the learning rate of MQ is set to 0.05 and the maximum number of iterations is given as 200; the weights and biases of IRVFL are generated from the uniform distribution over $[-1, 1]$; the $r$ and $\lambda$ of SCN and DSCN are determined from set $\{0.9, 0.99, 0.9999, 0.99999, 0.999999\}$ and $\{0.5, 1, 5, 10, 30, 50, 100, 150, 200, 250\}$ automatically; the maximum number of candidate nodes ($T_{\max}$) in SCN and DSCN are set to 200; the tolerance error ($\varepsilon$) of SCN and DSCN are set to $1e-3$; the maximum of hidden layers of DSCN is set as 2; In CSSA-DSCN, CSSA-DSCNE the upper bound (ub) and lower bound (lb) of $r$ are set as $0.9, 0.9999$ respectively, while the upper and lower bounds of $\lambda$ are $0.5, 250$.

The training and test results of MQ, IRVFL, SCN, CSSA-DSCN and CSSA-DSCNE on four datasets are given in Tables 10.2–10.5, in which $L_{\max}$ represents the maximum hidden nodes.

From Tables 10.2–10.5, in addition to the Stock dataset, the training results of the CSSA-DSCN is slightly worse than DSCN, but its test performance is significantly improved compared to DSCN. it is obvious that CSSA-DSCN outperforms MQ, IRVFL, SCN and DSCN in terms of both training and test results on real-valued function $f(x)$, Concrete and Computer Activity datasets.

At the same time, the CSSA-DSCNE model based on AdaBoost has optimal training results and test results on different datasets,

**Table 10.2.** Performance comparison of different algorithms on function $f(x)$.

| | Training results ↓ | | Test results ↓ | |
|---|---|---|---|---|
| Algorithms | $L_{\max} = 25$ | $L_{\max} = 50$ | $L_{\max} = 25$ | $L_{\max} = 50$ |
| MQ | $0.1031 \pm 0.0001$ | $0.1030 \pm 0.0001$ | $0.1011 \pm 0.0003$ | $0.1011 \pm 0.0003$ |
| IRVFL | $0.1630 \pm 0.0008$ | $0.1626 \pm 0.0005$ | $0.1622 \pm 0.0012$ | $0.1617 \pm 0.0008$ |
| SCN | $0.0392 \pm 0.0031$ | $0.0091 \pm 0.0034$ | $0.0392 \pm 0.0031$ | $0.0091 \pm 0.0034$ |
| DeepSCN | $0.0063 \pm 0.0030$ | $0.0009 \pm 0.0001$ | $0.0064 \pm 0.0030$ | $0.0009 \pm 0.0001$ |
| CSSA-DSCN | $0.0012 \pm 0.0005$ | $0.0008 \pm 0.0002$ | $0.0012 \pm 0.0005$ | $0.0008 \pm 0.0002$ |
| CSSA-DSCNE | $\mathbf{0.0006 \pm 0.0003}$ | $\mathbf{0.0001 \pm 0.0000}$ | $\mathbf{0.0006 \pm 0.0003}$ | $\mathbf{0.0001 \pm 0.0000}$ |

**Table 10.3.** Performance comparison of different algorithms on Stock dataset.

| | Training results ↓ | | Test results ↓ | |
|---|---|---|---|---|
| Algorithms | $L_{\max} = 25$ | $L_{\max} = 50$ | $L_{\max} = 25$ | $L_{\max} = 50$ |
| MQ | $0.0624 \pm 0.0058$ | $0.0410 \pm 0.0014$ | $0.0611 \pm 0.0061$ | $0.0407 \pm 0.0017$ |
| IRVFL | $0.2121 \pm 0.0260$ | $0.1853 \pm 0.0248$ | $0.2057 \pm 0.0268$ | $0.1787 \pm 0.0237$ |
| SCN | $0.0399 \pm 0.0010$ | $0.0309 \pm 0.0006$ | $0.0440 \pm 0.0013$ | $0.0374 \pm 0.0015$ |
| DeepSCN | $0.0308 \pm 0.0006$ | $0.0233 \pm 0.0005$ | $0.0356 \pm 0.0025$ | $0.0321 \pm 0.0027$ |
| CSSA-DSCN | $0.0308 \pm 0.0009$ | $0.0235 \pm 0.0004$ | $0.0337 \pm 0.0016$ | $0.0280 \pm 0.0012$ |
| CSSA-DSCNE | $\mathbf{0.0290 \pm 0.0003}$ | $\mathbf{0.0212 \pm 0.0003}$ | $\mathbf{0.0328 \pm 0.0008}$ | $\mathbf{0.0275 \pm 0.0005}$ |

**Table 10.4.** Performance comparison of different algorithms on Concrete dataset.

| | Training results ↓ | | Test results ↓ | |
|---|---|---|---|---|
| Algorithms | $L_{\max} = 25$ | $L_{\max} = 50$ | $L_{\max} = 25$ | $L_{\max} = 50$ |
| MQ | $0.1096 \pm 0.0042$ | $0.0910 \pm 0.0014$ | $0.0999 \pm 0.0048$ | $0.0869 \pm 0.0021$ |
| IRVFL | $0.2045 \pm 0.0189$ | $0.1929 \pm 0.0135$ | $0.2109 \pm 0.0214$ | $0.1983 \pm 0.0166$ |
| SCN | $0.0934 \pm 0.0013$ | $0.0789 \pm 0.0014$ | $0.0980 \pm 0.0019$ | $0.0904 \pm 0.0030$ |
| DeepSCN | $0.0786 \pm 0.0021$ | $0.0605 \pm 0.0016$ | $0.0895 \pm 0.0041$ | $0.0880 \pm 0.0086$ |
| CSSA-DSCN | $0.0775 \pm 0.0021$ | $0.0593 \pm 0.0015$ | $0.0873 \pm 0.0044$ | $0.0824 \pm 0.0055$ |
| CSSA-DSCNE | $\mathbf{0.0739 \pm 0.0010}$ | $\mathbf{0.0544 \pm 0.0006}$ | $\mathbf{0.0781 \pm 0.0019}$ | $\mathbf{0.0741 \pm 0.0016}$ |

**Table 10.5.** Performance comparison of different algorithms on Computer Activity dataset.

| Algorithms | Training results ↓ | | Test results ↓ | |
|---|---|---|---|---|
| | $L_{\max} = 25$ | $L_{\max} = 50$ | $L_{\max} = 25$ | $L_{\max} = 50$ |
| MQ | $0.0840 \pm 0.0052$ | $0.0600 \pm 0.0071$ | $0.0394 \pm 0.0016$ | $0.0624 \pm 0.0075$ |
| IRVFL | $0.2002 \pm 0.0391$ | $0.1924 \pm 0.0283$ | $0.1958 \pm 0.0386$ | $0.1882 \pm 0.0281$ |
| SCN | $0.0876 \pm 0.0069$ | $0.0386 \pm 0.0016$ | $0.0931 \pm 0.0079$ | $0.0429 \pm 0.0031$ |
| DeepSCN | $0.0331 \pm 0.0020$ | $0.0256 \pm 0.0005$ | $0.0364 \pm 0.0036$ | $0.0309 \pm 0.0049$ |
| CSSA-DSCN | $0.0304 \pm 0.0014$ | $0.0249 \pm 0.0005$ | $0.0318 \pm 0.0019$ | $0.0274 \pm 0.0009$ |
| CSSA-DSCNE | $\mathbf{0.0267 \pm 0.0004}$ | $\mathbf{0.0237 \pm 0.0003}$ | $\mathbf{0.0278 \pm 0.0006}$ | $\mathbf{0.0248 \pm 0.0003}$ |

and has a smaller standard deviation, which shows strong stability. Therefore, we may come to the conclusions that although the parameter optimization process of DSCN based on chaotic sparrow search algorithm may take some time, once the best parameters are decided, the optimized deep stochastic configuration network model which is first proposed in this chapter, however, it can not only helpful to enhance the regression accuracy of DSCN, but also has better training efficiency. Moreover, the generalization and stability performance of the CSSA-DSCN can be further improved by ensembel strategy of AdaBoost.

## 10.5  Summary

This chapter proposes a chaotic sparrow search algorithm-based deep stochastic configuration networks ensemble model, named CSSA-DSCNE, for increasing the regression performance of DSCN in solving large-scale data problems. To improve the optimization ability, logistic mapping, self-adaptive hyper-parameters and mutation operator are employed to the sparrow search algorithm. Then, random parameters selection of DSCN, optimized by chaotic sparrow search algorithm, guarantee the regression accuracy of the CSSA-DSCN model. Moreover, to enhance the generalization performance of CSSA-DSCN, AdaBoost method is employed to construct the deep stochastic configuration networks ensemble model via chaotic sparrow search algorithm, named as CSSA-DSCNE. Numerous experiments are used to verify the performance of CSSA-DSCN and CSSA-DSCNE. Finally, the performance evaluation in a realvalued function and three KEEL datasets, the DSCN model, with optimized parameters by CSSA and AdaBoost, has been proved of outstanding performance compared with DSCN, SCN and other contrast algorithms.

In future work, firstly, as the parameter selection process of CSSA-DSCNE wastes a lot of computation time, simplify CSSA will be the focus of our research to reduce computational time. Secondly, classification problems are also valuable in the current study, CSSA-DSCNE will be used to solve these kind of problems for obtaining a higher classification accuracy.

Chapter 11

# Deep Stochastic Configuration Networks Ensemble via Boosting Negative Correlation Learning

Deep stochastic configuration networks (DSCNs) employ data-dependent supervision mechanism to randomly assign node parameters and incrementally construct the deep neural network structure, thereby ensuring the model's universal approximation property (UAP). To build a random neural networks ensemble model with better generalization performance, we propose a novel greedy deep stochastic configuration networks ensemble model based on boosting negative correlation learning, termed as GDSCNE. Firstly, greedy optimization strategy based on inequality constraints is utilized to generate random parameters of base components with multi-layer architecture, which can accelerate the decline of network residuals when configuring a new node. Additionally, boosting negative correlation learning framework is presented for the base components ensemble process, which uses least square approach with negative correlation learning penalty term to update the ensemble output weights for each base component, subsequently, boosting method is applied to construct a stronger ensemble model by adaptive weighting through the results of base components. Finally, we evaluated GDSCNE on the popular regression benchmark datasets from the KEEL, experimental results demonstrate that GDSCNE outperforms state-of-the-art random learning algorithms in terms of

229

regression accuracy and generalization performance across several regression datasets with varying sizes.


## 11.1    Introduction

Nowadays, various parameter optimization strategies have been used in the SCNs and DSCNs to enhance the performance of single learner. Chaotic sparrow search algorithm (CSSA) and beetle antennae search algorithm were applied to select the optimal random parameter scopes and contraction factor respectively (Zhang and Ding, 2021; Zhang *et al.*, 2021a). Wang *et al.* (2023) presented a regularized stochastic configuration network and utilized the weighted mean of vectors (INFO) to optimize hyper-parameters. Chen *et al.* (2022) used variational mode decomposition (VMD) for feature extraction from non-stationary time series, while employed an improved whale optimization algorithm (IWOA) to determine the number of input dimensions, maximum number of neurons and candidate parameters. Furthermore, Zhou *et al.* (2023) proposed a novel greedy stochastic configuration network (GSCN), which utilized hunter-prey optimization (HPO) algorithm to assign input weights and biases. Wu *et al.* (2022a) employed improved sparrow search algorithm (ISSA) to select input parameters of all nodes under the supervision mechanism of SCN at one time. Felicetti and Wang (2022b) utilized Monte-Carlo tree search (MCTS) and random search strategy to get suitable hyper-parameters of DSCN, and Felicetti and Wang (2022a) simultaneously demonstrated superiority of random parameters based on normal distribution and logistic distribution. Otherwise, to address prediction intervals problem regarding carbon residual in crude oil analysis, Lu and Ding (2019a) combined lower-upper bound estimation method with DSCNs, and designed a modified backtracking search optimization algorithm (MBSA) to determine optimal prediction intervals.

Compared to single SCN-based models, ensemble models have better generalization performance by combining multiple SCNs through ensemble learning algorithms. At present, the ensemble models based on SCNs mainly employ bagging, boosting, stacking, negative correlation learning (NCL), etc. Among them, bagging models usually employ bootstrap approach to generate sub-training data and training several SCN-based models independently, the ensemble results of bagging models can be calculated by voting or averaging method (Guo *et al.*, 2022; Jiao *et al.*, 2023; Qu *et al.*, 2019). Similar to above SCN-based bagging models, Dai *et al.* (2024) presented a cloud oversampling approach to expand the training samples, and designed a cloud ensemble learning model via voting method with SCNs. Lu and Ding (2019b); Lu *et al.* (2021) adopted bootstrap ensemble method to the prediction intervals construction of the target variables, moreover, bootstrap was employed to generate sub-training data for base SCNs, the output weights of ensemble model are updated through simultaneous robust training method (Lu *et al.*, 2020). Meanwhile, boosting models adopt adaptive weighting strategies to update the ensemble weights of each base learner for the calculation of final results, which can effectively improve the generalization of the models (Guo *et al.*, 2022; Jiao *et al.*, 2023). To improve the robustness of SCN, Qu *et al.* (2019) combined bootstrap and boosting methods to construct ensemble model, different from the other boosting models, boosting was applied in the node configuration process. Otherwise, Pratama and Wang (2019) designed deep stacked stochastic configuration networks (DSSCNs), which simplify data stream learning and automatically construct the deep stack network structure based on the data stream. Additionally, Huang *et al.* (2021) proposed a novel ensemble method for stochastic configuration networks, which can select some better models from the pool of candidates to improve the performance of ensemble model.

Unlike bagging, boosting and stacking models, the bias-variance-covariance decomposition method can be employed to identify an ensemble model with minimal covariance among the base learners (Rosen, 1996). Negative correlation learning is commonly used in neural network ensembles to control the trade-off between bias, variance, and covariance through a penalty term (Liu and Yao, 1999; Zhang *et al.*, 2019b). Alhamdoosh and Wang (2014) presented a negative correlation learning model using random weights for the first time, in which the input parameters of base networks are generated randomly, the output weights of ensemble model were calculated using least square method with negative correlation learning scheme . Moreover, to address large-scale data problems, Wang and Li (2017b) proposed ensemble framework with heterogeneous feature based on SCNs, which utilized negative correlation learning to determine the output weights of the heterogeneous feature ensemble model. Although negative correlation learning scheme can trade-off among the bias, variance and covariance in the random neural networks ensemble learning, deep neural networks ensemble with optimized parameters can further improve the model performance (Zhang *et al.*, 2016). Besides, boosting approach can be employed to construct a stronger model by weighting the results of base learners instead of averaging operation (Gao *et al.*, 2010).

To sum up, although negative correlation learning scheme can trade-off among the bias, variance and covariance in the random neural networks ensemble learning, ensemble models based on SCNs utilize inequality constraints without optimization to determine input parameters of base learners may overlook some superior parameters. Moreover, deep neural networks ensemble with multi-layer structure and optimized parameters can further improve the model performance (Zhang *et al.*, 2016). Besides, boosting approach can be employed to construct a stronger model by weighting the results of base learners instead of averaging operationGao *et al.* (2010). Therefore, in this paper, to construct a better generalized ensemble model, we proposed a novel greedy deep stochastic configuration networks ensemble model based on boosting negative correlation learning, termed GDSCNE.

In a word, the major contributions of proposed GDSCNE are listed as follows:

- We present a novel deep stochastic configuration networks ensemble model which using boosting negative correlation learning and greedy optimization strategy.
- We use greedy optimization strategy based on the data-dependent inequality constraints to configure the input weights and biases of the base models with deep architecture, which can accelerate the reduction of network residual errors when adding a new node.
- We combine negative correlation learning with boosting method to construct an adaptive weighted ensemble model and calculate the ensemble output results.

## 11.2  Preliminaries

### 11.2.1  *Generalization Performance of Ensemble Learning*

It is assumed that $V = \{\tilde{X}, \tilde{Y}\}$ represents the validation data, $\tilde{X} = \{\tilde{x}_1, \tilde{x}_2, \ldots, \tilde{x}_{\tilde{N}}\}$ denotes the feature of validation data; $\tilde{Y} = \{\tilde{y}_1, \tilde{y}_2, \ldots, \tilde{y}_{\tilde{N}}\}$ indicates the label of validation data; $\tilde{N}$ is sample size of validation data.

The generalization error of an ensemble model $\bar{f}$ can be described as Eq. (11.1):

$$E_f(V) = E_D \left\{ \frac{1}{\tilde{N}} \sum_{i=1}^{\tilde{N}} \left( \bar{f}(\tilde{x}_i; D) - \tilde{y}_i \right)^2 \right\}, \tag{11.1}$$

$$\bar{f}(\tilde{x}_i; D) = \frac{1}{K} \sum_{k=1}^{K} f_k(\tilde{x}_i; D), \tag{11.2}$$

where $E_D\{\cdot\}$ indicates the expectation about the random sequence distribution $D$; $\bar{f}(\tilde{x}_i; D)$ represents the ensemble output of $\tilde{x}_i$ under the training dataset $D = \{X, Y\}$.

Bagging or Boosting aims at minimizing the errors of each base learner, while the generalization capacity of ensemble learning can be formulated as in Theorem 11.1.

**Theorem 11.1 Ueda and Nakano (1996):** *The generalization error of ensemble learning as Eq. 11.1 can be decomposed into bias/variance/covariance form as Eq. (11.3):*

$$E_{\bar{f}}(V) = \frac{1}{\tilde{N}} \sum_{i=1}^{\tilde{N}} \frac{1}{K} \overline{\mathrm{Var}}(\tilde{x}_i)$$

$$+ \frac{1}{\tilde{N}} \sum_{i=1}^{\tilde{N}} \frac{K-1}{K} \overline{\mathrm{Cov}}(\tilde{x}_i) + \frac{1}{\tilde{N}} \sum_{i=1}^{\tilde{N}} \overline{\mathrm{Bias}}(\tilde{x}_i)^2, \tag{11.3}$$

$$\overline{\mathrm{Var}}(\tilde{x}_i) = \frac{1}{K} \sum_{k=1}^{K} E_D\{(f_k - E_D\{f_k\})^2\}, \tag{11.4}$$

$$\overline{\mathrm{Cov}}(\tilde{x}_i) = \frac{1}{K(K-1)}$$

$$\sum_{k=1}^{K}\sum_{j \neq k} E_D\left\{\left(f_k - E_D\{f_k\}\right)\left(f_j - E_D\{f_j\}\right)\right\}, \tag{11.5}$$

$$\overline{\mathrm{Bias}}(\tilde{x}_i) = \frac{1}{K}\sum_{k=1}^{K}\left(E_D\{f_k\} - \tilde{y}_i\right), \tag{11.6}$$

*where $\overline{\mathrm{Var}}(\tilde{x}_i)$, $\overline{\mathrm{Bias}}(\tilde{x}_i)$ are the mean value of individual variances and biases, respectively, managing the covariance term $\overline{\mathrm{Cov}}(\tilde{x}_i)$ explicitly helps control the disagreement among ensemble components' outputs and constructs an better ensemble model.*

### 11.2.2  *Negative Correlation Learning*

Generally, the bagging-based and boosting-based ensemble models aim to minimize the training errors of base components, which overlook the interplay between bias, variance, and covariance (Liu and Yao, 1999; Rosen, 1996).

However, researches show that ensemble models with minimum covariance can retain the optimal performance of base learners. Negative correlation learning (NCL) frame adopts cost function with a penalty term to control the trade-off among bias, variance, and covariance and weakens the relationship with other individuals as Eq. (11.7) (Alhamdoosh and Wang, 2014; Wang and Li, 2017b):

$$E_k = \sum_{i=1}^{N}\left(\frac{1}{2}(f_k(x_i) - y_i)^2 - \gamma p_k(x_i)\right), \tag{11.7}$$

where $\gamma$ indicates a regularization parameter; $p_k$ represents a penalty term which can be set according to the need.

## 11.3  Methodology

### 11.3.1  *Issues and Motivations*

It is well known that the generalization performance of ensemble models is particularly relevant to base components and ensemble approaches. However, the current neural networks ensemble models based on SCNs mainly have two drawbacks: Firstly, existing ensemble models often utilize original inequality constraints to configure node parameters of base components, which may overlook some superior parameters; Secondly, ensemble models consisted of single-hidden layer base learners cannot acquire rich feature representation. As neural networks ensemble with deep framework and suitable parameters can obtain better generalization, hence, this part aims at developing a novel deep ensemble model based on DSCNs with optimal parameters for solving regression problems. In the first place, greedy searching strategy is adopted to configure more suitable input weights and biases of nodes in each layer, which can reduce network residual errors more efficiently; moreover, a boosting negative correlation learning approach for regression is demonstrated for GDSCN to improve the generalization performance and regression accuracy. The overview of the proposed GDSCNE framework is presented as Fig. 11.1.

### 11.3.2 *Parameter Configuration Through Greedy Searching Strategy*

The constructive process of DSCNs mainly use data-dependent inequality constraints to select suitable node parameters in each layer. According to the stochastic configuration theory (Dai *et al.*, 2021; Wang and Li, 2018): A larger value of $\xi_{L_n}^n$ can accelerate the current network residual reduction, however, only using random parameter generation mode may overlook some superior parameters that can reduce network residual errors more efficiently. In this section, as a greedy optimization strategy has demonstrated the excellent performance in parameter selection of SCNs (Zhou *et al.*, 2023), the input parameters of base models are randomly generated through greedy searching strategy firstly.

Assuming that DSCNs with $n - 1$ layers and $L_{n-1}$ nodes have already been constructed, the network residual errors of DSCNs can be expressed as Eq. (11.8) when adding a new node in the next layer $n$:

$$e_1^n = Y - f_1^n = Y - f_{L_{n-1}}^{n-1} - h_1^n \beta_1^n = e_{L_{n-1}}^{n-1} - h_1^n \beta_1^n. \qquad (11.8)$$

Meanwhile, supposed that DSCNs with $n$ layer and $L_n - 1$ nodes have been configured, Eq. (11.9) presents the network residual errors

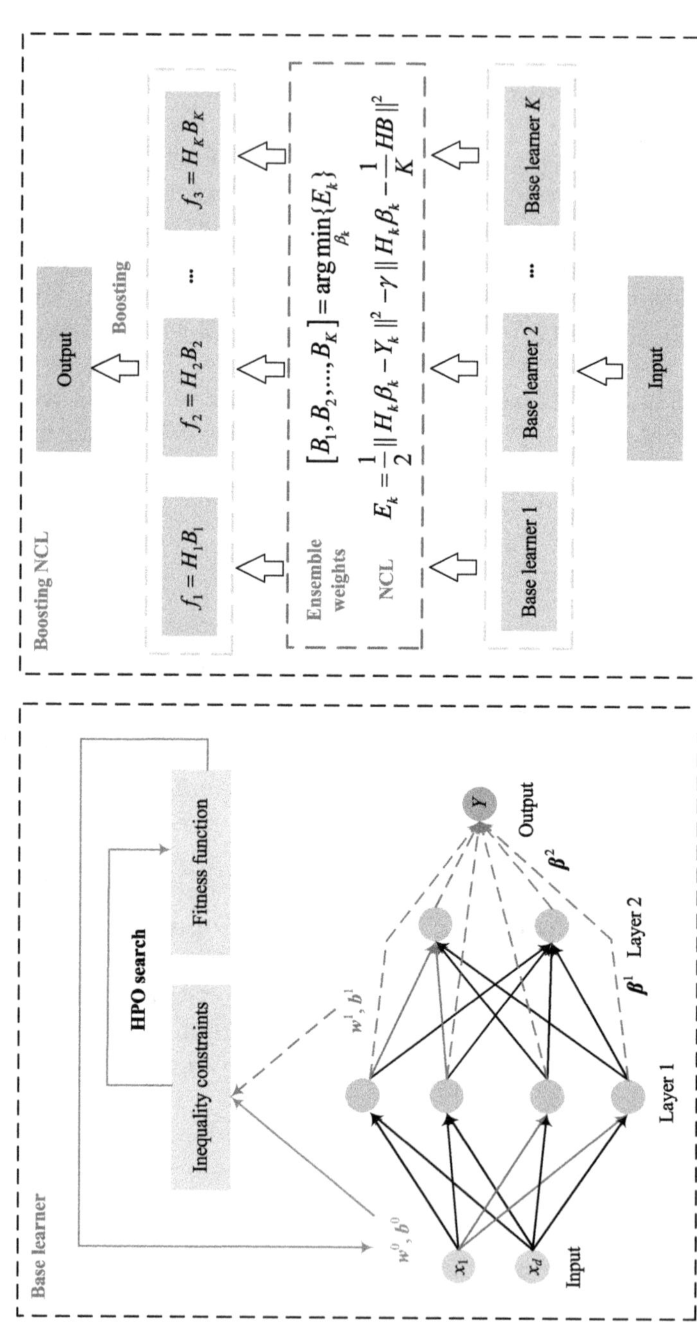



**Fig. 11.1.** The framework of proposed GDSCNE. (a) On the left side, we use greedy optimization based on the data-dependent supervision mechanism to assign node parameters of base models. (b) On the right side, boosting negative correlation learning is utilized to construct a stronger decorrelated ensemble model.

of DSCNs when adding a new node $L_n$ in the same layer $n$:

$$e_{L_n}^n = Y - f_{L_n-1}^n = Y - f_{L_n-1}^n - h_{L_n}^n \beta_{L_n}^n = e_{L_n-1}^n - h_{L_n}^n \beta_{L_n}^n. \tag{11.9}$$

According to the network residual errors as Eqs. (11.8) and (11.9), we can come to the following conclusions as Eqs. (11.11) and (11.11):

$$\begin{aligned} \|e_1^n\|^2 &= \langle e_{L_{n-1}}^{n-1} - h_1^n \beta_1^n, e_{L_{n-1}}^{n-1} - h_1^n \beta_1^n \rangle \\ &= \langle e_{L_{n-1}}^{n-1}, e_{L_{n-1}}^{n-1} \rangle - \frac{\langle e_{L_{n-1}}^{n-1}, h_1^n \rangle}{\langle h_1^n, h_1^n \rangle}. \end{aligned} \tag{11.10}$$

$$\begin{aligned} \|e_{L_n}^n\|^2 &= \langle e_{L_n-1}^n - h_{L_n}^n \beta_{L_n}^n, e_{L_n-1}^n - h_{L_n}^n \beta_{L_n}^n \rangle \\ &= \langle e_{L_n-1}^n, e_{L_n-1}^n \rangle - \frac{\langle e_{L_n-1}^n, h_{L_n}^n \rangle}{\langle h_{L_n}^n, h_{L_n}^n \rangle}. \end{aligned} \tag{11.11}$$

Therefore, to reduce the current residual errors to the greatest extent, we can generate weights and biases of node 1 and node $L_n$ in the layer $n$ randomly, then use greedy searching strategy to get the suitable parameters, the fitness functions of greedy searching can be defined as Eqs. (11.12) and (11.13):

$$\begin{aligned} Fit_1 = \langle e_{L_{n-1}}^{n-1}, e_{L_{n-1}}^{n-1} \rangle &- \frac{\langle e_{L_{n-1}}^{n-1}, h_1^n \rangle^2}{\langle h_1^n, h_1^n \rangle} \\ &+ \eta(L_1)(\|w_1^n\|^2 + \|b_1^n\|^2), \end{aligned} \tag{11.12}$$

$$\begin{aligned} Fit_2 = \langle e_{L_n-1}^n, e_{L_n-1}^n \rangle &- \frac{\langle e_{L_n-1}^n, h_{L_n}^n \rangle^2}{\langle h_{L_n}^n, h_{L_n}^n \rangle} \\ &+ \eta(L_n)(\|w_{L_n}^n\|^2 + \|b_{L_n}^n\|^2), \end{aligned} \tag{11.13}$$

where $Fit_1$ and $Fit_2$ are consisted of network residual errors and regularization terms for adding a new node in the new layer and same layer respectively, $\eta(\cdot)$ demonstrates a step function with positive range.

As HPO has shown excellent performance in parameter optimization of SCN Zhou *et al.* (2023), we choose HPO to assign the parameters of base learners of ensemble model, the flowchart of the parameter configuration process with greedy searching strategy is demonstrated as follows:

(1) The input weights and biases of the new node are initialized from a uniform distribution over $[-\lambda, \lambda]^d$ and $[-\lambda, \lambda]$ respectively;

(2) We use Eq. 11.11 to calculate the network residual errors and Eq. 11.12 is adopted as the fitness function of HPO when adding a new node in the new layer $n$. When adding a new node $L_n$ in the layer $n$, we use Eqs. 11.11 and 11.13 to calculate the network residual errors and fitness value of HPO;

(3) The iterative process for searching the node parameters that satisfy $\xi_{L_n,j}^n \geq 0$ will continue until reaching the maximum number of iterations, $T_{\max}$, as described in HPO;

(4) Select $P_{\text{best}}$ with the best fitness value as the parameter of the new node, then greedy searching the parameters of next node until meet the preset conditions of base learners.

(5) In the last, we combine the output of each layer $H_k = [H^1, H^2, \ldots, H^n]$ for the model ensembles.

**Remark 11.1.** In this part, the input parameters of base learners can be assigned by greedy optimization based on the data-dependent supervision mechanism proposed by Professor Wang (Wang and Li, 2017b, 2018), which ensures universal approximation property of base learner. However, greedy configuration optimization strategy with point increment mode has higher computational complexity compared with original supervision mechanism, which affects the computational efficiency when applied to very large datasets or highly complex network architectures. In addition, this part aims to present a parameter optimization strategy for DSCNs, the swarm intelligence optimization algorithm selection and improvement is not focus of our research.

### 11.3.3  *Boosting Negative Correlation Learning*

Negative correlation learning (NCL) have been employed to control the trade-off between bias, variance, and covariance through a penalty term for RVFLs-based ensemble model and SCNs-based ensemble model (Alhamdoosh and Wang, 2014; Wang and Li, 2017b). To get a better GDSCNE model, a boosting negative correlation ensemble method is demonstrated, the boosting negative correlation ensemble learning process can be divided into the determination of ensemble output weights $[B_1, B_2, \ldots, B_K]$, and the adaptive boosting construction of stronger ensemble model.

First of all, as the initial weights and biases of base components are determined by greedy searching, assuming that the number of base learners is set as $K$, the proposed GDSCNE model aims to minimize the cost function $E_k$, the $[B_1, B_2, \ldots, B_K]$ of ensemble learning can be obtained by minimizing the training errors of each base learner as Eq. (11.14) (Alhamdoosh and Wang, 2014; Wang and Li, 2017b):

$$[B_1, B_2, \ldots, B_K] = \arg\min_{B_k} \{E_k\}, \quad k = 1, 2, \ldots, K. \tag{11.14}$$

Among them, the cost function $E_k$ of the base learner $k$ can be demonstrated as Eq. (11.15) (Alhamdoosh and Wang, 2014; Wang and Li, 2017b):

$$E_k = \frac{1}{2}||H_k\beta_k - Y||^2 - \gamma\left\|H_k\beta_k - \frac{1}{K}HB\right\|^2, \tag{11.15}$$

where $H_k$ is denoted as the output of base learner $k$; $\beta_k$ indicates the original output weights of base learner $k$, $Y$ is the training label; $0 < \gamma < 1$ represents the regularization parameter; $H = [H_1, H_2, \ldots, H_K]_{N \times L}$ is denoted as the outputs of ensemble model; $L$ denotes the whole number of the nodes in each learners.

Negative correlation learning ensemble model will obtain optimal performance when the cost function gradient in Eq. (11.15) vanishes concerning the output weights. Therefore, the cost function $E_k$ of ensemble framework can be solved as Alhamdoosh and Wang (2014); Wang and Li (2017b):

By taking the partial derivative of the cost function $E_k$ as Eq. (11.16):

$$\frac{\partial E_k}{\partial \beta_k} = c_1 H_k^T H_k \beta_k + c_2 H_k^T \hat{H}_k B - H_k^T Y_k = 0, \tag{11.16}$$

where $c_1$ and $c_2$ are two constants as Eq. (11.17); $\hat{H}_k = [H_1, \ldots, H_{k-1}, 0_{N \times L}, H_{k+1}, \ldots, H_K]$.

$$c_1 = 1 - \frac{2\gamma(K-1)^2}{K^2}, \quad c_2 = \frac{2\gamma(K-1)^2}{K^2}. \tag{11.17}$$

According to Eq. (11.16), we can get a huge system of linear equations as Eq. (11.18):

$$\mathbb{H}B = H^T Y, \tag{11.18}$$

$$\mathbb{H} = \begin{bmatrix} c_1 H_1{}^T H_1 & c_2 H_1{}^T H_2 & \cdots & c_2 H_1{}^T H_K \\ c_2 H_2{}^T H_1 & c_1 H_2{}^T H_2 & \cdots & c_2 H_2{}^T H_K \\ \vdots & \vdots & \ddots & \vdots \\ c_2 H_K{}^T H_1 & c_2 H_K{}^T H_2 & \cdots & c_1 H_K{}^T H_K \end{bmatrix}. \tag{11.19}$$

Then, we can use pseudo-inverse to calculate the output weights $B = [B_1, B_2, \ldots, B_K]$ of base learners as Eq. (11.20):

$$B = \mathbb{H}^\dagger H^T Y, \tag{11.20}$$

where $\mathbb{H}^\dagger$ expresses the pseudo-inverse of the matrix $\mathbb{H}$.

In addition, to enhance generalization performance of base learners and ensemble model, regularization strategies are adopted in least squares models to avoid over-fitting (Ding *et al.*, 2023). We can modify the objective function by introducing a regularization parameter $C$, the output weights of base learners and ensemble output weights can be obtained as Eqs. (11.21) and (11.22):

$$\beta_k = (H_k^T H_k + CI)^{-1} H_k^T Y. \tag{11.21}$$

$$B = (\mathbb{H}^T \mathbb{H} + CI)^{-1} \mathbb{H} H^T Y. \tag{11.22}$$

According to the above process, we can obtain the ensemble output weights $[B_1, B_2, \ldots, B_K]$ for each base learners, the original learning method is to calculate the average outputs of base learners based on Eq. (11.23):

$$f_k = H_k B_k, \tag{11.23}$$

Furthermore, to construct a stronger ensemble deep model, boosting, as a classical ensemble learning method is employed to calculate the outputs through the outputs of each base learner. Hence, the boosting process is described as follows (Gao *et al.*, 2010):

Generate the initial weights of each sample by using Eq. (11.24):

$$\omega_k = [\omega_{k,1}, \omega_{k,2}, \ldots, \omega_{k,N}], \quad \omega_{k,i} = \frac{1}{N}, \tag{11.24}$$

where $k = 1, 2, \ldots, K$, $K$ denotes the total number of base models; $i = 1, 2, \ldots, N$, $N$ represents the number of samples.

Using Eq. (11.25) to compute the weighted loss $\varsigma_k$ of $f_k$, and update the distribution weights of each sample through Eq. (11.26):

$$\varsigma_k = \sum_{i=1}^{N} \frac{\omega_{k,i}}{\sum_{i=1}^{N} \omega_{k,i}} [|Y_i - f_{k,i}| > \mu], \qquad (11.25)$$

$$\omega_{k+1,i} = \begin{cases} \omega_{k,i} \times e^{-\alpha_k}, & \text{if } |Y_i - f_{k,i}| < \mu \\ \omega_{k,i} \times e^{\alpha_k}, & \text{if } |Y_i - f_{k,i}| \geq \mu, \end{cases} \qquad (11.26)$$

where $\alpha_k$ defines the weight of base learner $k$ which can be determined by Eq. 11.27; $\mu$ expresses a error threshold which is applied to reduce the negative effects of base learners.

The adaptive weights of base learners can be determined by Eq. (11.27), then we can construct a stronger ensemble model by using Eq. (11.28):

$$\alpha_k = \frac{1}{2} \ln \left( \frac{1 - \varsigma_k}{\varsigma_k} \right), \qquad (11.27)$$

$$f = \frac{\sum_{k=1}^{K} \alpha_k f_k}{\sum_{k=1}^{K} \alpha_k}, \qquad (11.28)$$

where $f$ denotes the outputs of boosting negative correlation learning ensemble model.

### 11.3.4 *Theoretical Analysis*

#### 11.3.4.1 *Generalization Performance Analysis*

The generalization performance of ensemble model is closely related to the base leaners, as Professor Wang has demonstrated the universal approximation property of SCNs and DeepSCNs with data-dependent supervision mechanism (Wang and Li, 2017b, 2018), the input parameters of GDSCNE are assigned by greedy optimization based on the supervision mechanism which can ensure the universal approximation property of base learner. Moreover, using negative correlation learning (NCL) to balance the trade-off of variance and bias, reduce the covariance of base leaners can get an ensemble model with better generalization performance (Alhamdoosh and Wang, 2014; Liu and Yao, 1999; Rosen, 1996; Wang and Li, 2017b; Zhang *et al.*, 2019b). Besides, we combine negative correlation learning

(NCL) with boosting regression method, the introduction of boosting regression method can further improve the generalization of the model (Gao *et al.*, 2010). In addition, $L_2$ regularization strategy is employed to avoid over-fitting and ill-conditioned problems (Ding *et al.*, 2023).

### 11.3.4.2 *Computational Complexity Analysis*

Suppose that $N$ denotes the number of training samples; $L_s$ indicates the number of each base learner; $K$ is the number of base leaners. As the main computational demands of GDSCNE is used to calculate the output weights of base leaners and ensemble model by singular value decomposition (SVD), the base leaner of GDSCNE employs greedy configuration optimization strategy with point increment mode, the computational complexity of base learners can be expressed as $O(\sum_{L=1}^{L_s} L \times N^2)$, therefore, the computational complexity of simpler ensemble methods with $K$ base leaners can be demonstrated as $O(K \times \sum_{L=1}^{L_s} L \times N^2)$, while as the negative correlation learning frame still need singular value decomposition (SVD) method to determine the ensemble output weights, the computational complexity of negative correlation learning frame is $O((K \times L_s)^3)$, hence, the total computational complexity of GDSCNE can be illustrated as $O(K \times \sum_{L=1}^{L_s} L \times N^2 + (K \times L_s)^3)$.

**Remark 11.2.** In the proposed GDSCNE, we use boosting regression method and $L_2$ regularization strategy to avoid over-fitting and ill-conditioned problems for solving regression questions (Ding *et al.*, 2023; Gao *et al.*, 2010). However, in practical industrial process, the acquired data may be contaminated by various levels of noise, the corresponding training error will seriously deviate from the normal error when we use least squares approach to determine the output weights for minimizing training errors, robust techniques can be introduced to the GDSCNE framework to deal with noise problems (Li *et al.*, 2019b; Wang and Li, 2017a).

## 11.4   Experimental Results and Discussion

In this section, to demonstrate the regression accuracy of the GDSCNE model, we compare GDSCNE with some state-of-the-art

**Table 11.1.** The attributes of benchmark datasets.

| Datasets | Input features | Instances |
|---|---|---|
| ANACALT | 7 | 4052 |
| MV | 10 | 40768 |
| Elevators | 18 | 16599 |
| Compactiv | 21 | 8192 |
| Pole | 26 | 14998 |
| Puma32h | 32 | 8192 |

random neural networks on several popular benchmark regression datasets. The related experimental codes of compared algorithm are programed based on MATLAB 2017b (PC with Intel (R) Core (TM) i7-12700 2.10 GHz CPU, NVIDIA GPU RTX3050 and 32 GB RAM).

### 11.4.1 *Experimental Settings*

#### 11.4.1.1 *Benchmark Datasets*

To verify the performance of GDSCNE, we select several benchmark regression datasets from the Knowledge Extraction based on Evolutionary Learning (KEEL),[1] include ANACALT, MV, Elevators, Compactiv, Pole and Puma32h. Table 11.1 presents the attributes information of the experimental datasets. Meanwhile, we employ normalization method to normalize the input and output of the datasets obtained from KEEL into the range of $[0, 1]$. Then, we randomly choose 75% of the data samples as the training datasets, while the rest are selected as the test datasets.

#### 11.4.1.2 *Parameter settings*

To demonstrate the regression performance of the proposed GDSCNE model, we choose IRVFL (Inremental version of RVFLN) (Li and Wang, 2017), RVFLN (Pao *et al.*, 1994; Pao and Take-fuji, 1992), DRVFL (Deep version of RVFLN) (Cecotti, 2016), SCN

---

[1]http://www.keel.es/.

(Wang and Li, 2017b), DSCN (Wang and Li, 2018), GSCN (Zhou *et al.*, 2023), BSCN (SCN based on sparse feature mappings) (Zhang *et al.*, 2022b) and SCNE (Wang and Li, 2017b) as the contrast algorithms.

Among them, we employ sigmoidal function $S(x) = 1/(1 + e^{-x})$ as activation function of all models; The deep models (DRVFL, DSCN and GDSCNE) adopt two hidden layers, the number of nodes in each layer are chosen from $\{25, 50, 75, 100\}$ for all deep and single layer models; For avoiding the over-fitting phenomenon of random neural networks, except for the IRVFL, we use $L_2$ regularization approach to calculate the output weights, and the regularization parameters are selected from $\{2^{-20}, 2^{-18}, \ldots, 2^{18}, 2^{20}\}$; The $T_{\max}$ of SCN, DSCN, GSCN, BSCN, SCNE and GDSCNE are set as 20; The parameter scope $\lambda$ of SCN, DSCN, BSCN and SCNE are chosen from $\{0.5, 1, 5, 10, 30, 50, 100, 150, 200\}$ and the shrinkage factor $r$ are selected from the set $\{0.9, 0.99, 0.999, 0.9999, 0.99999, 0.999999\}$ adaptively. As greedy optimization method can generate parameters iteratively, the shrinkage factor $r$ and the parameter scope $\lambda$ are set with fixed values for reduce the training time, the number of agents is set as 30.

Then, we run each algorithm 20 times, and the mean values and standard deviations (STD) of root mean square error ($RMSE$), mean square error ($MSE$), mean absolute error ($MAE$), $R$-squared ($R^2$) are recorded as the final results.

### 11.4.2 *Main Results and Discussion*

In this section, we present the performance evaluation of GDSCNE with three components. The test results, including the average $RMSE$, $MSE$, $MAE$ and $R^2$ values of GDSCNE in comparison with various models across six different sizes of regression datasets are presented in Tables 11.2–11.7. Among them, the smaller of $RMSE$, $MSE$, $MAE$, and the lager of $R^2$ can demonstrate the regression performance of models.

As can be seen from the Tables 11.2–11.7, the proposed GDSCNE gains the optimal average test RMSE, test $MSE$, test $MAE$ and test $R^2$ results compared with other models. Hence, the experimental results demonstrate that the proposed GDSCNE with greedy optimization method and boosting negative correlation learning can

**Table 11.2.** Performance comparison of all models on the ANACALT dataset.

| Models | Test RMSE | Test MSE | Test MAE | Test $R^2$ |
| --- | --- | --- | --- | --- |
| IRVFL | $2.17e\text{-}01 \pm 1.60e\text{-}02$ | $4.75e\text{-}02 \pm 7.23e\text{-}03$ | $1.45e\text{-}01 \pm 1.18e\text{-}02$ | $1.94e\text{-}01 \pm 1.20e\text{-}01$ |
| RVFLN | $9.90e\text{-}02 \pm 6.00e\text{-}03$ | $9.80e\text{-}03 \pm 1.20e\text{-}03$ | $7.20e\text{-}02 \pm 2.20e\text{-}03$ | $8.31e\text{-}01 \pm 2.23e\text{-}02$ |
| SCN | $7.73e\text{-}02 \pm 1.89e\text{-}02$ | $6.32e\text{-}03 \pm 3.85e\text{-}03$ | $3.43e\text{-}02 \pm 3.13e\text{-}03$ | $8.88e\text{-}01 \pm 7.15e\text{-}02$ |
| DRVFL | $8.54e\text{-}02 \pm 2.68e\text{-}02$ | $8.00e\text{-}03 \pm 6.10e\text{-}03$ | $4.93e\text{-}02 \pm 2.40e\text{-}03$ | $8.60e\text{-}01 \pm 9.09e\text{-}02$ |
| DSCN | $6.39e\text{-}02 \pm 1.33e\text{-}02$ | $4.25e\text{-}03 \pm 1.77e\text{-}03$ | $2.92e\text{-}02 \pm 4.18e\text{-}03$ | $9.25e\text{-}01 \pm 3.21e\text{-}02$ |
| BSCN | $7.58e\text{-}02 \pm 1.65e\text{-}02$ | $6.00e\text{-}03 \pm 2.08e\text{-}03$ | $1.76e\text{-}02 \pm 1.07e\text{-}03$ | $8.97e\text{-}01 \pm 3.62e\text{-}02$ |
| GSCN | $3.92e\text{-}02 \pm 6.30e\text{-}03$ | $1.60e\text{-}03 \pm 5.08e\text{-}04$ | $1.72e\text{-}02 \pm 2.60e\text{-}03$ | $9.72e\text{-}01 \pm 7.60e\text{-}03$ |
| SCNE | $6.78e\text{-}02 \pm 1.33e\text{-}02$ | $4.77e\text{-}03 \pm 1.94e\text{-}03$ | $3.22e\text{-}02 \pm 3.33e\text{-}03$ | $9.19e\text{-}01 \pm 3.02e\text{-}02$ |
| GDSCNE | $\mathbf{3.42e\text{-}02 \pm 5.30e\text{-}03}$ | $\mathbf{1.20e\text{-}03 \pm 3.85e\text{-}04}$ | $\mathbf{1.05e\text{-}02 \pm 9.83e\text{-}04}$ | $\mathbf{9.78e\text{-}01 \pm 7.00e\text{-}03}$ |

**Table 11.3.** Performance comparison of all models on the MV dataset.

| Models | Test RMSE | Test MSE | Test MAE | Test $R^2$ |
|---|---|---|---|---|
| IRVFL | $1.73\text{e-}01 \pm 2.76\text{e-}02$ | $3.07\text{e-}02 \pm 9.74\text{e-}03$ | $1.39\text{e-}01 \pm 2.14\text{e-}02$ | $4.44\text{e-}01 \pm 1.78\text{e-}01$ |
| RVFLN | $2.43\text{e-}02 \pm 2.70\text{e-}03$ | $5.98\text{e-}04 \pm 1.29\text{e-}04$ | $1.78\text{e-}02 \pm 2.00\text{e-}03$ | $9.89\text{e-}01 \pm 2.40\text{e-}03$ |
| SCN | $1.45\text{e-}02 \pm 6.16\text{e-}04$ | $2.11\text{e-}04 \pm 1.77\text{e-}05$ | $1.03\text{e-}02 \pm 4.40\text{e-}04$ | $9.96\text{e-}01 \pm 3.16\text{e-}04$ |
| DRVFL | $1.40\text{e-}02 \pm 1.10\text{e-}03$ | $1.97\text{e-}04 \pm 3.07\text{e-}05$ | $1.02\text{e-}02 \pm 8.33\text{e-}04$ | $9.96\text{e-}01 \pm 5.61\text{e-}04$ |
| DSCN | $9.65\text{e-}03 \pm 5.85\text{e-}04$ | $9.34\text{e-}05 \pm 1.12\text{e-}05$ | $6.81\text{e-}03 \pm 4.44\text{e-}04$ | $9.98\text{e-}01 \pm 2.02\text{e-}04$ |
| BSCN | $1.52\text{e-}02 \pm 5.36\text{e-}04$ | $2.30\text{e-}04 \pm 1.74\text{e-}05$ | $1.09\text{e-}02 \pm 5.21\text{e-}04$ | $9.96\text{e-}01 \pm 3.20\text{e-}04$ |
| GSCN | $9.20\text{e-}03 \pm 1.30\text{e-}03$ | $8.61\text{e-}05 \pm 2.45\text{e-}05$ | $7.00\text{e-}03 \pm 9.95\text{e-}04$ | $9.98\text{e-}01 \pm 4.36\text{e-}04$ |
| SCNE | $1.18\text{e-}02 \pm 3.99\text{e-}04$ | $1.41\text{e-}04 \pm 9.35\text{e-}06$ | $8.08\text{e-}03 \pm 3.32\text{e-}04$ | $9.97\text{e-}01 \pm 1.76\text{e-}04$ |
| GDSCNE | $\mathbf{5.20\text{e-}03 \pm 4.98\text{e-}04}$ | $\mathbf{2.70\text{e-}05 \pm 5.21\text{e-}06}$ | $\mathbf{3.80\text{e-}03 \pm 3.93\text{e-}04}$ | $\mathbf{1.00\text{e-}00 \pm 9.27\text{e-}05}$ |

**Table 11.4.** Performance comparison of all models on the Elevators dataset.

| Models | Test RMSE | Test MSE | Test MAE | Test $R^2$ |
|---|---|---|---|---|
| IRVFL | $8.24\text{e-}02 \pm 3.22\text{e-}03$ | $6.81\text{e-}03 \pm 5.24\text{e-}04$ | $5.51\text{e-}02 \pm 2.67\text{e-}03$ | $3.39\text{e-}01 \pm 5.55\text{e-}02$ |
| RVFLN | $3.72\text{e-}02 \pm 5.10\text{e-}03$ | $1.40\text{e-}03 \pm 4.51\text{e-}04$ | $2.65\text{e-}02 \pm 4.10\text{e-}04$ | $8.64\text{e-}01 \pm 4.17\text{e-}02$ |
| SCN | $3.69\text{e-}02 \pm 3.29\text{e-}03$ | $1.37\text{e-}03 \pm 2.66\text{e-}04$ | $2.67\text{e-}02 \pm 4.08\text{e-}04$ | $8.70\text{e-}01 \pm 2.46\text{e-}02$ |
| DRVFL | $3.84\text{e-}02 \pm 7.30\text{e-}03$ | $1.50\text{e-}03 \pm 6.72\text{e-}04$ | $2.58\text{e-}02 \pm 4.33\text{e-}04$ | $8.49\text{e-}01 \pm 7.20\text{e-}02$ |
| DSCN | $3.57\text{e-}02 \pm 7.91\text{e-}04$ | $1.27\text{e-}03 \pm 5.62\text{e-}05$ | $2.64\text{e-}02 \pm 3.83\text{e-}04$ | $8.79\text{e-}01 \pm 5.53\text{e-}03$ |
| BSCN | $3.55\text{e-}02 \pm 8.52\text{e-}04$ | $1.26\text{e-}03 \pm 6.10\text{e-}05$ | $2.68\text{e-}02 \pm 2.75\text{e-}04$ | $8.79\text{e-}01 \pm 4.26\text{e-}03$ |
| GSCN | $3.56\text{e-}02 \pm 1.10\text{e-}03$ | $1.30\text{e-}03 \pm 7.94\text{e-}05$ | $2.64\text{e-}02 \pm 6.56\text{e-}04$ | $8.76\text{e-}01 \pm 8.30\text{e-}03$ |
| SCNE | $3.52\text{e-}02 \pm 1.09\text{e-}03$ | $1.24\text{e-}03 \pm 7.68\text{e-}05$ | $2.61\text{e-}02 \pm 3.24\text{e-}04$ | $8.80\text{e-}01 \pm 7.29\text{e-}03$ |
| GDSCNE | $\mathbf{3.02\text{e-}02 \pm 5.81\text{e-}04}$ | $\mathbf{9.12\text{e-}04 \pm 3.65\text{e-}05}$ | $\mathbf{2.27\text{e-}02 \pm 3.49\text{e-}04}$ | $\mathbf{9.09\text{e-}01 \pm 4.60\text{e-}03}$ |

**Table 11.5.** Performance comparison of all models on the Compactiv dataset.

| Models | Test RMSE | Test MSE | Test MAE | Test $R^2$ |
|---|---|---|---|---|
| IRVFL | 2.26e-01 ± 2.04e-02 | 5.16e-02 ± 9.45e-03 | 1.77e-01 ± 1.82e-02 | 5.25e-01 ± 8.79e-02 |
| RVFLN | 5.45e-02 ± 7.30e-03 | 3.00e-03 ± 8.35e-04 | 3.41e-02 ± 2.90e-03 | 9.72e-01 ± 7.70e-03 |
| SCN | 3.45e-02 ± 3.27e-03 | 1.20e-03 ± 2.43e-04 | 2.16e-02 ± 8.19e-04 | 9.89e-01 ± 2.20e-03 |
| DRVFL | 3.38e-02 ± 5.80e-03 | 1.20e-03 ± 4.49e-04 | 2.14e-02 ± 1.40e-03 | 9.89e-01 ± 4.00e-03 |
| DSCN | 3.07e-02 ± 2.93e-03 | 9.51e-04 ± 1.90e-04 | 1.96e-02 ± 6.47e-04 | 9.91e-01 ± 1.74e-03 |
| BSCN | 2.57e-02 ± 5.85e-04 | 6.60e-04 ± 3.01e-05 | 1.74e-02 ± 3.04e-04 | 9.94e-01 ± 3.95e-04 |
| GSCN | 2.51e-02 ± 5.70e-04 | 6.31e-04 ± 2.86e-05 | 1.75e-02 ± 4.8060e-04 | 9.94e-01 ± 3.17e-04 |
| SCNE | 3.07e-02 ± 2.33e-03 | 9.47e-04 ± 1.52e-04 | 2.02e-02 ± 5.25e-04 | 9.91e-01 ± 1.45e-03 |
| GDSCNE | **2.27e-02 ± 6.08e-04** | **5.14e-04 ± 2.74e-05** | **1.55e-02 ± 3.15e-04** | **9.95e-01 ± 3.19e-04** |

**Table 11.6.** Performance comparison of all models on the Pole dataset.

| Models | Test RMSE | Test MSE | Test MAE | Test $R^2$ |
|---|---|---|---|---|
| IRVFL | $3.94e\text{-}01 \pm 7.60e\text{-}03$ | $1.55e\text{-}01 \pm 5.99e\text{-}03$ | $3.48e\text{-}01 \pm 8.96e\text{-}03$ | $1.09e\text{-}01 \pm 3.40e\text{-}02$ |
| RVFLN | $2.51e\text{-}01 \pm 5.10e\text{-}03$ | $6.32e\text{-}02 \pm 2.50e\text{-}03$ | $2.06e\text{-}01 \pm 4.20e\text{-}03$ | $6.37e\text{-}01 \pm 1.47e\text{-}02$ |
| SCN | $1.82e\text{-}01 \pm 6.62e\text{-}03$ | $3.31e\text{-}02 \pm 2.43e\text{-}03$ | $1.43e\text{-}01 \pm 6.11e\text{-}03$ | $8.10e\text{-}01 \pm 1.33e\text{-}02$ |
| DRVFL | $2.15e\text{-}01 \pm 5.10e\text{-}03$ | $4.64e\text{-}02 \pm 2.20e\text{-}03$ | $1.69e\text{-}01 \pm 4.00e\text{-}03$ | $7.34e\text{-}01 \pm 1.31e\text{-}02$ |
| DSCN | $1.48e\text{-}01 \pm 7.30e\text{-}03$ | $2.20e\text{-}02 \pm 2.15e\text{-}03$ | $1.12e\text{-}01 \pm 6.53e\text{-}03$ | $8.73e\text{-}01 \pm 1.26e\text{-}02$ |
| BSCN | $1.52e\text{-}01 \pm 9.18e\text{-}04$ | $2.32e\text{-}02 \pm 2.83e\text{-}04$ | $1.14e\text{-}01 \pm 6.55e\text{-}04$ | $8.67e\text{-}01 \pm 1.42e\text{-}03$ |
| GSCN | $1.02e\text{-}01 \pm 7.70e\text{-}03$ | $1.04e\text{-}02 \pm 1.70e\text{-}03$ | $7.14e\text{-}02 \pm 3.70e\text{-}03$ | $9.40e\text{-}01 \pm 9.70e\text{-}03$ |
| SCNE | $1.55e\text{-}01 \pm 3.90e\text{-}03$ | $2.41e\text{-}02 \pm 1.21e\text{-}03$ | $1.20e\text{-}01 \pm 3.05e\text{-}03$ | $8.61e\text{-}01 \pm 7.58e\text{-}03$ |
| GDSCNE | $\mathbf{5.06e\text{-}02 \pm 1.90e\text{-}03}$ | $\mathbf{2.50e\text{-}03 \pm 2.00e\text{-}04}$ | $\mathbf{3.16e\text{-}02 \pm 1.10e\text{-}03}$ | $\mathbf{9.85e\text{-}01 \pm 1.10e\text{-}03}$ |

**Table 11.7.** Performance comparison of all models on the Puma32h dataset.

| Models | Test RMSE | Test MSE | Test MAE | Test $R^2$ |
|---|---|---|---|---|
| IRVFL | 2.15e-01 $\pm$ 3.32e-02 | 4.71e-02 $\pm$ 1.43e-02 | 1.69e-01 $\pm$ 2.42e-02 | -6.26e-01 $\pm$ 5.03e-01 |
| RVFLN | 1.53e-01 $\pm$ 2.30e-03 | 2.34e-02 $\pm$ 7.16e-04 | 1.20e-01 $\pm$ 2.10e-03 | 2.07e-01 $\pm$ 2.13e-02 |
| SCN | 1.53e-01 $\pm$ 1.73e-03 | 2.33e-02 $\pm$ 5.28e-04 | 1.20e-01 $\pm$ 1.70e-03 | 2.12e-01 $\pm$ 1.31e-02 |
| DRVFL | 1.53e-01 $\pm$ 2.40e-03 | 2.34e-02 $\pm$ 7.45e-04 | 1.20e-01 $\pm$ 2.00e-03 | 2.05e-01 $\pm$ 1.73e-02 |
| DSCN | 1.52e-01 $\pm$ 2.11e-03 | 2.32e-02 $\pm$ 6.44e-04 | 1.20e-01 $\pm$ 1.91e-03 | 2.12e-01 $\pm$ 1.42e-02 |
| BSCN | 1.50e-01 $\pm$ 1.19e-05 | 2.26e-02 $\pm$ 3.56e-06 | 1.18e-01 $\pm$ 2.78e-04 | 2.37e-01 $\pm$ 6.75e-03 |
| GSCN | 9.94e-02 $\pm$ 6.40e-03 | 9.90e-03 $\pm$ 1.30e-03 | 7.72e-02 $\pm$ 5.00e-03 | 6.63e-01 $\pm$ 4.47e-02 |
| SCNE | 1.52e-01 $\pm$ 2.22e-03 | 2.31e-02 $\pm$ 6.75e-04 | 1.19e-01 $\pm$ 2.11e-03 | 2.15e-01 $\pm$ 1.95e-02 |
| GDSCNE | **7.27e-02 $\pm$ 3.20e-03** | **5.30e-03 $\pm$ 4.75e-04** | **5.64e-02 $\pm$ 2.30e-03** | **8.20e-01 $\pm$ 1.42e-02** |

achieve the best performance in terms of test RMSE, test *MSE*, test *MAE* and test $R^2$ results.

Moreover, as the performance of the base learners significantly impacts the generalization ability of the ensemble models, we conduct a comparative analysis between GDSCNE and IRVFL, RVFLN, DRVFL, SCN, DSCN, GSCN, SCNE in this section. The experimental results also indicate that SCN and its variants with supervisory mechanism can enhance the regression accuracy of IRVFL, RVFLN, and DRVFL; the combination of greedy optimization approach and boosting negative correlation learning method in GDSCNE further enhances the regression performance of SCNE, thereby facilitating the construction of an ensemble model with superior generalization capability. All experimental results demonstrate that GDSCNE outperforms IRVFL, RVFLN, DRVFL, SCN, DSCN, GSCN, BSCN and SCNE, highlighting the significant performance improvement achieved by incorporating greedy optimization strategy and boosting learning method into SCNE.

### 11.4.3 *Ablation Experiments*

In this section, we verify the effectiveness of GDSCNE with greedy searching strategy and boosting negative correlation learning by comparing some variants of GDSCNE: GDSCNE-E, GDSCNE-B, GDSCNE-D, GDSCNE-G, the differences between these variants are listed in Table 11.8. Among them, GDSCNE-E denotes the GDSCNE model without any ensemble strategy, GDSCNE-B indicates the

**Table 11.8.**  GDSCNE and its variants without specific modules.

| Models | Greedy Searching | Deep Framework | Negative Correlation | Boosting |
|---|---|---|---|---|
| GDSCNE | ✓ | ✓ | ✓ | ✓ |
| GDSCNE-E | ✓ | ✓ | ✗ | |
| GDSCNE-B | ✓ | ✓ | ✓ | ✗ |
| GDSCNE-D | ✓ | ✗ | ✓ | ✓ |
| GDSCNE-G | ✗ | ✓ | ✓ | ✓ |

GDSCNE model that only adopts the negative correlation learning, GDSCNE-D expresses the GDSCNE model without a deep framework, GDSCNE-G is an ensemble model with boosting negative correlation learning but does not employ the greedy searching strategy. Ablation experimental results are presented in Table 11.9, it is obvious that compared with GDSCNE-E, GDSCNE-B, GDSCNE-D, GDSCNE-G on the regression datasets, the test $MAE$ of GDSCNE achieves the smallest values, which illustrates the effectiveness of greedy optimization strategy and boosting negative correlation learning while also validating the validity of a deep framework.

### 11.4.4   *Parameter Analysis*

The number of base learners, denoted as $K$, is the most critical parameter in our proposed model. If $K$ is set too small, the model accuracy becomes insufficient; whereas if $K$ is set too large, it leads to increased computational complexity and over-fitting issues. To analyze the impact of parameter $K$, we conduct experiments on the experimental datasets with different number of components in GDSCNE. Then, we utilize test $MAE$ values as a metric to demonstrate how different values for $K$ affect GDSCNE.

The test results of different $K$ on GDSCNE are presented in Table 11.10. shows the test $MAE$ values of GDSCNE with varying number of components on the benchmark datasets. From Table 11.10, we can conclude that GDSCNE with only one component can also been executed, however, there is no clear difference compared with GDSCNE-E in regression performance. Meanwhile, with the increase number of components, the performance of GDSCNE improved. Although GDSCNE with $K = 3$ may not gets optimal results for all datasets, the bar chart of different datasets demonstrate that it effectively balances test accuracy and computational complexity of ensemble models.

**Remark 11.3.** As previous studies (Li and Wang, 2017; Wang and Li, 2017b, 2018) have already proven the significance of parameter scope $\lambda$ and maximum number $T_{\max}$ of weights and biases in random neural networks. Our main focus is to construct a deep ensemble

**Table 11.9.** Test *MAE* of GDSCNE and its variants.

| Models | ANACALT | MV | Elevators |
| --- | --- | --- | --- |
| GDSCNE | **1.05e-02 $\pm$ 9.83e-04** | **3.80e-03 $\pm$ 3.93e-04** | **2.27e-02 $\pm$ 3.49e-04** |
| GDSCNE-E | 1.35e-02 $\pm$ 1.10e-03 | 5.80e-03 $\pm$ 8.85e-04 | 2.48e-02 $\pm$ 5.53e-04 |
| GDSCNE-B | 1.46e-02 $\pm$ 1.50e-03 | 4.30e-03 $\pm$ 1.00e-03 | 2.33e-02 $\pm$ 3.13e-04 |
| GDSCNE-D | 1.44e-02 $\pm$ 1.60e-03 | 4.90e-03 $\pm$ 3.69e-04 | 2.49e-02 $\pm$ 4.07e-04 |
| GDSCNE-G | 1.87e-02 $\pm$ 1.93e-03 | 6.65e-03 $\pm$ 2.18e-04 | 2.58e-02 $\pm$ 4.49e-04 |
| Models | Compactiv | Pole | Puma32h |
| GDSCNE | **1.55e-02 $\pm$ 3.15e-04** | **3.16e-02 $\pm$ 1.10e-03** | **5.64e-02 $\pm$ 2.30e-03** |
| GDSCNE-E | 1.61e-02 $\pm$ 3.35e-04 | 4.42e-02 $\pm$ 3.20e-03 | 7.17e-02 $\pm$ 3.20e-03 |
| GDSCNE-B | 1.59e-02 $\pm$ 4.35e-04 | 3.23e-02 $\pm$ 1.20e-03 | 5.71e-02 $\pm$ 2.70e-03 |
| GDSCNE-D | 1.66e-02 $\pm$ 4.11e-04 | 5.61e-02 $\pm$ 1.80e-03 | 6.33e-02 $\pm$ 2.90e-03 |
| GDSCNE-G | 1.74e-02 $\pm$ 4.76e-04 | 1.10e-01 $\pm$ 2.64e-03 | 1.20e-01 $\pm$ 1.87e-03 |

**Table 11.10.** Performance comparison of GDSCNE with different number of components.

| Number of components | ANACALT | MV | Elevators |
| --- | --- | --- | --- |
| 1 | 1.37e-02 $\pm$ 2.10e-04 | 5.70e-03 $\pm$ 8.43e-04 | 2.49e-02 $\pm$ 5.05e-04 |
| 3 | 1.05e-02 $\pm$ 9.83e-04 | 3.80e-03 $\pm$ 3.93e-04 | 2.27e-02 $\pm$ 3.49e-04 |
| 5 | 1.05e-02 $\pm$ 8.94e-04 | 3.40e-03 $\pm$ 2.42e-04 | 2.30e-02 $\pm$ 4.10e-04 |
| 7 | 1.06e-02 $\pm$ 8.69e-04 | 3.00e-03 $\pm$ 1.68e-04 | 2.28e-02 $\pm$ 3.56e-04 |
| 9 | 1.06e-02 $\pm$ 9.66e-04 | 3.00e-03 $\pm$ 1.35e-04 | 2.26e-02 $\pm$ 2.98e-04 |
| Number of components | Compactiv | Pole | Puma32h |
| 1 | 1.62e-02 $\pm$ 5.06e-04 | 4.35e-02 $\pm$ 2.50e-03 | 7.43e-02 $\pm$ 6.70e-03 |
| 3 | 1.55e-02 $\pm$ 3.15e-04 | 3.16e-02 $\pm$ 1.10e-03 | 5.64e-02 $\pm$ 2.30e-03 |
| 5 | 1.52e-02 $\pm$ 2.05e-04 | 2.93e-02 $\pm$ 6.85e-04 | 5.19e-02 $\pm$ 1.50e-03 |
| 7 | 1.51e-02 $\pm$ 2.79e-04 | 2.79e-02 $\pm$ 9.00e-04 | 5.17e-02 $\pm$ 1.80e-03 |
| 9 | 1.52e-02 $\pm$ 4.23e-04 | 2.72e-02 $\pm$ 7.32e-04 | 5.02e-02 $\pm$ 1.70e-03 |

model using greedy optimization strategy and boosting negative correlation learning; therefore, we do not explore different parameter scopes $\lambda$ or maximum numbers $T_{\max}$ for GDSCNE.

## 11.5 Summary

This chapter proposes a novel deep greedy stochastic configuration networks ensemble model, known as GDSCNE, based on boosting negative correlation learning with greedy configuration parameters. Firstly, we employ HPO to assign weights and biases of nodes and construct multi-layer architecture under the supervision mechanism, which ensures universal approximation propertyand enhances regression performance of base models. Subsequently, we adopt the least square method with boosting negative correlation learning approach to determine output weights and construct a stronger ensemble model for improving generalization performance of base learners. Finally, performance evaluation on various regression datasets demonstrates that GDSCNE outperforms IRVFL, RVFLN, DRVFL, SCN, DSCN, BSCN, GSCN, SCNE and some variants of GDSCNE, in terms of regression accuracy.

However, GDSCNE adopts greedy configuration optimization method with point increment mode, which result in high computational complexity and affects the computational efficiency of the model. Besides, the current version of GDSCNE is not applicable to classification problems due to the regression boosting algorithm and optimization objective function. In the future, we can expand GDSCNE with heterogeneous features and block increment mode to solve multi-classification problems for reducing computational complexity and improving learning efficiency, moreover, as the superiority of Normal distribution and Logistic distribution for parameter configuration purposes, we can use greedy optimization idea to determine input parameters with Normal distribution and Logistic distribution.

Chapter 12

# Ensemble Intuitionistic Fuzzy Deep Stochastic Configuration Network

The intuitionistic fuzzy deep stochastic configuration network (IFD-SCN) has demonstrated significant improvements in generalization and robustness for solving binary classification problems compared to traditional deep stochastic configuration networks. However, as the number of nodes and hidden layers increases, IFDSCN remains susceptible to over-fitting. While ensemble learning techniques are known to enhance model generalization, they often come with substantial computational overhead, particularly in training time, due to the need to train multiple base models. In this chapter, we propose a novel self-ensemble deep model based on IFDSCN, termed ensemble intuitionistic fuzzy deep stochastic configuration network (EIFD-SCN). Unlike conventional ensemble strategies, EIFDSCN employs a multi-layer structure that simultaneously trains multiple sub-models, enabling effective feature extraction from the original input while preserving the fast learning capability of deep stochastic configuration networks. Experimental results demonstrate that this self-ensemble strategy significantly improves classification accuracy and robustness.

## 12.1  Introduction

Deep learning architectures with randomized weights have gained widespread success due to their superior feature representation

255

capabilities (Huang *et al.*, 2023; Li and Zeng, 2023). Among these, the intuitionistic fuzzy deep stochastic configuration network (IFD-SCN) leverages a fuzzy-based weighted least squares approach and weighted inequality constraints to randomly assign parameters, effectively mitigating the impact of outliers and enhancing model robustness. Despite its advantages, IFDSCN, like other randomized neural networks, struggles with over-fitting as the number of nodes and layers increases, which limits its generalization performance.

Ensemble learning, which combines multiple individual models to achieve better generalization, has shown promise in improving model performance. Deep ensemble learning models, in particular, integrate the strengths of deep learning and ensemble techniques, resulting in superior generalization capabilities (Ganaie *et al.*, 2022).Common ensemble methods such as bagging, boosting, and stacking have been widely adopted to construct ensemble learning models. These methods combine the predictions of multiple models, often resulting in the "$1 + 1 > 2$" effect, where the ensemble outperforms any single constituent model (Zhou, 2012).

However, ensembling deep neural networks is computationally expensive, as training multiple networks can require weeks of GPU-accelerated computation. To address this, implicit and explicit ensemble methods have been proposed. Implicit ensembles train a single model to approximate the behavior of multiple networks, while explicit ensembles combine predictions from independently trained models. Ganaie *et al.* (2022). Explicit ensembles, such as those based on random vector functional link, diversify predictions through different random initializations of hidden layer weights (Shi *et al.*, 2021).

To enhance the generalization capability of IFDSCN while minimizing computational costs, we propose a novel explicit ensemble model called the ensemble intuitionistic fuzzy deep stochastic configuration network (EIFDSCN). Similar to the constructive processes of IFSCN and IFDSCN, EIFDSCN employs intuitionistic fuzzy methods to calculate membership and non-membership degrees for each sample. Node parameters are then assigned using intuitionistic fuzzy weighted inequality constraints. The output of each layer serves as the input for the next, constructing a deep architecture where each layer acts as a sub-model. Finally, EIFDSCN integrates these sub-models using voting methods to produce the final classification results.

The main contributions of this section are as follows:

- We introduce EIFDSCN, a self-ensemble deep model that leverages the outputs of each layer to determine final classification results, enhancing generalization and robustness.
- We employ intuitionistic fuzzy techniques to calculate membership and non-membership degrees for each sample, enabling more effective parameter determination.
- We demonstrate the robustness of EIFDSCN through extensive experiments on real-world datasets with noise, showcasing its superior performance in challenging scenarios.

## 12.2  Preliminaries

Ensemble learning is an important paradigm in machine learning, with its fundamental idea being to complete learning tasks by constructing and combining multiple learners to achieve better generalization capability than single models. Ensemble learning trains multiple different base learners, also called weak learners, and employs various strategies to combine them into a strong learner, thereby significantly improving machine learning performance and reducing generalization error.

Ensemble learning is primarily based on the following two theoretical foundations (Ganaie *et al.*, 2022):

**Bias-variance decomposition:** The model's generalization error can be decomposed into bias, variance, and noise. Through combining multiple learners, ensemble learning can effectively reduce variance while maintaining relatively low bias, thereby decreasing the overall generalization error.

**Diversity theory:** The performance of an ensemble system depends not only on the capability of individual learners but also on the diversity among learners. Greater diversity leads to stronger complementarity between learners, resulting in better ensemble effects.

Voting is a basic and straightforward combination strategy in ensemble learning. The fundamental idea of voting is that for a given test sample, multiple learners provide their own prediction results, which are then combined through certain voting rules to obtain the final prediction result.

There are three main voting rules:

**Absolute majority voting:** If a class receives more than half of the votes, it is selected as the final prediction result.

**Plurality voting:** The class that receives the most votes is selected, without requiring an absolute majority.

**Weighted voting:** Different learners have different weights, typically determined by their performance on the validation set. The prediction result is determined by the weighted sum of votes.

## 12.3   Methodology

The framework of EIFDSCN is shown in Fig. 12.1. Similar to IFD-SCN, this ensemble architecture consists of multiple hidden layers. The parameters of these hidden layers are configured through the same supervisory mechanism as IFDSCN to ensure the network's

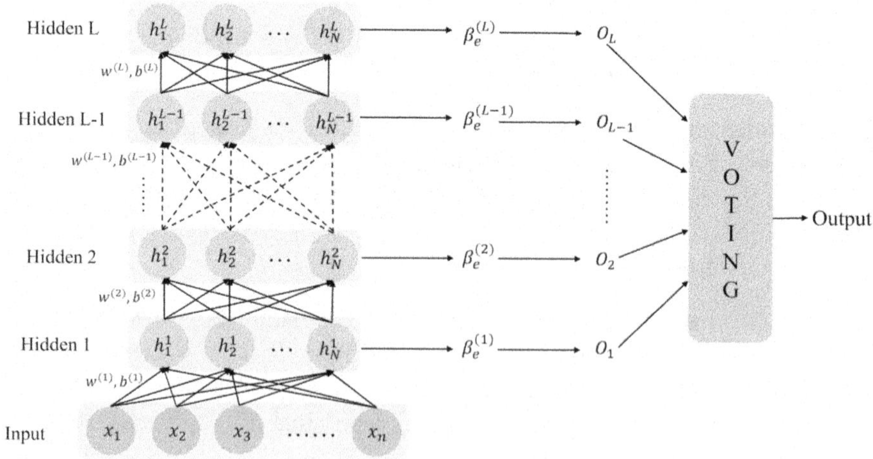


**Fig. 12.1.**   Framework of EIFDSCN.

universal approximation capability and good generalization ability. However, what distinguishes it from IFDSCN is that each hidden layer corresponds to an independent sub-model.

After all sub-models complete learning, EIFDSCN employs voting methods to integrate these sub-models and obtain the final classification results. Specifically, each sub-model learns different feature representations and patterns from the data to make predictions on input samples. EIFDSCN then aggregates the prediction results from all sub-models using absolute majority voting to determine the final classification results, where the class receiving the most votes becomes the final decision. This voting-based ensemble strategy cleverly utilizes the diversity and complementarity between sub-models. Since each sub-model learns different feature representations and patterns from the data, their predictions also differ. By comprehensively considering these different predictions, EIFDSCN can reduce potential bias and limitations of individual models. Meanwhile, the diversity between sub-models also enhances EIFDSCN's generalization ability and robustness. While a single model may be sensitive to certain feature types or noise, leading to classification errors, through ensemble learning of multiple diverse sub-models, EIFDSCN can effectively balance and eliminate such individual inadequacies, improving classification accuracy and reliability. Even if some sub-models make incorrect judgments, as long as the majority of sub-models can make correct predictions, EIFDSCN can obtain accurate final classification results through the voting mechanism.

The detailed algorithm description of EIFDSCN is as follows:

Given training sample input $X = \{x_1, x_2, \ldots, x_N\}$, $x_i = [x_{i,1}, \ldots, x_{i,d}]$; output $Y = \{y_1, y_2, \ldots, y_N\}$, $y_i = [y_{i,1}, y_{i,2} \ldots, y_{i,m}]$.

Hidden layer 1 takes the training samples as input, and its output is calculated by

$$H^{(L)} = g(XW^{(L)}), \tag{12.1}$$

where $W^{(L)}$ is the weight of hidden layer 1 selected through supervisory mechanism, and $g(\cdot)$ is the activation function.

For deeper hidden layer $L$, taking the nonlinear features from hidden layer $L - 1$ as input, the output of hidden layer $L$ is calculated by

$$H^{(L)} = g(H^{(L-1)}W^{(L)}). \tag{12.2}$$

The output weight of hidden layer $L$ is calculated by

$$\beta_e^{(L)} = \begin{cases} D^T \left(\frac{I}{C} + SDD^T\right)^{-1} SY, & N < L \\ \left(\frac{I}{C} + D^T SD\right)^{-1} D^T SY, & N \geq L, \end{cases} \tag{12.3}$$

where $D = H^{(L)}$; $S = \mathrm{diag}\{s_1, s_2, \ldots, s_N\}$, is the intuitionistic fuzzy evaluation weight matrix.

For each hidden layer corresponding to an independent sub-model, the model output of hidden layer $L$ is calculated by

$$O_L = H^{(L)} \beta_e^{(L)}. \tag{12.4}$$

EIFDSCN differs significantly from IFDSCN in network structure: while IFDSCN considers hidden layers as a whole, EIFDSCN treats each hidden layer independently as a sub-model. Moreover, EIFDSCN differs from traditional deep learning models. Traditional deep learning models typically only utilize high-level representations from the final hidden layer for classification decisions. While this approach can capture abstract features, it ignores the rich information contained in intermediate layers. In contrast, EIFDSCN not only utilizes high-level features from the final hidden layer but also fully exploits the rich features and kernel information provided by intermediate model layers. By integrating features from different layers with different abstraction levels, EIFDSCN can more comprehensively and precisely capture the internal patterns and relationships in data, greatly enhancing the network's feature utilization capability.

Compared to the IFDSCN, EIFDSCN has reduced both time and space complexity as it does not need to repeatedly calculate global output weights but rather decomposes the output weights.

Based on the above algorithm description, one key advantage of EIFDSCN is that it can achieve effects equivalent to multiple model ensembles by training a single model, thereby improving model generalization ability. This unique implicit ensemble technique shares some similarities with snapshot ensemble learning. In snapshot ensemble learning, the system preserves the current model state at the end of each learning rate cycle. During prediction, all preserved model states are combined to improve prediction accuracy. Through this approach, snapshot ensemble learning can achieve model ensemble effects based on a single model. However, EIFDSCN's algorithm has one important distinction from snapshot ensemble learning. Unlike traditional ensemble learning methods, EIFDSCN does not rely on learning rate decay for model training. Instead, it utilizes SCN's supervisory mechanism and realizes model training through closed-form solution of hidden layer output weights. This unique training strategy avoids some complex calculations in traditional training processes, such as gradient computation and learning rate adjustment, making the training process more efficient and stable.

## 12.4    Experimental Results and Discussion

### 12.4.1    *Experimental Setup*

All experiments were conducted on a platform with MATLAB R2022b, Intel® Core® CPU 12900H 2.50 GHz, 32GB RAM, and Windows 11 operating system. The Gaussian kernel function was adopted in the experiments:

$$K(x_1, x_2) = \exp(-\|x_1 - x_2\|^2/\mu^2), \tag{12.5}$$

where $\mu$ is the kernel parameter.

Different from prior chapter, eight UCI datasets were selected for experiments, covering various data types and feature dimensions to comprehensively evaluate the algorithm's generalization ability. While SCN has been compared with other algorithmic models previously, this section focuses on verifying the classification accuracy of EIFDSCN improved from IFDSCN. SCN (Wang and Li, 2017b), IFSCN (Guo *et al.*, 2024), and IFDSCN are selected as comparison models. Through performance comparison with these models, the advantages and improvement effects of EIFDSCN can be more clearly demonstrated. The experiments divide each dataset into training and test sets according to a 7:3 ratio to ensure the reliability and validity of experimental results. Detailed dataset information is summarized in Table 12.1.

Other experimental settings are described as follows:

**Parameter settings:** The parameters $C$ and $\mu$ are selected from $\{10^{-5}, \ldots, 10^5\}$ and $\{2^{-6}, \ldots, 2^6\}$ respectively. The maximum number of nodes $L_{\max}$ is selected from $\{10, 20, 50, 100, 200, 500\}$.

**Table 12.1.** Details of datasets.

| Dataset | Samples | Negative samples | Positive samples | Features |
|---|---|---|---|---|
| sonar | 208 | 111 | 97 | 60 |
| fourclass | 862 | 555 | 307 | 2 |
| segment | 2310 | 1320 | 990 | 19 |
| aus | 690 | 383 | 307 | 14 |
| spambase | 4601 | 2788 | 1813 | 57 |
| satimage | 4508 | 1908 | 2600 | 36 |
| ionosphere | 351 | 126 | 225 | 34 |
| breastcancer | 683 | 239 | 444 | 10 |

Considering the balance between model complexity and computational efficiency, the maximum number of layers $M$ for IFDSCN and EIFDSCN is uniformly set to 3, and their maximum number of candidate nodes $T_{\max}$ is set to 100.

**Hyperparameter optimization:** Grid search is employed to optimize hyperparameters for each model. Five-fold cross-validation is used during parameter tuning to ensure reliability and stability of results.

**Evaluation metrics:** Using accuracy and average ranking to evaluate model classification performance.

## 12.4.2 *Main Results and Discussion*

As shown in Table 12.2, when compared with other models, the proposed EIFDSCN demonstrates superior performance. Among the eight UCI evaluation datasets, EIFDSCN achieves the best classification results on six datasets and reaches the second-best level on the remaining two datasets. These results strongly validate EIFDSCN's versatility in handling various classification tasks, showing stable performance even when dealing with complex heterogeneous data features.

To comprehensively evaluate EIFDSCN's robustness and adaptability in handling practical problems, four representative datasets from Table 12.1 were selected as test objects: sonar, aus, breastcancer, and segment. These datasets come from different application domains, with varying data scales and feature dimensionality,

**Table 12.2.** Performance comparison of different models on classification datasets.

| Dataset | SCN | IFSCN | IFDSCN | EIFDSCN |
|---|---|---|---|---|
| sonar | 0.812 | 0.825 | **0.828** | **0.828** |
| fourclass | 0.982 | **0.985** | 0.981 | <u>0.984</u> |
| segment | 0.956 | 0.961 | <u>0.968</u> | **0.970** |
| aus | 0.850 | 0.856 | <u>0.860</u> | **0.865** |
| spambase | 0.958 | 0.970 | **0.975** | <u>0.972</u> |
| satimage | 0.910 | 0.923 | <u>0.934</u> | **0.938** |
| ionosphere | 0.932 | 0.947 | <u>0.952</u> | **0.961** |
| breastcancer | 0.965 | 0.970 | <u>0.972</u> | **0.983** |
| Average accuracy | 0.921 | 0.930 | <u>0.934</u> | **0.939** |
| Average rank | 3.875 | 2.75 | <u>2</u> | **1.25** |

*Note*: Best results are shown in **bold**, second best results are <u>underlined</u>.

thus enabling a more comprehensive assessment of the algorithm's performance. To simulate real-world data complexity and uncertainty, random noise at three different levels (5%, 10%, and 20%) was introduced to each dataset. By controlling the noise ratio, we can systematically evaluate the algorithm's performance under different noise levels, thereby assessing its robustness and anti-interference capability. This experimental design not only considers data diversity and complexity but also closely approximates practical application scenarios, providing important reference for the algorithm's performance in real-world problems.

Through detailed observation of Tables 12.3–12.6, it is evident that EIFDSCN demonstrates advantages in handling noisy data. Even with continuously increasing noise ratios, EIFDSCN maintains the highest accuracy levels, exhibiting superior robustness. For a more intuitive display of performance differences under noisy environments, the numerical results are plotted as line graphs, as shown in Fig. 12.2.

Through in-depth analysis of Fig. 12.2, a significant trend can be observed: as the noise level in the data continuously increases, all models show varying degrees of performance degradation. This phenomenon aligns with theoretical expectations, as noise interferes with the model's feature extraction and classification accuracy during the learning process, thus adversely affecting the overall performance.

**Table 12.3.** Performance comparison of four models on Sonar dataset.

| Model | 0% | 5% | 10% | 20% |
|---|---|---|---|---|
| SCN | 0.812 | 0.793 | 0.785 | 0.760 |
| IFSCN | 0.825 | 0.811 | <u>0.804</u> | 0.781 |
| IFDSCN | 0.828 | <u>0.816</u> | 0.802 | <u>0.788</u> |
| EIFDSCN | 0.828 | **0.819** | **0.808** | **0.790** |

**Table 12.4.** Performance comparison of four models on AUS dataset.

| Model | 0% | 5% | 10% | 20% |
|---|---|---|---|---|
| SCN | 0.850 | 0.812 | 0.783 | 0.744 |
| IFSCN | 0.856 | <u>0.848</u> | <u>0.824</u> | 0.796 |
| IFDSCN | 0.860 | 0.846 | 0.825 | <u>0.799</u> |
| EIFDSCN | 0.865 | **0.853** | **0.830** | **0.812** |

**Table 12.5.** Performance comparison of four models on Breastcancer dataset.

| Model | 0% | 5% | 10% | 20% |
|---|---|---|---|---|
| SCN | 0.965 | 0.922 | 0.907 | 0.881 |
| IFSCN | 0.970 | 0.943 | 0.924 | 0.892 |
| IFDSCN | 0.972 | <u>0.946</u> | <u>0.930</u> | <u>0.901</u> |
| EIFDSCN | 0.983 | **0.974** | **0.953** | **0.929** |

**Table 12.6.** Performance comparison of four models on Segment dataset.

| Model | 0% | 5% | 10% | 20% |
|---|---|---|---|---|
| SCN | 0.956 | 0.942 | 0.931 | 0.917 |
| IFSCN | 0.961 | 0.958 | <u>0.949</u> | 0.933 |
| IFDSCN | 0.968 | <u>0.960</u> | 0.946 | 0.935 |
| EIFDSCN | 0.970 | **0.965** | **0.959** | **0.948** |

*Note*: Best results are shown in **bold**, second best results are <u>underlined</u>.

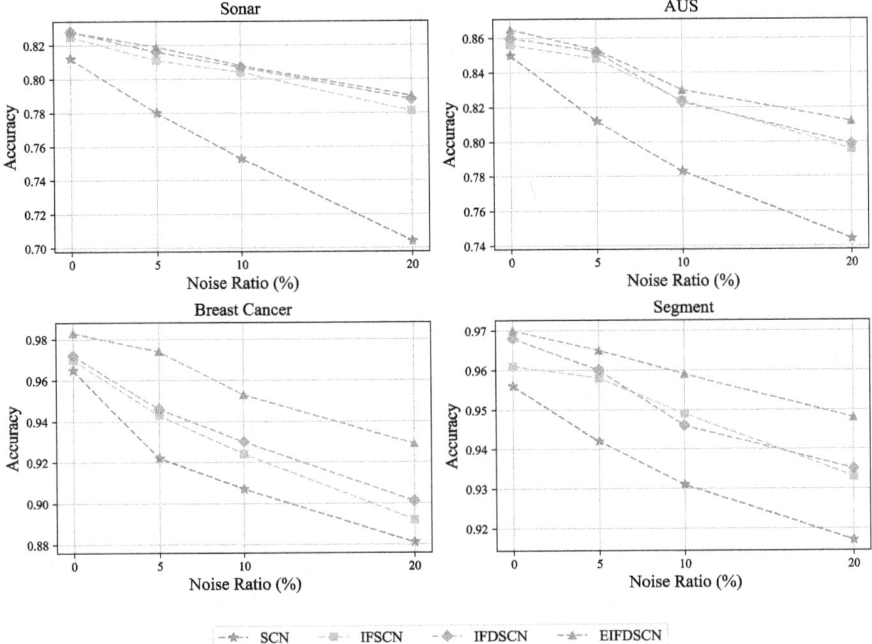



**Fig. 12.2.** Performance comparison of different models under various noise levels.

However, notably, while all models' accuracy is affected by noise, EIFDSCN's rate of accuracy decline is significantly lower than other models. This finding demonstrates EIFDSCN's outstanding advantages in robustness, indicating that when processing noisy data, it can effectively combine features learned from each hidden layer, better preserve key feature information, and thus minimize the negative impact of noise on model performance.

### 12.4.3 *Statistical Tests*

Based on the experimental results from Tables 12.3–12.6, this section employs the Wilcoxon signed-rank test to conduct statistical analysis on the classification accuracy performance of EIFDSCN compared with SCN, IFSCN and IFDSCN.

The Wilcoxon signed-rank test is a non-parametric statistical method used to assess whether the differences between two related samples, paired observations or repeated measurements have statistical significance. This test does not require assumptions about specific data distributions, therefore, compared to parametric test methods that rely on normal distribution assumptions, such as paired $t$-test, it has broader applicability. When the sample size is relatively small, the Wilcoxon signed-rank test is more appropriate.

The basic principle of the Wilcoxon signed-rank test is to rank and mark the differences in paired data. First calculate the difference for each pair of data, ignoring cases where the difference is zero. Then, rank these differences by their absolute values while preserving the sign (positive or negative) of the original difference. The test statistic is the smaller of the sums of positive and negative ranks, enabling detection of median differences between two datasets.

The hypotheses are set as follows: the null hypothesis assumes no difference between the two samples, meaning their medians are equal; the alternative hypothesis assumes there is a difference, meaning unequal medians. The calculated $p$-value can be used to decide whether to reject the null hypothesis and conclude that there is a significant difference in medians between the two samples.

The Wilcoxon signed-rank test is calculated as follows:

$$R^+ = \sum_{\theta_i > 0} \text{rank}(\theta_i) + \frac{1}{2} \sum_{\theta_i = 0} \text{rank}(\theta_i), \qquad (12.6)$$

$$R^- = \sum_{i < 0} \text{rank}(\theta_i) + \frac{1}{2} \sum_{\theta_i = 0} \text{rank}(\theta_i), \qquad (12.7)$$

where $R^+$ and $R^-$ represent the sums of positive and negative ranks respectively, $\theta_i$ represents the difference in accuracy between two algorithms, $\text{rank}(\theta_i)$ is the rank value of $\theta_i$. The test statistic $R = \min\{R^+, R^-\}$, and the $p$-value is obtained from the statistical table based on $R$. If $p$ is less than the significance level $\alpha$, the null hypothesis is rejected.

As observed from the Table 12.7, under the specified significance level $\alpha = 0.05$, all test results show $p$-values less than 0.05. This statistical result demonstrates that the proposed EIFDSCN model exhibits significant differences in classification accuracy compared to existing models like SCN, IFSCN, and IFDSCN. In other words, the superior performance demonstrated by the EIFDSCN model not only

**Table 12.7.**  $p$-value of Wilcoxon signed-rank test.

|  | SCN | IFSCN | IFDSCN |
|---|---|---|---|
| EIFDSCN | <0.001 | <0.001 | <0.001 |

surpasses other models but also shows statistical significance rather than being a simple random phenomenon.

## 12.5   Summary

Inspired by ensemble learning ideas, this section improves upon the IFDSCN and presents an ensemble learning-based algorithm EIFD-SCN. EIFDSCN features a unique network architecture design that not only fully exploits and utilizes the rich information and kernel information embedded in network intermediate layers but also enhances the model's noise resistance capability through clever model ensemble strategies. Through ensemble learning, EIFDSCN can effectively denoise and extract commonalities from different learners, achieving more accurate and stable classification decisions than single models. This ensemble strategy not only improves the model's generalization ability but also demonstrates strong adaptability and robustness when facing complex and noisy environments.

This section first describes EIFDSCN's network structure and deeply explores the uniqueness and advantages of this structure. Compared to traditional ensemble learning methods, EIFDSCN adopts an implicit ensemble strategy, achieving more compact and efficient model fusion. Subsequently, a series of experiments were conducted on UCI datasets, including comparative experiments with different noise levels. The experimental results fully demonstrate EIFDSCN's superior performance on various datasets, especially showing significant robustness and anti-interference capability when facing noise challenges. Whether on clean data or noisy data, EIFD-SCN can achieve higher classification accuracy and stability than other algorithms, demonstrating the effectiveness and superiority of the ensemble method proposed in this section.

**Chapter 13**

# Stacked Deep Stochastic Configuration Networks with Multi-Level Feature Fusion

Stochastic configuration network (SCN) is an incremental learning approach with universal approximation property for analyzing high-dimensional and large-scale data. It can start with a small structure and gradually increasing hidden layer nodes through the supervision mechanism. To enhance the feature learning capability of the SCN, this chapter proposes a stacked deep stochastic configuration network based on sparse feature fusion by stacking random sparse autoencoder and SCN. Specifically, the original features are transformed into mapping features in the feature layer and the mapping features are enhanced in the enhancement layer, then the input weights and biases of enhancement nodes are determined according to the supervision mechanism and the output weight matrix can be calculated through the standard least squares. The experimental results on function approximation problems and real-world datasets indicate that SDSCN improves the performance of SCN, and it has higher regression accuracy and stability.

## 13.1  Introduction

Nowadays, with the growth of the data scale, how to extract appropriate features is facing great challenges. Deep learning (DL) models can extract multi-level abstract features from high-dimensional, large-scale data. However, classical multi-layer perceptron (MLP) with BP algorithm has a large number of network parameters and requires more training time compared with randomized neural networks (Arora *et al.*, 2014; Giryes *et al.*, 2016; Wang and Li, 2018). Hence, Wang and Li (2018) first used supervision mechanism to incrementally assign the parameters of deep stochastic configuration networks (DSCNs). Exploring essential features is widely used in deep stacking of stochastic neural network models, with better feature representation capabilities. However, how to improve the model's feature learning ability while ensuring learning efficiency remains a significant challenge.

In addition to traditional multi-model fusion methods, single-model fusion based on feature fusion is conducive to improving the generalization of the model while reducing the training cost of deep neural networks (Ganaie *et al.*, 2022; Shi *et al.*, 2021). Lin *et al.* (2020) proposed a new deep ensemble feature (DEF) network. DEF is divided into two sub-networks: an ensemble feature network and a decision network. The ensemble feature network uses multiple CNN models to learn deep ensemble features, and the decision network implements image classification tasks. Xue *et al.* (2021) proposed a deep ensemble model and designed a fully convolutional neural network (FCN) ensemble module to extract effective features by training multiple FCN models with different initializations, and combined multiple loss and coarse-fine compensation modules to improve the model's segmentation accuracy.

Therefore, to ensure the learning efficiency of SCN while improving its feature learning ability, this chapter introduces stacked deep stochastic configuration networks based on sparse feature fusion (SDSCNs). Firstly, multiple R-SAEs are used to extract sparse features from the original input data in parallel to construct feature layers by taking advantage of the randomness of R-SAE feature learning. Secondly, the fused sparse features are enhanced using the SC algorithm, and the weights and biases of the enhancement nodes are stochastic configured using the supervision mechanism and the standard least squares method is used to calculate the output matrix of SDSCNs. Finally, the performance of SDSCN is verified through experiments on function approximation problems and KEEL benchmark datasets. In short, the main contributions of this chapter are as follows:

- We design stacked deep stochastic configuration networks based on sparse feature fusion (SDSCNs) which can determine the enhancement nodes adaptively without human intervention.
- The input features are converted to mapping features in feature layer, and the weights and biases of the enhancement nodes are assigned by SC algorithm, and then the enhancement nodes are gradually increased by the supervision mechanism.
- Standard least squares approach is used to compute the output weight matrix of SDSCNs with multi-group of enhancement nodes quickly.
- Numerous experiments demonstrate the regression performance of SDSCNs. The analysis of experimental results are analyzed in detail.

## 13.2  Preliminaries

Autoencoder (AE) can extract high-level abstract feature information from input data through unsupervised learning for supervised tasks such as classification and regression. Pan *et al.* (2020) proposed an SCN-AE model for feature learning, which improved the accuracy of the SCN model. To ensure learning efficiency, SCN-AE uses randomized parameters, incrementally increases hidden layer nodes, and outputs the results as the input of the SCN classifier. Compared with SCN-AE, Randomized sparse autoencoder (R-SAE)can extract sparse features of the original data and has better feature representation capabilities (Chen and Liu, 2018).

The structure of R-SAE can be regarded as a single hidden layer neural network model, whose input is the original feature and output is the extracted feature. As an unsupervised learning model, it uses randomized input node parameters and reconstructs features through an objective function based on the $L_1$ regularization parameter to obtain sparse features. Since the objective function is non-convex and non-smooth, the ADMM algorithm is required to update the model output weights.

The specific algorithm process is described as follows:

Given the training sample feature $X = \{x_1, x_2, \ldots, x_N\}$, where $x_i = [x_{1,1}, x_{1,2}, \ldots, x_{i,4}] \in \mathbb{R}^d$, $d$ represents the original feature dimension; $i = 1, 2, \ldots, N$, $N$ represents the number of samples.

Assuming that the number of R-SAE hidden layer nodes is $L$, the input weights and biases of the hidden layer nodes $L$ are randomly assigned according to Eqs. (13.1) and (13.2):

$$w_L = 2 \times \text{rand}(d, 1) - 1. \tag{13.1}$$

$$b_L = 2 \times \text{rand}(1, 1) - 1. \tag{13.2}$$

The output matrix $H$ of hidden layer can be calculated through Eqs. (13.3) and (13.4):

$$h_L = \left[\varphi_L(x_1 w_L + b_L), \ldots, \varphi_L(x_N w_L + b_L),\right]^T \tag{13.3}$$

$$H = \left[h_1, h_2, \ldots, h_L\right] = \begin{bmatrix} \varphi_1(x_1) & \cdots & \varphi_L(x_1) \\ \vdots & \ddots & \vdots \\ \varphi_1(x_N) & \cdots & \varphi_L(x_N) \end{bmatrix}, \tag{13.4}$$

where $h_L$ represents the output of node $L$; $\varphi_L$ is expressed as the activation function; $w_L$ and $b_L$ are denoted as the input weights and biases of node $L$, respectively.

To ensure feature sparsity, the output weights $\beta$ of R-SAE is denoted as Eq. (13.5):

$$\beta = \arg \min_{\beta} \|H\beta - X\|^2 + C_1 \|\beta\|_1, \tag{13.5}$$

where $\beta = [\beta_1, \beta_2, \ldots, \beta_L]^T$; $C_1$ represents the $L_1$ regularization parameter, which is used to balance the importance between the regularization term and the error term.

Then the the output features $X'$ can be obtained by Eq. (13.6):

$$X' = X\beta, \tag{13.6}$$

where $X' = \{x'_1, x'_2, \ldots, x'_N\}$, $x'_i = \{x'_{i,1}, x'_{i,2}, \ldots, x'_{i,d}\} \in \mathbb{R}^{d'}$; $d'$ represents the output feature dimension.

To solve the objective function shown in Eq. (13.5), the ADMM solution process is as follows (Gong *et al.*, 2015; Yang *et al.*, 2015):

Convert the objective function of Eq. (13.5) into the ADMM form of Eq. (13.7):

$$\arg \min_{\beta} u(\beta) + v(o), \text{s.t.} \beta - o = 0, \tag{13.7}$$

where $u(\beta) = \|H\beta - X\|^2$; $v(o) = C_1 \|\beta\|_1$.

Use the iterative process of Eq. (13.8) to iteratively optimize Eq. (13.7):

$$\begin{cases} \beta_{k+1} = (H^T H + \rho I)^{-1} \left( H^T X + \rho(o^k - z^k) \right) \\ o_{k+1} = S_{\frac{C_1}{\rho}} (\beta_{k+1} + z_k) \\ z_{k+1} = z_k + (\beta_{k+1} - o_{k+1}), \end{cases} \tag{13.8}$$

where $\rho > 0$; $S$ represents the soft threshold operator, see (13.9).

$$S_\kappa(a) = \begin{cases} a - \kappa, a > \kappa \\ 0, \quad |a| \le \kappa \\ a + \kappa, a < \kappa. \end{cases} \tag{13.9}$$

## 13.3 Methodology

To improve the representation ability and ensure learning efficiency of SCN, in this section, we propose stacked deep stochastic configuration networks with multi-level sparse Feature fusion, termed as SDSCNs. Different from the DSCN (Wang and Li, 2018), SDSCNs combine stochastic neural network model with randomized sparse autoencoder (R-SAE). The learning process of SDSCNs mainly divided into two stages: unsupervised representation learning and supervised learning.

Unsupervised learning sets up an multi-level representation learning module, which is similar to the deep feature fusion model based on multiple CNNs (Lin *et al.*, 2020; Xue *et al.*, 2021). SDSCNs use multiple R-SAEs to learn the input data in parallel, which can overcome the shortcomings of insufficient learning ability of a single R-SAE and extract more effective high-level features from the original data; in the supervised learning stage, the SC algorithm is used to enhance the sparse features and generate one or more groups of enhanced nodes for supervised learning tasks such as regression, ensuring the universal approximation of the model.

The structure of SDSCNs with one or multi-group of enhancement nodes are demonstrated in Figs. 13.1–13.2, including input layer, feature layer, enhancement layer and output layer. The feature layer has multiple groups of feature nodes, which are obtained by mapping the original features through multiple R-SAE projections; the

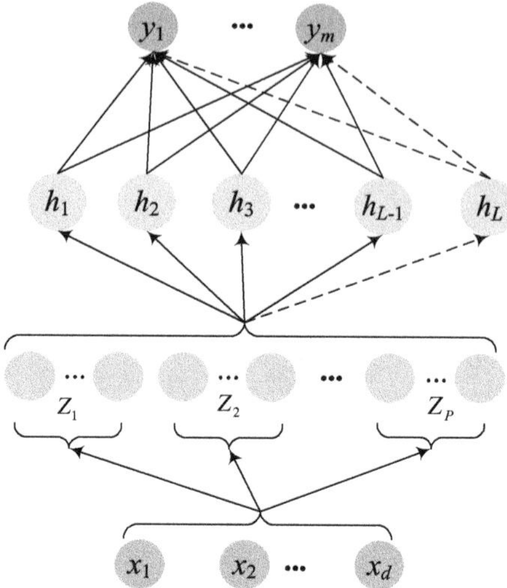

**Fig. 13.1.** The structure of SDSCN with one group of enhancement nodes.

feature nodes can be enhanced through the enhancement layer, in the enhancement process, we use SC algorithm to assign the parameters of each nodes for ensuring universal approximation property of the model. Similar to the feature layer, the enhancement layer of SDSCNs can be presented with one group of enhancement nodes as Fig. 13.1 and multi-groups of enhancement nodes in Fig. 13.2, so as to realize incremental configuration of the model and ensemble learning of multiple groups of nodes, further improving model performance.

The specific algorithm process of SDSCNs are described as follows:

Given training data $\{X, Y\}$, $X = \{x_1, x_2, \ldots, x_N\}$, where $x_i = [x_{i,1}, x_{i,2}, \ldots, x_{i,d}] \in \mathbb{R}^d$, $d$ is the original feature dimension; $Y = \{y_1, y_2, \ldots, y_N\}$, where $y_i = [y_{i,1}, y_{i,2}, \ldots, y_{i,m}] \in \mathbb{R}^m$, $m$ represents the original feature dimension; $i = 1, 2, \ldots, N$, $N$ indicates the number of samples.

**Sparse feature fusion:** In the process of sparse feature fusion, we use multiple R-SAEs in parallel to perform feature mapping $Z_p, p = 1, 2, \ldots, P$ on the input data $X$, each group generates $K$ dimension features. All the sparse features learned from R-SAEs are fused to generate fusion features using Eq. (13.10). Due to the feed-forward random learning method of R-SAE, the feature fusion of multiple

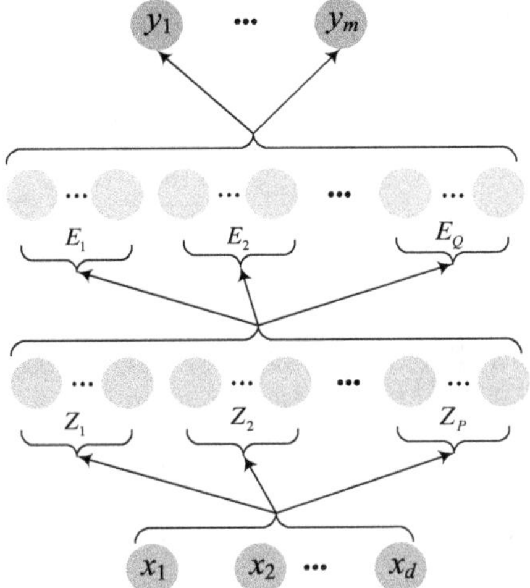


**Fig. 13.2.** The structure of SDSCN with multi-group of enhancement nodes.

R-SAEs is conducive to the rapid learning of diverse features.

$$Z^p = [Z_1, Z_2, \ldots, Z_p]. \tag{13.10}$$

**Feature enhancement:** In the enhancement layer, the fusion features obtained by Eq. (13.10) are enhanced multiple times, where multiple sets of feature enhancements can be regarded as multiple SCN ensemble learning. For each set of enhancement features, the parameter configuration process can be demonstrated as follows:

Assuming that the $q$th group of $L - 1$ enhancement nodes has been configured, the current network outputs can be defined as $f_q^{L-1}$ as Eq. (13.11):

$$f_q^{L-1} = \sum_{l=1}^{L-1} \varphi_q \left( Z^P w_q^I + b_q' \right) \beta_q^l, \tag{13.11}$$

where, $L = 1, 2, \ldots, L_{\max}$, $L_{\max}$ represents the maximum number of enhanced nodes in the $q$th group; $f_q^0 = 0$ indicates the initialization output of the network; $\beta_q^l = [\beta_q^{l,1}, \beta_q^{l,2}, \ldots, \beta_q^{l,m}]$ represents the output weight of node $l$; $\varphi_q(\cdot)$ denotes the activation function; $w_q^l$ and $b_q^l$ are the input weights and biases of node $l$, respectively.

Then, the current residual vector $e_q^{L-1}$ can be calculated by Eq. (13.12), then add the enhancement node $L$ to the $q$th group incrementally, until satisfy $L = L_{\max}$ or $\|e_L\|^2 \leq \varepsilon$.

$$
\begin{aligned}
e_q^{L-1} &= Y - f_q^{L-1} \\
&= \left[ e_q^{L-1,1}\left(Z^P\right), e_q^{L-1,2}\left(Z^P\right), \ldots, e_q^{L-1,m}\left(Z^P\right) \right] \in R^{N \times m}.
\end{aligned}
\tag{13.12}
$$

According to Eqs. (13.13) and (13.14), we can generate candidate weights $w_q^L$ and biases $b_q^L$ of node $L$ randomly,

$$
w_q^L = \lambda \times \left(2 \times \text{rand}\left(d, T_{\max}\right) - 1\right),
\tag{13.13}
$$

$$
b_q^L = \lambda \times \left(2 \times \text{rand}\left(1, T_{\max}\right) - 1\right),
\tag{13.14}
$$

where $\lambda$ is the parameter range control factor; $T_{\max}$ represents the maximum number of candidate node parameters.

Based on the supervisory mechanism of SCNs, we select the weights $w_q^L$ and biases $b_q^L$ with largest values of $\xi_q^L = \sum_{j=1}^{m} \xi_q^{L,j}$ as the final parameters of node $L$:

$$
h_q^L = \varphi_q \left(Z^P w_q^L + b_q^L\right).
\tag{13.15}
$$

$$
\xi_q^{L,j} = \frac{\langle e_q^{L-1,j}, h_q^L \rangle^2}{\| h_q^L \|^2} - (1 - r - \mu_L) \| e_q^{L-1,j} \|^2,
\tag{13.16}
$$

where $h_q^L$ indicates the outputs of the $q$th group of $L$th enhancement nodes; $j = 1, 2, \ldots, m$; $r \in (0, 1)$; $\{\mu_L\}$ represents a non-negative real number sequence, satisfying $\mu_L \leq 1 - r$, $\lim_{L \to +\infty} \mu_L = 0$.

The output of group $q$ and all the enhancement nodes can be defined as Eqs. (13.17) and (13.18):

$$
E_q = [h_q^1, h_q^2, \ldots, h_q^L].
\tag{13.17}
$$

$$
E^Q = [E_1, E_2, \ldots, E_Q].
\tag{13.18}
$$

The connecting weight matrix for the SDSCNs can be evaluated through the standard least squares approach as Eq. (13.19):

$$
\beta^Q = \arg\min_{\beta^Q} \left\| E^Q \beta^Q - Y \right\|_F^2 = E^{Q\dagger} Y,
\tag{13.19}
$$

where, $E^{Q\dagger}$ is the Moore–Penrose inverse of $E^Q$.

Therefore, the target output $f$ of SDSCNs can be calculated by Eq. (13.20):

$$f = E^Q \beta^Q. \tag{13.20}$$

## 13.4 Experimental Results and Discussion

### 13.4.1 *Experimental Settings*

#### 13.4.1.1 *Parameter Settings*

Several experiments are designed to illustrate the effectiveness of SDSCNs, we compare SDSCNs to RVFLN (Pao *et al.*, 1994), BLS (Chen and Liu, 2018) and SCN (Wang and Li, 2017b) and multi-layer perceptron (MLP) (Ren *et al.*, 2017) to illustrate the effectiveness of SDSCNs. All the programs are developed based on MATLAB 2019b and Python 3.7 on a PC with Intel (R) Core (TM) i7-9750H 2.60 GHz CPU, NVIDIA GPU GTX1650 and 64 GB RAM.

The main parameters of related models are set as follows:

RVFLN: The number of hidden layer nodes is set to 50, and the input weights and biases determined from the uniform distribution over $[-1, 1]$ and $[0, 1]$, respectively.

BLS: The input parameters of feature nodes and enhancement nodes obey the uniform distribution over $[-1, 1]$; the number of enhancement node groups $Q$ is set to 1; the number of enhancement nodes in each group $L$ is set to 50; the number of feature mappings $P$ and the number of nodes $K$ in each feature mapping group are set according to different training data for obtaining a better performance.

**SCN:** The maximum number of hidden layer nodes is set to 50; the tolerance error is set as $1e - 10$; the maximum number of candidate nodes is set to 200; the parameter ranges $\Upsilon$ is set to $\{1, 5, 10, 20, 30, \ldots, 100, 150, 200\}$, which is used to configure node parameters based on supervision mechanism.

**MLP:** The number of hidden layers is set to 3; the number of nodes in each hidden layer are set to 100, 50, and 30 respectively; the maximum number of iterations is set to 1000; and some other parameters are set as general settings.

**SDSCN-1:** The number of enhancement node groups $Q$ is set to 1; the number of enhancement nodes in each group $L$ is set to 50; the tolerance error is set to $1e - 10$; the maximum number of candidate nodes is set to 200; the parameter range control factor array $\Upsilon$ is set to $\{1, 5, 10, 20, 30, \ldots, 100, 150, 200\}$; the number of feature mappings $P$ and the number of feature nodes $K$ in each feature mapping group are determined as BLS.

**SDSCN-2:** the parameters of SDSCN-2 are similar to those of SDSCN-1, except the number of enhancement nodes in each group $L$ is in the range of $10, 20, 30, \ldots, 100$, which is determined automatically in the SDSCN-2.

**SDSCN-3:** It is the same as SDSCN-1, except the number of enhancement node groups $Q$ is set as 2 for illustrating the scalability of the proposed SDSCNs. To ensure the fairness of the experiments, RVFLN, SCN, BLS, and SDSCNs all use the Sigmoid function of Eq. (13.21) as the activation function.

$$S(x) = \frac{1}{1 + e^{-x}} \tag{13.21}$$

### 13.4.1.2 *Benchmark Datasets*

To verify the regression performance of SDSCNs, two function approximation problems as Eqs. (13.22) and (13.23), and some different scales of real-world datasets from KEEL (http://www.keel.es/), including Laser, Friedman, Concrete, Stock, Wizmir, MV, Treasury, Pole, Delta_elv, Compactiv and Elevators in Table 13.1 are selected as experimental datasets.

Function approximation problems (Igelnik and Pao, 1995; Tyukin and Prokhorov, 2009):

$$f_1(x) = \begin{cases} \sin(x)/x, & x \neq 0 \\ 1, & x = 0 \end{cases}, x \in [-10, 10] \tag{13.22}$$

$$f_2(x) = 0.2e^{-(10x-4)^2} + 0.5e^{-(80x-40)^2} + 0.3e^{-(80x-20)^2}, \quad x \in [0, 1] \tag{13.23}$$

For the function approximation problem, the training dataset and test dataset are generated according to the real-valued functions (Eqs. (13.22) and (13.23)), in which training dataset has 1000

**Table 13.1.** Attributes of KEEL benchmark datasets.

| Datasets | Type | Dimension | Number |
|---|---|---|---|
| Laser | Regression | 4 | 993 |
| Friedman | Regression | 5 | 1200 |
| Delta_elv | Regression | 6 | 9517 |
| Concrete | Regression | 8 | 1020 |
| Stock | Regression | 9 | 950 |
| Wizmir | Regression | 9 | 1461 |
| MV | Regression | 10 | 40768 |
| Treasury | Regression | 15 | 1049 |
| Elevators | Regression | 18 | 16599 |
| Compactiv | Regression | 21 | 8192 |
| Pole | Regression | 26 | 14998 |

samples, all the sample points of x are generated from the uniform distribution over the domain, while the test dataset consists of 300 points which are subject to a regularly spaced grid over the domain.

For the real-world datasets, normalization preprocessing is applied to reduce the influences of different scales of the data, the input and output vectors are converted into $[0, 1]$. Then, 75% samples of all real-world datasets are selected as training data while other samples are used as test data.

### 13.4.1.3 *Evaluation Indicators*

To evaluate the proposed SDSCNs, several well-known evaluation indicators for regression performance are used, including mean absolute error (MAE) (Eq. (13.24)), root mean square error (RMSE) (Eq. (13.25)), mean square error (MSE) (Eq. (13.26)) and determination coefficient ($R^2$) (Eq. (13.27)). Among them, smaller results of MAE, MSE and RMSE indicate better regression accuracy. $R2$ with a range of is $[0, 1]$, the value of $R^2$ closer to 1 demonstrates the model has a remarkable fitting degree.

To ensure the validity of the experiments, SDSCNs and related comparison models are executed 100 times independently. The average evaluation indicators and its standard deviation are utilized to estimate the generalization capacity of the proposed model.

$$\text{MAE} = \frac{1}{N} \sum_{i=1}^{N} \mid y_i - f_i \mid, \tag{13.24}$$

$$\text{RMSE} = \sqrt{\frac{1}{N} \sum_{i=1}^{N} (y_i - f_i)^2}, \tag{13.25}$$

$$\text{MSE} = \frac{1}{N} \sum_{i=1}^{N} (y_i - f_i)^2, \tag{13.26}$$

$$\text{R}^2 = 1 - \frac{\sum_{i=1}^{N} (y_i - f_i)^2}{\sum_{i=1}^{N} (\overline{y} - y_i)^2}, \tag{13.27}$$

where $y_i$ represents the actual value of sample $i$; $\overline{y}$ denotes the average value of all samples; $f_i$ is the regression result of sample $i$; $N$ indicates the total number of samples.

### 13.4.2  *Function Approximation Problems*

To get a better regression performance on the function approximation problems, the number of feature mappings $P$ and the number of nodes $K$ in each feature mapping are selected from $1, 2, 3, \ldots, 50$ through grid search for SDSCNs. For SDSCN-2, except that the number of enhancement nodes in each group is automatically determined within the range of $10, 20, 30, \ldots, 100$, the other parameters of SDSCN-2 remain the same as those of SDSCN-1. In addition, for the SDSCN-3, the number of enhancement node groups is set to 2, the other parameters of SDSCN-3 remain the same as those of SDSCN-1.

The specific parameter settings of SDSCNs for function approximation problems are shown in Table 13.2.

Figures 13.3 and 13.4 show the approximation performance of SDSCN-1 on two function approximation problems, respectively, where the points represent the actual values and the regression results are represented by lines. It can be seen from the fitting curves of Figs. 13.3 and 13.4 that SDSCN-1 has a strong fitting ability for function approximation problems.

**Table 13.2.** Parameter settings of SDSCNs for function approximation problems.

| | SDSCN-1 | | | | SDSCN-2 | | | | SDSCN-3 | | | |
|---|---|---|---|---|---|---|---|---|---|---|---|---|
| $f(x)$ | $P$ | $K$ | $Q$ | $L$ | $P$ | $K$ | $Q$ | $L$ | $P$ | $K$ | $Q$ | $L$ |
| $f_1(x)$ | 25 | 1 | 1 | 50 | 1 | 1 | 1 | 100 | 1 | 1 | 2 | 50 |
| $f_2(x)$ | 44 | 41 | 1 | 50 | 30 | 25 | 1 | 100 | 38 | 21 | 2 | 50 |

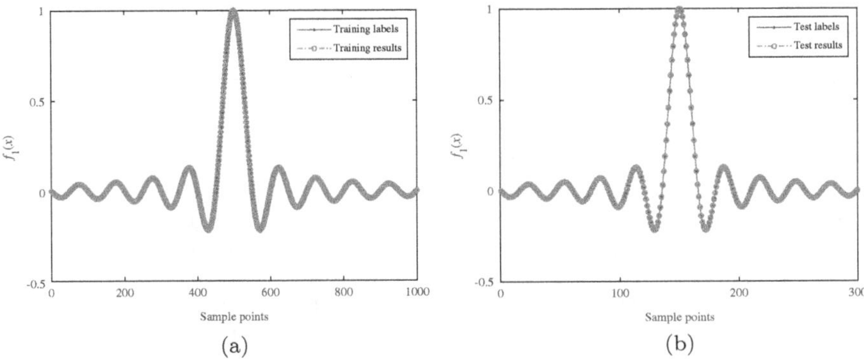

**Fig. 13.3.** Approximation performance of SDSCN-1 on $f_1(x)$ function.

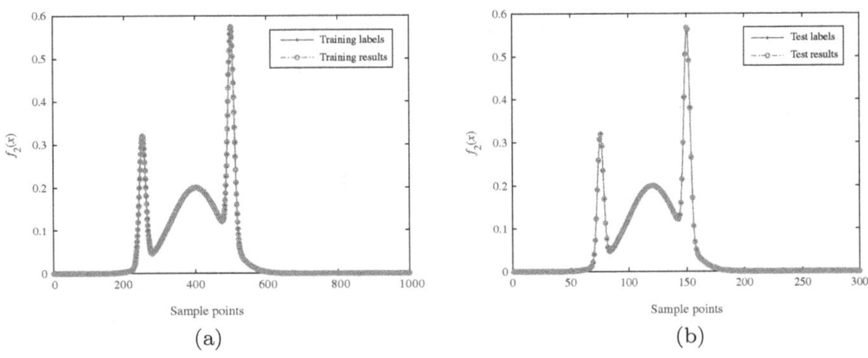

**Fig. 13.4.** Approximation performance of SDSCN-1 on $f_2(x)$ function.

Tables 13.3 and 13.4 present the performance comparison of related models on 2 function approximation problems, in which all the results in Tables 13.3 and 13.4 are average results of each evaluation index.

**Table 13.3.**    Performance comparison of different models on function $f_1(x)$.

| $f(x)$ | Models | MAE↓ | RMSE↓ | MSE↓ | $R^2$↑ | Training times |
|---|---|---|---|---|---|---|
| $f_1(x)$ | RVFLN | 1.69E-02 | 2.08E-02 | 4.31E-04 | 9.91E-01 | **0.1610 s** |
| | BLS | 7.41E-04 | 9.17E-04 | 8.41E-07 | 1.00E + 00 | 0.2841 s |
| | SCN | 5.99E-04 | 8.31E-04 | 7.89E-07 | 1.00E + 00 | 0.5293 s |
| | MLP | 4.94E-02 | 6.69E-02 | 4.47E-03 | 9.05E-01 | 79.9059 s |
| | SDSCN-1 | 4.67E-05 | 5.77E-05 | 3.33E-09 | **1.00E + 00** | 0.6716 s |
| | SDSCN-2 | 1.51E-06 | 1.99E-06 | 3.98E-12 | **1.00E + 00** | 1.8789 s |
| | SDSCN-3 | **3.04E-08** | **4.39E-08** | **1.93E-15** | **1.00E + 00** | 1.5020 s |

**Table 13.4.**    Performance comparison of different models on function $f_2(x)$.

| $f(x)$ | Models | MAE↓ | RMSE↓ | MSE↓ | $R^2$↑ | Training times |
|---|---|---|---|---|---|---|
| $f_2(x)$ | RVFLN | 2.98E-02 | 5.86E-02 | 3.44E-03 | 6.35E-01 | **0.1612 s** |
| | BLS | 9.72E-03 | 2.05E-02 | 4.19E-04 | 9.55E-01 | 0.3950 s |
| | SCN | 4.81E-03 | 8.96E-03 | 8.94E-05 | 9.91E-01 | 0.8118 s |
| | MLP | 2.60E-02 | 5.66E-02 | 3.20E-03 | 6.60E-01 | 84.2750 s |
| | SDSCN-1 | 1.15E-04 | 2.36E-04 | 5.58E-08 | 1.00E + 00 | 1.3336 s |
| | SDSCN-2 | 3.79E-06 | 6.92E-06 | 4.78E-11 | **1.00E + 00** | 2.0110 s |
| | SDSCN-3 | **1.88E-06** | **3.08E-06** | **9.51E-12** | **1.00E + 00** | 1.8307 s |

As can be seen from Tables 13.3 and 13.4, the performance of SDSCN-1, SDSCN-2 and SDSCN-3 are better than RVFLN, BLS, SCN and MLP. Compared with SCN, the multi-level sparse feature fusion module based on R-SAE of SDSCN-1 enhances the feature learning capacity of SCN; compared with SDSCN-2, the adaptive selection of enhancement nodes in SDSCN-1 can further improve the model regression accuracy; among all models, the MSE, MAE, RMSE and other errors of SDSCN-3 are the smallest, and the $R^2$ value is the largest, which shows the effectiveness of the collaboration of the two groups of enhancement nodes of SDSCN-3.

In addition to the MSE, MAE, RMSE and $R^2$ evaluation indicators, Tables 13.3 and 13.4 analyzes the computational efficiency(training time) of different models. Although the enhanced nodes of SDSCN-1, SDSCN-2 and SDSCN-3 adopt point increment configuration method, which consumes some time compared

**Table 13.5.** Parameter settings of SDSCNs for KEEL benchmark datasets.

| Datasets | SDSCN-1 | | | | SDSCN-2 | | | | SDSCN-3 | | | |
| --- | --- | --- | --- | --- | --- | --- | --- | --- | --- | --- | --- | --- |
| | $P$ | $K$ | $Q$ | $L$ | $P$ | $K$ | $Q$ | $L$ | $P$ | $K$ | $Q$ | $L$ |
| Laser | 23 | 12 | 1 | 50 | 40 | 2 | 1 | 80 | 16 | 2 | 2 | 50 |
| Friedman | 9 | 6 | 1 | 50 | 4 | 17 | 1 | 70 | 1 | 32 | 2 | 50 |
| Delta_elv | 3 | 23 | 1 | 50 | 3 | 23 | 1 | 50 | 13 | 5 | 2 | 50 |
| Concrete | 19 | 40 | 1 | 50 | 1 | 37 | 1 | 100 | 17 | 39 | 2 | 50 |
| Stock | 20 | 7 | 1 | 50 | 40 | 17 | 1 | 90 | 8 | 11 | 2 | 50 |
| Wizmir | 8 | 16 | 1 | 50 | 8 | 16 | 1 | 50 | 8 | 17 | 2 | 50 |
| MV | 1 | 17 | 1 | 50 | 1 | 27 | 1 | 100 | 1 | 18 | 2 | 50 |
| Treasury | 4 | 28 | 1 | 50 | 2 | 18 | 1 | 100 | 4 | 17 | 2 | 50 |
| Elevators | 2 | 24 | 1 | 50 | 7 | 17 | 1 | 100 | 5 | 18 | 2 | 50 |
| Compactiv | 26 | 3 | 1 | 50 | 20 | 3 | 1 | 100 | 50 | 2 | 2 | 50 |
| Pole | 44 | 45 | 1 | 50 | 50 | 38 | 1 | 100 | 44 | 46 | 2 | 50 |

to BLS, they still maintain the computational efficiency comparable to RVFLN, BLS and SCN, and are better than MLP.

### 13.4.3 *KEEL Benchmark Datasets*

To achieve higher regression accuracy on the KEEL benchmark datasets, the parameter settings of SDSCNs are determined to be the same as those used for solving function approximation problems.

The specific parameter settings for the KEEL benchmark datasets are presented in Table 13.5.

The performance comparison results of RVFLN, BLS, SCN, MLP, and SDSCN-1, SDSCN-2, and SDSCN-3 are shown in Tables 13.6–13.16. From Tables 13.6–13.16, the test performance of SDSCN-1, RVFLN, BLS, and SCN on the Laser, Friedman, Delta_elv, Concrete, Stock, Wizmir, MV, Treasury, Elevators, Compactiv, and Pole datasets demonstrates that: except for BLS achieving the smallest MAE on the Stock, Treasury, Delta_elv, and Elevators datasets, SDSCN-1 has the smallest MSE, RMSE, and the largest $R^2$, indicating that its overall performance is superior to that of BLS. In terms of the remaining 7 datasets and various evaluation metrics, SDSCN-1 has the smallest MSE, MAE, RMSE, and the largest $R^2$ compared with the relevant models, achieving the best performance.

**Table 13.6.** Performance comparison of different models on Laser dataset.

| Dataset | Models | MAE↓ | RMSE↓ | MSE↓ | $R^2$ ↑ | Training times |
|---|---|---|---|---|---|---|
| Laser | RVFLN | 1.13E-02 | 2.84E-02 | 8.06E-04 | 9.73E-01 | 0.1478 s |
| | BLS | 9.20E-03 | 2.25E-02 | 5.04E-04 | 9.83E-01 | 0.1542 s |
| | SCN | 9.39E-03 | 2.72E-02 | 7.43E-04 | 9.75E-01 | 0.3655 s |
| | MLP | 1.16E-02 | 2.74E-02 | 7.50E-04 | 9.75E-01 | 83.8058 s |
| | SDSCN-1 | 7.86E-03 | 2.13E-02 | 4.54E-04 | 9.85E-01 | 0.4540 s |
| | SDSCN-2 | **7.23E-03** | **2.02E-02** | **4.10E-04** | **9.86E-01** | 0.6862 s |
| | SDSCN-3 | 7.37E-03 | 2.08E-02 | 4.33E-04 | 9.86E-01 | 0.7732 s |

**Table 13.7.** Performance comparison of different models on Friedman dataset.

| Dataset | Models | MAE↓ | RMSE↓ | MSE↓ | $R^2$ ↑ | Training times |
|---|---|---|---|---|---|---|
| Friedman | RVFLN | 3.63E-02 | 4.62E-02 | 2.13E-03 | 9.39E-01 | 0.2357 s |
| | BLS | 3.05E-02 | 3.84E-02 | 1.47E-03 | 9.58E-01 | **0.1690 s** |
| | SCN | 3.58E-02 | 4.59E-02 | 2.11E-03 | 9.40E-01 | 0.3685 s |
| | MLP | 3.46E-02 | 4.44E-02 | 1.97E-03 | 9.44E-01 | 82.3388 s |
| | SDSCN-1 | 3.01E-02 | 3.82E-02 | 1.46E-03 | 9.59E-01 | 0.4246 s |
| | SDSCN-2 | **2.97E-02** | **3.79E-02** | **1.43E-03** | **9.59E-01** | 0.5146 s |
| | SDSCN-3 | 3.05E-02 | 3.86E-02 | 1.49E-03 | 9.58E-01 | 0.6667 s |

**Table 13.8.** Performance comparison of different models on Delta_elv dataset.

| Dataset | Models | MAE↓ | RMSE↓ | MSE↓ | $R^2$ ↑ | Training times |
|---|---|---|---|---|---|---|
| Delta_elv | RVFLN | 3.96E-02 | 5.32E-02 | 2.83E-03 | 6.53E-01 | 7.0143 s |
| | BLS | **3.89E-02** | 5.26E-02 | 2.76E-03 | 6.61E-01 | **1.2491 s** |
| | SCN | 3.94E-02 | 5.30E-02 | 2.81E-03 | 6.55E-01 | 3.3705 s |
| | MLP | 3.89E-02 | 5.38E-02 | 2.89E-03 | 6.46E-01 | 43.6924 s |
| | SDSCN-1 | 3.89E-02 | **5.25E-02** | **2.75E-03** | **6.62E-01** | 1.5673 s |
| | SDSCN-2 | 3.89E-02 | **5.25E-02** | **2.75E-03** | **6.62E-01** | 1.5673 s |
| | SDSCN-3 | 3.88E-02 | 5.27E-02 | 2.77E-03 | 6.60E-01 | 2.4116 s |

**Table 13.9.** Performance comparison of different models on Concrete dataset.

| Dataset | Models | MAE↓ | RMSE↓ | MSE↓ | $R^2$ ↑ | Training times |
|---|---|---|---|---|---|---|
| Concrete | RVFLN | 7.71E-02 | 9.88E-02 | 9.77E-03 | 7.86E-01 | 0.1709 s |
| | BLS | 6.16E-02 | 8.11E-02 | 6.57E-03 | 8.56E-01 | **0.1292 s** |
| | SCN | 6.89E-02 | 9.01E-02 | 8.14E-03 | 8.21E-01 | 0.3281 s |
| | MLP | **4.71E-02** | 6.80E-02 | 4.63E-03 | 8.98E-01 | 81.8601 s |
| | SDSCN-1 | 5.86E-02 | 7.37E-02 | 5.43E-03 | 8.81E-01 | 0.7415 s |
| | SDSCN-2 | 4.97E-02 | **6.35E-02** | **4.04E-03** | **9.11E-01** | 0.6920 s |
| | SDSCN-3 | 5.25E-02 | 6.95E-02 | 4.84E-03 | 8.94E-01 | 1.2575 s |

**Table 13.10.** Performance comparison of different models on Stock dataset.

| Dataset | Models | MAE↓ | RMSE↓ | MSE↓ | $R^2$↑ | Training times |
|---|---|---|---|---|---|---|
| Stock | RVFLN | 2.96E-02 | 4.06E-02 | 1.65E-03 | 9.71E-01 | **0.1661 s** |
| | BLS | 2.53E-02 | 3.43E-02 | 1.18E-03 | 9.79E-01 | 0.1766 s |
| | SCN | 2.81E-02 | 3.71E-02 | 1.38E-03 | 9.76E-01 | 0.3178 s |
| | MLP | 2.86E-02 | 3.58E-02 | 1.28E-03 | 9.77E-01 | 87.7872 s |
| | SDSCN-1 | 2.58E-02 | 3.31E-02 | 1.09E-03 | 9.81E-01 | 0.4712 s |
| | SDSCN-2 | **2.27E-02** | **2.99E-02** | **8.97E-04** | **9.84E-01** | 1.1975 s |
| | SDSCN-3 | 2.41E-02 | 3.02E-02 | 9.14E-04 | 9.84E-01 | 0.7452 s |

**Table 13.11.** Performance comparison of different models on Wizmir dataset.

| Dataset | Models | MAE↓ | RMSE↓ | MSE↓ | $R^2$ ↑ | Training times |
|---|---|---|---|---|---|---|
| Wizmir | RVFLN | 1.44E-02 | 1.98E-02 | 3.91E-04 | 9.93E-01 | 0.2243 s |
| | BLS | 1.37E-02 | 1.85E-02 | 3.41E-04 | 9.94E-01 | **0.1724 s** |
| | SCN | 1.42E-02 | 1.94E-02 | 3.75E-04 | 9.94E-01 | 0.4191 s |
| | MLP | 2.25E-02 | 2.85E-02 | 8.11E-04 | 9.86E-01 | 90.5737 s |
| | SDSCN-1 | 1.37E-02 | **1.81E-02** | **3.28E-04** | **9.94E-01** | 0.5112 s |
| | SDSCN-2 | 1.37E-02 | **1.81E-02** | **3.28E-04** | **9.94E-01** | 0.5112 s |
| | SDSCN-3 | **1.36E-02** | 1.82E-02 | 3.32E-04 | 9.94E-01 | 0.9023 s |

**Table 13.12.**  Performance comparison of different models on MV dataset.

| Dataset | Models | MAE$\downarrow$ | RMSE$\downarrow$ | MSE$\downarrow$ | $R^2\uparrow$ | Training times |
|---|---|---|---|---|---|---|
| MV | RVFLN | 2.90E-02 | 3.84E-02 | 1.47E-03 | 9.74E-01 | 158.6448 s |
|  | BLS | 2.05E-02 | 2.86E-02 | 8.18E-04 | 9.85E-01 | **1.3238 s** |
|  | SCN | 1.57E-02 | 2.16E-02 | 4.68E-04 | 9.92E-01 | 4.5675 s |
|  | MLP | 8.90E-03 | **1.11E-02** | **1.23E-04** | **9.98E-01** | 146.3915 s |
|  | SDSCN-1 | 1.40E-02 | 1.89E-02 | 3.58E-04 | 9.94E-01 | 5.4577 s |
|  | SDSCN-2 | **8.50E-03** | 1.21E-02 | 1.46E-04 | 9.97E-01 | 11.2690 s |
|  | SDSCN-3 | 1.01E-02 | 1.46E-02 | 2.14E-04 | 9.96E-01 | 10.4340 s |

**Table 13.13.**  Performance comparison of different models on Treasury dataset.

| Dataset | Models | MAE$\downarrow$ | RMSE$\downarrow$ | MSE$\downarrow$ | $R^2\uparrow$ | Training times |
|---|---|---|---|---|---|---|
| Treasury | RVFLN | 7.68E-03 | 1.27E-02 | 1.61E-04 | 9.96E-01 | 0.1920 s |
|  | BLS | 7.31E-03 | 1.16E-02 | 1.35E-04 | 9.96E-01 | **0.1791 s** |
|  | SCN | 7.63E-03 | 1.26E-02 | 1.60E-04 | 9.96E-01 | 0.3686 s |
|  | MLP | 1.16E-02 | 1.78E-02 | 3.18E-04 | 9.91E-01 | 86.9754 s |
|  | SDSCN-1 | 7.35E-03 | 1.16E-02 | 1.34E-04 | 9.96E-01 | 0.4526 s |
|  | SDSCN-2 | **6.48E-03** | **1.07E-02** | **1.14E-04** | **9.97E-01** | 0.8585 s |
|  | SDSCN-3 | 6.69E-03 | 1.07E-02 | 1.13E-04 | 9.97E-01 | 0.7764 s |

**Table 13.14.**  Performance comparison of different models on Elevators dataset.

| Dataset | Models | MAE$\downarrow$ | RMSE$\downarrow$ | MSE$\downarrow$ | $R^2\uparrow$ | Training times |
|---|---|---|---|---|---|---|
| Elevators | RVFLN | 2.70E-02 | 3.64E-02 | 1.32E-03 | 8.70E-01 | 53.7180 s |
|  | BLS | 2.64E-02 | 3.56E-02 | 1.27E-03 | 8.75E-01 | **1.6586 s** |
|  | SCN | 2.65E-02 | 3.55E-02 | 1.26E-03 | 8.76E-01 | 2.4850 s |
|  | MLP | **2.57E-02** | 3.72E-02 | 1.39E-03 | 8.64E-01 | 50.4479 s |
|  | SDSCN-1 | 2.68E-02 | 3.55E-02 | 1.26E-03 | 8.76E-01 | 1.7747 s |
|  | SDSCN-2 | 2.60E-02 | **3.45E-02** | **1.19E-03** | **8.83E-01** | 4.5106 s |
|  | SDSCN-3 | 2.61E-02 | 3.47E-02 | 1.20E-03 | 8.82E-01 | 3.5546 s |

**Table 13.15.** Performance comparison of different models on Compactiv dataset.

| Dataset | Models | MAE↓ | RMSE↓ | MSE↓ | $R^2$↑ | Training times |
|---|---|---|---|---|---|---|
| Compactiv | RVFLN | 3.08E-02 | 4.77E-02 | 2.28E-03 | 9.78E-01 | 13.9480 s |
| | BLS | 1.84E-02 | 2.66E-02 | 7.07E-04 | 9.93E-01 | **0.5928 s** |
| | SCN | 2.65E-02 | 4.15E-02 | 1.73E-03 | 9.84E-01 | 2.4504 s |
| | MLP | 1.81E-02 | 2.45E-02 | 5.98E-04 | 9.94E-01 | 40.9778 s |
| | SDSCN-1 | 1.71E-02 | 2.45E-02 | 6.00E-04 | 9.94E-01 | 4.9714 s |
| | SDSCN-2 | **1.62E-02** | **2.37E-02** | **5.59E-04** | **9.95E-01** | 3.2497 s |
| | SDSCN-3 | 1.66E-02 | 2.40E-02 | 5.76E-04 | 9.95E-01 | 3.5407 s |

**Table 13.16.** Performance comparison of different models on Pole dataset.

| Dataset | Models | MAE↓ | RMSE↓ | MSE↓ | $R^2$↑ | Training times |
|---|---|---|---|---|---|---|
| Pole | RVFLN | 1.98E-01 | 2.43E-01 | 5.90E-02 | 6.61E-01 | 57.5874 s |
| | BLS | 1.29E-01 | 1.69E-01 | 2.86E-02 | 8.39E-01 | **0.3700 s** |
| | SCN | 1.90E-01 | 2.35E-01 | 5.54E-02 | 6.82E-01 | 3.6292 s |
| | MLP | **2.42E-02** | **5.47E-02** | **2.99E-03** | **9.83E-01** | 125.7626 s |
| | SDSCN-1 | 1.18E-01 | 1.55E-01 | 2.40E-02 | 8.60E-01 | 7.0725 s |
| | SDSCN-2 | 1.01E-01 | 1.36E-01 | 1.84E-02 | 8.93E-01 | 15.9510 s |
| | SDSCN-3 | 9.90E-02 | 1.33E-01 | 1.78E-02 | 8.97E-01 | 14.5320 s |

In addition, by comparing the training times of different models on the KEEL benchmark datasets, although the incremental configuration of network parameters through the SC algorithm consumes some time, the learning process of SDSCN-1 and SCN requires more computing time but still maintains a learning efficiency comparable to that of BLS. Therefore, it can be concluded that compared with RVFLN, BLS, and SCN, the proposed SDSCN-1 performs well on the KEEL benchmark datasets, and its feature learning ability can be significantly enhanced by introducing feature optimization integration.

To demonstrate the scalability and effectiveness of SDSCNs, Tables 13.6 to 13.16 also present three SDSCN models with different network parameters or structures, namely SDSCN-1, SDSCN-2, and SDSCN-3. Except for the Friedman, Wizmir, and Delta_elv datasets, SDSCN-2 and SDSCN-3 perform better than SDSCN-1 on the remaining datasets. SDSCN-2 obtained the same results as

SDSCN-1 on the Wizmir and Delta_elv datasets. The performance of SDSCN-3 on the Friedman, Wizmir, and Delta_elv datasets was slightly weaker than that of SDSCN-1, but it performed better than SDSCN-1 on the other datasets, indicating that the integrated performance based on two sets of enhanced nodes is superior to that of SDSCN-1 with a single set of enhanced nodes.

In addition, we compared SDSCN-1, SDSCN-2, and SDSCN-3 with the classic MLP model based on the BP algorithm to demonstrate the effectiveness of the SDSCNs. From the performance comparison results in Tables 13.6 to 13.16, SDSCNs achieved 7 optimal test results out of 11 datasets, all of which were superior to those of MLP. On the Concrete and Elevators datasets, except for the MAE result, SDSCNs were weaker than MLP, but the MSE, RMSE, and $R^2$ were all better than those of MLP. At the same time, the overall training times of the SDSCNs are much shorter than those of MLP.

## 13.5   Summary

SCN adopts an incremental learning method, which can start from a smaller network structure, use supervision mechanism to allocate hidden layer node parameters, and gradually increase the number of hidden layer nodes. The introduction of supervision mechanism makes SCN have a sound generalization performance. Although the training process of SCN has less manual intervention and faster learning efficiency, the single layer framework affects the representation learning ability of the model. In this chapter, stacked deep stochastic configuration networks (SDSCNs) based on multi-level feature fusion are proposed to address the problem of insufficient representation learning ability of SCN. SDSCNs adopt stacking framework, in which the input features of training data are mapped as the feature nodes and the mapped features are enhanced as the enhancement nodes through the stochastic configuration algorithm, ensuring the universal approximation property of the model. The experimental results on function approximation problems and real-world datasets demonstrate that SDSCNs have higher regression performance compared with RVFLN, BLS, SCN, LightGBM, MLP and the stability of SDSCNs have been improved significantly compared to SCN. Although the regression accuracy of SDSCNs are not as good as LightGBM and MLP in some larger-scale datasets, it has a training efficiency compared with LightGBM and MLP on almost all datasets.

# Chapter 14

# Stochastic Configuration Network with Long Short-Term Memory Feature Embedding

Short-term load forecasting (STLF) is essential for the efficient management of power systems, as it improves forecasting accuracy while optimizing power scheduling efficiency. Despite significant recent advancements in STLF models, forecasting accuracy in high-volatility regions remains a key challenge. To address this issue, this chapter introduces a hybrid load forecasting model that integrates the long short-term memory network (LSTM) with the stochastic configuration network (SCN). We first reconstruct the features and input them into the LSTM for feature extraction. Subsequently, these extracted feature vectors are then used as inputs for SCN-based STLF. Finally, we evaluate the performance of the LSTM-SCN model against other baseline models using the Australian Electricity Load dataset. We also select five high-volatility regions in the test set to validate the LSTM-SCN model's advantages in such scenarios. The results show that the LSTM-SCN model achieved an RMSE of 56.970, MAE of 43.033, and MAPE of 0.492% on the test set. Compared to the next best model, the LSTM-SCN model reduced errors by 6.016, 8.846, and 0.053% for RMSE, MAE, and MAPE, respectively. Additionally, the model consistently outperformed across all five high-volatility regions analyzed. These findings highlight its contribution to improved power system management, particularly in challenging high-volatility scenarios.

## 14.1   Introduction

Power load forecasting is an important area of research within the field of power systems. The field has received increasing academic attention due to its critical role in the efficient and economical operation of power systems (Zeng *et al.*, 2020). Electrical load forecasting can be categorized into three categories based on the forecasting horizon (Wang *et al.*, 2018): short-term load forecasting (STLF), medium-term load forecasting (MTLF), and long-term load forecasting (LTLF). STLF, which ranges from one hour to one week, is significantly influenced by weather conditions and recent load data. These forecasts play a crucial role in real-time grid management. MTLF, typically spanning from one week to several months, is influenced by factors such as seasonal variations in electricity consumption, holidays, and working days. These forecasts are essential for maintenance scheduling and fuel reserve management. LTLF, which extends beyond one year, is influenced by factors such as demographic changes, economic growth, and energy policies. These forecasts are crucial for system planning and optimization. This chapter focuses on STLF. The proposed model leverages deep learning techniques, specifically integrating the stochastic configuration network (SCN), to achieve high accuracy in load forecasting results.

With the growth in global electricity demand, improving the accuracy of load forecasting has become increasingly critical (Mei *et al.*, 2024). Many factors affect electricity load, such as regional differences, socio-economic activities, weather, and prices (Li *et al.*, 2023a). Therefore, power load data are characterized by randomness, volatility, periodicity, and diversity. Extracting the intrinsic patterns of load change from historical power load data and developing an accurate forecasting method are key to successful load forecasting (Wan *et al.*, 2023). Various power load forecasting methods have been proposed to address specific challenges, each offering unique advantages based on different technologies, algorithms, or data types. Currently, power load forecasting methods are mainly divided into four categories (Wan *et al.*, 2015): statistical methods, artificial intelligence techniques, knowledge-based expert systems, and hybrid approaches.

Statistical methods require the construction of explicit data models to represent the relationship between the electric load and contributing factors. Classical statistical methods include multiple regression analysis, exponential smoothing, and stochastic time series, among others. Krstonijević (2022) proposed an adaptive load forecasting method based on the generalized additive model (GAM) and big data estimation techniques. Shi *et al.* (2019) introduced a very short-term bus load forecasting model that utilizes phase space reconstruction (PSR) and a deep belief network (DBN). Barta *et al.* (2016) aimed to establish a national energy consumption forecasting framework using open-access data from the European Network of Transmission System Operators for Electricity (ENTSO-E). To construct the forecast density, they employed gradient boosting regression trees (GBRTs) and conducted benchmarking based on actual load data and forecasts provided by each country. Wijaya *et al.* (2015) extended the generalized additive model (GAM) to GAM2, where a second GAM is applied to the squared residuals. Many statistical methods rely on linear models, which limit their ability to handle nonlinear relationships and complex patterns. Therefore, the nonlinear characteristics of complex electric loads cannot be precisely characterized using traditional methods (Farrag and Elattar, 2021).

Artificial intelligence methods used in power load forecasting include artificial neural networks (ANNs), fuzzy logic, neuro-fuzzy systems, and support vector machines (SVMs) (Guan *et al.*, 2021; Kazemzadeh *et al.*, 2020; Wen *et al.*, 2020). Andriopoulos *et al.* (2020) leveraged convolutional neural networks (CNNs) to optimize neural network hyper-parameters for power load forecasting. Duan *et al.* (2024) proposed a power load forecasting model based on the sparrow search algorithm (SSA), variational mode decomposition (VMD), attention mechanism, and long short-term memory (LSTM). Initially, the SSA is used to optimize VMD parameters; then, LSTM is employed for load forecasting, and an attention mechanism is introduced to enhance the model. Pavlatos *et al.* (2023) applied bidirectional long short-term memory (BiLSTM) to power load forecasting and proposed combining bidirectional memory with advanced neural network architectures. Shi *et al.* (2017) applied a pooling-based deep recurrent neural network (PDRNN) to household load forecasting and suggested that adding more hidden layers to the neural network could improve forecasting performance. Chen *et al.* (2018) applied an improved deep residual network to power load forecasting to enhance prediction results. Although the above models show good performance on their respective datasets, they suffer from limited applicability and poor generalization ability (Zeng *et al.*, 2020).

Expert systems, a notable achievement in artificial intelligence, rely on rule-based logic to mimic the decision-making processes of domain experts. These systems are commonly used as decision support tools. Qiu *et al.* (2021) applied expert system theory to analyze load transfer in regional power grids during transformer, busbar, and line faults, providing load transfer schemes. A study utilized a knowledge-based reasoning expert system to assist decision-makers in selecting the most appropriate load forecasting model for long-term planning in power systems (Kandil *et al.*, 2002). Additionally, researchers have developed a rule-driven method that incorporates prior knowledge from experts on load curves, integrating this knowledge into statistical models to enhance forecasting accuracy (Arora and Taylor, 2013). These research outcomes demonstrate that expert systems play a significant role in power load forecasting, enhancing the credibility and precision of forecasting results by combining expert insights with statistical analysis.

Electricity load data are characterized by temporal correlation, volatility, and uncertainty, with volatility leading to significant forecasting errors in models (Song *et al.*, 2024). Statistical methods and traditional machine learning approaches often fail to account for these characteristics simultaneously, resulting in insufficient load forecasting accuracy, indicating room for further improvement (Liyun *et al.*, 2021). A single method to deal with power load data will result in low computational efficiency, high computational complexity, and high error rates. Over the years, numerous scholars have developed hybrid load forecasting models with the goal of achieving higher forecasting accuracy and lower error rates. Song *et al.* (2024) proposed a hybrid model based on the improved complete ensemble empirical mode decomposition with adaptive noise (ICEEMDAN), combined with CNN, BiLSTM, and self-attention (SA) techniques, along with wavelet domain denoising (WDD) to enhance data smoothing, applied to household electricity load data. This model leverages the spatial feature extraction capabilities of the CNN, the bidirectional temporal sequence extraction capabilities of BiLSTM, and the ability of SA to focus on key historical time points to reduce information loss. Ma *et al.* (2024) proposed a hybrid model based on the CNN, improved chaotic particle swarm optimization (ICPSO), and LSTM for electric load forecasting. CNNs are used for feature extraction, ICPSO is employed to optimize LSTM parameters, and LSTM is then used for load forecasting. Goh *et al.* (2021) proposed a forecasting model that combines the CNN and LSTM, where CNNs are used to identify and extract local features from time series data, which are then input into LSTM for STLF. Chen *et al.* (2023) proposed a hybrid load forecasting model integrating a residual neural network (ResNet) and LSTM, using a ResNet for feature extraction and LSTM for STLF. Zhou and Zhang (2024) proposed an improved ARIMA-LSTM model that allocates weights based on the forecasting errors of the two models in the training set. Shin *et al.* (2024) proposed a hybrid approach combining variational mode decomposition (VMD) to decompose complex data into intrinsic mode functions (IMFs) and an RVFL network to predict each IMF, thereby improving load forecasting accuracy and robustness.

The SCN, a stochastic learning method, was proposed by Wang and Li (2017b). Common stochastic learning algorithms include radial basis function (RBF) networks (Lowe and Broomhead, 1988) and RVFL networks (Pao and Takefuji, 1992). The SCN learning algorithm outperforms other methods due to its supervision mechanism (Dai *et al.*, 2019a; Li and Wang, 2024a; Wang, 2016; Wang and Li, 2017b). However, the lack of supervision mechanisms and the challenge of setting appropriate parameter ranges can lead to poor model performance (Li and Wang, 2017), as demonstrated mathematically in Gorban *et al.* (2016). The SCN exhibits faster convergence and superior forecasting ability compared to other stochastic networks (Lowe and Broomhead, 1988). The SCN has achieved great success in various fields, including software implementation, computer vision, medical data analysis, fault detection and diagnosis, and the modeling and forecasting of various systems. In the realm of power load forecasting, Wang and Dang (2024b) developed a recurrent version of the SCN for time series problems. However, when dealing with power load data, comparing it with only a single model does not sufficiently demonstrate its superiority in handling such data. Our aim is to contribute an effective and accurate hybrid load forecasting model to the field.

The proposed LSTM-SCN approach offers distinct advantages over traditional statistical methods. Conventional statistical models typically assume linearity or stationarity in the data and focus on capturing dependencies and seasonal variations in time series, making them more suitable for simpler load forecasting scenarios. In contrast, LSTM-SCN, as a hybrid model, is capable of handling complex nonlinear relationships and data heterogeneity, enabling it to deliver more accurate predictions in challenging power load forecasting tasks. Compared to existing hybrid models, the LSTM-SCN approach introduces the SCN model innovatively to enhance predictive performance.

The main contributions of this chapter are as follows:

- We propose an innovative fusion method for STLF by combining LSTM and the SCN. We extract features using LSTM, which are then fed into the SCN for forecasting.
- We introduce the SCN as an alternative to traditional forecasting methods, leveraging its Universal Approximation Property to enhance forecasting accuracy in STLF.
- We contribute to the literature by comparing the LSTM-SCN model with other baseline models, particularly examining its performance in high-volatility regions, and thereby highlighting its superior predictive accuracy.

## 14.2  Preliminaries

Long short-term memory (LSTM) is a specialized type of recurrent neural network (RNN) architecture that excels in time series analysis and forecasting. LSTM's ability to learn long-term dependencies enables it to outperform traditional RNNs in capturing such dependencies within sequential data. LSTM was originally designed to address the issues of gradient vanishing and explosion in traditional RNNs when processing long sequences. By introducing a special memory unit, LSTM can retain information from previous states.

The LSTM cell incorporates three gating mechanisms: the forget gate, the input gate, and the output gate. The role of the forget gate is to determine whether information should be discarded or retained in the cell state, based on the hidden state from the previous time step and the current input. The input gate consists of a sigmoid layer and a tanh layer. The sigmoid layer decides which values to

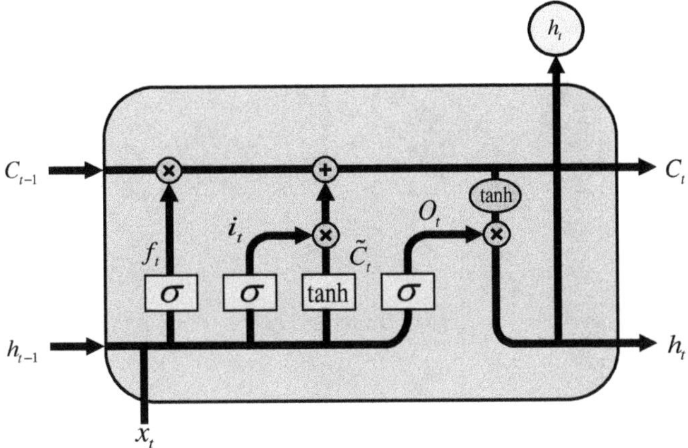

**Fig. 14.1.**   Cell structure of the LSTM model.

update, and the tanh layer generates a new vector of candidate values for updating the cell state. The output gate determines the value of the next hidden state. The interaction of these three gates enables LSTM to efficiently capture long-term dependencies in time series data while mitigating the effects of noise. The LSTM unit is depicted in Fig. 14.1. The mathematical representation of the LSTM is presented as follows.

$$\begin{cases} f_t = \sigma\left(W_f \cdot [h_{t-1}, x_t] + b_f\right) \\ i_t = \sigma\left(W_i \cdot [h_{t-1}, x_t] + b_i\right) \\ C_t' = \tanh\left(W_C \cdot [h_{t-1}, x_t] + b_C\right) \\ C_t = f_t \cdot C_{t-1} + i_t \cdot C_t' \\ O_t = \sigma\left(W_O \cdot [h_{t-1}, x_t] + b_O\right) \\ h_t = O_t \cdot \tanh\left(C_t\right). \end{cases} \tag{14.1}$$

## 14.3   Methodology

In this section, we provide a comprehensive overview of the LSTM-SCN models. The LSTM-SCN model consists of two main components: the LSTM, which acts as a feature extractor, and the SCN, which performs load forecasting using these features. The structure of the model is illustrated in Fig. 14.2.

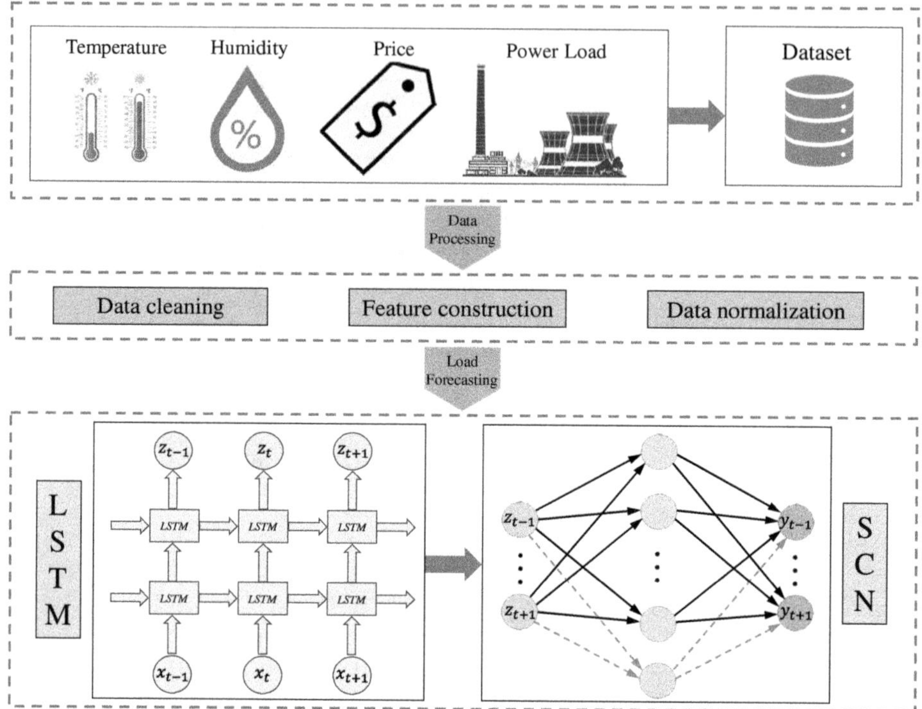


**Fig. 14.2.** The structure of LSTM-SCN model.

Data are preprocessed before being input into the model. Missing values, outliers, and noise in the data can affect the accuracy of the results, necessitating preprocessing operations. Additionally, data normalization can improve the performance of the LSTM model and prevent issues with vanishing or exploding gradients.

The proposed model employs an LSTM network for feature extraction. The internal architecture of the LSTM network consists of two layers Chen *et al.* (2023): the first layer contains 1024 units, and the second layer contains 256 units. To mitigate over-fitting, dropout is applied between the two LSTM layers. The output from the second layer, representing the extracted features, serves as the final output of the model.

This chapter dispenses with the fully connected layers commonly used in most models, opting instead for an innovative approach that employs the SCN for forecasting. In traditional models that use fully connected layers for forecasting, it is necessary to frequently set and adjust the number of hidden layers. The SCN allows for a relatively large number of hidden layer nodes, enabling the model to autonomously identify the optimal network structure within the permissible range of node configurations. This process not only consumes time but also requires significant computational resources. In contrast, the SCN structure is determined by setting a maximum number of hidden nodes and a tolerance level. The number of hidden nodes in the SCN will incrementally increase until the specified tolerance is achieved or the maximum node limit is reached. The SCN is set with the following parameters: the maximum number of hidden layers $L_{\max} = 200$, weights scale sequence Lambdas $=$ $[0.5, 1, 5, 10, 30, 50, 100, 150, 200, 250]$, training tolerance $\varepsilon = 0.001$, contractive sequence r $= [0.9, 0.99, 0.999, 0.9999, 0.99999, 0.999999]$, and maximum number of candidate nodes $T_{\max} = 100$.

## 14.4   Experimental Results and Discussion

This section utilizes the Queensland electricity load dataset (Australia Load. Available online: https://github.com/weiran4/Australi aData (accessed on 22 June 2024)) to evaluate the performance of the proposed model. The effectiveness of the model in predicting the electricity load is also compared against other established baseline models.

### 14.4.1   *Benchmark Datasets*

The dataset contains electrical load data from Queensland, Australia, spanning from 1 January 2006, to 31 December 2010. Sampled at 30 min intervals, the dataset provides 48 sampling points per day and contains 87,649 entries. The dataset includes tariff, temperature, humidity, and power load information, as detailed in Table 14.1. In this section, data from 1 January 2006, to 30 June 2009, are used as the training set; data from 1 July 2009, to 31 December 2009, are used as the validation set; and data from the year 2010 are used as the test set.

### 14.4.2   *Experimental Settings*

The experiments presented in this chapter were conducted on the Ubuntu 22.04 LTS platform within an experimental environment that

**Table 14.1.**  Dataset characteristics.

| Feature Name | Unit | Description |
| --- | --- | --- |
| Power Load | MW | The rate of electrical energy consumption of electrical devices |
| Dry Bulb Temperature | °C | The air temperature measured by a conventional thermometer |
| Dew Point Temperature | °C | The temperature at which water vapor in the air condenses into dew |
| Wet Bulb Temperature | °C | Wet bulb temperature indicates humidity and cooling potential |
| Humidity | $/MWh | The amount of water vapor in the air |
| Price | | The cost per unit of electricity consumed by the user per hour |

**Table 14.2.**  Experimental environment configuration.

| Experimental environment | Experimental setup |
| --- | --- |
| OS | Ubuntu 22.04 |
| Development Environment | VS code |
| Experimental Setup | Intel(R)Xeon® Silver 4116 CPU @ 2.10 GHz |
| Graphics Card Model | NVIDIA GeForce RTX 3090, RTX(24GB) |
| Programming Language | Python3.10 |
| Deep Learning Framework | Pytorch |

included Python 3.10 and PyTorch 2.1.0. The precise specifications of the experimental setup are detailed in Table 14.2.

### 14.4.2.1  *Evaluation Metrics*

The performance of the proposed model is evaluated using three commonly utilized metrics: the root mean square error (RMSE), mean absolute error (MAE), and mean absolute percentage error (MAPE). These metrics are widely recognized for assessing the accuracy of forecasting models. In the fourth part of the experiment, these metrics are also applied to further evaluate the model's performance. The RMSE quantifies the magnitude of discrepancies between predicted and actual values, the MAE calculates the mean of absolute differences, and the MAPE measures percentage errors. The formulas for these metrics are as follows:

$$\mathrm{RMSE} = \frac{1}{n} \sum_{i=1}^{n} (y_i - \hat{y}_i)^2 , \tag{14.2}$$

$$\mathrm{MAE} = \sqrt{\frac{1}{n} \sum_{I=1}^{N} (y_i - \hat{y}_i)^2}, \tag{14.3}$$

$$\mathrm{MAPE} = \frac{1}{n} \sum_{i=1}^{n} \left| \frac{y_i - \hat{y}_i}{y_i} \right|. \tag{14.4}$$

#### 14.4.2.2 *Parameter Settings*

In this section, we use the sigmoid activation function for the SCN, RVFL, and FC models. The parameter settings for each model are as follows Wang and Li (2017b): for the FC model, we set the number of iterations to 200 and specify 200 nodes in the hidden layer. For the RVFL model, we also set the number of iterations to 200 and use 200 hidden nodes. For SVR, we determine the optimal parameter combinations through a grid search method, and then apply these optimal parameters to perform regression analysis. For GBRTs, we set the number of trees to 200.

### 14.4.3 **Data Preprocessing**

We preprocessed the dataset to ensure the accuracy and reliability of subsequent analyses. This involved cleaning the data to remove inconsistencies or errors, extracting time series features to capture temporal patterns, and normalizing the data to standardize the scale of variables.

#### 14.4.3.1 *Data Cleaning*

In the data cleaning section, we inspected the data to confirm that there were no missing values in the dataset. Additionally, we identified potential outliers by calculating the interquartile range (IQR) and applying the $1.5 \times$ IQR rule. For detected outliers, we replaced them with the mean of the preceding and succeeding data points.

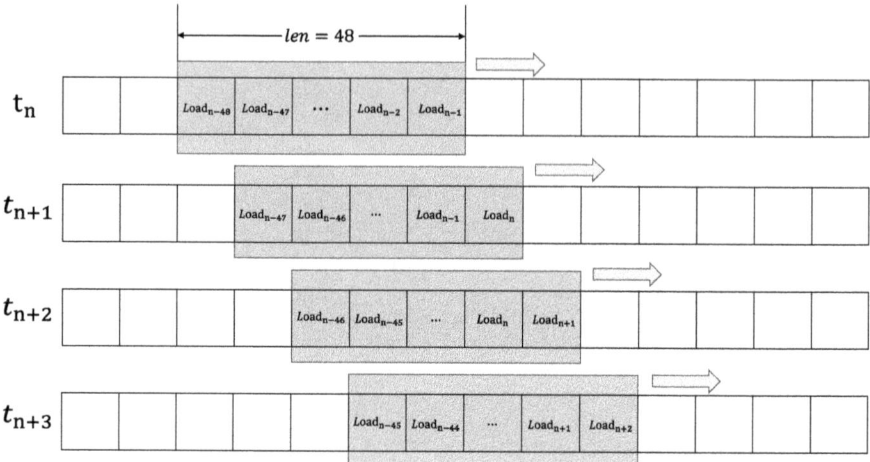



**Fig. 14.3.** Feature acquisition using the sliding window method.

This approach reduces the impact of outliers on the overall data distribution while maintaining data continuity and stability.

### 14.4.3.2 *Time Series Feature Construction*

It is recognized that power load data exhibit significant time series characteristics and interdependence between neighboring data points. Therefore, in addition to selecting environmental factors such as weather and humidity as features, we employ a sliding window method to construct features from the power load data. Specifically, we define a sliding window of 48 time units (Zhou and Zhang, 2024) that moves step by step along the time series. Consequently, the feature vector at each time point includes data from the previous 48 time units, capturing the dynamic changes in the historical data at that point. This process is illustrated in Fig. 14.3. For instance, the feature vector for the nth data point is $\alpha_n = [\text{Load}_{n-48}, \text{Load}_{n-47}, \ldots, \text{Load}_{n-1}]$. Using the sliding window method to construct features enhances the model's ability to capture temporal dependencies and reveals potential patterns and trends in the data. This approach provides richer and more accurate feature information for electricity load forecasting. The feature vectors for the first 48 data points are incomplete due to missing values within the sliding window. Therefore, we remove the first 48 records from the dataset after feature construction to prevent any potential impact of these missing values on subsequent data analysis and model training. The 48 load features we constructed, combined with factors such as weather and humidity, result in a total of 55 features for each electricity load value.

### 14.4.3.3   *Data Normalization*

For the power load data, we normalize both the training and test sets before inputting them into the model. We use the min-max normalization method to scale the data to the $[0, 1]$ range with the following formula:

$$X_{\text{norm}} = \frac{X - X_{\min}}{X_{\max} - X_{\min}}. \tag{14.5}$$

The normalized value $X_{\text{norm}}$ is calculated from the original value $X$, where $X$ is the original value, $X_{\max}$ is the maximum value, and $X_{\min}$ is the minimum value in the dataset.

In this section, we back-normalize the model forecasts to revert the data to their original scale. All model performance metrics are calculated on the back-normalized data, and the visualization of results is also based on these data. Performing the inverse normalization provides a more intuitive and clearer view of the model's forecasting performance. The inverse normalization formula is as follows:

$$X = X_{\text{norm}} \times (X_{\max} - X_{\min}) + X_{\min}. \tag{14.6}$$

### 14.4.4   **Main Results and Discussion**

We compared the proposed LSTM-SCN model with other baseline models, and Table 14.3 presents the performance metrics of each model on the forecasting set. The LSTM-SCN model demonstrated the best performance across all metrics, with an RMSE of 56.970, an MAE of 43.033, and a MAPE of 0.492%. The RMSE and MAPE values of the LSTM-SCN model are reduced by 6.016 and 0.053%, respectively, compared to the second-best performing CNN-LSTM model. Additionally, the MAE of the LSTM-SCN model is decreased by 8.846 compared to the second-best performing GRU model. These

**Table 14.3.** Dataset characteristics.

| Model | RMSE | MAE | MAPE (%) |
| --- | --- | --- | --- |
| LSTM | 93.797 | 72.175 | 0.819 |
| BiLSTM | 124.220 | 100.635 | 1.179 |
| GRU | 69.620 | 51.879 | 0.593 |
| SCN | 97.626 | 74.071 | 0.847 |
| CNN-LSTM | 62.986 | 57.829 | 0.545 |
| LSTM-RVFL | 187.695 | 167.114 | 1.866 |
| LSTM-SCN (ours) | 56.970 | 43.033 | 0.492 |

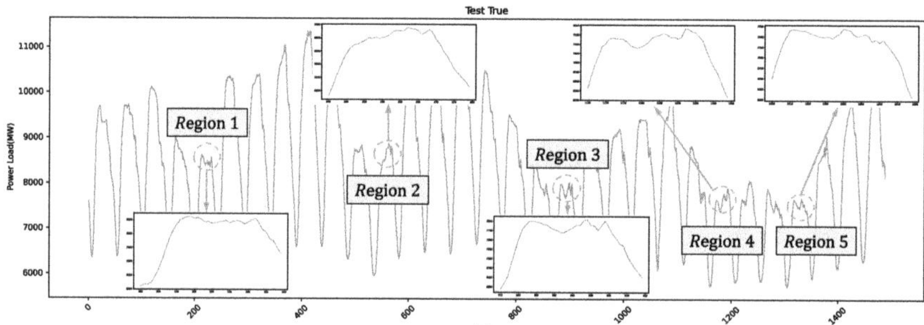


**Fig. 14.4.** Selection process for five high-volatility regions.

**Table 14.4.** Data ranges for selected high-volatility regions.

| Region name | Region 1 | Region 2 | Region 3 | Region 4 | Region 5 |
| --- | --- | --- | --- | --- | --- |
| Data range | $[200, 240)$ | $[540, 580)$ | $[875, 915)$ | $[1165, 1205)$ | $[1310, 1350)$ |

results demonstrate the superior performance of the LSTM-SCN model compared to the others.

In the field of electricity load forecasting, while most models achieve good forecasting performance in low-volatility regions, their true performance is often revealed in high-volatility regions. To fully evaluate LSTM-SCN's performance, we selected five highvolatility periods from the last month of the test set, each with 40 data points. Fig. 14.4 and Table 14.4 detail the selection of these regions and their data ranges, respectively. This detailed analysis enables us to more accurately assess the model's applicability and accuracy in real-world scenarios with high volatility.

Table 14.5 displays the performance metrics for each model in the five selected highvolatility regions. The analysis results indicate that the LSTM-SCN model demonstrates optimal performance across all five high-volatility regions. In Region 1, we compare the LSTM-SCN model to the second-best performing model. The LSTM-SCN model achieves reductions of 37.901 in RMSE, 29.781 in MAE, and 0.391% in MAPE, respectively. In Regions 2, 3, 4, and 5, the reductions in these three metrics for the LSTM-SCN model are as follows: 39.923 in RMSE, 31.502 in MAE, and 0.389% in MAPE for Region 2; 42.201 in RMSE, 29.990 in MAE, and 0.420 % in MAPE for Region 3; 34.951 in RMSE, 24.734 in MAE, and 0.332% in MAPE for Region 4; and 34.552 in RMSE, 24.074 in MAE, and 0.325% in MAPE for Region 5. These results demonstrate that the LSTM-SCN model exhibits excellent performance in handling high-volatility regions, thereby highlighting the advantages of the LSTM-SCN model in the field of power load forecasting.

To explain why the LSTM-SCN model exhibits optimal performance across the five high-volatility regions, we offer the following analysis: (1) Adaptive Dynamic Network Structure: The LSTM-SCN model relies on a supervision mechanism during prediction, whereas other models depend on the backpropagation mechanism of fully connected layers. Backpropagation requires gradient optimization and relies on a fixed network structure, while the supervision mechanism can dynamically adjust the network structure based on data and task requirements. This adaptability allows the model to construct an optimal network architecture during learning, avoiding over-fitting and unnecessary complexity. (2) Robustness to Gradient Issues: Backpropagation in deep networks often faces challenges like vanishing or exploding gradients, which hinder model convergence and learning efficiency. In contrast, the supervision mechanism does not rely entirely on gradients but adjusts through a feedback-driven process, making the model more robust to these issues. (3) Enhanced Interpretability: The supervision mechanism offers higher interpretability. Its dynamic structural adjustments can reveal the relationship between data features and model behavior, providing a more transparent and efficient learning process.

**Table 14.5.** Comparative performance indicators of models across different regions.

| Region name | Model | RMSE | MAE | MAPE (%) |
|---|---|---|---|---|
| Region 1 | LSTM | 69.503 | 56.357 | 0.723 |
|  | BiLSTM | 43.366 | 34.632 | 0.453 |
|  | GRU | 49.503 | 40.009 | 0.511 |
|  | SCN | 82.894 | 69.422 | 0.894 |
|  | CNN-LSTM | 48.532 | 36.188 | 0.454 |
|  | LSTM-RVFL | 120.833 | 111.067 | 1.391 |
|  | LSTM-SCN (ours) | 5.465 | 4.851 | 0.062 |
| Region 2 | LSTM | 77.431 | 55.698 | 0.666 |
|  | BiLSTM | 63.474 | 46.654 | 0.566 |
|  | GRU | 47.208 | 36.597 | 0.451 |
|  | SCN | 58.148 | 47.428 | 0.591 |
|  | CNN-LSTM | 52.001 | 41.473 | 0.517 |
|  | LSTM-RVFL | 158.725 | 149.760 | 1.853 |
|  | LSTM-SCN (ours) | 7.285 | 5.095 | 0.062 |
| Region 3 | LSTM | 66.255 | 48.467 | 0.632 |
|  | BiLSTM | 48.305 | 36.094 | 0.477 |
|  | GRU | 53.502 | 43.131 | 0.573 |
|  | SCN | 86.465 | 81.428 | 0.794 |
|  | CNN-LSTM | 53.183 | 41.249 | 0.542 |
|  | LSTM-RVFL | 154.871 | 146.592 | 1.947 |
|  | LSTM-SCN (ours) | 6.104 | 6.104 | 0.057 |
| Region 4 | LSTM | 109.402 | 93.140 | 1.262 |
|  | BiLSTM | 56.048 | 37.506 | 0.506 |
|  | GRU | 71.450 | 54.467 | 0.733 |
|  | SCN | 93.136 | 82.856 | 1.492 |
|  | CNN-LSTM | 42.403 | 30.666 | 0.412 |
|  | LSTM-RVFL | 156.803 | 148.207 | 2.012 |
|  | LSTM-SCN (ours) | 7.452 | 5.932 | 0.080 |
| Region 5 | LSTM | 95.331 | 84.480 | 1.166 |
|  | BiLSTM | 41.727 | 30.050 | 0.406 |
|  | GRU | 60.292 | 46.030 | 0.625 |
|  | SCN | 79.458 | 69.475 | 0.916 |
|  | CNN-LSTM | 58.118 | 45.542 | 0.617 |
|  | LSTM-RVFL | 112.343 | 104.097 | 1.418 |
|  | LSTM-SCN (ours) | 7.175 | 5.976 | 0.081 |

## 14.5 Summary

With the growing demand for higher accuracy in STLF in power systems, particularly in high-volatility regions, this study introduces a hybrid forecasting model based on the LSTM-SCN. Abandoning the traditional fully connected layer forecasting method, this study innovatively adopts the SCN, known for its universal approximation property, for the forecasting process. This approach not only reduces the time and effort required to set up the network structure by eliminating the need for repeated attempts but also enables the identification of the optimal network structure among various configurations. The LSTM-SCN model utilizes the LSTM to extract data features, which are then used as inputs to the SCN for forecasting. In this study, we selected the Australian electricity load dataset for the experiments and used three metrics-the RMSE, MAE, and MAPE-to evaluate the model's performance. The RMSE, MAE, and MAPE values of the LSTM-SCN model on the Australian dataset are 56.970, 43.033, and 0.492%, respectively, outperforming other models. To evaluate the predictive performance of the LSTM-SCN model in high-volatility regions, five high-volatility areas were selected from the test set for analysis. The LSTM-SCN model achieved the best performance metrics across all selected regions. In Region 1, the RMSE, MAE, and MAPE values for the LSTMSCN model were $5.465, 4.851$, and 0.062%, respectively. Compared to the second-best model, the LSTM-SCN model achieved reductions in errors of 37.901, 29.781, and 0.391% for the RMSE, MAE, and MAPE, respectively. Similarly, in Region 2, the LSTM-SCN model obtained RMSE, MAE, and MAPE values of $7.285, 5.095$, and 0.062%, respectively, with reductions in errors of $39.923, 31.502$, and 0.389% compared to the second-best model. For the remaining three regions, the LSTM-SCN model consistently outperformed all other models across the three evaluation metrics.

In summary, the proposed LSTM-SCN hybrid model demonstrates strong performance in short-term power load forecasting, particularly in capturing data variation trends in high-volatility regions, thereby improving forecasting accuracy in these challenging areas. Additionally, the LSTM-SCN model offers a novel solution for STLF, with significant practical application value and promising development potential. This model has the potential to drive new breakthroughs in the field of power load forecasting.

# Chapter 15

# Book Review and Future Work

What are advanced randomized neural networks, and why are they important? This book offers a comprehensive exploration of these questions. Randomized neural networks can be categorized into two types based on their parameter learning mechanisms: data-dependent and data-independent. Advanced randomized neural networks (ARNNs) utilize data-dependent stochastic configuration algorithms to assign random parameters and incrementally build network structures, thereby preserving the universal approximation property (UAP) of randomized neural networks. To further enhance the performance of ARNNs in various pattern analysis tasks, our research provides systematic solutions across three key areas: neural network optimization, robust data analysis, and deep fusion learning.

## Part 1: Neural Networks Optimization

This part explores neural networks optimization techniques for ARNNs across four chapters, addressing challenges such as hyper-parameter optimization, over-fitting phenomenon, efficient block-incremental learning, and ill-posed problem.

## Part 2: Robust Data Analysis

Focused on robust data analysis, this part comprises four chapters that introduce techniques like intuitionistic fuzzy theory, weighted least squares methods, noise-robust regularization, and robust semi-supervised learning for handling outliers.

## Part 3: Deep Fusion Learning

This part delves into deep fusion learning techniques for ARNNs, spanning five chapters that cover single-model and multi-model ensemble learning, multi-level feature fusion, boosting negative correlation learning and long short-term memory embedding.

In this chapter, we summarize the content of the book and explore future directions for advanced randomized neural networks. Section 15.1 provides an overview of the previous chapters, while Section 15.2 discusses the challenges and future research opportunities in the field of advanced randomized neural networks.

## 15.1  Book Recapitulation

Advanced randomized neural networks (ARNNs) play a crucial role in pattern analysis. Chapter 1 of this book serves as a guideline, highlighting the differences between randomized neural networks and advanced randomized neural networks. The book is divided into three parts, focusing on typical models for neural networks optimization, robust data analysis, and deep fusion learning.

Part 1 delves into neural networks optimization techniques for ARNNs and consists of four chapters (Chapters 2–5).

**Chapter 2:** This chapter introduces an adaptive decay regularized stochastic configuration network (DRSCN) with multi-level signal processing for predicting the remaining useful life (RUL) of UAV batteries. We first detail the development of a multi-level signal enhancement framework (MLSEF) and the application of decay regularization to enhance the SCN model's output layer. Moreover, we present the convex lens and dual-mechanism enhanced sand cat swarm optimization algorithm (CLDM-SCSO) for hyperparameter tuning. Extensive experiments using the NASA HIRF battery dataset demonstrate the framework's accuracy and reliability for UAV battery health monitoring.

**Chapter 3:** This chapter focuses on establishing a regularized stochastic configuration network based on the weighted mean of vectors (RSCN-INFO) to optimize parameter selection and network structure. The introduction of a regularization term that combines the ridge method with residual error feedback can dynamically adjust the training parameters. The INFO algorithm is employed to explore an appropriate four-dimensional parameter vector for RSCN, leading to a compact network architecture with faster residual error reduction. Simulation results on benchmark datasets showcase the superior performance of RSCN-INFO in parameter setting, convergence, and network compactness.

**Chapter 4:** This chapter presents efficient block-incremental stochastic configuration networks (EBSCN) with group lasso regularization (EBSCNGL) to address issues in the original SCNs. We first introduce a new set of inequalities without matrix generalized inverse to ensure the universal approximation capability of EBSCN. Then group lasso regularization is applied to prune redundant nodes in the hidden layer, and the regularized least-squares solution is transformed into an efficient form using the Woodbury matrix identity. Empirical results on various applications verify the efficiency and sparsity of the proposed method.

**Chapter 5:** This chapter investigates the supervisory mechanism of stochastic configuration networks and the algebraic properties of the hidden output matrix to address instability issues in SCNs. A new greedy stochastic configuration network (GSCN) for ill-posed problems is proposed, utilizing the hunter–prey optimization (HPO) algorithm to optimize hidden parameters. Singular value decomposition (SVD) and orthogonal-triangular (QR) decomposition with column pivoting are introduced to extract linearly independent subsets of the hidden output matrix. Experimental results on multiple datasets demonstrate GSCN's superior performance in convergence, generalization, and stability.

Part 2 mainly presents robust data analysis methods for ARNNs, comprising four chapters (Chapters 6–9).

**Chapter 6:** This chapter introduce intuitionistic fuzzy stochastic configuration network (IFSCN) and intuitionistic fuzzy deep stochastic configuration network (IFDSCN) to enhance the precision and robustness for binary classification tasks. In the proposed IFSCN and IFDSCN, intuitionistic fuzzy numbers (IFNs) are used as penalty weights for samples to measure data reliability and mitigate the adverse effects of noise and outliers. Moreover, we disign intuitionistic fuzzy based weighted supervision mechanisms for assign the parameters of IFSCN and IFDSCN. Numerous experiments indicate IFSCN and IFDSCN have higher classification accuracy on eight benchmark binary classification datasets.

**Chapter 7:** This chapter introduces weighted deep stochastic configuration networks (WDSCN) based on M-Estimator functions. First of all, we adopt two common M-estimator functions (i.e., Huber and Bisquare) to acquire the sample weights for reducing the negative impact of outliers. Meanwhile, the weighted least square method and $L_2$ regularization strategy are introduced to calculate output weight vector replace the least square method. For further improve the representation ability of WDSCN, a stochastic configuration sparse autoencoder (SC-SAE) is designed, SC-SAE use the supervision mechanism of DSCN to assign input parameters, at the same time, we adopt the $L_1$ regularization technique to objective function for getting sparse features, consequently effective feature representation can be acquired through fusion features from multiple SC-SAE for the training of WDSCN. Finally, experimental results on real-world datasets show that the proposed WDSCN-Huber and WDSCN-Bisquare have higher generalization performances and regression accuracies than DSCN, SCN, and other weighted models (e.g., RSC-KDE, RSC-Huber, RSC-IQR, RDSCN-KDE, WBLS-KDE and RBLS-Huber).

**Chapter 8:** This chapter introduces the robust deep stochastic configuration network (RDSCN) for enhancing the regression accuracy and robustness of DSCN in handling industrial noise data. Unlike other robust stochastic configuration network (RSCN) models that use weighted methods, RDSCN employs the $L_1$ norm loss function to process outliers with sparse characteristics, while the $L_2$ regularization technique is used to mitigate over-fitting. Additionally, the slime mould algorithm (SMA) is applied to select appropriate parameter scales for weights and biases, further enhancing RDSCN's robustness. Experiments on real-world regression datasets with various contamination rates demonstrate that RDSCN, with the $L_1$ norm loss function and $L_2$ regularization technique, achieves higher regression accuracy in addressing outlier data with uniformly distributed noise. The SMA-optimized RDSCN further improves the model's robustness.

**Chapter 9:** This chapter presents a novel robust semi-supervised stochastic configuration network to improve regression performance in real-world pattern analysis scenarios with missing labels and noise.The proposed model uses kernel density estimation (KDE) to evaluate the density of labeled training samples, reducing the influence of noise and outliers. Manifold regularization is employed to learn features from unlabeled data, enhancing SCN's generalization performance. Additionally, $L_2$ regularization term is introduced to manage outliers in sparse features, reducing over-fitting. The universal approximation property is demonstrated within an improved robust semi-supervised optimization framework. Simulation experiments on benchmark datasets show significant improvements in semi-supervised learning and robustness for proposed model compared to the original algorithm.

Part 3 mainly presents deep fusion learning approaches for ARNNs, which including five parts (Chapters 10–14).

**Chapter 10:** This chapter proposes a deep stochastic configuration network ensemble model based on the chaotic sparrow search algorithm (CSSA-DSCN). The chaotic sparrow search algorithm, utilizing logistic mapping, self-adaptive hyper-parameters, and mutation operator, enhances the global optimization capability. The performance of DSCN is optimized by adjusting the regularization parameter $r$ and scale factor $\lambda$ of weights and biases using CSSA. The optimal hyper-parameters are used to train base models and construct an adaptive boosting model, reducing generalization error and improving regression accuracy. Experimental results on various datasets demonstrate the feasibility and validity of CSSA-DSCN compared to SCN and other contrast algorithms.

**Chapter 11:** This chapter introduces the greedy deep stochastic configuration networks ensemble model based on boosting negative correlation learning (GDSCNE). The model uses a greedy optimization strategy based on inequality constraints to generate random parameters of base components with a multi-layer architecture, accelerating the decline of network residuals. A boosting negative correlation learning framework is presented for the ensemble process, using a least squares approach with a negative correlation learning penalty term to update ensemble output weights for each base component. Experimental results on regression benchmark datasets from KEEL show that GDSCNE outperforms state-of-the-art random learning algorithms in regression accuracy and generalization performance.

**Chapter 12:** This chapter introduces the ensemble intuitionistic fuzzy deep stochastic configuration network (EIFDSCN), a self-ensemble deep model based on IFDSCN. Unlike conventional ensemble strategies, EIFDSCN employs a multi-layer structure that simultaneously trains multiple sub-models, enabling effective feature extraction from the original input while preserving the fast learning capability of deep stochastic configuration networks. Experimental results demonstrate that this self-ensemble strategy significantly improves classification accuracy and robustness.

**Chapter 13:** This chapter proposes a stacked deep stochastic configuration network (SDSCN) based on sparse feature fusion, combining random sparse autoencoders and SCNs. The original features are transformed into mapping features in the feature layer, which are then enhanced in the enhancement layer. Input weights and biases are determined according to the supervision mechanism, and the output weight matrix is calculated through standard least squares. Experimental results on function approximation problems and real-world datasets show that SDSCN improves SCN's performance, with higher regression accuracy and stability.

**Chapter 14:** This chapter introduces a hybrid load forecasting model that integrates the long short-term memory network (LSTM) with the stochastic configuration network (SCN) for short-term load forecasting (STLF). Features are reconstructed and input into the LSTM for extraction, with the extracted feature vectors used as inputs for SCN-based STLF. The LSTM-SCN model's performance is evaluated against baseline models using the Australian Electricity Load dataset, particularly in high-volatility regions. Results show that the LSTM-SCN model achieves superior forecasting accuracy, reducing errors and consistently outperforming across high-volatility regions, contributing to improved power system management.

## 15.2 Challenges and Future Work

Advanced randomized neural networks (ARNNs) have achieved notable success in pattern analysis, thanks to their constructive architecture and data-dependent random weights, which offer advantages such as low training costs and rapid deployment. However, with the advent of multi-modal learning, reinforcement learning, and edge computing — particularly in the era of large language models — ARNNs face new challenges that must be addressed to fully unlock their potential. Despite these challenges, ARNNs, when appropriately designed and integrated with innovative mechanisms such as attention models, dynamic adaptation strategies, and resource-efficient optimization, hold significant promise for success in these domains.

**ARNNs in multi-modal learning:** In multi-modal learning, ARNNs struggle with effectively modeling heterogeneous data distributions due to their architecture. However, incorporating attention mechanisms can significantly enhance their ability to dynamically allocate weights across different modalities (e.g., text, images, and sensor signals). This enables ARNNs to perform more effective cross-modal alignment, making them suitable for applications such as autonomous driving and healthcare diagnostics, where prioritizing critical information dynamically is essential. Additionally, attention-enhanced ARNNs can better handle asynchronous or partially observed data streams, improving their robustness in real-world multi-modal scenarios. By combining the efficiency of random projections with the adaptability of trainable models, ARNNs offer a scalable and efficient solution for complex multi-modal learning tasks.

**ARNNs in reinforcement learning:** Stability and adaptability remain key challenges for ARNNs in reinforcement learning (RL), as random weights limit their ability to model dynamic environments. However, by integrating adaptive attention mechanisms, ARNNs can refine policy representations and improve value function estimation, leading to more stable gradient-based updates. In high-dimensional tasks such as robotic manipulation and real-time game playing, ARNNs can dynamically adjust exploration strategies based on environmental feedback, enhancing the exploration-exploitation balance. Moreover, attention-enhanced ARNNs can capture long-term dependencies and temporal correlations, which are critical for sequential decision-making. When properly designed, ARNNs can merge the computational efficiency of randomized architectures with the adaptability of attention-driven models, making them a viable approach for RL applications.

**ARNNs in edge computing:** Deploying ARNNs in edge computing environments presents unique challenges, such as hardware constraints and the need for energy-efficient algorithms. However, ARNNs can be optimized for edge deployment by leveraging lightweight attention mechanisms that dynamically adjust computational complexity. For real-time inference tasks in IoT or autonomous drones, ARNNs can focus on the most relevant features, reducing energy consumption while maintaining performance. Furthermore, efficient use of non-volatile memory allows for on-chip storage of attention weights and random matrices, enabling resource-constrained applications without significant performance degradation. Advances in quantization techniques for attention weights and random projections further enhance their deployability on low-precision edge chips, paving the way for scalable and efficient edge AI solutions.

In summary, while ARNNs face challenges in adapting to emerging AI paradigms, their inherent efficiency, combined with mechanisms for dynamic adaptation, positions them as a promising approach for multi-modal learning, reinforcement learning, and edge computing. Future research should focus on further refining these models to fully harness their potential in complex, resource-constrained, and dynamically evolving environments. With continued innovation, ARNNs are poised to achieve significant success in these cutting-edge fields.

# Bibliography


Abdi, H., Valentin, D., and Edelman, B. (1999). *Neural Networks*, p. 124 (Sage).

Ahmadianfar, I., Heidari, A. A., Noshadian, S., Chen, H., and Gandomi, A. H. (2022). INFO: An efficient optimization algorithm based on weighted mean of vectors, *Expert Systems with Applications* **195**, p. 116516.

Ai, W. and Wang, D. (2020). Distributed stochastic configuration networks with cooperative learning paradigm, *Information Sciences* **540**, pp. 1–16.

Alhamdoosh, M. and Wang, D. (2014). Fast decorrelated neural network ensembles with random weights, *Information Sciences* **264**, pp. 104–117.

Alsahanova, N., Yarkin, V., Spodarev, E., Bronov, O., Bychenko, V., Marinets, A., Syrkashev, E., Karpov, O., Burnaev, E., Bernstein, A., Alferova, V., and Sharaev, M. (2025). Knowledge-informed randomized machine learning and data fusion for anomaly areas detection in multimodal 3D images, *Information Sciences* **686**, p. 121354.

Alvarez, J. M. and Salzmann, M. (2016). Learning the number of neurons in deep networks, *Advances in Neural Information Processing Systems* **29**, pp. 1–9.

Andriopoulos, N., Magklaras, A., Birbas, A., Papalexopoulos, A., Valouxis, C., Daskalaki, S., Birbas, M., Housos, E., and Papaioannou, G. P. (2020). Short term electric load forecasting based on data transformation and statistical machine learning, *Applied Sciences* **11**, 1, p. 158.

Ansal, V. (2020). ALO-optimized artificial neural network-controlled dynamic voltage restorer for compensation of voltage issues in distribution system, *Soft Computing* **24**, 2, pp. 1171–1184.

Arora, S., Bhaskara, A., Ge, R., and Ma, T. (2014). Provable bounds for learning some deep representations, in *International Conference on Machine Learning* (PMLR), pp. 584–592.

Arora, S. and Taylor, J. W. (2013). Short-term forecasting of anomalous load using rule-based triple seasonal methods, *IEEE Transactions on Power Systems* **28**, 3, pp. 3235–3242.

Atanassov, K. T. (1986). Intuitionistic fuzzy sets, *Fuzzy Sets & Systems* **20**, 1, pp. 87–96.

Barron, A. R. (1993). Universal approximation bounds for superpositions of a sigmoidal function, *IEEE Transactions on Information Theory* **39**, 3, pp. 930–945.

Barta, G., Nagy, G., Papp, G., and Simon, G. (2016). Forecasting framework for open access time series in energy, in *2016 IEEE International Energy Conference (ENERGYCON)* (IEEE), pp. 1–6.

Belkin, M., Niyogi, P., and Sindhwani, V. (2006). Manifold regularization: A geometric framework for learning from labeled and unlabeled examples, *Journal of Machine Learning Research* **7**, 11.

Bengio, Y., Courville, A., and Vincent, P. (2013). Representation learning: A review and new perspectives, *IEEE Transactions on Pattern Analysis and Machine Intelligence* **35**, 8, pp. 1798–1828.

Cai, S., Zhang, L., Zuo, W., and Feng, X. (2016). A probabilistic collaborative representation based approach for pattern classification, in *Proceedings of the IEEE conference on computer vision and pattern recognition*, pp. 2950–2959.

Cao, F., Ye, H., and Wang, D. (2015). A probabilistic learning algorithm for robust modeling using neural networks with random weights, *Information Sciences* **313**, pp. 62–78.

Cao, W., Xie, Z., Li, J., Xu, Z., Ming, Z., and Wang, X. (2021). Bidirectional stochastic configuration network for regression problems, *Neural Networks* **140**, pp. 237–246.

Cecotti, H. (2016). Deep random vector functional link network for handwritten character recognition, in *2016 International Joint Conference on Neural Networks (IJCNN)* (IEEE), pp. 3628–3633.

Chen, C. L. P. and Liu, Z. (2018). Broad learning system: An effective and efficient incremental learning system without the need for deep architecture, *IEEE Transactions on Neural Networks and Learning Systems* **29**, 1, pp. 10–24.

Chen, K., Chen, K., Wang, Q., He, Z., Hu, J., and He, J. (2018). Short-term load forecasting with deep residual networks, *IEEE Transactions on Smart Grid* **10**, 4, pp. 3943–3952.

Chen, T. and Chen, H. (1995). Universal approximation to nonlinear operators by neural networks with arbitrary activation functions and its application to dynamical systems, *IEEE Transactions on Neural Networks* **6**, 4, pp. 911–917.

Chen, X., Chen, W., Dinavahi, V., Liu, Y., and Feng, J. (2023). Short-term load forecasting and associated weather variables prediction using ResNet-LSTM based deep learning, *IEEE Access* **11**, pp. 5393–5405.

Chen, Z., Xiao, F., Wang, X., Deng, M., Wang, J., and Li, J. (2022). Stochastic configuration network based on improved whale optimization algorithm for nonstationary time series prediction, *Journal of Forecasting* **41**, 7, pp. 1458–1482.

Chu, F., Liang, T., Chen, C. P., Wang, X., and Ma, X. (2019). Weighted broad learning system and its application in nonlinear industrial process modeling, *IEEE Transactions on Neural Networks and Learning Systems* **31**, 8, pp. 3017–3031.

chuan Wang, W., Xu, L., wing Chau, K., and mei Xu, D. (2020). Yin-yang firefly algorithm based on dimensionally cauchy mutation, *Expert Systems with Applications* **150**, p. 113216.

Cui, J., Peng, G., Lu, Q., and Huang, Z. (2020). A special modified tikhonov regularization matrix for discrete ill-posed problems, *Applied Mathematics and Computation* **377**, p. 125165.

Cybenko, G. (1989). Approximation by superpositions of a sigmoidal function, *Mathematics of control, signals and systems* **2**, 4, pp. 303–314.

Dai, W., Li, D., Zhou, P., and Chai, T. (2019a). Stochastic configuration networks with block increments for data modeling in process industries, *Information Sciences* **484**, pp. 367–386.

Dai, W., Li, D.-P., Chen, Q.-X., and Chai, T.-Y. (2019b). Data driven particle size estimation of hematite grinding process using stochastic configuration network with robust technique, *Journal of Central South University* **26**, 1, pp. 43–62.

Dai, W., Liu, J., and Wang, L. (2024). Cloud ensemble learning for fault diagnosis of rolling bearings with stochastic configuration networks, *Information Sciences* **658**, p. 119991.

Dai, W., Liu, Q., and Chai, T. (2015). Particle size estimate of grinding processes using random vector functional link networks with improved robustness, *Neurocomputing* **169**, pp. 361–372.

Dai, W., Zhou, X., Li, D., Zhu, S., and Wang, X. (2021). Hybrid parallel stochastic configuration networks for industrial data analytics, *IEEE Transactions on Industrial Informatics* **18**, 4, pp. 2331–2341.

Dai, X., Li, M., Zhai, P., Tong, S., Gao, X., Huang, S.-L., Zhu, Z., You, C., and Ma, Y. (2022). Revisiting sparse convolutional model for visual recognition, *arXiv preprint arXiv:2210.12945*.

Dang, G. and Wang, D. (2025). Online self-learning fuzzy recurrent stochastic configuration networks for modeling nonstationary dynamics, *IEEE Transactions on Fuzzy Systems*.

Demšar, J. (2006). Statistical comparisons of classifiers over multiple data sets, *The Journal of Machine Learning Research* **7**, pp. 1–30.

Deng, L. and Yu, D. (2014). Deep learning: Methods and applications, *Foundations and Trends® in Signal Processing* **7**, 3–4, pp. 197–387.

Deng, X., Zhang, J., Huang, L., Zhao, Y., and Wang, P. (2024a). Transfer learning soft sensor modeling based on two-dimensional domain-adaption stochastic configuration network, *IEEE Sensors Journal.* **24**, pp. 42511–42522.

Deng, X., Zhao, Y., Zhang, J., Li, X., and Wang, Z. (2024b). A holistic global-local stochastic configuration network modeling framework with antinoise awareness for efficient semi-supervised regression, *Information Sciences* **661**, p. 120132.

Depcik, C., Cassady, T., Collicott, B. (2020). Comparison of lithium ion batteries, hydrogen fueled combustion engines, and a hydrogen fuel cell in powering a small unmanned aerial vehicle, *Energy Conversion and Management* **207**, p. 112514.

Ding, S., Zhang, C., Guo, L., Zhang, J., and Ding, L. (2023). Weighted deep stochastic configuration networks based on m-estimator functions, *Chinese Journal of Computers* **46**, 11, pp. 2476–2487.

Duan, Q., He, X., Chao, Z., Tang, X., and Li, Z. (2024). Short-term power load forecasting based on sparrow search algorithm-variational mode decomposition and attention-long short-term memory, *International Journal of Low-Carbon Technologies* **19**, pp. 1089–1097.

Eleftheroglou, N., Mansouri, S. S., Loutas, T., Karvelis, P., Georgoulas, G., Nikolakopoulos, G., and Zarouchas, D. (2019). Intelligent data-driven prognostic methodologies for the real-time remaining useful life until the end-of-discharge estimation of the lithium-polymer batteries of unmanned aerial vehicles with uncertainty quantification, *Applied Energy* **254**, p. 113677.

Farrag, T. A. and Elattar, E. E. (2021). Optimized deep stacked long short-term memory network for long-term load forecasting, *IEEE Access* **9**, pp. 68511–68522.

Felicetti, M. J. and Wang, D. (2022a). Deep stochastic configuration networks with different random sampling strategies, *Information Sciences* **607**, pp. 819–830.

Felicetti, M. J. and Wang, D. (2022b). Deep stochastic configuration networks with optimised model and hyper-parameters, *Information Sciences* **600**, pp. 431–441.

Fu, Y., Ying, F., Huang, L., and Liu, Y. (2023). Multi-step-ahead significant wave height prediction using a hybrid model based on an innovative two-layer decomposition framework and LSTM, *Renewable Energy* **203**, pp. 455–472.

Ganaie, M., Sajid, M., Malik, A., and Tanveer, M. (2024). Graph embedded intuitionistic fuzzy random vector functional link neural network for class imbalance learning, *IEEE Transactions on Neural Networks and Learning Systems* **35**, 9, pp. 11671–11680.

Ganaie, M. A., Hu, M., Malik, A. K., Tanveer, M., and Suganthan, P. N. (2022). Ensemble deep learning: A review, *Engineering Applications of Artificial Intelligence* **115**, p. 105151.

Gao, L., Kou, P., Gao, F., and Guan, X. (2010). Adaboost regression algorithm based on classification-type loss, in *2010 8th World Congress on Intelligent Control and Automation* (IEEE), pp. 682–687.

Gao, S., Yu, Y., Wang, Y., Wang, J., Cheng, J., and Zhou, M. (2019a). Chaotic local search-based differential evolution algorithms for optimization, *IEEE Transactions on Systems, Man, and Cybernetics: Systems* **51**, 6, pp. 3954–3967.

Gao, S., Zhou, M., Wang, Y., Cheng, J., Yachi, H., and Wang, J. (2019b). Dendritic neuron model with effective learning algorithms for classification, approximation, and prediction, *IEEE Transactions on Neural Networks and Learning Systems* **30**, 2, pp. 601–614.

Gao, Y., Luan, F., Pan, J., Li, X., and He, Y. (2020a). FPGA-based implementation of stochastic configuration networks for regression prediction, *Sensors* **20**, 15, p. 4191.

Gao, Y., Xie, L., Zhang, Z., and Fan, Q. (2020b). Twin support vector machine based on improved artificial fish swarm algorithm with application to flame recognition, *Applied Intelligence* **50**, pp. 2312–2327.

Giryes, R., Sapiro, G., and Bronstein, A. M. (2016). Deep neural networks with random gaussian weights: A universal classification strategy? *IEEE Transactions on Signal Processing* **64**, 13, pp. 3444–3457.

Goh, H. H., He, B., Liu, H., Zhang, D., Dai, W., Kurniawan, T. A., and Goh, K. C. (2021). Multi-convolution feature extraction and recurrent neural network dependent model for short-term load forecasting, *IEEE Access* **9**, pp. 118528–118540.

Golub, G. H. and Van Loan, C. F. (2013). *Matrix Computations* (JHU press).

Goluguri, N. R. R., Devi, K. S., and Srinivasan, P. (2021). Ricenet: An efficient artificial fish swarm optimization applied deep convolutional neural network model for identifying the oryza sativa diseases, *Neural Computing and Applications* **33**, 11, pp. 5869–5884.

Gong, M., Liu, J., Li, H., Cai, Q., and Su, L. (2015). A multiobjective sparse feature learning model for deep neural networks, *IEEE Transactions on Neural Networks and Learning Systems* **26**, 12, pp. 3263–3277.

Gorban, A. N., Tyukin, I. Y., Prokhorov, D. V., and Sofeikov, K. I. (2016). Approximation with random bases: Pro et contra, *Information Sciences* **364**, pp. 129–145.

Gribonval, R., Jenatton, R., and Bach, F. (2015). Sparse and spurious: Dictionary learning with noise and outliers, *IEEE Transactions on Information Theory* **61**, 11, pp. 6298–6319.

Gu, Q., Li, Z., and Han, J. (2011). Joint feature selection and subspace learning, in *22nd International Joint Conference on Artificial Intelligence, IJCAI 2011*, pp. 1294–1299.

Guan, Y., Li, D., Xue, S., and Xi, Y. (2021). Feature-fusion-kernel-based gaussian process model for probabilistic long-term load forecasting, *Neurocomputing* **426**, pp. 174–184.

Guo, J. and Yan, A. (2021). Robust deep stochastic configuration network modeling method based on kernel density estimation, in *2021 33rd Chinese Control and Decision Conference (CCDC)* (IEEE), pp. 575–579.

Guo, L., Zhu, J., Zhang, C., and Ding, S. (2024). Intuitionistic fuzzy stochastic configuration networks for solving binary classification problems, *IEEE Transactions on Fuzzy Systems* **32**, 8, pp. 4210–4219.

Guo, W. and Xu, T. (2023). M-estimator-based robust broad learning system, *Control and Decision* **38**, 4, pp. 1039–1046.

Guo, X., Wang, X., Ao, Y., Dai, W., and Gao, Y. (2022). Short-term photovoltaic power forecasting with adaptive stochastic configuration network ensemble, *Wiley Interdisciplinary Reviews: Data Mining and Knowledge Discovery* **12**, 6, p. e1477.

Haghnegahdar, L. and Wang, Y. (2020). A whale optimization algorithm-trained artificial neural network for smart grid cyber intrusion detection, *Neural Computing and Applications* **32**, 13, pp. 9427–9441.

Han, F., Jiang, J., Ling, Q.-H., and Su, B.-Y. (2019). A survey on metaheuristic optimization for random single-hidden layer feedforward neural network, *Neurocomputing* **335**, pp. 261–273.

Hazarika, B. B., Gupta, D., and Borah, P. (2021). An intuitionistic fuzzy kernel ridge regression classifier for binary classification, *Applied Soft Computing* **112**, p. 107816.

Hazarika, B. B., Gupta, D., and Gupta, U. (2023). Intuitionistic fuzzy kernel random vector functional link classifier, in *Machine Intelligence Techniques for Data Analysis and Signal Processing: Proceedings of the 4th International Conference MISP 2022, Volume 1* (Springer), pp. 881–889.

He, K., Zhang, X., Ren, S., and Sun, J. (2016). Deep residual learning for image recognition, in *Proceedings of the IEEE Conference on Computer Vision and Pattern Recognition*, pp. 770–778.

Hinton, G. and Salakhutdinov, R. (2012). An efficient learning procedure for deep boltzmann machines, *Neural Computation* **24**, 8, pp. 1967–2006.

Hinton, G. E., Osindero, S., and Teh, Y.-W. (2006). A fast learning algorithm for deep belief nets, *Neural Computation* **18**, 7, pp. 1527–1554.

Hochstenbach, M. E., Reichel, L., and Rodriguez, G. (2015). Regularization parameter determination for discrete ill-posed problems, *Journal of Computational and Applied Mathematics* **273**, pp. 132–149.

Hornik, K., Stinchcombe, M., and White, H. (1989). Multilayer feedforward networks are universal approximators, *Neural Networks* **2**, 5, pp. 359–366.

Huang, C., Li, M., Cao, F., Fujita, H., Li, Z., and Wu, X. (2023). Are graph convolutional networks with random weights feasible? *IEEE Transactions on Pattern Analysis and Machine Intelligence* **45**, 3, pp. 2751–2768.

Huang, C., Li, M., and Wang, D. (2021). Stochastic configuration network ensembles with selective base models, *Neural Networks* **137**, pp. 106–118.

Husmeier, D. (1999). Random vector functional link (RVFL) networks, *Neural Networks for Conditional Probability Estimation: Forecasting Beyond Point Predictions*, pp. 87–97.

Ibrahim, R. A., Elaziz, M. A., and Lu, S. (2018). Chaotic opposition-based grey-wolf optimization algorithm based on differential evolution and disruption operator for global optimization, *Expert Systems with Applications* **108**, pp. 1–27.

Igelnik, B. and Pao, Y.-H. (1995). Stochastic choice of basis functions in adaptive function approximation and the functional-link net, *IEEE Transactions on Neural Networks* **6**, 6, pp. 1320–1329.

Jiao, W., Li, R., Wang, J., Wang, D., and Zhang, K. (2023). Activity recognition in rehabilitation training based on ensemble stochastic configuration networks, *Neural Computing and Applications* **35**, 28, pp. 21229–21245.

Kandil, M., El-Debeiky, S. M., and Hasanien, N. (2002). Long-term load forecasting for fast developing utility using a knowledge-based expert system, *IEEE Transactions on Power Systems* **17**, 2, pp. 491–496.

Kang, Q., Fan, Q., Zurada, J. M., and Huang, T. (2022). A pruning algorithm with relaxed conditions for high-order neural networks based on smoothing group $L_{1/2}$ regularization and adaptive momentum, *Knowledge-Based Systems* **257**, p. 109858.

Kazemzadeh, M.-R., Amjadian, A., and Amraee, T. (2020). A hybrid data mining driven algorithm for long term electric peak load and energy demand forecasting, *Energy* **204**, p. 117948.

Kiani, F., Anka, F. A., and Erenel, F. (2023). PSCSO: Enhanced sand cat swarm optimization inspired by the political system to solve complex problems, *Advanced Engineering Software* **178**, p. 103423.

Krizhevsky, A., Sutskever, I., and Hinton, G. E. (2012). Imagenet classification with deep convolutional neural networks, *Advances in Neural Information Processing Systems* **25**, pp. 1–9.

Krstonijević, S. (2022). Adaptive load forecasting methodology based on generalized additive model with automatic variable selection, *Sensors* **22**, 19, p. 7247.

Kulkarni, C., Hogge, E., Quach, C., and Goebel, K. (2020). HIRF battery data set, NASA ames prognostics data repository, NASA Ames Research Center, Moffett Field, CA, http://ti.arc.nasa.gov/project/prognostic-data-repository.

Kwok, T.-Y. and Yeung, D.-Y. (1997). Objective functions for training new hidden units in constructive neural networks, *IEEE Transactions on Neural Networks* **8**, 5, pp. 1131–1148.

LeCun, Y., Bengio, Y., and Hinton, G. (2015). Deep learning, *Nature* **521**, 7553, pp. 436–444.

Lei, Z., Gao, S., Gupta, S., Cheng, J., and Yang, G. (2020). An aggregative learning gravitational search algorithm with self-adaptive gravitational constants, *Expert Systems with Applications* **152**, p. 113396.

Li, C., Li, S., Feng, Y., Gryllias, K., Gu, F., and Pecht, M. (2024a). Small data challenges for intelligent prognostics and health management: A review, *Artificial Intelligence Review* **57**, 8, pp. 1–52.

Li, D. and Zeng, Z. (2023). CRNet: A fast continual learning framework with random theory, *IEEE Transactions on Pattern Analysis and Machine Intelligence* **45**, 9, pp. 10731–10744.

Li, J., Li, X., Chen, Y., Wang, Y., Wang, B., Zhang, X., and Zhang, N. (2024b). Mesothelin expression prediction in pancreatic cancer based on multimodal stochastic configuration networks, *Medical & Biological Engineering & Computing*, pp. 1–13.

Li, J. and Wang, D. (2024a). 2D convolutional stochastic configuration networks, *Knowledge-Based Systems* **300**, p. 112249.

Li, J. and Wang, D. (2024b). Stochastic configuration networks with cpu-gpu implementation for large-scale data analytics, *Information Sciences* **667**, p. 120497.

Li, K., Huang, W., Hu, G., and Li, J. (2023a). Ultra-short term power load forecasting based on CEEMDAN-SE and LSTM neural network, *Energy and Buildings* **279**, p. 112666.

Li, K., Qiao, J., and Wang, D. (2023b). Fuzzy stochastic configuration networks for nonlinear system modeling, *IEEE Transactions on Fuzzy Systems* **32**, 3, pp. 948–957.

Li, K., Wang, W., and Lin, S. (2018). Soft measurement of ammonia nitrogen concentration based on ga-scn, in *2018 IEEE Symposium on Product Compliance Engineering-Asia (ISPCE-CN)* (IEEE), pp. 1–4.

Li, K., Yang, C., Wang, W., and Qiao, J. (2023c). An improved stochastic configuration network for concentration prediction in wastewater treatment process, *Information Sciences* **622**, pp. 148–160.

Li, L., Qin, L., Qu, X., Zhang, J., Wang, Y., and Ran, B. (2019a). Day-ahead traffic flow forecasting based on a deep belief network optimized by the multi-objective particle swarm algorithm, *Knowledge-Based Systems* **172**, pp. 1–14.

Li, M., Huang, C., and Wang, D. (2019b). Robust stochastic configuration networks with maximum correntropy criterion for uncertain data regression, *Information Sciences* **473**, pp. 73–86.

Li, M. and Wang, D. (2017). Insights into randomized algorithms for neural networks: Practical issues and common pitfalls, *Information Sciences* **382**, pp. 170–178.

Li, M. and Wang, D. (2019). 2-D stochastic configuration networks for image data analytics, *IEEE Transactions on Cybernetics* **51**, 1, pp. 359–372.

Li, S., Chen, H., Wang, M., Heidari, A. A., and Mirjalili, S. (2020). Slime mould algorithm: A new method for stochastic optimization, *Future generation computer systems* **111**, pp. 300–323.

Li, W. and Chu, M. (2023). A pruning feedforward small-world neural network by dynamic sparse regularization with smoothing $L_{1/2}$ norm for nonlinear system modeling, *Applied Soft Computing* **136**, p. 110133.

Li, W., Zeng, Z., Qu, H., and Sun, C. (2019c). A novel fiber intrusion signal recognition method for ofps based on SCN with dropout, *Journal of Lightwave Technology* **37**, 20, pp. 5221–5230.

Li, X., Yu, D., Byg, V. S., and Ioan, S. D. (2023d). The development of machine learning-based remaining useful life prediction for lithium-ion batteries, *Journal of Energy Chemistry* **82**, pp. 103–121.

Li, Y., Du, W., Wang, X., Yang, M., and Zhao, Y. (2025). Adaptive robust stochastic configuration networks for near-infrared multivariate analysis, *IEEE Transactions on Neural Networks and Learning Systems*. Doi: 10.1109/TNNLS.2024.3512492.

Liang, W., Tadesse, G. A., Ho, D., Fei-Fei, L., Zaharia, M., Zhang, C., and Zou, J. (2022). Advances, challenges and opportunities in creating data for trustworthy ai, *Nature Machine Intelligence* **4**, 8, pp. 669–677.

Lin, T.-H., Jhang, J.-Y., Huang, C.-R., Tsai, Y.-C., Cheng, H.-C., and Sheu, B.-S. (2020). Deep ensemble feature network for gastric section classification, *IEEE Journal of Biomedical and Health Informatics* **25**, 1, pp. 77–87.

Lipu, M. S. H., Hannan, M. A., Hussain, A., Ayob, A., Saad, M. H., Karim, T. F., and How, D. N. (2020). Data-driven state of charge estimation of lithium-ion batteries: algorithms, implementation factors, limitations and future trends, *Journal of Cleaner Production* **277**, p. 124110.

Liu, J., Liu, Y., Ma, Y., and Fu, Y. (2024). Stochastic configuration networks based on smoothed L1 regularization, *Control and Decision* **39**, 03, pp. 813–818.

Liu, J.-W., Liu, Y., and Luo, X.-L. (2015). Semi-supervised learning methods, *Chinese Journal of Computers* **38**, 8, pp. 1592–1617.

Liu, X., Chen, S., Song, L., Woźniak, M., and Liu, S. (2022). Self-attention negative feedback network for real-time image super-resolution, *Journal of King Saud University-Computer and Information Sciences* **34**, 8, pp. 6179–6186.

Liu, Y. and Yao, X. (1999). Ensemble learning via negative correlation, *Neural networks* **12**, 10, pp. 1399–1404.

Liyun, P., Wenjun, Z., Sining, W., and Lu, H. (2021). Short-term load forecasting based on densenet-LSTM fusion model, in *2021 IEEE International Conference on Energy Internet (ICEI)* (IEEE), pp. 84–89.

Lowe, D. and Broomhead, D. (1988). Multivariable functional interpolation and adaptive networks, *Complex Systems* **2**, 3, pp. 321–355.

Lu, J. and Ding, J. (2019a). Construction of prediction intervals for carbon residual of crude oil based on deep stochastic configuration networks, *Information Sciences* **486**, pp. 119–132.

Lu, J. and Ding, J. (2019b). Mixed-distribution-based robust stochastic configuration networks for prediction interval construction, *IEEE Transactions on Industrial Informatics* **16**, 8, pp. 5099–5109.

Lu, J., Ding, J., Dai, X., and Chai, T. (2020). Ensemble stochastic configuration networks for estimating prediction intervals: A simultaneous robust training algorithm and its application, *IEEE Transactions on Neural Networks and Learning Systems* **31**, 12, pp. 5426–5440.

Lu, J., Ding, J., Liu, C., and Chai, T. (2021). Hierarchical-bayesian-based sparse stochastic configuration networks for construction of prediction intervals, *IEEE Transactions on Neural Networks and Learning Systems* **33**, 8, pp. 3560–3571.

Lukoševičius, M. and Jaeger, H. (2009). Reservoir computing approaches to recurrent neural network training, *Computer Science Review* **3**, 3, pp. 127–149.

Luo, T., Liu, M., Shi, P., Duan, G., and Gao, X. (2024). A hybrid data preprocessing-based hierarchical attention bilstm network for remaining useful life prediction of spacecraft lithium-ion batteries, *IEEE Transactions on Neural Networks and Learning Systems* **35**, 12, pp. 18076–18089.

Ma, L., Wang, L., Zeng, S., Zhao, Y., Liu, C., Zhang, H., Wu, Q., and Ren, H. (2024). Short-term household load forecasting based on attention mechanism and CNN-ICPSO-LSTM. *Energy Engineering* **121**, 6, p. 1473.

Mahoney, M. W. *et al.* (2011). Randomized algorithms for matrices and data, *Foundations and Trends® in Machine Learning* **3**, 2, pp. 123–224.

Malik, A. K., Ganaie, M., Tanveer, M., Suganthan, P. N. (2024). Alzheimer's disease diagnosis via intuitionistic fuzzy random vector functional link network, *IEEE Transactions on Computational Social Systems* **11**, 4, pp. 4754–4765.

Mao, S., Wang, B., Tang, Y., and Qian, F. (2019). Opportunities and challenges of artificial intelligence for green manufacturing in the process industry, *Engineering* **5**, 6, pp. 995–1002.

Marx, V. (2013). The big challenges of big data, *Nature* **498**, 7453, pp. 255–260.

McAfee, A., Brynjolfsson, E., Davenport, T. H., Patil, D., and Barton, D. (2012). Big data: The management revolution, *Harvard Business Review* **90**, 10, pp. 60–68.

Mei, T., Si, Z., Yan, J., and Lu, L. (2024). Short-term power load forecasting study based on IWOA optimized CNN-BILSTM, in *International Conference on Intelligent Computing* (Springer), pp. 502–510.

Mirjalili, S. (2015). Moth-flame optimization algorithm: A novel nature-inspired heuristic paradigm, *Knowledge-Based Systems* **89**, pp. 228–249.

Mirjalili, S. (2016). SCA: A sine cosine algorithm for solving optimization problems, *Knowledge-Based Systems* **96**, pp. 120–133.

Mirjalili, S. and Lewis, A. (2016). The whale optimization algorithm, *Advances in Engineering Software* **95**, pp. 51–67.

Mirjalili, S., Mirjalili, S. M., and Hatamlou, A. (2016). Multi-verse optimizer: A nature-inspired algorithm for global optimization, *Neural Computing and Applications* **27**, pp. 495–513.

Mirjalili, S., Mirjalili, S. M., and Lewis, A. (2014). Grey wolf optimizer, *Advances in Engineering Software* **69**, pp. 46–61.

Mishra, U., Gupta, D., and Hazarika, B. B. (2023). An intuitionistic fuzzy random vector functional link classifier, *Neural Processing Letters* **55**, 4, pp. 4325–4346.

Mohamed, A.-A. A., Hassan, S., Hemeida, A., Alkhalaf, S., Mahmoud, M., and Eldin, A. M. B. (2020). Parasitism–predation algorithm (PPA): A novel approach for feature selection, *Ain Shams Engineering Journal* **11**, 2, pp. 293–308.

Naruei, I., Keynia, F., and Sabbagh Molahosseini, A. (2022). Hunter–prey optimization: algorithm and applications, *Soft Computing* **26**, 3, pp. 1279–1314.

Nematollahi, A. F., Rahiminejad, A., and Vahidi, B. (2017). A novel physical based meta-heuristic optimization method known as lightning attachment procedure optimization, *Applied Soft Computing* **59**, pp. 596–621.

Nie, F., Huang, H., Cai, X., and Ding, C. (2010). Efficient and robust feature selection via joint $L_{2,1}$-norms minimization, in *Proceedings of the 23rd International Conference on Neural Information Processing Systems-Volume 2*, pp. 1813–1821.

Niu, H., Wei, J., and Chen, Y. (2020). Optimal randomness for stochastic configuration network (SCN) with heavy-tailed distributions, *Entropy* **23**, 1, p. 56.

Niu, Y., Yan, X., Wang, Y., and Niu, Y. (2024). An improved sand cat swarm optimization for moving target search by UAV, *Expert Systems with Applications* **238**, p. 122189.

Pan, J., Luan, F., Gao, Y., and Wei, Y. (2020). FPGA-based implementation of stochastic configuration network for robotic grasping recognition, *IEEE Access* **8**, pp. 139966–139973.

Pan, Z. F., An, L., and Wen, C. Y. (2019). Recent advances in fuel cells based propulsion systems for unmanned aerial vehicles, *Applied Energy* **240**, pp. 473–485.

Pao, Y.-H., Park, G.-H., and Sobajic, D. J. (1994). Learning and generalization characteristics of the random vector functional-link net, *Neurocomputing* **6**, 2, pp. 163–180.

Pao, Y.-H. and Takefuji, Y. (1992). Functional-link net computing: Theory, system architecture, and functionalities, *Computer* **25**, 5, pp. 76–79.

Park, J. and Sandberg, I. W. (1991). Universal approximation using radial-basis-function networks, *Neural Computation* **3**, 2, pp. 246–257.

Park, Y., Reichel, L., Rodriguez, G., and Yu, X. (2018). Parameter determination for tikhonov regularization problems in general form, *Journal of Computational and Applied Mathematics* **343**, pp. 12–25.

Pavlatos, C., Makris, E., Fotis, G., Vita, V., and Mladenov, V. (2023). Enhancing electrical load prediction using a bidirectional LSTM neural network, *Electronics* **12**, 22, p. 4652.

Pratama, M. and Wang, D. (2019). Deep stacked stochastic configuration networks for lifelong learning of non-stationary data streams, *Information Sciences* **495**, pp. 150–174.

Qiao, J. and Chen, Y. (2023). Stochastic configuration networks with chaotic maps and hierarchical learning strategy, *Information Sciences* **629**, pp. 96–108.

Qiu, X., Zhao, Q., Wang, Y., Tian, J., Ding, H., Zhang, J., and Zhao, H. (2021). Load transfer analysis of regional power grid based on expert system theory, in *2021 6th Asia Conference on Power and Electrical Engineering (ACPEE)* (IEEE), pp. 557–561.

Qu, H., Feng, T., Zhang, Y., and Wang, Y. (2019). Ensemble learning with stochastic configuration network for noisy optical fiber vibration signal recognition, *Sensors* **19**, 15, p. 3293.

Reichel, L. and Ugwu, U. O. (2022). The tensor Golub–Kahan–Tikhonov method applied to the solution of ill-posed problems with at-product structure, *Numerical Linear Algebra with Applications* **29**, 1, p. e2412.

Ren, L., Cui, J., Sun, Y., and Cheng, X. (2017). Multi-bearing remaining useful life collaborative prediction: A deep learning approach, *Journal of Manufacturing Systems* **43**, pp. 248–256.

Ren, Y., Zhu, X., Bai, K., and Zhang, R. (2022). A new random forest ensemble of intuitionistic fuzzy decision trees, *IEEE Transactions on Fuzzy Systems* **31**, 5, pp. 1729–1741.

Reyes, O., Altalhi, A. H., and Ventura, S. (2018). Statistical comparisons of active learning strategies over multiple datasets, *Knowledge-Based Systems* **145**, pp. 274–288.

Rezvani, S., Wang, X., and Pourpanah, F. (2019). Intuitionistic fuzzy twin support vector machines, *IEEE Transactions on Fuzzy Systems* **27**, 11, pp. 2140–2151.

Rezvani, S. and Wu, J. (2023). Handling multi-class problem by intuitionistic fuzzy twin support vector machines based on relative density information, *IEEE Transactions on Pattern Analysis and Machine Intelligence* **45**, 12, pp. 14653–14664.

Rosen, B. E. (1996). Ensemble learning using decorrelated neural networks, *Connection Science* **8**, 3–4, pp. 373–384.

Rumelhart, D. E., Durbin, R., Golden, R., and Chauvin, Y. (1995). Backpropagation: The basic theory, *Backpropagation: Theory, Architectures and Applications*, pp. 1–34.

Sagiroglu, S. and Sinanc, D. (2013). Big data: A review, in *2013 International Conference on Collaboration Technologies and Systems (CTS)* (IEEE), pp. 42–47.

Saha, B., Koshimoto, E., Quach, C. C., Hogge, E. F., Strom, T. H., Hill, B. L., Vazquez, S. L., and Goebel, K. (2011). Battery health management system for electric UAVs, in *2011 IEEE Aerospace Conference, Big Sky, MT, USA*, pp. 1–9.

Saunders, C., Gammerman, A., and Vovk, V. (1998). Ridge regression learning algorithm in dual variables, in *Proceedings of the Fifteenth International Conference on Machine Learning*, pp. 515–521.

Scardapane, S., Comminiello, D., Hussain, A., and Uncini, A. (2017). Group sparse regularization for deep neural networks, *Neurocomputing* **241**, pp. 81–89.

Scardapane, S. and Wang, D. (2017). Randomness in neural networks: An overview, *Wiley Interdisciplinary Reviews: Data Mining and Knowledge Discovery* **7**, 2, p. e1200.

Schadt, E. E., Linderman, M. D., Sorenson, J., Lee, L., and Nolan, G. P. (2010). Computational solutions to large-scale data management and analysis, *Nature Reviews Genetics* **11**, 9, pp. 647–657.

Schmidt, W. F., Kraaijveld, M. A., and Duin, R. P. (1992). Feed forward neural networks with random weights, in *International Conference on Pattern Recognition* (IEEE Computer Society Press), pp. 1–1.

Seyyedabbasi, A. and Kiani, F. (2023). Sand cat swarm optimization: A nature-inspired algorithm to solve global optimization problems, *Engineering with Computers* **39**, 4, pp. 2627–2651.

Shi, H., Xu, M., and Li, R. (2017). Deep learning for household load forecasting — A novel pooling deep RNN, *IEEE Transactions on Smart Grid* **9**, 5, pp. 5271–5280.

Shi, Q., Katuwal, R., Suganthan, P. N., and Tanveer, M. (2021). Random vector functional link neural network based ensemble deep learning, *Pattern Recognition* **117**, p. 107978.

Shi, T., Mei, F., Lu, J., Lu, J., Pan, Y., Zhou, C., Wu, J., and Zheng, J. (2019). Phase space reconstruction algorithm and deep learning-based very short-term bus load forecasting, *Energies* **12**, 22, p. 4349.

Shi, Y. and Eberhart, R. C. (1999). Empirical study of particle swarm optimization, in *Proceedings of the 1999 Congress on Evolutionary Computation-CEC99 (Cat. No. 99TH8406)*, Vol. 3 (IEEE), pp. 1945–1950.

Shibl, M. M., Ismail, L. S., and Massoud, A. M. (2023). A machine learning-based battery management system for state-of-charge prediction and state-of-health estimation for unmanned aerial vehicles, *Journal of Energy Storage* **66**, p. 107380.

Shin, S. M., Rasheed, A., Kil-Heum, P., and Veluvolu, K. C. (2024). Fast and accurate short-term load forecasting with a hybrid model, *Electronics* **13**, 6, p. 1079.

Sierra, G., Orchard, M., Goebel, K., and Kulkarni, C. (2019). Battery health management for small-size rotary-wing electric unmanned aerial vehicles: An efficient approach for constrained computing platforms, *Reliability Engineering and System Safety* **182**, pp. 166–178.

Solomatine, D. P. and Shrestha, D. L. (2004). AdaBoost. RT: A boosting algorithm for regression problems, in *2004 IEEE International Joint Conference on Neural Networks (IEEE Cat. No. 04CH37541)*, Vol. 2 (IEEE), pp. 1163–1168.

Song, X., Wang, Z., and Wang, H. (2024). Short-term load prediction with LSTM and FCNN models based on attention mechanisms, in *Journal of Physics: Conference Series*, Vol. 2741 (IOP Publishing), p. 012026.

Sun, K., Zhao, L., Tian, P., Zhao, J., and Wang, D. (2024). Prediction of X-ray fluorescence copper grade using regularized stochastic configuration networks, *Information Sciences* **659**, p. 120098.

Tang, X., Zhang, N., Zhou, J., and Liu, Q. (2017). Hidden-layer visible deep stacking network optimized by PSO for motor imagery eeg recognition, *Neurocomputing* **234**, pp. 1–10.

Tyukin, I. Y. and Prokhorov, D. V. (2009). Feasibility of random basis function approximators for modeling and control, in *2009 IEEE Control Applications, (CCA) & Intelligent Control, (ISIC)* (IEEE), pp. 1391–1396.

Ueda, N. and Nakano, R. (1996). Generalization error of ensemble estimators, in *Proceedings of International Conference on Neural Networks (ICNN'96)*, Vol. 1 (IEEE), pp. 90–95.

Van Engelen, J. E. and Hoos, H. H. (2020). A survey on semi-supervised learning, *Machine learning* **109**, 2, pp. 373–440.

Wan, A., Chang, Q., Khalil, A.-B., and He, J. (2023). Short-term power load forecasting for combined heat and power using CNN-LSTM enhanced by attention mechanism, *Energy* **282**, p. 128274.

Wan, C., Zhao, J., Song, Y., Xu, Z., Lin, J., and Hu, Z. (2015). Photovoltaic and solar power forecasting for smart grid energy management, *CSEE Journal of Power and Energy Systems* **1**, 4, pp. 38–46.

Wang, B., Zhao, D., Li, W., Wang, Z., Huang, Y., You, Y., and Becker, S. (2020a). Current technologies and challenges of applying fuel cell hybrid propulsion systems in unmanned aerial vehicles, *Progress in Aerospace Sciences* **116**, p. 100620.

Wang, D. (2016). Randomized algorithms for training neural networks, *Information Sciences* **100**, 364-365, pp. 126–128.

Wang, D. and Cui, C. (2017). Stochastic configuration networks ensemble with heterogeneous features for large-scale data analytics, *Information Sciences* **417**, pp. 55–71.

Wang, D. and Dang, G. (2024a). Fuzzy recurrent stochastic configuration networks for industrial data analytics, *IEEE Transactions on Fuzzy Systems*, **33**, 4, pp. 1178–1191.

Wang, D. and Dang, G. (2024b). Recurrent stochastic configuration networks for temporal data analytics, *arXiv preprint arXiv:2406.16959*.

Wang, D. and Li, M. (2017a). Robust stochastic configuration networks with kernel density estimation for uncertain data regression, *Information Sciences* **412**, pp. 210–222.

Wang, D. and Li, M. (2017b). Stochastic configuration networks: Fundamentals and algorithms, *IEEE Transactions on Cybernetics* **47**, 10, pp. 3466–3479.

Wang, D. and Li, M. (2018). Deep stochastic configuration networks with universal approximation property, in *2018 International Joint Conference on Neural Networks (IJCNN)* (IEEE), pp. 1–8.

Wang, D., Luo, H., Grunder, O., and Zhang, Y. Z. (2017a). Multi-step ahead electricity price forecasting using a hybrid model based on two-layer decomposition technique and BP neural network optimized by firefly algorithm, *Applied Energy* **190**, pp. 390–407.

Wang, J., Wang, J. Q., Chen, Y. Q., and Zhang, Y. Z. (2022a). Fractional stochastic configuration networks-based nonstationary time series prediction and confidence interval estimation, *Expert Systems with Applications* **192**, p. 116357.

Wang, J., Xu, C., Yang, X., and Zurada, J. M. (2017b). A novel pruning algorithm for smoothing feedforward neural networks based on group lasso method, *IEEE Transactions on Neural Networks and Learning Systems* **29**, 5, pp. 2012–2024.

Wang, J., Zhang, H., Wang, J., Pu, Y., and Pal, N. R. (2020b). Feature selection using a neural network with group lasso regularization and controlled redundancy, *IEEE Transactions on Neural Networks and Learning Systems* **32**, 3, pp. 1110–1123.

Wang, Q., Dai, W., Lu, Q., Fu, X., and Ma, X. (2022b). A sparse learning method for SCN soft measurement model, *Control and Decision* **37**, 12, pp. 3171–3182.

Wang, Q., Dai, W., Ma, X., and Shang, Z. (2020c). Driving amount based stochastic configuration network for industrial process modeling, *Neurocomputing* **394**, pp. 61–69.

Wang, Q., Yang, C., Ma, X., Zhang, C., and Peng, S. (2021). Underground airflow quantity modeling based on SCN, *Acta Automatica Sinica* **47**, pp. 1963–975.

Wang, W., Xu, L., Chau, K.-w., and Xu, D. (2020d). Yin-yang firefly algorithm based on dimensionally cauchy mutation, *Expert Systems with Applications* **150**, p. 113216.

Wang, Y., Chen, Q., Zhang, N., and Wang, Y. (2018). Conditional residual modeling for probabilistic load forecasting, *IEEE Transactions on Power Systems* **33**, 6, pp. 7327–7330.

Wang, Y., Wang, M., Wang, D., and Chang, Y. (2022c). Stochastic configuration network based cascade generalized predictive control of main steam temperature in power plants, *Information Sciences* **587**, pp. 123–141.

Wang, Y., Zhou, T., Yang, G., Zhang, C., and Li, S. (2023). A regularized stochastic configuration network based on weighted mean of vectors for regression, *PeerJ Computer Science* **9**, p. e1382.

Wen, Z., Xie, L., Fan, Q., and Feng, H. (2020). Long term electric load forecasting based on TS-type recurrent fuzzy neural network model, *Electric Power Systems Research* **179**, p. 106106.

Wijaya, T. K., Sinn, M., and Chen, B. (2015). Forecasting uncertainty in electricity demand, in *Workshops at the Twenty-Ninth AAAI Conference on Artificial Intelligence*.

Wu, H., Zhang, A., Han, Y., Nan, J., and Li, K. (2022a). Fast stochastic configuration network based on an improved sparrow search algorithm for fire flame recognition, *Knowledge-Based Systems* **245**, p. 108626.

Wu, R., Lv, B., Dai, C., and Wang, W. (2022b). Bayesian stochastic configuration networks for robust data modeling, *Concurrency and Computation: Practice and Experience* **34**, 1, p. e6495.

Xie, J. and Zhou, P. (2020). Robust stochastic configuration network multi-output modeling of molten iron quality in blast furnace ironmaking, *Neurocomputing* **387**, pp. 139–149.

Xu, L., Wu, F., Chen, R., and Li, L. (2023a). Data-driven-aided strategies in battery lifecycle management: Prediction, monitoring, and optimization, *Energy Storage Materials* , p. 102785.

Xu, Q., Wu, M., Khoo, E., Chen, Z., and Li, X. (2023b). A hybrid ensemble deep learning approach for early prediction of battery remaining useful life, *IEEE/CAA Journal of Automatica Sinica* **10**, 1, pp. 177–187.

Xu, Y., Chen, H., Luo, J., Zhang, Q., Jiao, S., and Zhang, X. (2019). Enhanced moth-flame optimizer with mutation strategy for global optimization, *Information Sciences* **492**, pp. 181–203.

Xu, Z., Chang, X., Xu, F., and Zhang, H. (2012). $L_{1/2}$ regularization: A thresholding representation theory and a fast solver, *IEEE Transactions on Neural Networks and Learning Systems* **23**, 7, pp. 1013–1027.

Xue, J. and Shen, B. (2020). A novel swarm intelligence optimization approach: Sparrow search algorithm, *Systems Science & Control Engineering* **8**, 1, pp. 22–34.

Xue, J., Wang, Z., Kong, D., Wang, Y., Liu, X., Fan, W., Yuan, S., Niu, S., and Li, D. (2021). Deep ensemble neural-like $p$ systems for segmentation of central serous chorioretinopathy lesion, *Information Fusion* **65**, pp. 84–94.

Yan, X. and Jia, M. (2018). A novel optimized SVM classification algorithm with multi-domain feature and its application to fault diagnosis of rolling bearing, *Neurocomputing* **313**, pp. 47–64.

Yang, W., Gao, Y., Shi, Y., and Cao, L. (2015). MRM-LASSO: A sparse multiview feature selection method via low-rank analysis, *IEEE Transactions on Neural Networks and Learning Systems* **26**, 11, pp. 2801–2815.

Yao, Y., Wang, J., Zhou, Z., Li, H., Liu. H., and Li, T. (2023). Grey Markov prediction-based hierarchical model predictive control energy management for fuel cell/battery hybrid unmanned aerial vehicles, *Energy* **262**, p. 125405.

Ye, Z. and Yu, J. (2022). Multi-level features fusion network-based feature learning for machinery fault diagnosis, *Applied Soft Computing* **122**, p. 108900.

Zeng, P., Jin, M., and Elahe, M. F. (2020). Short-term power load forecasting based on cross multi-model and second decision mechanism, *IEEE Access* **8**, pp. 184061–184072.

Zhang, C. and Ding, S. (2021). A stochastic configuration network based on chaotic sparrow search algorithm, *Knowledge-Based Systems* **220**, p. 106924.

Zhang, C., Ding, S., and Ding, L. (2022a). An AdaBoost based-deep stochastic configuration network, in *International Conference on Intelligent Information Processing* (Springer), pp. 3–14.

Zhang, C., Ding, S., and Du, W. (2022b). Broad stochastic configuration network for regression, *Knowledge-Based Systems* **243**, p. 108403.

Zhang, C., Ding, S., Guo, L., and Zhang, J. (2024). Research progress on stochastic configuration network, *Journal of Software* **35**, 5, pp. 2379–2399.

Zhang, C., Ding, S., Zhang, J., and Jia, W. (2021a). Parallel stochastic configuration networks for large-scale data regression, *Applied Soft Computing* **103**, p. 107143.

Zhang, C., Lim, P., Qin, A. K., and Tan, K. C. (2016). Multiobjective deep belief networks ensemble for remaining useful life estimation in prognostics, *IEEE Transactions on Neural Networks and Learning Systems* **28**, 10, pp. 2306–2318.

Zhang, D., Chen, B., Zhu, H., Goh, H. H., Dong, Y., and Wu, T. (2023). Short-term wind power prediction based on two-layer decomposition and BiTCN-BiLSTM-attention model, *Energy* **285**, p. 128762.

Zhang, D., Zheng, Z., Li, M., and Liu, R. (2021b). CSART: Channel and spatial attention-guided residual learning for real-time object tracking, *Neurocomputing* **436**, pp. 260–272.

Zhang, H., Wang, J., Sun, Z., Zurada, J. M., and Pal, N. R. (2019a). Feature selection for neural networks using group lasso regularization, *IEEE Transactions on Knowledge and Data Engineering* **32**, 4, pp. 659–673.

Zhang, J., Ghosh, R., and Kulkarni, C. S. (2021c). Application of a hybrid between residual RNN and regression methods in predicting battery state of health in autonomous aircrafts, in *AIAA Scitech 2021 Forum*, p. 0271.

Zhang, L., Shi, Z., Cheng, M.-M., Liu, Y., Bian, J.-W., Zhou, J. T., Zheng, G., and Zeng, Z. (2019b). Nonlinear regression via deep negative correlation learning, *IEEE Transactions on Pattern Analysis and Machine Intelligence* **43**, 3, pp. 982–998.

Zhang, Z., Ding, S., and Sun, Y. (2020). A support vector regression model hybridized with chaotic krill herd algorithm and empirical mode decomposition for regression task, *Neurocomputing* **410**, pp. 185–201.

Zhao, L., Zou, S., Huang, M., and Wang, G. (2021). Distributed regularized stochastic configuration networks via the elastic net, *Neural Computing and Applications* **33**, 8, pp. 3281–3297.

Zhao, Y., Deng, X., and Li, S. (2023). A nonlinear industrial soft sensor modeling method based on locality preserving stochastic configuration network with utilizing unlabeled samples, *ISA Transactions* **139**, pp. 548–560.

Zhou, R. and Zhang, X. (2024). Short-term power load forecasting based on ARIMA-LSTM, in *Journal of Physics: Conference Series*, Vol. 2803 (IOP Publishing), p. 012002.

Zhou, T., Wang, Y., Yang, G., Zhang, C., and Wang, J. (2023). Greedy stochastic configuration networks for ill-posed problems, *Knowledge-Based Systems* **269**, p. 110464.

Zhou, Z.-H. (2012). *Ensemble Methods: Foundations and Algorithms* (CRC press).

Zhu, X., Feng, X., Wang, W., Jia, X., and He, R. (2019). A further study on the inequality constraints in stochastic configuration networks, *Information Sciences* **487**, pp. 77–83.

Zhu, Z., Liu, L., Free, R. C., Anjum, A., and Panneerselvam, J. (2024). OPT-CO: Optimizing pre-trained transformer models for efficient COVID-19 classification with stochastic configuration networks, *Information Sciences* **680**, p. 121141.

# Index